Twice Condemned

Twice Condemned

Slaves and the Criminal Laws of Virginia, 1705–1865

Philip J. Schwarz

Copyright © 1988 by Louisiana State University Press
All rights reserved
Manufactured in the United States of America
10 9 8 7 6 5 4 3 2 1
Designer: Patricia Douglas Crowder
Typeface: Linotron Aster
Typesetter: The Composing Room of Michigan, Inc.
Printer: Thomson-Shore, Inc.
Binder: John H. Dekker & Sons, Inc.

LIBRARY OF CONGRESS CATALOGING-IN-PUBLICATION DATA
Schwarz, Philip J., 1940–
    Twice condemned : slaves and the criminal laws of Virginia,
1705–1865 / Philip J. Schwarz.
        p. cm.
    Bibliography: p.
    Includes index.
    ISBN 0-8071-1401-4 (alk. paper)
    1. Slavery—Law and legislation—Virginia—Cases.   2. Criminal
law—Virginia—Cases.   3. Criminal justice, Administration of—
Virginia—Cases.   I. Title.
KFV2801.6.S55S39 1988
346.75501'3—dc19
[347.550613]   87-36442
                                                       CIP

Portions of this study were originally published as "Gabriel's Challenge: Slaves and Crime in Late Eighteenth-Century Virginia," *Virginia Magazine of History and Biography*, XC (1982), 283–309.

The paper in this book meets the guidelines for permanence and durability of the Committee on Production Guidelines for Book Longevity of the Council on Library Resources.∞

To the memory of my mother,
Constance Harrigan Schwarz,
1906–1986

Contents

Preface

A Roman epigram—"As many slaves, so many enemies"—illuminates the central feature of what Orlando Patterson has called the political psychology of slavery.[1] The white authorities of Virginia appear to have accepted the Roman perception. That helps to explain why they ordered that untold thousands and thousands of slaves be whipped or given other corporal punishments, sent at least 983 slaves into exile between 1801 and 1865, and condemned at least 555 to death between 1706 and 1784 and executed 628 between 1785 and 1865. Free whites and white servants received corporal punishment and the death penalty through the same period, but definitely less often—dramatically so between 1785 and 1865. White authorities singled out enslaved defendants because they were slaves. While accusing them of being dangerous to property and people, those whites also regarded them as guilty of being dangerous to slavery.

Between 1706 and 1865, those people whom white authorities in Virginia called slaves and then also judged to be criminals killed at least 199 white people, 98 other slaves, and 14 free blacks. Another 160 poisoned or were feared to have poisoned other people, and 149 resorted to arson in order to attack whites only. More than 211 had physically attacked white people. Some 1,277 were convicted of felonious stealing or other property crimes. Particularly threatening to

1. Orlando Patterson, *Slavery and Social Death: A Comparative Study* (Cambridge, Mass., 1982), 39, 339. Seneca made the proverb famous in *Ad Lucilium epistulae morales,* Epistle XLVII, "On Master and Slave": "totidem hostes esse quot servos." The original and Richard M. Gunmere's translation are in the Loeb Classical Library edition (3 vols.; London, 1917–30), I, 302–303. See also Keith Hopkins, *Conquerors and Slaves* (Cambridge, England, 1978), 119n43; and William Watts, "Seneca on Slavery," *Downside Review,* XC (1972), 183–95.

slavery were the more than 181 slaves convicted of plotting or raising insurrection. Given that these figures do not include unprosecuted or undetected behavior, it is clear that whites, and even other slaves, had something to fear from some slaves. These figures of official violence or action in conflict with defiant, aggressive, or enraged slaves depict a clash of enemies. The most obvious foes were the enslavers and the enslaved. Many whites involved regarded the suspected and convicted slaves as domestic enemies, or the "internal enemy." Many slaves perceived white authorities as enemies, albeit not authoritative. Some of the fury fell on other slaves.

Because of my belief that conflict is quite often a most revealing indication of the nature of any society, I decided to look at the trials of slaves, the most numerous records of such conflict in the large slave society of Virginia. Many historians have depicted dramatic examples of the fundamental, sometimes deadly, conflict that was endemic to societies based primarily on slave labor. Few, however, have attempted to focus on the prevalence, longevity, and variety of such discord. My purpose has been to obtain a better, but obviously not complete, idea of how often slaves in Virginia engaged in behavior defined as criminal.[2] Essential to this question of "how often" is a measure of changes over time and place as well as differences among various slaves or groups of slaves. The main point of my analysis of this behavior is that the tensions, hostility, and conditions involved profoundly influenced the slave society of Virginia, both as a whole and in its constituent parts. I mean to suggest some implications of my conclusions for the study of slavery in the Old Dominion and the Old South. My study also bears on the legacy of slaves' illegal behavior and white authorities' reactions to it for later Virginian and American history.

Held to slavery by the law, some men and women broke the law. Whether committed rebels or not, many of these people stood trial in slaveholders' courts for criminal offenses. The courtroom actions were parts of battles in which both slaves and slaveowners used their strongest weapons against each other. This conflict between lawbreaking slaves and the defenders of the law of slavery changed over time and differed over space. Using more than four thousand trials that took

2. Winthrop Jordan is only one among those who have called for this sort of study. *White Over Black: American Attitudes Toward the Negro, 1550–1812* (Chapel Hill, 1968), 392.

place in the 160 years between 1705 and 1865, this study traces the manner in which diverse slaves and whites developed opposing perceptions of legitimate behavior and then acted on the basis of those perceptions.

It was one thing for this sort of conflict to occur in the seventeenth century, when blacks made up so small a percentage of the colony's population and whites tried black suspects in much the same way they did lower-class white suspects. But as the slave and the white communities developed, members of both groups pursued shifting strategies to deal with each other. At any given time, there were major variations in slaves' attacks on whites or even on other slaves, depending on where they lived, how long they had been there, and the previous behavior of other slaves there. Vincent Harding has convincingly demonstrated in *There Is a River* that the interaction of Afro-Americans and Euro-Americans has been in constant flux.[3] So also was the relationship between slaves and the criminal justice system controlled by whites. The history of the conflict between the legally subjugated and dominant peoples of Virginia, the largest slave society in North America from 1705 through 1865, shows why.

A disclaimer is essential. The purpose of my study is by no means to characterize slaves as criminal or deviant. The damage done by such characterization of free or enslaved Afro-Americans is incalculable. I have written in accordance with certain moral assumptions and I have made the implicit moral judgments that any historian must, especially when dealing with slavery, but I do not mean for such judgments to be the primary emphasis here. My most fundamental tenet about black defendants whom slave court justices found guilty is that they are still morally innocent unless proved guilty beyond the shadow of a doubt. I have neither implicitly nor explicitly attempted to establish such guilt. I do not claim the authority to judge the morality of any of those defendants. It might be unwise to leave such judgments to those who know less about some slaves' allegedly criminal behavior than I do, but I am left with no impression stronger than that I still know too little to pass off glib moral generalizations about peo-

---

3. Vincent Harding, *There Is a River: The Black Struggle for Freedom in America* (New York, 1981), esp. 107. In George P. Rawick (ed.), *The American Slave: A Composite Autobiography* (41 vols.; Westport, Conn., 1972–79), Ser.1, Vol. IV, Pt. 1, p.139, a former slave in Texas explained it in another way: "Slavery, one to 'nother, was purty rough. Every plantation have to answer for itself."

ple who lived through what I merely analyze and who suffered oppression that I have never experienced.

I have accordingly relied on a nonpejorative definition of slave crimes as those actions of slaves that were in conflict with Virginia's slave code and that normally resulted in public prosecution and, frequently, in public punishments that ranged from whippings to various forms of execution. We must remember, as did slaves, that those who held ultimate power in slave societies made every effort to treat as crimes those acts of slaves that they deemed flagrantly immoral, impossible to prevent through private means, liable to encourage similar behavior among other slaves if neither suppressed nor publicly punished, dangerous to white society if not sometimes to other slaves, and threatening to the very authority of owners and other powerful whites. Such behavior was historically criminal—*i.e.*, in conflict with criminal laws of the time—even if most such behavior might be positively characterized as "convictional crime," deriving from laudable or reasonable motives or convictions.[4] Slaves knew what the slave codes meant whether they had read a word of them or not. Those codes were part of the world that slaveholders made and defended. In trying to make their own world, slaves could defiantly resist these codes, but they could not ignore them. Neither can historians.

4. Useful historical or political studies of the problem of defining political crime are: Barton L. Ingraham, *Political Crime in Europe: A Comparative Study of France, Germany, and England* (Berkeley, 1979); Stephen Schafer, *The Political Criminal: The Problem of Morality and Crime* (New York, 1974), the source of the term *convictional crime*; Austin T. Turk, *Political Criminality: The Defiance and Defense of Authority* (Beverly Hills, 1982). I found Ingraham to be the most helpful, but my definition of slave crime differs from his definition of political crime because of the different circumstances involved.

Acknowledgments

When expressing gratitude to those who have contributed to a book, one addresses a widespread community of scholars and professionals on whom one has relied for so long and so often. Many colleagues have shown constant willingness to guide me out of the wilderness. That I may still be lost is certainly not their fault.

I received especially good directions from James T. Moore, Thomas Doerflinger, Thomas Armstrong, Philip Morgan, and the anonymous readers for LSU Press, all of whom read the entire manuscript in one version or another. Commentators on papers that support, or became part of, the manuscript include Edward Ayers, John Boles, Paul Clemens, Eugene D. Genovese, David Konig, Daniel C. Littlefield, Pauline Maier, A. E. Keir Nash, Juliet E. K. Walker, and Peter H. Wood. Many other people pointed out the need for both major and minor changes in various chapters. David Bodenhamer, Reggie Butler, T. J. Davis, James W. Ely, Jr., Stanley Engerman, Susan Rosenfeld Falb, Douglas Greenberg, Peter Hoffer, Norrece Jones, Jr., Paul Keve, Allan Kulikoff, Michael Mullin, Bill Pease, Kathryn Preyer, Marcus Rediker, A. G. Roeber, Fredrika Teute, Mark Tushnet, and several anonymous readers had their say. Especially helpful were the members of the 1978–79 NEH-sponsored seminar on Values and Social Development in Pre-Industrial America, ably directed by T. H. Breen at Northwestern University. Besides Breen, seminar members Thomas Armstrong, Gerald Moran, Mark Noll, Howard Rock, Joel Shufro, and James Walsh urged me on at an important stage of my research. Joseph W. Bendersky, Warren Billings, Marijean Hawthorne, John M. Hemphill, Kevin Kelly, John Lowe, and Harry M. Ward provided me with important leads. I wish I could also mention all the people with whom I have discussed my topic at one time or another. Foremost among these are my colleagues in the Department of History and Geography at Virginia Commonwealth University.

There are many librarians and archivists to thank as well. At the Archives and Manuscripts Division of the Virginia State Library, Robert Clay, Conley Edwards, Emily Salmon, and Brent Tarter deserve most honorable mention. Howson W. Cole, the late William M. E. Rachal, E. Lee Shepard, Paul C. Nagel, and Waverly K. Winfree of the Virginia Historical Society were most helpful and supportive. Fred Anderson of the Virginia Baptist Historical Society familiarized me with the underused minute books of the many Baptist churches of Virginia. The librarians and staff of Colonial Williamsburg's Research Department and the Alderman Library at the University of Virginia enabled me to make effective use of their materials, while Katherine Mandusic McDonell, researcher at Conner Prairie Pioneer Settlement in Noblesville, Indiana, provided many leads in my search for George Boxley, and Marie E. Windell of the Archives and Manuscripts Department, Earl K. Long Library, University of New Orleans, made it possible for me to learn more about the fate of a group of twenty transported slaves. I am grateful also for the diverse kinds of assistance I received from Dr. Marcella F. Fierro, Deputy Chief Virginia Medical Examiner; William P. Schaffer of Richmond; Gilbert Francis and other members of the Southampton Historical Society; Frank V. Emmerson, Clerk of Surry Circuit Court, and Mrs. Emmerson; and Gary M. Williams, Clerk of Sussex Circuit Court. The Interlibrary Loan departments at the James Branch Cabell Library of Virginia Commonwealth University and at the Northwestern University Library secured many books and microfilms for me. Edward Kopf, the staff of VCU's Academic Computing Center, and Paul Minton, then Director of VCU's Institute of Statistics, gave me helpful advice concerning strategies of statistical analysis. I am also grateful to Barbara O'Neil Phillips, editor at LSU Press, for distinguishing *that* from *which* more times than I care to remember, and for substantially cleaning up my writing act—no small achievement. To Margaret Fisher Dalrymple, senior editor, and to the other staff members at LSU Press, I owe a great debt for the high quality of their work.

Abbreviations

AHR	*American Historical Review*
AJLH	*American Journal of Legal History*
C.C.M.B.	County Court Minute Book
C.C.O.B.	County Court Order Book
C.M.B.	Court Minute Book
C.O.B.	Court Order Book
C.S.	Condemned Slaves, Virginia State Library, Richmond
CVSP	*Calendar of Virginia State Papers*
CWRD	Colonial Williamsburg Research Department
EJC	*Executive Journals of the Council of Colonial Virginia*
JAH	*Journal of American History*
JHB	*Journals of the House of Burgesses*
JNH	*Journal of Negro History*
JSH	*Journal of Southern History*
LJC	*Legislative Journals of the Council of Colonial Virginia*
MCGC	*Minutes of the Council and General Court of Colonial Virginia*
NEQ	*New England Quarterly*
UVa	University of Virginia
VBHS	Virginia Baptist Historical Society, Richmond
VCRP	Virginia Colonial Records Project microfilms
VEPLR	Virginia Executive Papers, Letters Received, Virginia State Library, Richmond
VHS	Virginia Historical Society, Richmond
VMHB	*Virginia Magazine of History and Biography*
VSL	Virginia State Library, Richmond
WMQ	*William and Mary Quarterly*

PART I

The Slave Code and the Slave Courts

Introduction

The salient feature of both private and courtroom confrontations between enslaved blacks and free whites was the diametrically opposed points of view of the Afro-Americans and their accusers, judges, and owners. From the first time a Virginian slave "raised his hand against a white Christian" in the obscure depths of the seventeenth century, the same potential existed for deep-seated conflict of perspectives and values between slaves accused of crimes and whites of various ranks and stations in the earliest North American slave society. This conflict was played out in similar informal and formal contexts from the seventeenth through the nineteenth century. Each action by a slave that threatened the property or safety of other people also had the potential, and often the clear power, to weaken, even destroy slavery. Thus the informal and the formal contexts took on a character that differed distinctly in many respects from the character of both legal and illegal interaction among white people.

Slaves and white authorities as well had to develop their understanding of slave societies. This was no less true of what whites called slave crimes than of other aspects of perpetual bondage. Not only did different people live in slave societies but they did so at different times. Informal and formal modes of interaction changed over time, requiring new perceptions and responses. The institution of slavery may look timeless, as if it had always existed and always would, should no epic event such as the Civil War intervene. But everywhere it existed it began, took certain forms, changed, and sometimes even died a natural death. Although slavery died anything but a natural death in Virginia, it developed from an inchoate, vague form in the seventeenth century to a hardened yet flexible form in the nineteenth. So it was with the phenomenon of slave crime. It was not always there. The separate code for slaves did not take form until 1705, even though criminal laws concerning slaves had started to appear some years before. The slave code went through several revisions, those of 1748 and 1848–1850 being among the most important. Revisions reflected behavioral and perceptual transformations among slaves, whites, and also free blacks and Native Americans.

The hybrid nature of Virginia's people and institutions evolved over the seventeenth and eighteenth centuries. If the colony was an English outpost in the early seventeenth century, it was "home" to most of its inhabitants by the mid-eighteenth century. Dependent on indentured servants for labor in the 1600s, it relied almost exclusively on slave labor in the 1700s. But it had thereby become a biracial society, a combination of dominant whites and enslaved blacks, with Native Americans nearly forgotten and free blacks living in between as "slaves without masters." So it was with slave crime. The regular courts and laws served those who dealt with blacks in the early seventeenth century. They even served some blacks, such as Anthony Johnson, in their dealings with whites. The law was completely in the hands of whites by the time the colony became a state; separate courts and distinctive laws, even if hybrids of English law, the slave laws of Caribbean island governments, and the pragmatic notions of Virginian planters, covered slaves. But more and more slaves ignored or defied these laws and courts.

Chapters 1 and 2 try to show that slave crime did not exist in a historical vacuum. White Virginians employed a combination of Old World and New World experiences and values in order to shape the shackles they fastened onto their new slaves. They obviously learned how to defend slavery against slaves, as the survival of the institution for so long testifies, but their constant modification of the slave code and courts shows that they had to be ready to react to new movements among slaves. Chapter 2 explores the manner in which Creoles and newly imported enslaved Virginians confronted free Virginians in and out of criminal courts in ways that had a social significance larger than the significance of the acts alone. That chapter deals with the difficult question of how historians can discern such significance in the trial records of the criminal courts for slaves in spite of the obvious bias of those courts.

The perspective of African and Afro-American bondspeople is generally absent from these first chapters. It is possible to recount the African experience with laws, crimes, and courts in some detail.[1] That rich aspect of newly imported Africans' culture undoubtedly shaped their perception of slaveowners' courts. But we unfortunately lack evidence of how Afro-Virginians applied the legal and judicial values of their ancestors to the new society they encountered along the Chesapeake. Instead, we have to study what a large number of enslaved Virginians did in defiance of or in conflict with the slave code of the Old Dominion.

1. P. J. Schwarz, "Adaptation of Afro-American Slaves to the Anglo-American Judiciary" (Paper delivered at the forty-first Conference of the Institute of Early American History and Culture, April 30, 1981, Millersville [Pa.] State College).

1. *The Shape of the Shackles*

It is possible to match, horror for horror, many of the punishments that slaveowners inflicted upon defiant slaves with those that other authorities in European and American—indeed, African—societies administered to the people under their control. The leaders of slave societies relied on everything from leg-irons and the pillory to drawing and quartering or hanging in chains to control aggressive slaves. But military officers, English county justices, tribal judges in West Africa, and even ecclesiastical officials also resorted to such means to suppress those who endangered their rule or their societies. There is no point, then, in analyzing the means slaveowners used to control slaves to demonstrate the obvious: that transplanted Europeans and their descendants relied on legal and judicial practices long since established in their homelands in order to subordinate the laboring class in their plantation societies. Nor do we need any more proof of the almost self-evident proposition that slavery was by nature a brutal system, based on and ultimately maintained by the ruthless use of force.

It is the functioning of the slaveowners' mode of domination that needs to be analyzed. The nature of the system of control on which slaveowners relied for self-protection and for the perpetuation of slavery depended largely on the nature of slavery in their societies. Was the society so dependent on lifetime bondage that it was a slave society? The more any society was based on slavery, the greater was the chance that legislators would develop an independent set of laws and courts for slaves alone. Virginia was just such a society by 1700. Did the slave society change dramatically over time? If so, then the system of control would also change in an adaptive fashion, as did Virginia's. If the slave society maintained itself from the seventeenth through two-thirds of the nineteenth century, as happened in the Old Dominion, then many adaptive changes took place not only because the society— including any larger society of which it became a part—changed but also because the behavior of slaves varied in accordance with the development of their own communities. Did plantation owners employ their slaves in the production of one crop or diverse crops? Were there many skilled slaves in the society, especially in urban areas? Both diversification and urbanization meant that slaves could normally operate more independently than those who worked in rural, group-labor conditions. Independent slaves certainly would influence the structure and day-to-day operation of the judicial system for all bondspeople and the manner in which blacks dealt with that system.

The central questions, then, are the influence of slaves' criminalized behavior on slavery, the slave code, and the judicial system, the impact of slavery on the criminal code and judicial system for slaves, and the impact of that code and system on slaves. What difference did it make that slaves engaged in illegal behavior in a society controlled by slaveholders? Did such behavior truly endanger slavery? To what extent did white leaders use the system for the perpetuation of slavery as well as for the protection of life and property? In what ways did the code and judicial system for slaves differ from as well as resemble the code and judicial system for free people, both black and white? What was the significance of this system of control existing in Virginia, a society based on racial slavery?

While slavery in North America was primarily a system of forced, lifetime labor, central to the perpetuation of this method of extracting work from human beings were the means of trying to coerce the absolute subservience of slave to owner. The coercion of labor and of obedience overlapped to create the total slave society within which so many bondspeople had to live, no matter what their wishes or values were. As the statistics of official whippings, hangings, and sentences of transportation reveal, even many of those slaves who aggressively challenged the system of slavery fell to the power that defended it. However much attention subsequent chapters will give to defiant slaves, it is essential to begin with an analysis of the particulars and development of the system of control with which they collided. The slaves knew that system in its operation. Thorough knowledge of it is the prerequisite of trying to understand the manner in which a large number of enslaved blacks attempted to deal with it.

Prisoners wear shackles and chains. Instruments of physical restraint are prominent among symbols of penal control. Some slaves occasionally or even permanently had to carry these signs of punishment. But slaveholders weighed down all their victims with invisible shackles even before they actually administered punishments for particular offenses. "The white man was the slave's jail," recalled one former slave.[1] Slaveholders spent an extraordinary amount of time trying to prevent bondspeople from acting in conflict with the norms invented or perpetuated by masters. They also expended a great deal of energy in imposing negative sanctions on those slaves who nevertheless allegedly did commit offenses against the slaveholders' society.

The owners or their surrogates were the first rule-makers, the corrections officers, and even sometimes the executioners. "Every master is born a petty tyrant," George Mason of Virginia told the Constitutional Convention in 1787.[2] Slaveholders had to answer to few people; they could rule in almost complete privacy. They were implacable, sometimes unpredictable, and truly powerful. Because of their ultimate role as supreme authorities, like monarchs who assumed that all power and right flowed through them, owners inevitably became involved in the process of punishment. And that prevented anyone from being actually a kind master. Any master could show kindness on occasion; some masters were regularly kind. But to remain a master, to defend slavery, almost all slaveholders would sooner or later have to wield the whip or direct or participate in the many other processes of suppressing defiant slaves.

The case of Dr. Richard Eppes of Hopewell, Virginia, is instructive. One of his former slaves remembered him as a "nice old man." As a physician, Eppes did show concern for human suffering and he encountered more than his share of personal pain. His sensitivity informed his opinions concerning slavery as well. "The worst feature in the system of slavery," he wrote in 1852, "is the punishments to be

---

1. Rawick (ed.), *The American Slave*, VII (Oklahoma), 112–13. See J. Thorsten Sellin, *Slavery and the Penal System* (New York, 1976).
2. Max Farrand (ed.), *The Records of the Federal Convention of 1787* (4 vols.; New Haven, 1937), II, 370.

inflicted, which give me a dista[s]te for the whole institution." About three months after expressing this uneasiness, however, Eppes recorded his own whipping of George. That George had not provided milk for Eppes's morning coffee fails to account for the disproportion between offense and punishment. The real reason for Eppes's cruelty was that between the time he confessed to abhorrence for the fundamental security that violence provided slaveholders and the morning he had wantonly employed one omnipresent means of securing that protection, his young wife and newborn daughter had suddenly died. Those deaths, he would later lament, had made him "reckless and miserable."[3]

No one could fail to be moved by the suffering Eppes endured after he lost his family. Yet what legal protection was there for the many slaves who, like George, had to suffer the effects of owners' "reckless and miserable" states? It was apparent to even the most fanatical defender of slavery that evil people could abuse their position as slaveholders and inflict abominable and barbaric punishments upon slaves. But the deepest evil of slavery, which Eppes himself partly understood, was that even in the hands of a kind master, the whip lacerated the skin of fellow human beings.[4]

A host of eighteenth-century planters such as William Byrd II and Landon Carter rationalized their arbitrary powers by assuming the role of benevolent patriarch. Lesser planters apparently tried with varying degrees of success to follow the example set by the grandees.[5] As a man who inherited his father's estate in 1850, Eppes tried to combine the eighteenth-century ideal of planter-patriarch with the antebellum concept of the expert farmer and manager. Eppes regarded all his "people" as part of his "family," but he also tried to regularize and systematize all aspects of plantation life. Criticizing the leniency of a new overseer, Eppes concluded that he lacked "system." This slaveowner tried to train his slaves and regulate their con-

---

3. *Weevils in the Wheat: Interviews with Virginia Ex-Slaves*, ed. Charles L. Perdue (Charlottesville, 1976), 269–73; Richard Eppes Diary, January 8, April 16, 1852, in Eppes Family Muniments, 1722–1948, VHS.

4. See Michael L. Nicholls, " 'In the Light of Human Beings': Richard Eppes and His Island Plantation Code of Laws," *VMHB*, LXXXIX (1981), 67–78.

5. Rhys Isaac, *The Transformation of Virginia, 1740–1790* (Chapel Hill, 1982), 328–57; Gerald W. Mullin, *Flight and Rebellion: Slave Resistance in Eighteenth-Century Virginia* (New York, 1972), 62–80; Daniel Blake Smith, *Inside the Great House: Planter Family Life in Eighteenth-Century Chesapeake Society* (Ithaca, 1980); Michael Zuckerman, "William Byrd's Family," *Perspectives on American History*, XII (1979), 279–87.

duct just as he bought the best new machinery and kept it in good repair.[6]

But Eppes's slave George could testify to the limited worth of his master's rational systematizing. It ultimately could not control Eppes's use of power. People such as George knew where the shackles were because they knew who fastened them to slaves. While the owner was the supreme authority on the plantation, the overseers and drivers (both black and white) often exercised day-to-day authority. The latter men resembled policemen on the beat. Some of them, especially the whites, consented to the patriarchal and managerial values of the owners. All of them would keep their jobs, maintain their "professional" reputations, and retain their privileges only as long as they controlled the slaves. So the overseers and drivers did what they believed in or what they could get away with. Those who hired slaves from other owners acted similarly.[7]

Plantation authorities actually had many powers. Fundamentally, they could inflict a wide variety of pain. They could deprive blacks of basic needs, such as family or food. They could withdraw "privileges"—overnight passes to visit family members, liquor allowances, or holidays. Switches and whips were the most prevalent instruments of administering corrective suffering. No amount of debate over how much the whip was actually used can obscure the fact that, as slaves knew, it could always be used. As Herbert Gutman has put it, the whip had high "social visibility." A Virginian former slave interviewed in 1925 explained that he "lived in fear of the whipping post and for this reason made himself the most docile of servants."[8]

Former slaves have testified to the gruesome variety of corporal punishments to which owners and their surrogates could resort. Stocks, plantation jails, "hot boxes" (iron enclosures that baked the

6. Michael Mullin discusses the systematic planter-manager in his collection of documents, *American Negro Slavery* (New York, 1976), 151–210. Eppes Diary, April 26, 1852.

7. Eugene D. Genovese, *Roll, Jordan, Roll: The World the Slaves Made* (New York, 1974), 12–22; Mullin, *Flight and Rebellion*, 29–31; William Kauffman Scarborough, *The Overseer: Plantation Management in the Old South* (Baton Rouge, 1966); Kenneth M. Stampp, *The Peculiar Institution: Slavery in the Ante-Bellum South* (New York, 1956), 36–40, 106–108, 175–83.

8. Stampp, *The Peculiar Institution*, 171–91, a standard survey of punishments; Leon F. Litwack, *"Been in the Storm So Long": The Aftermath of Slavery* (New York, 1979), 158, 238, 371–74; Herbert Gutman, *Slavery and the Numbers Game: A Critique of Time on the Cross* (Urbana, 1975), 19–20; John W. Blassingame (ed.), *Slave Testimony: Two Centuries of Letters, Speeches, Interviews, and Autobiographies* (Baton Rouge, 1977), 568.

victim in the sun), stringing up by the thumbs, iron collars, shackles, and other instruments of torture awaited slaves who dared to defy their owners or overseers. Ultimately and most tragically, owners and others could sometimes murder troublesome slaves and never have to answer to anyone for doing so. Before Virginia law allowed manslaughter convictions of those who killed slaves while ostensibly correcting them, owners and their allies were virtually untouchable. Afterwards, a few spent several-year terms in the Virginia Penitentiary, but several fled to other states. There was a continuing problem with this extreme mode of discipline. Who would pay for the loss of the slave? What overseer could afford to? Why not just sell recalcitrant slaves, or let the government execute them and pay compensation?[9] The punishment that could cause the most lasting pain to the Virginian slave was being "sold to Georgia." This private, unregulated action presented bondspeople with the uncertainties of new surroundings and owners at best, and at worst with separation of families and the lifelong specter of working under the harsh and sometimes brutal conditions of gang labor on a West Indies sugar plantation or later on a cotton or sugar plantation in the Deep South.[10]

Slaves who managed to evade or overcome plantation authorities' sanctions faced several kinds of public, collective controls. Ecclesiastical institutions exerted strong influence on the lives of a significant minority of slaves. That minority was small in the early eighteenth century but became somewhat larger in Virginia by the Civil War. Bondspeople baptized in the eighteenth-century Anglican parish churches later heard ministers sermonize against stealing from owners and other sins. Some accepted these admonitions against theft, but others created an ethical rationale for rejecting them. After

9. On whites' killing slaves, see William Waller Hening, *The Statutes at Large, Being a Collection of All the Laws of Virginia* (13 vols.; Richmond, 1809–23), II, 270, IV, 132–33, XII, 681; Anthony Benezet to John Wesley, May 23, 1774, in Roger Bruns (ed.), *Am I Not a Man and a Brother: The Antislavery Crusade of Revolutionary America, 1688–1788* (New York, 1977), 315; Benjamin Rush, *An Address to the Inhabitants of the British Settlements in America on Slave-Keeping* (Philadelphia, 1773), *ibid.*, 236; Philip J. Schwarz, "Forging the Shackles: The Development of Virginia's Criminal Code for Slaves," in David J. Bodenhamer and James W. Ely, Jr. (eds.), *Ambivalent Legacy: A Legal History of the South* (Jackson, Miss., 1984), 125–46.

10. Norrece Thomas Jones, Jr., "Control Mechanisms in South Carolina Slave Society, 1800–1865" (Ph.D. dissertation, Northwestern University, 1981), 26–54, finds the same to have been true in South Carolina. For a reflection of how prevalent was the fear of such sale from Virginia, see trial of Ned, May 21, 1836, Preston County (now West Virginia), and Petition for clemency, received May 23, 1836, both in 1836 rejected claims folder, VEPLR.

the Great Awakening (the first and the second) spread into the black community, more and more Afro-Americans joined Baptist and Methodist churches. Both bodies eventually tried to justify their failure to abolish slaveholding among their white members by claiming to be the special means of morally uplifting the slave members. Through careful attention to slave members' behavior, Baptists and Methodists hoped to render slaves acceptable to God if not to humanity.[11]

The Baptists exercised church discipline over black members for the straightforward reason that they disciplined any and all of their members. The problem was that abstractly equal rules fell unequally on enslaved and free members. Various congregations agonized over whether to punish slaves who took new spouses after old ones had been sold to distant or unknown owners. There was no hesitation, however, about censuring or dismissing those slaves whom slaveowning members accused of fighting, cursing, lying, gaming, drunkenness, stealing, insolence, assault, or other offenses.[12] Punishment of personal sins also effectively defended the institution of slavery. As the members of Tomahawk Baptist Church of Chesterfield County testified, "We have . . . taken under consideration the state of hereditary slavery and think it is not the business of the church, but the legislators." As a result, many Baptists supported slavery in practice.[13]

During many nonworking hours, slaves well knew they could encounter still another collective body designed by whites to control Afro-Americans' every move at certain times. Patrollers are a part of black folklore either as symbols of evil or as examples of people whom slaves could outsmart. It depended upon time, place, and size of plantation. Most patrollers in eighteenth-century and antebellum Virginia served during weekends, which were frequently slaves' "time off." As might be expected, the number of patrollers and the hours of service

11. The most recent general treatment is Mechal Sobel, *Trabelin' On: The Slave Journey to an Afro-Baptist Faith* (Westport, Conn., 1979).
12. Sobel, *Trabelin' On*; Boar's Head Swamp (Antioch, Henrico County) Baptist Church Minute Book (1787, 1791–1828), in VBHS, shows that 15.9 percent of the white members were excommunicated for various offenses, while 23.5 percent of the black members were so disciplined. South Quay (Nansemond County) Baptist Church Minute Book (1775–1827), photostat in VSL, shows the percentages of 19.3 for the former and 19.0 for the latter.
13. For good examples, see Boar's Head Swamp Church Minute Book, July–August, 1818; Henrico C.C.M.B. (1816–19), 393, 410; South Quay Church Minute Book, 30; Tomahawk (Chesterfield County) Baptist Church Minute Book (1787–1842), 3, microfilm in VSL; and Piney Branch (Spotsylvania County) Baptist Church Minute Book (1813–51), November, 1815, photostat in VSL.

rose dramatically during insurrections or insurrection scares. In some counties, virtually no notice of patrollers' actions appears in the record books. Perhaps their activities were taken for granted, or there were too few slaves to require patrollers' surveillance, or whites felt so secure that they failed to keep up patrols. Those few detailed records that have survived indicate that patrollers concentrated on the largest plantations. That was a practical approach not only because the larger slaveowners controlled the counties but because a few patrollers could thereby watch a large number of slaves.[14]

Some slaves had to deal with the patrollers more often than did others. It was runaways who had the most to fear from them. Slaves going to and from church meetings, especially hidden ones, had to be careful, as did husbands or wives going to meet their spouses on other plantations. Patrollers were the ultimate means of preventing insurrection, so conspirators had to watch them closely. So did any slaves planning to steal goods from outside their own "territory."[15] Patrollers were of virtually no use in preventing killing, poisoning, rape, or arson, however. Most such actions either occurred on a plantation or happened unpredictably and in secret.

When masters, overseers, churches, and patrollers all failed to prevent slaves from violating slaveholders' rules, many whites chose to punish blacks with the full majesty of the law. Anomalous, anachronistic "monarchists" though they were in their assumption about their powers and rights, Virginian slaveholders from the beginning of the legally supported institution in the 1660s until the enforced end in the 1860s insisted that slavery must be based on the law. That could not be common law, of course, since it did not recognize lifetime bondage. But slaveholders thus had all the more power to shape the legal system because they and they almost alone would create the necessary positive law. As a result, not only was slavery as a form of property ownership supposed to exist under the law, but slaves as human beings

---

14. Arthur P. Scott, *Criminal Law in Colonial Virginia* (Chicago, 1930), 307–308, reviews the patrol laws. Some of the most detailed records of patrollers' activities are in Patrol Accounts, 1758, and "A Jornel of Pattroling," April–November, 1763, Sussex County Court [Loose] Papers, 1758, 1763–64, microfilm in VSL. Detailed papers on costs are in "Patrollers, 1806–35, Accounts, etc., Certificates," Caroline County Historical Papers, box 3, VSL. For extra patrols after an insurrection, see Southampton C.C.M.B. (1830–35), 170–77, 264–71.

15. See, for example, trial of Caleb, June 1, 1826, Amherst County, C.S., box 5, and VEPLR at April 22, 1826.

were, in spite of their legally defined status as chattel, also supposed to exist under the law.

Official hangings of slaves made obvious the ultimate power of legal punishment that white authorities could exercise. The aggregate statistics in Table 1 show that slaves could face execution by hanging, the final punishment, for consistent reasons before the 1780s and for a new group of fairly predictable reasons between the 1780s and 1865. Between 1706 and 1784, of the alleged victims of slaves condemned to hang, 91.4 percent were white. Amelioration in the judicial system stands out in the reversal of the proportion of hanging sentences for offenses against property and offenses against persons between the first and second eighty-year segments. That change is, however, prefigured in the percentages for the infrequently used and extreme methods—hanging convicts and displaying their severed heads, or that and quartering—and is less sharp than might appear since I could not verify that all sentences in the first period were carried out.

The legal and judicial shackles were particularly complicated in structure but rather simple in intention. Evolving over the entire history of the "peculiar institution" in the Old Dominion, the statutes and courts changed in numerous ways, as much in reaction to slaves' actual and feared behavior as to shifts in the jurisprudential stance of Virginia's leaders. Modifications appeared frequently in the categorization of crimes—which were felonies and which were also capital offenses—the empowerment of courts, the length of time permitted between indictment and trial, the forms, functions, and rituals of the actual trial, the recording of testimony, and the number or percentage of votes required for conviction or condemnation. Virginia's legislators also regularly altered mandatory and discretionary sentences, the manner of execution, the availability of pardons, the use of transportation as an alternative sentence, the conferral of benefit of clergy, gubernatorial pardoning powers, and the payment of compensation for executed or transported slaves. Good Anglo-Saxons all and supporters of the emerging bourgeois ideology of individual rights before the law, Virginia's white authorities did provide some due process protection for slave defendants, or at least for masters whose slave property faced court action. Their intention, however, seems to have been to control all slaves and to defend slavery.[16]

16. Schwarz, "Forging the Shackles."

Table 1. Slaves Sentenced to Hang, Crimes, and Executions, 1706–1865

| Crime charged | Sentence: Hang, 1706–1784[a] | % This Sentence | Hanged, 1785–1865 | % Slaves Hanged | Extraordinary Sentences, 1706–1809 | | | |
					Body or Head Displayed	% This Sentence	Body Quartered and Displayed	% This Sentence
Against property	312	56.2%	84	13.4%	3	12.0%	0	—
Against persons	137	24.7	432	68.8	22	88.0	5[b]	71.4%
Against system	7	1.3	0	—	0	—	0	—
Insurrection	13	2.3	81	12.9	0	—	2	28.6
Unspecified felony	85	15.3	31	4.9	0	—	0	—
Robbery and treason	1	trace	0	—	0	—	0	—
Total	555	100.0	628	100.0	25	100.0	7	100.0

SOURCES: For Extraordinary Sentences—county court records; C.S., boxes 1–2; *Virginia Gazette,* February 4, 27, 1737. Known pardons excluded; 15 (45.5 percent) verified; no instances found after 1809. The reported dissection of Nat Turner's corpse was not ordered by the court (Oates, *The Fires of Jubilee,* 143). For Hanged, 1785–1865—C.S., boxes 1–10, Treasury Cash Journal, VEPLR, and county court records when possible. All verified.

NOTE: Crimes against property include all forms of stealing and arson; crimes against persons are murder and attempted murder, poisoning or illegal medication, rape and attempted rape, and assault; aiding a runaway, forging a pass, and perjury are the crimes against the system; unspecified crimes are those which clerks designated as felonies but which they did not further identify. Destruction of seventeenth- and eighteenth-century General Court records and the decentralization of the state's criminal courts for free people after the 1780s have made it impossible to collect comparative data on executions of free people in Virginia. Figures painstakingly gathered from a variety of sources by Watt Espy, of the Capital Punishment Research Project, indicate at least 77 executions of free people between 1706 and 1784 and 50 between 1785 and 1864.

[a]Hanging sentences only, according to county records. Verification available in 131 (23.6 percent) of the 555 cases. Known pardons excluded. Figures in first four columns include extraordinary sentences.

[b]Includes one slave woman burned to death after being convicted of poisoning her master in 1746 and another female slave burned to death after conviction for murder in 1737.

The development of laws and judicial institutions for slaves in Virginia was rather dynamic. Changes in society certainly influenced that development. As the oldest British-American colony, the first North American colony to introduce and legalize slavery, and the colony or state with the largest slave population in North America, the Old Dominion necessarily underwent a long and massive process of becoming and sustaining itself as a slave society. In spite of Virginia's distinctive size, the ratio of slaves to whites varied from county to county and from decade to decade, contributing in another way to the development of the laws and the courts. Finally, the departure, either forced or voluntary, legal or illegal, of thousands and thousands of bondspeople from Virginia between the American Revolution and the Civil War also changed, sometimes dramatically, the social circumstances to which changes in the slave code and court system were in part a response.

Whites created and expanded Virginia's criminal code for slaves primarily to control slaves in the interest of peace and order in the slave society. There are parallel developments in the criminal codes for free whites, free blacks, and enslaved blacks, but the slave code had something of a life of its own.[17] One of the first laws relative to slaves passed in Virginia established that subordination of chattels would require separate criminal sanctions. Laws concerning servants would not work when applied to slaves, the 1669 "Act about the casuall killing of slaves" declared. Masters who killed slaves while correcting them, therefore, would be exempt from prosecution. Eleven years later, the House of Burgesses reserved for bondspeople the special punishment of thirty lashes should they lift their hand against *any* Christian.[18]

The second and equally important point is that even though no slave served in the House of Burgesses, voted for a single burgess, or sat on a judge's bench in any county, slaves did influence the creation and development of the criminal code reserved for them alone. The 1669 and 1680 laws reflect the manner in which the behavior of slaves moved legislators to act as they did. According to the 1669 law, the "obstinacy" of many blacks meant that they could not be "supprest" by "other than violent means." Whites would be able to keep the law

17. *Ibid.* Like English law, which county judges tried to exploit, slave law was intrinsically subject to only so much bending. E. P. Thompson, *Whigs and Hunters: The Origins of the Black Act* (New York, 1975), 258–69; Mark Tushnet, *The American Law of Slavery, 1810–1860: Considerations of Humanity and Interest* (Princeton, 1981), 27–30.
18. Hening, *The Statutes at Large*, II, 270, 481–82.

in their own hands in order to deal with lawless blacks. The wording may amount to nothing more than rationalization; the law itself was still a response. From the perspective of the twentieth century, it is easy to infer from this response that some black Virginians had already mounted firm resistance to their subordination. This resistance could take a collective form as well. The 1680 law against slaves who attacked Christians also proscribed unlawful meetings of blacks, since "the frequent meeting of considerable numbers of negroe slaves under the pretence of feasts and burials is judged of dangerous consequence."[19]

The culmination of white Virginians' efforts to segregate the prosecution of slaves came in the 1692 "Act for the more speedy prosecution of slaves committing Capitall Crimes." Speed was "absolutely necessary in such cases," the preamble stated, because other slaves needed to be "affrighted to commit the like crimes" and because previous prosecutions in the centralized General Court or in special bodies had caused too much expense and delay. Thereafter, slaves accused of capital offenses would be tried by county courts of oyer and terminer—that is, county notables, usually the justices of the peace, acted under a gubernatorial commission issued expressly for the trial of the slave in question and empowering them to try and sentence the defendant "without the solemnitie of the jury." The judges would issue orders for execution, loss of member, or other punishment. Almost all would be done according to the laws of England, including the categorization of the offense as capital, the form of the court of oyer and terminer, and the passing of final judgment "as the law of England provides in the like case." The one exception was that jury trials would be refused to all slave defendants in capital cases, not just in instances of treason or sedition. Englishmen would apply some English laws to "heathen" Africans in a special way.[20]

19. *Ibid.*
20. *Ibid.*, III, 102–103. The best description of Virginia's oyer and terminer court system is in Peter C. Hoffer's introduction to *Criminal Proceedings in Colonial Virginia*, ed. Peter Charles Hoffer and William B. Scott, American Historical Association, American Legal Records, X (Athens, Ga., 1984), xliv–lii. Thad W. Tate, Jr., *Negro in Eighteenth-Century Williamsburg* (Charlottesville, 1972), 93–96, is another excellent description of the judicial system for slaves. Warren M. Billings, "Pleading, Procedure, and Practice: The Meaning of Due Process of Law in Seventeenth-Century Virginia," *JSH*, XLVII (1981), 577, places this creation in the context of Virginia governors' having used the oyer and terminer commission. See also *JHB*, 1692, pp. 384–86, 389–90, 396; and *EJC*, I, 171–72. White Virginians had attempted in 1646 to set up a separate judicial process for Indians, but it is not clear whether or how the system worked (Edmund S. Morgan, *American Slavery—American Freedom: The Ordeal of Colonial Virginia* [New York, 1975], 232).

Virginia's white leaders preserved the basic aspects of slave tribunals intact for the rest of the life of slavery—more than 170 years. Numerous bondspeople would appear in courtrooms as suspects and leave after having been legally exonerated. Others would face scenes of near hysteria in spite of the purported rationality of written law and formal institutions. Until the 1840s, accused rapists had little chance of legal survival in a court of oyer and terminer. A speedy trial often would not allow time for the eventual appearance of conflicting evidence in such cases. The slave prosecuted for poisoning had a much better chance, for the court's ability to convict was only as great as its capacity to elicit testimony that judges who claimed at least rudimentary acquaintance with the law might likely accept in the presence of their peers and with the realization that the governor and the council might review the case.

Only certain actions would lead to the prosecution of slaves in courts of oyer and terminer. As the title of the 1692 law indicated, any capital offense required this mode of prosecution. Since the laws of England then in force made many crimes capital, slaves could do a fairly large number of things that would bring on court action. Yet their circumscribed lives allowed them to violate the criminal code only in certain ways. The "usual" capital offenses were burglary, robbery, theft of items of high value, arson, manslaughter, murder, poisoning, and rape. The House of Burgesses became more specific in later years. In addition, by legislation of 1691, which allowed designated persons to kill any outlawed slave—one proclaimed to be a runaway with no intention of returning—with absolute legal impunity, the burgesses had created a new kind of extrajudicial punishment.[21] In 1723 the house responded to the growing problem of insurrection and established that any group of five or more slaves who might "consult, advise, or conspire, to rebel or make insurrection, or shall plot or conspire the murder of any person or persons whatever" would receive the mandatory sentence of death. No such statutes appeared in English codes; Old Dominion Anglo-Americans had just confronted a dangerous slave plot, however. They would apply their legal originality to Africans and Afro-Americans.[22]

21. Sir Leon Radzinowicz, *A History of the English Criminal Law and Its Administration from 1750* (3 vols.; London, 1948–56), I, 628–57; Hening, *The Statutes at Large*, III, 86–88; George Webb, *The Office and Authority of a Justice of the Peace* (Williamsburg, 1736); Richard Starke, *The Office and Authority of a Justice of the Peace* (Williamsburg, 1774).

22. Hening, *The Statutes at Large*, IV, 126. English gentry and their allies did create

But Virginian slaves dealt with peculiar owners. For more than a century, blacks would have a chance to escape the full force of the law. Officially debased, mostly illiterate, probably mostly non-Christian, and certainly non-European, Afro-Virginians would, in changing circumstances, be able to plead benefit of clergy. It was a situation created by British subjects who were somewhat inconsistent about applying English laws and traditions to slaves.[23] In 1731, Lieutenant Governor William Gooch began the process by which slaves received a guarantee of the privilege of being able to "plead their clergy." Knowing that Mary Aggie, a slave defendant in a York County theft case, was a professed Christian, Gooch unsuccessfully tried to support her plea for mercy on the grounds that her faith cancelled out the already traditional impediments of race and status. He then moved the case through a divided General Court and an uncertain council and appealed to the attorney general and the solicitor general of England, who gave Gooch a favorable opinion.[24] The 1732 House of Burgesses consequently laid down the rule that slaves could receive the same benefit of clergy that whites enjoyed, but, of course, in fewer cases. Benefit would be confined to whites, and thus denied to slaves, for manslaughter, burglary at night, and daytime burglary involving goods worth more than five shillings.[25]

As if regretting the necessity to confer English legal privileges on transplanted Africans and their descendants, the burgesses took the opportunity to include in the same act the prohibition of blacks' testimony in any court case except a trial of a slave for a capital offense. In spite of the law's implicit recognition that a growing number of blacks were converting to Christianity, it nevertheless concluded that "they are people of such base and corrupt natures, that the credit of their

---

many new capital statutes during the same years (Douglas Hay, "Property, Authority and the Criminal Law," in Hay et al. [eds.], Albion's Fatal Tree: Crime and Society in Eighteenth-Century England [New York, 1975], 17–63).

23. Hening, The Statutes at Large, IV, 325–27.

24. In spite of the question Gooch raised, at least one slave had received benefit of clergy as early as 1726 (Lancaster C.C.O.B. [1721–29], 192–93). For his account of the search, see Gooch to Bishop of London, May 31, 1731, in Correspondence of the Bishop of London, III, Fulham Palace Papers, 15, VCRP, also printed in VMHB, XXXII (1924), 322–25. See also EJC, IV, 243; and King George C.C.O.B. (1721–34), 566.

25. Jordan, White Over Black, 188, 191, 208, on the values of the bishop of London and metropolitan administrators; Hening, The Statutes at Large, IV, 325–27. General treatments include Landon C. Bell, "Benefit of Clergy" (Typescript in VSL); William K. Boyd, "Documents and Comments on Benefit of Clergy as Applied to Slaves," JNH, VIII (1923), 443–47; and Tate, Negro in Eighteenth-Century Williamsburg, 94–96.

testimony cannot be certainly depended upon." White leaders would accept benefit because it could protect the property of slaveowners. But blacks' testimony in cases involving white people could only make trouble for slaveowners. Legislators would later realize the inconsistency in not allowing blacks to testify in civil and noncapital cases involving other Afro-Americans, but before 1866 they would not relent on the exclusion of black witnesses, slave or free, from any trial involving whites.[26]

The construction of such safeguards did not stop with features that would merely appeal to slaveowners' interests. The House of Burgesses early made certain that successfully trying a slave for a capital offense would literally contribute to the interest of those who possessed slave property. The 1705 legislation and all subsequent renewals ensured in one way or another that if the government destroyed the life of a slave convicted of a capital crime, it would nevertheless make every effort to maintain the owner's original capital investment. That is, the government would compensate the owners of condemned slaves for their monetary loss. The intention of this provision was to persuade slaveholders not to conceal their slaves' offenses for fear of economic injury. Instead, public trials could ensure the public safety. This measure probably conferred some real protection on slaves from arbitrary and inconsistent private punishment by uncommunicative masters who acted independent of one another, but it was relative protection, since consistency and fairness by no means prevailed at all times in the courts.[27]

By 1748, however, legal and judicial shackles so carefully constructed by whites had clearly failed to live up to their creators' and beneficiaries' expectations. It was "absolutely necessary," announced the lieutenant governor, the council, and the burgesses, "that effectual provision should be made for the better ordering and governing of slaves, free negroes, mulattoes, and Indians, and detecting and punishing their secret plots, and dangerous combinations, and for the speedy trial of such of them as commit capital crimes." What kind of improvement was needed? The third section of the 1748 act made clear that poisoning had become a special problem.[28] During the same year, a

26. Hening, *The Statutes at Large*, IV, 25–27, VI, 107; Franklin Johnson, *The Development of State Legislation Concerning the Free Negro* (Westport, Conn., 1979), 193.
27. Hening, *The Statutes at Large*, III, 269–70; *The Code of Virginia* (2nd ed.; Richmond, 1860), 815–17.
28. Hening, *The Statutes at Large*, VI, 104–105; Radzinowicz, *A History of the English Criminal Law*, I, 628–29.

particularly ominous threat to slaves emerged from Williamsburg. Hog stealing was a traditional activity for all the "lower sort" in Virginia. Laws existed that promised many stripes—*i.e.*, strokes of the whip—for enslaved first offenders and several kinds of mutilation for second offenders. But public punishment was infrequent, with predictable results. The "Act against stealing hogs" of October, 1748, consequently decreed that after June 10, 1751, any slave convicted a third time of hog stealing would suffer death without benefit of clergy. Whether this terrifying language had the desired result cannot be measured. No slave ever received such a sentence in any court whose record has survived, and we have no way to determine whether there would otherwise have been any or many third offenders. Suffice it to point out that as was true for the whip, the availability of this penal weapon was undoubtedly well known to slaves.[29]

Any amelioration that occurred thereafter was a sure sign not only of the influence of the Enlightenment and perhaps the Great Awakening but also of planters' increasing confidence that they could control bondspeople who seemed decreasingly alien to them. But it is not always possible to distinguish amelioration from increasing rigor. In 1765, for example, the burgesses streamlined the procedure by which county officials could secure commissions for justices of oyer and terminer. No longer would a sheriff or his agent have to journey all the way to Williamsburg each time there was a need for a commission. From then on, governors issued blanket commissions to specific judges who would hear those cases in their counties. This legislation would save time and money, of course, but would it affect due process? The same act also recognized that even slaves accused of having "base and corrupt natures" could kill someone without malice aforethought. In other words, it was possible for slaves to be guilty of manslaughter. By the legislation of 1765, then, slaves would be able to plead for benefit of clergy when convicted of manslaughter. Yet the burgesses restrained themselves in the interest of white safety and supremacy. Benefit of clergy would be available only to slaves convicted of manslaughter for killing a slave.[30]

The same sharp but deadly distinction characterized the next major modification of the Old Dominion's criminal code for the enslaved. Legislation of 1769, whose title revealed the layers of change already

29. Morgan, *American Slavery*, 217–18, 237; Hening, *The Statutes at Large*, VI, 121–24; Schwarz, "Gabriel's Challenge," 296–98.
30. Hening, *The Statutes at Large*, VIII, 137–39.

incorporated into the slave code—"An Act to amend the Act, intituled an Act to amend the Act for the better government of Servants and slaves"—explained that the previously conferred power to dismember outlying slaves (*i.e.*, those runaways who defied owners' and courts' orders to return and who lived off the land and by raiding plantations) was a punishment "often disproportioned to the offence, and contrary to the principles of humanity." No longer would such a punishment be employed to discipline outlying slaves. The act went on, however, to destroy any misconception free or enslaved Virginians might have that the burgesses had softened their attitude toward "deviant" slaves. County courts of oyer and terminer could order the castration of any slave convicted of *attempting* to rape a white woman. The act read as if it left untouched a power justices already had. In fact, it conferred new authority on them, and a rise in the number of rape convictions encouraged them to hold that authority in reserve and eventually use it.[31]

Before the American Revolution, the legislators of Virginia made two more major and possibly ameliorative revisions in the legal and judicial system on which whites relied to suppress defiant slaves. Legislation of February, 1772, seemingly preserved more slaves from the gallows, making it more difficult for justices to sentence slaves to death, and extending benefit of clergy for one other offense. Thereafter, at least four justices, being also a majority, must vote for condemnation. Landon Carter fumed in private that this law, merely an effort to save money, would make nearly impossible the courts' use of the sanction of hanging. The more than seventeen slaves sentenced to death between March and December, 1772, would undoubtedly have disagreed with Carter, especially since that was twice the number condemned to death during the same period in 1771. Amelioration was rather unpredictable. Lawmakers write on the human skin, Catherine the Great reportedly wrote to Diderot at about this time.[32]

The language of the same act's extension of benefit of clergy to slaves "convicted of breaking and entering houses in the night time, without stealing goods or chattels from thence" reveals the central theme of

31. *Ibid.*, 358–61. Rape continued to be a capital offense.

32. Hening, *The Statutes at Large*, VIII, 522; Landon Carter, *The Diary of Colonel Landon Carter of Sabine Hall, 1752–1778*, ed. Jack P. Greene (2 vols.; Charlottesville, 1965), II, 676; Louis Philippe, Comte de Ségur, *Mémoires, ou souvenirs et anecdotes* (5th ed.; 2 vols.; Paris, 1844), II, 127 ("je travaille sur la peau humaine").

almost every change made between the 1780s and the 1860s in Virginia's criminal code for slaves. "A slave who shall break any house in the night time," the act established, "shall not be excluded from clergy, unless the same breaking, in the case of a freeman, would be a burglary." In spite of the postrevolutionary reform of the criminal code, revision of the judiciary, and development of the state penitentiary— all for free people only—the system of suppressing dangerous behavior among slaves would not simultaneously match the system for whites. Errant bondspeople were in greater jeopardy of capital punishment. One can find identical features in sections of the Commonwealth's codes for blacks and whites only if one juxtaposes a somewhat later set of laws for blacks and an earlier collection of statutes for whites. Reform for slaves existed, but it lagged behind reform for whites.[33]

The American Revolution's ambiguous legacy for slaves appears most starkly in the system of criminal laws and courts for slaves. The "amelioration" during the 1760s and 1770s was a well-sharpened, two-edged sword. Even though the simple conviction rate in trials of slaves dropped between the 1760s and 1770s, that was temporary. The rate began to rise again in the early 1780s. Data from representative counties for the years thereafter indicate that the simple conviction rate always fluctuated. What revolutionary humanitarianism may have done, therefore, was to provide a temporary breathing period, not a permanent change.

Officials did, however, make some improvements. Hanging, for example, did decline, even though sentences of hanging had not declined by the 1780s. (Only sentencing to the harsher forms of execution had begun to decrease.) By the 1780s, the state executive's granting of full pardons to many condemned slaves grew dramatically, saving many a person from the hangman. The reduction of felony charges to misdemeanor verdicts continued, as did the numerous grants of benefit of clergy. One reason for these trial results was that even though owners had long been able to speak in court on matters of fact concerning their slaves on trial, some were now beginning to send trained attorneys instead. This development was natural in a society whose property owners increasingly relied on professionals to protect all their prop-

---

33. Kathryn Preyer, "Crime, the Criminal Law and Reform in Post-Revolutionary Virginia," *Law and History Review*, I (1983), 53–85; Schwarz, "Forging the Shackles."

erty in courts. It could lead either to lesser sentences or to the result secured by young lawyer Luther Martin when he appeared on behalf of the slave Dick in Accomack County Court in August of 1775. Presented by, oddly enough, the grand jury for illegal preparation of medicines, Dick pleaded not guilty, and he and Martin won a continuance until November court. At that time, the king's attorney simply dropped the charges, whether intimidated by Martin's developing skills or acting from other motives is not known.[34]

Whatever its source, a heightened awareness of extenuating circumstances began to appear in the records of slave trials in the revolutionary era. Judges began to recognize some of the "temptations" slaves faced or take into account the "hard usages" a slave had received from a white person. One court even went so far as to drop the charges against Will, who had been accused of murdering another slave, on the grounds that at the time of the action "he was a Lunatic & not in his proper Senses." Similarly, due to the optimistic and libertarian emphases of revolutionary ideology, a party of humanity had begun to debate, and occasionally to do battle, with the party of the devil. The humanitarians made known their distaste for the cruelty exercised by many overseers. Some even joined efforts to secure pardons or reduced punishments for slaves who had violated the law either under the duress of depraved whites or in reaction to especially cruel superiors. In 1788 the legislature changed the law concerning whites who killed slaves in the process of correcting them. Now the Commonwealth could charge such people with manslaughter. Thereafter, scattered trials of such killers of slaves occurred in the assorted courts for free people. Legislators also built some more safeguards for slaveowners' human property, perhaps even for the slaves themselves, into the state's slave code.[35]

34. Accomack C.C.O.B. (1774–77), 377, 393. See A. G. Roeber, *Faithful Magistrates and Republican Lawyers: Creators of Virginia Legal Culture, 1680–1810* (Chapel Hill, 1981).
35. *EJC*, VI, 390; trial, October 15, 1776, Prince Edward C.C.O.B. (1773–81), 502–503; *EJCS*, I, 228; trial, December 21, 1785, Henrico C.C.O.B. (1784–87), 380 (I have seen no other such judgment of temporary insanity in the trial of a slave); Mullin (ed.), *American Negro Slavery*, 71–72; *The Letters of Elijah Fletcher*, ed. Martha von Briesen (Charlottesville, 1965), 23; Judge Nelson to Governor Cabell, December 21, 1805, and "Petition of Sundry the Inhabitants of the County of Prince George in behalf of Robin," November 16, 1786, both in VEPLR. On trials of whites for killing slaves, see Hening, *The Statutes at Large*, XII, 681; Brunswick C.C.O.B. (1784–88), 433 (to General Court); Spotsylvania C.C.O.B. (1792–95), 414 (to District Court); Spotsylvania C.C.M.B. (1815–19), 151–53 (to Superior Court), (1821–24), 308 (to Superior Court), (1826–29), 287–88, 313 (to Superior Court); Essex C.C.O.B. (1800–1801), 247 (acquitted); Petition of Franklin District cit-

But the problem was that all these apparent reforms effectively perpetuated bondage. They were intended to prevent another revolution. Mixed as the motives for the reforms may have been, white leaders would have an easier, but by no means assured, chance of controlling their slave society. It is the limitations on the reforms for slaves that reveal the character of the lawmakers' program. When those authorities completely revamped the criminal justice system for free people, creating district courts (1788), abolishing the death sentence for all offenses except first-degree murder (1796), ending benefit of clergy (1796), and eventually opening a penitentiary (1800) that was practically unique for a southern state, they left the nearly century-old oyer and terminer courts virtually intact. Local judges would still retain life-and-death powers over slaves. Segregated slave courts, among the most powerful in the slave South, would continue to exist partly so that slavery could continue to exist. The only other visible change resulting from the Revolution was that cases would now be tried in the name of the Commonwealth rather than the Crown.[36]

The most significant change effected in the 1786 law concerning trials of slaves was that thereafter only a unanimous court of oyer and terminer could condemn a slave to death.[37] The number of execution sentences did drop dramatically between 1786 and 1787, but that decline was deceptive since the same number of condemnations was

izens to Governor Cabell, 1807, Petition of Thomas Johns and others, September, 1807, William B. Williams to Governor Cabell, July 15, 1808, John T. Mason to Governor Cabell, November 17, 1808, Maryland governor's proclamation of December 20, 1808, and Daniel McLaren to Governor Tyler, September 2, 1810, all in VEPLR; Proclamation of Governor Preston, April 25, 1818, in Richmond *Enquirer*, May 29, 1818, p. 4; Petition of 109 Northampton County citizens to Governor Pleasants, December 4, 1822 (January, 1824, folder), Inquisition on body of Maria, slave of Fielding Curtis, February 11, 1826, Proclamation of Governor Tyler, March 27, 1826, Proclamation of Governor Giles, December 9, 1828, reward receipt, August 5, 1829, Inquisition on the body of Armistead, slave of William Conner, September 23, 1829, and Fredericksburg Mayor Thomas Goodwin to Governor Giles, September 24, 1829, all in VEPLR. For petitions against executions, see Edmund Randolph to Governor Beverley Randolph, January 14, 1790, in Miscellaneous Manuscripts, Chicago Historical Society (CWRD microfilm M-97); John Caruthers to Governor Cabell, June 10, 24, 1806, Petition of Norfolk citizens, October, 1807, Arthur Lee to Governor Cabell, October 11, 1807, William Sharp to Governor Cabell, October 29, 1807, Petition of Brunswick County citizens, March, 1808, Robert Tinsley to Governor Tyler, June 22, 1826, C. Anthony to Governor Tyler, June 22, 1826, Petition of Staunton citizens to Governor Giles, September, 1829, all in VEPLR.

36. Preyer, "Crime, the Criminal Law and Reform," 53–85; Daniel Flanigan, "The Criminal Law of Slavery and Freedom, 1800–1868" (Ph.D. dissertation, Rice University, 1973), 100, 103.

37. Hening, *The Statutes at Large*, XII, 345; *The Papers of Thomas Jefferson*, ed. Julian Boyd *et al.* (21 vols. to date; Princeton, 1950–), II, 616–17.

recorded in 1787 as in 1785, and the number rose again between 1788 and 1799, before Gabriel's Plot and prior to the legalization of transportation. One more change was intended to be ameliorative. Some new language appeared in the 1786 act. All previous legislation had empowered courts of oyer and terminer to try slaves accused of capital offenses alone. The "act directing the method of trying Slaves charged with treason or felony" covered a broader category of crimes than did the earlier statutes. Now justices could use oyer and terminer powers to try slaves accused of any felony. Court records from representative cities and counties indicate that justices did thereafter try more slaves per year. Perhaps this modification did have an ameliorative effect by taking more punishments out of unsupervised and unrestrained hands.[38]

After 1789, slaves would plead for benefit of clergy before unreformed tribunals, while free people would for a few years ask for the same privilege in completely reformed judicial bodies. As before, slaves faced a more rigid criminal justice system than did free people. As if to underscore this condition, authorities decided in 1796 to restrict the death penalty not only to those free persons convicted of murder in the first degree but also to all slaves convicted of "nonclergyable" offenses. In the 1856 edition of *A Sketch of the Laws Relating to Slavery*, George M. Stroud used the Old Dominion's statutes to make the overwhelmingly convincing point—a point that would be reiterated by an associate justice of the U.S. Supreme Court in the Civil Rights Cases of 1883—that slaves convicted of crimes were subject to grossly unequal punishment in comparison to whites and even to free blacks. He listed all the more than sixty offenses for which Afro-Virginian bondspeople could be condemned to death but for which no free white person could be executed. Stroud had to list that many offenses because Virginia's code made so many distinctions within the main categories of crime, such as the seventeen different kinds of arson.[39]

38. The courts were those of Brunswick, Essex, Henrico, Henry, Southampton, and Spotsylvania counties, and the city of Richmond, for 1786 through 1799. The totals reveal a spurt in 1787 and a slight rise thereafter: ten in 1786; thirty in 1787; nine in 1788; fifteen in 1789; eleven in 1790.

39. Hening, *The Statutes at Large*, XII, 532–38, XIII, 30–32; Roeber, *Faithful Magistrates*, 192–230; Samuel Shepherd, *Statutes at Large of Virginia, from October Session 1792, to December Session 1806, Inclusive* (3 vols.; Richmond, 1835), II, 8; George M. Stroud, *A Sketch of the Laws Relating to Slavery in the Several States of the United States of America* (1856; rpr. New York, 1968), 77–80. Justice Joseph P. Bradley maintained that punishments more severe for slaves than for free persons were one of slavery's "necessary incidents," or "inseparable incidents of the institution" (109 U.S. 3 [1883]).

Daniel J. Flanigan has characterized the Old Dominion's antebellum penal system for slaves as about the most repressive in all the slave South. The reason, he persuasively concludes, is that Virginians had one of the oldest criminal codes for slaves on the mainland of North America. They might revise certain secondary aspects of it, but they would be loath to modify its most basic features. Whites relied on the same fundamental categories of criminal statute—homicide, poisoning, assault, rape, arson, theft, and robbery—in order to curb any aggressive members of the "alien" population in their midst.[40] Two major changes did occur in the penal system for slaves between 1800 and 1865, however. One was a sea change that modified details in accordance with the development of the white, free black, and enslaved sectors of Virginia's population. The other was a colossal effort of white Virginians to have their cake and eat it too.

Changes in the slave code during this period could directly affect the rate of prosecution for certain crimes. In 1823, for instance, perhaps in response to the Vesey Plot in South Carolina, and probably in reaction to the rise in convictions of slaves for murdering whites in the previous eight years, an act passed that mandated transportation for slaves convicted of intentional and malicious assault of or beating a white person with intent to kill. The penalty for that offense became death without benefit of clergy in the spring of 1832, as shocked legislators reacted to Nat Turner's Revolt in August, 1831. Table 2 shows that in the years 1825 through 1829 the convictions for this offense had grown dramatically, and that in spite of the severe penalty after 1832, the number of convictions resulting in execution or transportation remained at about the same level until the 1850s, when it rose markedly since judges could no longer grant benefit of clergy to bondspeople for any offense.[41]

One might think, then, that a state with so many capital offenses of which to convict slaves would have been even busier at the gallows than it actually was. Yet in this area, Virginians' judiciary had their deterrence and looked like humanitarians as well. In early 1801, partly in response to Gabriel's Plot and partly as an effort to eliminate as much as possible the spectacle of public hangings, legislation went into effect that allowed the governor and the council, either upon rec-

40. Daniel J. Flanigan, "Criminal Procedure in Slave Trials in the Antebellum South," *JSH*, XL (1974), 546–47.

41. *Supplement to the Revised Code of the Laws* (Richmond, 1833), 147, 234; *The Code of Virginia* (Richmond, 1849), 753.

Table 2. Slaves Executed or Transported for Assaulting Whites with Intent to Kill, 1785–1864

1785–89	0	1825–29	14
1790–94	1	1830–34	12
1795–99	2	1835–39	11
1800–1804	6	1840–44	11
1805–1809	2	1845–49	11
1810–14	4	1850–54	23
1815–19	3	1855–59	33
1820–24	4	1860–64	16
Total	22	Total	131

SOURCES: C.S., boxes 1–10, and miscellaneous county court order and minute books.

ommendation of justices of oyer and terminer or on their own, to sell condemned slaves to persons who guaranteed to transport them out of the United States to places from which they could not return to Virginia. Such slaves would wait for purchasers in the Virginia Penitentiary, then go into exile from Virginia forever—out of sight, out of mind, and incapable of a second offense in the Old Dominion. Nearly nine hundred Afro-Virginians would become deportees before still another change occurred in 1858.[42]

By 1857 the market for convicted felons, especially insurrectionaries, had somewhat diminished outside the United States. Few European colonies desired Afro-Americans who had already shown what

42. I have treated this subject at greater length in "The Transportation of Slaves from Virginia, 1801–1865," *Slavery and Abolition: A Journal of Comparative Studies,* VII (1986), 215–40. For the basic sources, see *The Papers of Thomas Jefferson,* II, 504; Jefferson to Governor Monroe, September 20, 1800, in *The Writings of Thomas Jefferson,* ed. Paul L. Ford (10 vols.; New York, 1892–99), VII, 457; Shepherd, *Statutes at Large,* II, 279–80; "Letter from the Governor," *Journal of the House of Delegates,* 1841–42, pp. 87–88; "Statement Shewing the Number and Cost to the Commonwealth of Executed and Transported Slaves, For the Twenty Years Which Ended the 31st December 1840," *Journal of the House of Delegates,* 1841-42, docu. no. 43; Message of Governor Floyd, *Journal of the House of Delegates,* 1848–49, p. 24; *Governor's Biennial Messages to the General Assembly . . . December 7, 1857* (Richmond, 1857), 150–51; Stampp, *The Peculiar Institution,* 243–44, 258; Clement Eaton, *The Freedom-of-Thought Struggle in the Old South* (New York, 1964), 94; Helen T. Catterall, *Judicial Cases Concerning American Slavery and the Negro* (5 vols.; Washington, D.C., 1924–26), III, 558–59, covers *State v. William H. Williams,* 7 Rob. La. 252 (1844), a prosecution of a trader for sneaking into Louisiana some slaves transported from Virginia. The names of the slaves can be traced through "A List of Slaves and Free Persons of Color received into the Penitentiary . . . 1816 to . . . 1842," C.S., box 10; and papers concerning *State v. Williams,* in Supreme Court of Louisiana Collection, docket 4671, Earl K. Long Library, University of New Orleans.

they thought of docility. Slavery in the British and French West Indies had legally ended in the 1830s and 1840s; Spanish Florida was now in the Union; other areas had come under U.S. control; and, finally, Deep South states had objected loudly to slave traders' initially undetected practice of "dumping" transported slaves within their boundaries. Perhaps the most obvious disadvantage of the system for white Virginians was that it lost considerable money for the state. In one of the last efforts to shore up the criminal code for slaves, the Virginia General Assembly of 1858 declared that enslaved laborers who would previously have been condemned to sale and transportation could now benefit the public as state-owned laborers on public works. Strangely enough, still another revision of the law in 1864 allowed the governor to transport a "reprieved" slave outside the Confederate states. At least fourteen blacks were exiled in 1864 and 1865 as a result of this act, but there is no indication of where they could possibly have been taken outside the Confederacy.[43]

State officials regarded the sale and transportation of convict bondspeople as a reprieve. It is difficult to determine how much suffering resulted from this sentence, however. Little or no record survives of early destinations. Some went to Cuba, others to Spanish Florida, and a few even went to the Dry Tortugas, the future place of confinement for Dr. Samuel Mudd, who set John Wilkes Booth's broken leg. Transportation was no real punishment, declared Governor Wise in 1857. He did not ask the forced migrants how they felt; we cannot. But a persistent tradition said that there were more dangerous slaves in the Deep South simply because the upper South had sent so many slaves there in self-defense.[44]

Whatever happened to the enslaved exiles, the fate of Afro-Virginians who stood on the gallows is clear. After institution of the alternative of transportation, or between 1801 and 1865, the hangman's noose still granted 454 slaves the only kind of freedom for which many could hope. About two-thirds of them suffered the pain of death be-

43. *State* v. *Williams*, Supreme Court of Louisiana Collection; *Acts of the General Assembly*, 1857–58, pp. 39–40; *Acts of the General Assembly*, 1863, p. 54.

44. George Goosley to Governor Page, June 5, 24, 1802, Norfolk Mayor Thomas Newton to Governor Page, September 8, 1802, Memorial of William Fulcher, December, 1806 ("undated"), all in VEPLR; R. E. Griffith, Sr., "Notes on Rock Hill," *Proceedings of the Clarke County Historical Association*, III (1943), 47; Stephen Z. Starr, *Colonel Grenfell's Wars: The Life of a Soldier of Fortune* (Baton Rouge, 1971), 273–79; *Governor's Biennial Messages . . . 1857*, p. 151; Litwack, *"Been in the Storm,"* 138.

cause they had been convicted of crimes against persons—forcing pain, terror, or death on someone else. In relation to whites' standards then, at least some proportionality between punishment and crime existed in these cases. But the ugly look of double jeopardy, of being condemned once by slavery and then again in court, characterizes the entire process. One can hardly expect that white Virginians—and the small percentage of black victims—would not struggle for self-preservation. The problem is in the systematic refusal of slave laws and courts to acknowledge and protect the right of slaves to self-preservation.

At times, whites convinced themselves that their legal and judicial system succeeded in protecting them from the special and grave danger posed by the presence of a suppressed slave population. Surely that system did terrorize some people into submission. Slaves had to take seriously the risk of going to the gallows. But there were those who either ignored the system or recognized it for what it was and therefore set out to exploit, undermine, or utterly destroy it. Many black people perceived the shape of the shackles. For some, that shape meant complete restraint. Others attempted to learn how to move about, even to run, in spite of the irons. The men and women in this study sought to escape from or break these shackles.

Except in times of large-scale slave plots or fear thereof, the legal and judicial system created a kind of order in the lives of slaves. Systems of absolute power claim to provide safety in order, but slaves thus had a good idea of what to expect should they behave in certain ways. The most significant implication of the relative predictability of the system of *legal* control is that many of those slaves who chose to challenge it could do so on the basis of their own values. The seemingly omnipresent stealing by slaves exemplifies how such illegal behavior can appear to be merely a reaction but was in fact more than that. Those slaves who did not steal as well as those who distinguished between stealing from other slaves and stealing from whites, or even between stealing from their owners as opposed to other whites, could base their behavior on their own ethic.[45] Their decisions were not

---

45. Jacob Stroyer, *Sketches of My Life in the South* (Salem, Mass., 1890), 28–29, 44–45, 52–54; Albert J. Raboteau, *Slave Religion: The "Invisible Institution" in the Antebellum South* (New York, 1978), 294–97; Garry Wills, *Inventing America: Jefferson's Declaration of Independence* (Garden City, N.Y., 1978), 226–27; Michael Craton *et al.* (eds.), *Slavery, Abolition, and Emancipation: Black Slaves and the British Empire: A Thematic Documentary* (London, 1976), 141; Stanley Feldstein, *Once a Slave: The Slaves' View of Slavery* (New York, 1971), 172–78; Blassingame (ed.), *Slave Testimony*, 153, 170, 173, 219, 374,

necessarily reflexive reactions to their situations. According to a pre-scient white observer, there was a direct relationship between white relegation of blacks to the status of property and many slaves' re-taliatory appropriation of whites' property:

The man, in whose favour no laws of property exist, probably feels himself less bound to respect those made in the favour of others. When arguing for our-selves, we lay it down as a fundamental, that laws, to be just, must give a reciprocation of right: that, without this, they are mere arbitrary rules of conduct, founded in force, and not in conscience: and it is a problem which I give the master to solve, whether the religious precepts against the violation of property were not framed for him as well as his slave? And whether the slave may not as justifiably take a little from one, who has taken all from him, as he may slay one who would slay him?[46]

The problem with this formulation is that it places slaves in a subor-dinate position, dependent on white error or immorality as an excuse, guide, or justification for action. Like some of Jefferson's other at-tempts to solve the American dilemma, his reasoning here combined the assumptions of white supremacy and the theory of the social con-tract. Whites have violated the contract, so slaves can act for them-selves. But the situation of slaves required that they first act for them-selves and in accordance with their own notions if they wished to have any power over their own lives.

Still, it was against special shackles that many slaves would struggle in the effort to act for themselves. Other groups in North American, Western Hemisphere, and European societies would find themselves in legal and judicial shackles as well, but the simple fact that they were not slaves inevitably meant that their shackles differed from those fastened onto slaves. Those groups included free blacks,[47] Native

652; Rawick (ed.), *The American Slave*, Supp., Ser. 1, Vol. III (South Carolina), Pt. 3, p. 172, Pt. 4, pp. 179–80, Vol. II (South Carolina), Pt. 2, p. 161, among many other examples; Frederick Douglass, *The Life and Times of Frederick Douglass Written by Himself* (Rev. ed., 1892; London, 1962), 104–105; Litwack, *"Been in the Storm,"* 478, 522; Henry L. Swint (ed.), *Dear Ones at Home: Letters from the Contraband Camps* (Nashville, 1966), 22; Law-rence W. Levine, *Black Culture and Black Consciousness: Afro-American Folk Thought from Slavery to Freedom* (New York, 1977), 122–31; Ralph Roberts, "A Slave's Story," *Putnam's Monthly*, IX (June, 1857), 617–18; *Weevils in the Wheat*, 78, 116, 124, 139–40, 181, 244–45. Whether her remarks were tailored for white consumption is not clear, but one interviewed former slave did state that slaves did not think stealing was right. They only did it because they were driven to by hunger.

46. Thomas Jefferson, *Notes on the State of Virginia* (Chapel Hill, 1955), 142.

47. Ira Berlin, *Slaves Without Masters: The Free Negro in the Antebellum South* (New York, 1974), 183, 186–87, 360–62; John H. Russell, *The Free Negro in Virginia, 1619–1865* (1913, rpr. New York, 1969), 164–67; Schwarz, "Forging the Shackles," 125–46; June Purcell Guild, *Black Laws of Virginia* (Richmond, 1936), 161–70; Stroud, *A Sketch of the Laws*, 77–80.

Americans,[48] members of other ethnic groups,[49] contract servants, convict servants, the poor, military volunteers and draftees, laborers, especially union organizers, prisoners, and women, particularly those accused of witchcraft.[50] Numerous segments of European populations

48. U.S. Army, Military Commission, 1862, Papers, photostats, in Minnesota Historical Society, St. Paul (originals in Records of the Senate, RG 46, SEN 37A-F2, National Archives); David A. Nichols, *Lincoln and the Indians: Civil War Policy and Politics* (Columbia, Mo., 1978), 75–78, 94–118, 175; William W. Folwell, *History of Minnesota* (4 vols.; St. Paul, 1922–30), II, 109–241; the "Peach Gang" incident (1638), an episode of "Ourstory," a 1975 series that appeared on public television station WNET and is available as a feature film; Yasuhide Kawashima, "Forced Conformity: Puritan Criminal Justice and Indians," *Kansas Law Review*, XXV (1977), 361–73; Kawashima, "Jurisdiction of the Colonial Courts Over the Indians in Massachusetts, 1689–1763," *NEQ*, XLII (1969), 532–50; Kawashima, *Puritan Justice and the Indian: White Man's Law in Massachusetts, 1630–1763* (Middletown, Conn., 1983); Lyle Koehler, "Red-White Relations and Justice in the Courts of Seventeenth-Century New England," *American Indian Culture and Research Journal*, III (1979), 1–31; W. Stitt Robinson, Jr., "The Legal Status of the Indian in Colonial Virginia," *VMHB*, LXI (1953), 249–59; James P. Ronda, "Red and White at the Bench: Indians and the Law in Plymouth County, 1620–1691," *Essex Institute Historical Collections*, CX (1974), 200–215; Colonial Office, Class 5, No. 1314, fols. 208–209, No. 1341, fols. 16–17, in VCRP; Sussex County, Virginia, Court Papers, 1756–1757, bundle no. 5, microfilm reel 38, in VSL; Memorial of Edith Turner, Nottoway Indian, December, 1821, and Petition of Pamunkey Indians to protect "our laws, rules, and regulations," February 18, 1836, both in VEPLR; Timothy Morgan, "Turmoil in an Orderly Society: Colonial Virginia, 1607–1754: A History and Analysis" (Ph.D. dissertation, College of William and Mary, 1976), 35–51, 71–81, 97–104, 116–23, 148–55, 204–208; *Ex parte Crow Dog,* 109 U.S. 556 (1883), *U.S.* v. *Kagama,* 118 U.S. 375 (1886), *Keeble* v. *U.S.,* 412 U.S. 205 (1973), and *U.S.* v. *Antelope,* 430 U.S. 641 (1977); Wilcomb E. Washburn, "The Historical Context of American Indian Legal Problems," *Law and Contemporary Problems,* XL (1976), 12–24; U.S. Bureau of Indian Affairs, Division of Law Enforcement Services, *Indian Law Enforcement History* (Washington, D.C., 1975); William Thomas Kagan, *Indian Police and Judges: Experiments in Acculturation and Control* (New Haven, 1966), 88–89; Tim Vollmann, "Criminal Jurisdiction in Indian Country: Tribal Sovereignty and Defendants' Rights in Conflict," *Kansas Law Review,* XXII (1974), 387–412; Brend H. Gubler, *A Constitutional Analysis of the Criminal Jurisdiction and Procedural Guarantees of the American Indian* (Saratoga, Calif., 1974); Mary Beth West, *Manual of Indian Criminal Jurisdiction* (10 vols. to date; Washington, D.C., 1977–); Laurence French and Jim Hornbuckle, "An Analysis of Indian Violence: The Cherokee Example," *American Indian Quarterly,* III (1977–78), 335–56; *Voices from Wounded Knee, 1973: In the Words of the Participants* (Rooseveltown, N.Y., 1974); *New York Times Index,* 1973–86.

49. Divergent approaches include: David R. Johnson, *Policing the Urban Underworld: The Impact of Crime on the Development of the American Police, 1800–1887* (Philadelphia, 1979); James Francis Caye, "Crime and Violence in the Heterogeneous Urban Community: Pittsburgh, 1870–1899" (Ph.D. dissertation, University of Pittsburgh, 1977); Ronald Lee Boostrom, "The Personalization of Evil: The Emergence of American Criminology, 1865–1910" (Ph.D. dissertation, University of California, Berkeley, 1974); Eric H. Monkonnen, *The Dangerous Class: Crime and Poverty in Columbus, Ohio, 1860–1885* (Cambridge, Mass., 1975); Michael S. Hindus, *Prison and Plantation: Crime, Justice, and Authority in Massachusetts and South Carolina, 1767–1878* (Chapel Hill, 1980); Allen Steinberg, "History of Immigration and Crime," in U.S. Select Commission on Immigration and Refugee Policy, *U.S. Immigration Policy and the National Interest: Staff Report* (10 vols.; Washington, D.C., 1981), Appendix A, 463–630.

50. Two sources of voluminous citations from the growing literature on crime in early America are Douglas Greenberg, "Crime, Law Enforcement, and Social Control in Colo-

became marked people who knew judicial discrimination and oppression quite well. Serfs, peasants, women, again especially those accused of witchcraft, heretics, Jews, Muslims, Gypsies, and even colonists understood how their status affected their chances in a criminal court when their behavior threatened a member of a society's dominant group.[51] Noblesse oblige or genteel restraint may have saved some oppressed Europeans from the harshest penalties just as paternalism could protect some slaves from the worst punishments.[52] The fundamental similarity was that all such peoples were not equal before the law.

nial America"; and Kathryn Preyer, "Penal Measures in the American Colonies: An Overview," both in *AJLH*, XXVI (1982), 293–325, 326–353. See also T. H. Breen, James H. Lewis, and Keith Schlesinger, "Motive for Murder: A Servant's Life in Virginia, 1678," *WMQ*, 3rd ser., XL (1983), 106–20; Frederick Hall Schmidt, "British Convict Servant Labor in Colonial Virginia" (Ph.D. dissertation, College of William and Mary, 1976), 245–49; Marion Dargan, "Crime and the Virginia Gazette, 1736–1775," *University of New Mexico Bulletin, Sociological Series*, Vol. II, No. 1 (1934), 55; Fairfax Harrison, "When the Convicts Came," *VMHB*, XXX (1922), 250–60; Eli Faber, "Puritan Criminals: The Economic, Social, and Intellectual Background of Crime in 17th-Century Massachusetts," *Perspectives in American History*, XI (1977–78), 81–144; Faber, "The Evil That Men Do: Crime and Transgression in Colonial Massachusetts" (Ph.D. dissertation, Columbia University, 1974); Jules Zanger, "Crime and Punishment in Early Massachusetts," *WMQ*, 3rd ser., XXII (1965), 471–77; Nicholas Canny, "The Permissive Frontier: The Problem of Social Control in English Settlements in Ireland and Virginia, 1550–1650," in K. R. Andrews *et al.* (eds.), *The Westward Empire: English Activities in Ireland, the Atlantic, and America, 1480–1650* (Liverpool, England, 1978), 17–44; Richard B. Morris, *Government and Labor in Early America* (New York, 1946), 461–500; Lawrence Towner, "Fondness for Freedom: Servant Protest in Puritan Society," *WMQ*, 3rd ser., XIX (1962), 201–20; Towner, " 'A Good Master Well Served': A Social History of Servitude in Massachusetts, 1620–1750" (Ph.D. dissertation, Northwestern University, 1955), 118–45, 329, 397–430; John Putnam Demos, *Entertaining Satan: Witchcraft and the Culture of Early New England* (New York, 1982), esp. 401–409, "List of Known Witchcraft Cases in Seventeenth-Century New England"; Lyle Koehler, *A Search for Power: The 'Weaker Sex' in Seventeenth Century New England* (Urbana, 1980), 264–300, 383–417, 474–91; Morgan, "Turmoil in an Orderly Society," 124–29; Richard Slotkin, "Narratives of Negro Crime in New England, 1675–1800," *American Quarterly*, XXV (1973), 3–31. For some notion of the punishments to which various American soldiers were liable, see Douglas Southall Freeman, *George Washington: A Biography* (7 vols.; New York, 1948–57), II, 131, 138–39, 202, 259, V, 112.

51. Besides the work of such authors as Douglas Hay, among the best examples of the voluminous literature on crime in Europe is a comparative study, namely, Peter Kolchin's "The Process of Confrontation: Patterns of Resistance to Bondage in Nineteenth-Century Russia and the United States," *Journal of Social History*, XI (1978), 457–90. See also Douglas Hay, "Crime and Justice in Eighteenth- and Nineteenth-Century England," in Norval Morris and Michael Tonry (eds.), *Crime and Justice: An Annual Review of Research*, II (1980), 45–84; Albert Hartshorne, *Hanging in Chains* (London, 1891), which indicates (p. 110) that the last hanging in chains in England was in 1834; and Malise Ruthven, *Torture: The Grand Conspiracy* (London, 1978).

52. Hay, "Property, Authority and the Criminal Law," in Hay *et al.* (eds.), *Albion's Fatal Tree*, 17–63.

But no other system of legal and judicial discrimination was quite the same as that created by the slave code. Slavery, of course, made the difference in the shape of the shackles. Members of other groups in various societies fulfilled dominant groups' worst expectations of them when they violated criminal statutes. Like the deviants in Kai T. Erikson's study of seventeenth-century Massachusetts, those oppressed, exploited, or despised peoples of the world who committed crimes reinforced the dominant groups' perception of their own worth and values.[53] White authorities relied on separate and discriminatory codes and courts for slaves partly for the same reason, but they did so primarily because almost any defiant slave threatened whites' sense of control and superiority.

If the shackles were shaped mainly for political reasons and secondarily for social reasons, how did Virginian slaves deal with the shackles? Their actions were political in effect even when they were not politically motivated. That was because of white leaders' perceptions, which were stronger at some times and some places than others. Therefore only that behavior of slaves perceived by white authorities as dangerous, threatening, or destructive—*i.e.*, criminal—can show us how slaves dealt with the legal and judicial shackles.

53. Kai T. Erikson, *Wayward Puritans: A Study in Deviance* (New York, 1966).

2. *Slaves and Crime: A Problem of Evidence*

The nature of the historian's problem in analyzing the relationship between slaves and crime in Virginia is apparent in *White Over Black*, the pioneering work by Winthrop Jordan about whites' attitudes toward blacks in early America. In a chapter entitled "The Cancer of Revolution," Jordan explains how news of the Saint Domingue uprising directly stimulated slave rebelliousness, as well as white fear of rebelliousness, in the United States. "It is incontrovertibly evident . . . that a period of pronounced unrest among American slaves began not long after word arrived of racial turmoil in St. Domingo." Before and after making this direct statement, however, Jordan seems less sure of his evidence. Some newspapers suppressed news of revolts, he tells us; various witnesses might distort the facts for different reasons, and others may simply have been spreading groundless rumors. "But the vast bulk of information concerning slave rebelliousness completely eludes certainty of interpretation," Jordan soon asserts. He then is willing only to give examples of what happened. His final comment is that "the present need, of course, is for quantitative studies of these occurrences," that is, all examples of major slave resistance.[1]

Jordan's conclusions suggest the solution to the historian's problem of interpretation. Jordan is convinced that even though "we simply do not know" how much rebellion occurred, "even the most cursory reading in the newspapers suggests persuasively that there was enough of it to give contemporaries genuine cause for alarm." In his use of James Hugo Johnston's data for executed Virginia slaves from 1783 to 1814,

1. Jordan, *White Over Black*, 391–92.

Jordan implicitly recognizes that rebelliousness involved the interaction of conflicting perceptions and behavior. Deflated as were those data, they did reveal widespread and persistent challenges to white authorities. It is up to historians to analyze the confrontations between slaves and whites, and even among slaves, reflected in the trials of slaves for criminal offenses. But Jordan cautioned his readers that there was "little reason to think Virginia typical."[2] Understanding that there is little reason to think that any slave state was typical and realizing that we must therefore have the same kind of data for all, or perhaps nearly all, slave states before drawing valid conclusions for the entire slave South, we can at least begin the job of analysis with data from Virginia. The remaining question is, then, whether these data support generalizations about slave crime in that place. Several scholars have analyzed criminal cases concerning slaves in order to illuminate the criminal justice system as it affected enslaved defendants.[3] The present need is to determine whether scholars can also rely on these criminal cases as evidence for the interaction of slaves and whites and among slaves.[4]

In spite of all the hidden traps for the unwary historian as well as the wary, the trials do provide a measure of the minimum number of major illegal acts by slaves in Virginia between the early eighteenth and late nineteenth century. Unjust and biased though the slave code

2. *Ibid.*, 392–93.

3. Hindus, *Prison and Plantation;* Douglas Greenberg, *Crime and Law Enforcement in the Colony of New York, 1691–1776* (Ithaca, 1976), 72–76, 138–39, 142, 149–52; A. E. Keir Nash, "Reason of Slavery: Understanding the Judicial Role in the Peculiar Institution," *Vanderbilt Law Review,* XXXII (1979), 7–218, which cites a great deal of relevant secondary literature; Robert M. Saunders, "Crime and Punishment in Early National America: Richmond, Virginia, 1784–1820," *VMHB,* LXXXVI (1978), 33–44; Alan D. Watson, "Impulse Toward Independence: Resistance and Rebellion Among North Carolina Slaves, 1750–1775," *JNH,* LXIII (1978), 319–21; Watson, "North Carolina Slave Courts, 1715–1785," *North Carolina Historical Review,* LX (1983), 24–36; Duncan J. MacLeod, *Slavery, Race, and the American Revolution* (Cambridge, England, 1974), 152–53; Mark Tushnet, "Approaches to the Study of the Law of Slavery," *Civil War History,* XXV (1979), 329–38. See also William Cinque Henderson, "Spartan Slaves: A Documentary Account of Blacks on Trial in Spartanburg, South Carolina, 1830 to 1865" (Ph.D. dissertation, Northwestern University, 1978); Flanigan, "The Criminal Law of Slavery"; and James Hugo Johnston, *Race Relations in Virginia and Miscegenation in the South, 1776–1860* (Amherst, Mass., 1970).

4. As in the rest of this study, the word *crime* and the term *slave crime* refer only to behavior as evaluated by the slave code of Virginia. I reject any assumption that these means of historical identification also constitute my evaluation of the behavior I am analyzing. For an argument against the notion that historians can learn much about slaves' behavior from criminal trials of slaves, see Tushnet, *The American Law of Slavery,* 16–18.

and courts were, they were meant to serve the practical function of suppressing slaves who endangered people, property, or slavery itself. White authorities at least tried to make the system work correctly and accurately, even if not justly. Otherwise the system would not have served its purpose nearly as well. As a result, historians can make valid use of the trial records as evidence concerning the behavior of a significant number of slaves.

No one doubts the significance of the courts. The slave tribunals were the most formal and structured manifestation of the power of those who led white society. Such episodes as Gabriel's Plot and Nat Turner's Revolt forced overtly rebellious slaves into confrontations with the "hegemony of the law" in segregated criminal courts. But those were special cases. In the same bodies, judges also heard prosecutions of slave "property" for stealing other forms of property and censured those kinds of behavior the law defined as dangerous and antisocial. The major stumbling block to relying on the records of these courts as anything more than evidence for legal change, white racism, or legalized oppression is that they appear to be nothing more than kangaroo courts.[5] Slaveholders made no pretense of providing equality before the law to bondspeople even in the most lenient societies or calmest situations. That would have been self-contradictory behavior. Later constant discrimination by American courts of law against black people not only has made those institutions notorious examples of the judiciary's perpetuation of injustice but has rendered their records particularly suspect in the eyes of historians.[6] In addition, well-documented white reliance on private punishments to control Afro-American bondspeople gives historians good reason to ask whether the public trials of slaves on which generalizations are to be based can yield comprehensive data.[7]

5. See, for example, F. Nwabueze Okoye, "Chattel Slavery as the Nightmare of the American Revolutionaries," *WMQ*, 3rd ser., XXXVII (1980), 7, 20.
6. Justice Joseph P. Bradley in the Civil Rights Cases, 109 U.S. 3 (1883); Jack Greenberg, *Race Relations and American Law* (New York, 1959), 313–42; Guy B. Johnson, "The Negro and Crime," *Annals of the American Academy of Political and Social Science*, CCLXXI (1941), 93–104; Saunders, "Crime and Punishment," 33–44; Stroud, *A Sketch of the Laws*, 77–80.
7. Kenneth M. Stampp, *The Peculiar Institution: Slavery in the Ante-Bellum South* (New York, 1956), 171–77; Mullin, *Flight and Rebellion*, 20–33, 71; Michael Greenberg, "William Byrd II and the World of the Market," *Southern Studies*, XVI (1977), 451–56; Eugene D. Genovese, *Roll, Jordan, Roll: The World the Slaves Made* (New York, 1974), 383, 655. Good examples of private punishment appear in John Tayloe to Landon Carter, April 23, 1774, and Robert Wormeley Carter to Landon Carter, May 10, 1774, both in

The trials were certainly numerous. The papers of Virginia's county courts are available in large numbers and provide an excellent opportunity to test the utility and reliability of slave trials as evidence concerning slaves' behavior.[8] The records are voluminous because of Virginia's laws concerning court records and because Virginia had one of the largest slave populations of any European colony in the Western Hemisphere and continued to have the largest slave population in the United States until 1865.[9] Many more records of slave trials than of the trials of free persons have survived because of the Old Dominion's segregated judicial system. Free people stood trial for felonies at the centralized General Court until 1788, and later at the district or superior courts. Fire, war, theft, and mismanagement resulted in the destruction of the official records of all of the former sessions and many of the latter. Fortunately for historians, slave trial records did not generally meet the same fate.[10]

From 1692 until 1865, Virginia county justices of oyer and terminer ran capital trials—and other felony trials as well after 1786. Few such trials occurred before the first decade of the eighteenth century, so it is reasonable to consider the handful of cases from the early years of the oyer and terminer courts as skimpy evidence.[11] But after the colony's lawmakers promulgated the comprehensive slave code of 1705, partly because of the concomitant rapid rise in the slave population, justices presided over more and more slave trials each year.[12] The number of sessions reached a consistent annual level by the 1780s.

I have collected several sets of data in order to be as comprehensive as possible as well as to secure representative evidence from certain periods and places. The 1,988 trials related to 1,453 incidents con-

Landon Carter Papers, Alderman Library, UVa; Herbert G. Gutman, *The Black Family in Slavery and Freedom, 1750–1925* (New York, 1976), 262–63. See also Nicholls, " 'In the Light of Human Beings,' " 67–78, for an excellent example of the range of slave behavior that an antebellum Virginia planter hoped to control on his own.

8. David H. Flaherty, "A Select Guide to the Manuscript Court Records of Virginia," *AJLH*, XIX (1975), 112–37, provides a formal listing.

9. Hening, *The Statutes at Large*, I, 303–304, III, 511–12, XI, 464–66; Shepherd, *Statutes at Large*, II, 280.

10. Flaherty, "A Select Guide," 112–37; Tate, *Negro in Eighteenth-Century Williamsburg*, 91–99.

11. For example, Accomack C.C.O.B. (1690–97), 195–96, (1697–1703), 137; Morgan, *American Slavery*, 412–13, 422–23. See also Governor Nicholson to Board of Trade, with supporting documents, December 1, 1701, in Colonial Office, Class 5, No. 1312, Pt. 1, fols. 200, 243–50, Pt. 2. fols. 20–24, VCRP.

12. Hening, *The Statutes at Large*, III, 447–62.

stitute a large portion of all capital and noncapital trials of slaves held in eighteenth-century Virginia. As Table 3 indicates, the data cover an important period—1706 to 1785—and include cases from counties

Table 3. Trials in Courts of Oyer and Terminer, 1706–1785

Charge	Accused	Convicted	Simple Rate of Conviction	Percentage of All Convictions
I. Stealing	1,080	775	71.8%	
Arson	36	13	36.1	
Receiving stolen goods	20	14	70.0	
Hog stealing	89	80	89.9	
Other	19	8	42.1	
Against property	1,244	890	71.5	63.6%
II. Murder and attempted murder	155	109	70.3	
Poisoning and administering illegal medication	186	115	61.8	
Rape and attempted rape	59	50	84.7	
Assault	17	14	82.4	
Other	2	2	100.0	
Against persons	419	290	69.2	20.7
III. Perjury	10	9	90.0	
Escaping prison	9	7	77.8	
Comforting felon	2	2	100.0	
Running away	13	13	100.0	
Aiding runaway	1	0	0.0	
Against system	35	31	86.6	2.2
IV. Insurrection/conspiracy	28	25	89.3	1.8
V. Unspecified	262	163	62.2	11.7

SOURCES: Documents of counties and cities represented (Parentheses indicate those jurisdictions that did not exist until the late 1770s or whose records have mostly not survived): Accomack, (Albemarle), Amelia, Amherst, Augusta, Bedford, Botetourt, Brunswick, (Campbell), Caroline, (Charles City), Charlotte, Chesterfield, (Culpeper), Cumberland, Elizabeth City, Essex, Fairfax, Fauquier, (Fluvanna), Frederick, (Fredericksburg), Goochland, (Greensville), Halifax, Henrico, (Henry), Isle of Wight, King George, Lancaster, Loudoun, Louisa, Lunenburg, Mecklenburg, Middlesex, Montgomery, Norfolk, Norfolk city, Northampton, Northumberland, Orange, (Petersburg city), Pittsylvania, (Powhatan), Prince Edward, Prince William, Princess Anne, Richmond (county), (Rockbridge), (Rockingham), Shenandoah (Dunmore), Southampton, Spotsylvania, Surry, Sussex, (Warwick), (Washington), Westmoreland, York.
NOTE: In only nineteen instances was breaking and entering charged by itself. Any case of breaking and entering that also involved a theft was therefore counted only as a theft.

whose slave population had demographic and historical features in common with counties whose records have not survived. For example, regrettable as is the loss of court order books from such counties as James City and Prince George, documents from such counties as Lancaster and Spotsylvania help to compensate. Two rough measures of the availability of cases—extant years of records weighed against missing years of records, and the population of "lost-record" counties as a percentage of the population of all Virginia counties—suggest that the surviving record may amount to 60 or 75 percent of all capital as well as noncapital trials of slaves ever held in Virginia between 1706 and 1785. The records of certain counties contain gaps, but they do not occur with sufficient consistency to destroy the usefulness of the trial data.

Two different kinds of data cover the years 1786 to 1865. Table 4 indicates the origins of some comprehensive trial data. Like the sources from 1706 to 1785, these sources contain information that makes it possible to determine how many slaves faced trial, what charges were brought against them, and the simple rate of conviction—that is, the percentage of persons actually tried who were found guilty of various offenses.[13] Table 5 includes the records that the Old Dominion's Auditor's Office and the Treasury Office kept of public compensation paid to owners for the value of executed or transported slaves. While these records do not include all the convictions of slaves for serious offenses, they do include almost all of those regarded as the most serious by white county and state authorities—as indicated by the carrying out of the harshest sentences available. The total of all cases from 1706 to 1865 is 4,342; the total of convictions is 3,432.[14]

These records appear to have enormous utility for the historian. In many cases, they stand as the only available description of the attempts of otherwise anonymous slaves to defy the apparently overwhelming coercive power held by whites. But these records can be only as useful as they are valid, especially when relied on to support

13. For an explanation of the simple conviction rate, see Michael S. Hindus and Douglas Lamar Jones, "Quantitative and Theoretical Approaches to the History of Crime and Law," *Newberry Papers in Family and Community History*, No. 77–46 (Chicago, 1977), 25–26.

14. The simple conviction rate has meaning only for the data on trials. All the data in the Auditor's Office and the executive records concern convictions; only the data found in county court order and minute books support computation of the simple conviction rate for Virginia.

Table 4. Trials in Oyer and Terminer Courts, Selected
Jurisdictions, 1786–1865

	Accused	Convicted	Simple Conviction Rate	% of Convictions
I. Against Property				
Brunswick, 1786–99	17	6	35.29%	54.55%
Essex, 1786–1865	103	48	46.60	67.61
Henrico, 1786–1802	36	22	61.11	29.33
Henry, 1786–1865	23	18	78.26	46.16
Richmond (city), 1786–99	67	36	53.73	87.80
Southampton, 1786–1865	71	36	50.70	33.96
Spotsylvania, 1786–1859	81	50	61.73	54.47
II. Against Persons				
Brunswick	9	4	44.44	36.36
Essex	33	15	45.46	21.13
Henrico	11	9	81.82	12.00
Henry	34	20	58.82	51.28
Richmond (city)	1	1	100.00	2.44
Southampton	47	34	72.34	32.08
Spotsylvania	40	24	60.00	27.59
III. Against System				
Brunswick	1	1	100.00	9.09
Essex	6	6	100.00	8.45
Henrico	1	1	100.00	1.33
Henry	1	1	100.00	2.56
Richmond (city)	0	0	0.00	0.00
Southampton	0	0	0.00	0.00
Spotsylvania	0	0	0.00	0.00
IV. Insurrection				
Brunswick	0	0	0.00	0.00
Essex	2	0	0.00	0.00
Henrico	60	42	70.00	56.00
Henry	0	0	0.00	0.00
Richmond (city)	0	0	0.00	0.00

(*continued*)

Table 4.   (Continued)

	Accused	Convicted	Simple Conviction Rate	% of Convictions
Southampton	58	36	62.07	33.96
Spotsylvania	25	10	40.00	11.49
V. Unspecified Felony				
Brunswick	0	0	0.00	0.00
Essex	4	2	50.00	2.81
Henrico	2	1	50.00	1.34
Henry	5	0	0.00	0.00
Richmond (city)	6	4	66.67	9.76
Southampton	1	0	0.00	0.00
Spotsylvania	6	3	50.00	3.45

SOURCES: Documents of counties and the city represented.
NOTE: See Table 3 for the components of categories I–IV. Based on the number of trials in the four representative counties whose records were surveyed from 1786 to 1865, a rough estimate of the total number of trials and convictions for all 91 counties that existed by 1860 is 9,100 trials and 4,550 convictions. These figures are, of course, rather inexact. They are meant only to suggest how many trials and convictions might have occurred.

The years cited in I for each jurisdiction apply in the other categories.

generalizations. There are several ways to test that validity. One is implicit in this entire study. That is, if this study holds up well under critical evaluation, that will implicitly confirm the validity of the use made of the data. Explicit justification is still needed. A noted historian of slavery has articulated a set of standards for systematically evaluating the validity of data from trial documents. According to Kenneth Stampp, such "white sources" as plantation diaries, slave-management articles, and fugitive slave advertisements are "at least as valuable as the available black sources" as evidence concerning slaves' behavior because they reflect the pressure for accuracy and not for distortion, they were firsthand, and they were recorded soon after the event.[15]

Virginia's slave court records, certainly a "white source," meet Stampp's standards fairly well, even though they seem to suffer from extraordinary distortion. The authority of the trial judges did derive

15. Kenneth M. Stampp, "Slavery—The Historian's Burden," in Harry P. Owens (ed.), Perspectives and Irony in American Slavery (Jackson, Miss., 1976), 169.

Table 5. Trial Data, 1785–1865

	Executed	Transported or Public Works	Escaped	Died in Prison	Unknown Outcome	Total
I. Against Property						
Stealing	46	331	4	1	2	384
Robbery	14	19	0	0	0	33
Arson	24	121	0	0	0	145
Total	84	471	4	1	2	562
II. Against Persons						
Murder (unspecified or first degree)	274	96	0	1	3	374
Murder (second degree or manslaughter)	0	32	0	0	0	32
Infanticide	3	15	0	0	0	18
Attempted murder	33	119	0	0	2	154
Poisoning or illegal medication	35	49	1	0	0	85
Rape	59	22	0	0	0	81
Attempted rape	24	32	0	0	0	56
Assault	4	21	1	0	0	26
Total	432	386	2	1	5	826
III. Against System						
Aid runaway	0	5	0	0	0	5
Forge pass	0	1	0	0	0	1

(continued)

Table 5. (Continued)

	Executed	Transported or Public Works	Escaped	Died in Prison	Unknown Outcome	Total
Print abolitionist liter- ature	0	1	0	0	0	1
Total		7				7
IV. Insurrection	79	56	0	1	3	139
V. Unspecified	31	63	0	0	0	94
Totals	626	983	6	3	10	1,628
(Percentage of convicted)	(38.5)	(60.4)	(trace)	(trace)	(trace)	

SOURCES: C.S., boxes 1–10.
NOTE: These figures differ from those in Flanigan, "The Criminal Law of Slavery and Freedom," 404, because, using VEPLR, Treasury cash journals, and miscellaneous county court records, I could identify numerous cases that Flanigan had to list as "unspecified" and I could fill in 130 of the missing cases from 1855 to 1863.

only from white representatives' legislation; punishments administered by white court officials reflected only their conception of the
proper social order; and the entire judicial process certainly supported white slaveowners' domination of black slaves. Yet the judges'
bias is so obvious that it can be useful to historians. Criminalization of
certain slave behavior and the search by judges and prosecutors for
slaves' motives created a record of blacks' conscious decisions that
would otherwise not be available. Indeed, the trial records are prime
examples of "witnesses in spite of themselves."[16] Slaves could ordinarily ill afford to tell their owners what they intended to do for
themselves; they had to conceal their plans and dissemble. In trying to
protect the social order as defined by white leaders, justices unwit-
tingly chronicled the attempt of many slaves to operate outside of,
even to redefine, the social order imposed on them. Here were, for the
most part, slaves acting on their own behalf and according to their own
ethic. Criminal trials of slaves therefore frequently amounted to public confrontations, whether acknowledged or not, between conflicting
Afro-American and Euro-American cultures.

It was a fundamental conflict of values that led to many of the criminal prosecutions. First, newly imported Africans often brought with
them strongly developed conceptions of crime, justice, and judicial
institutions, so they could evaluate the slave code and courts. Second,
all slaves learned what it meant to be a slave. What a black person
might have called killing in self-defense a slave court often classified as
a capital crime. If slaves regarded their appropriation of a slave-
holder's property as "taking," the courts condemned such behavior as
criminal theft. Slaves who had actually done what judges said was a
crime knew—from county authorities' announcement of relevant statutes on the steps of the parish church, memorable court cases, the
slave grapevine, or some other means—that certain actions violated
the criminal code whether or not they were justified and whether or
not whites gave slaves fair trials and punishments.[17] Indeed, that is

16. Mullin, *Flight and Rebellion*, x, applies French historian Marc Bloch's definition of
"witnesses in spite of themselves" to primary evidence concerning slavery.
17. Hening, *The Statutes at Large*, III, 461, IV, 134; Rhys Isaac, "Dramatizing the
Ideology of Revolution: Popular Mobilization in Virginia, 1774 to 1776," *WMQ*, 3rd ser.,
XXXIII (1976), 357–85, esp. 364–67; A. G. Roeber, "Authority, Law, and Custom: The
Rituals of Court Day in Tidewater Virginia, 1720–1750," *WMQ*, 3rd ser., XXXVII (1980),
29–52; Philip J. Schwarz, "Adaptation of Afro-American Slaves to the Anglo-American
Judiciary" (Paper delivered at the forty-first Conference of the Institute of Early Ameri-
can History and Culture, April 30, 1981, Millersville [Pa.] State College).

what makes slaves' "criminal" behavior so interesting to historians. The conscious violation of formally or informally announced laws indicated intentions of the greatest social and historical significance. In 1802 a Goochland County slaveholder somehow managed to exclaim "You have killed me" to a slave who had just fractured his skull. "Damn you," replied Dick. "That's what I intended to do." Even though Dick had responded to his master's threat of renewed whipping, he probably knew that he would find no justification for his self-defense in the Old Dominion's slave code. Instead he would encounter conviction and punishment. Yet Dick apparently still intended to kill his master.[18]

In spite of the obvious bias of judges, several forces for accuracy competed with forces for distortion in the trials of slaves. The trial records partly meet one of Stampp's standards. First, the nature of the crime prosecuted influenced, but could not determine, the judges' decision to convict. The rank order of simple conviction rates for crimes of which more than twenty-five slaves were accused in Virginia between 1706 and 1785 bears this out. The extraordinarily threatening crime of insurrection (89.3 percent) and the much-feared crime of rape (84.7 percent) stand near the top, and the crimes against the system of control (88.6 percent), such as escaping from prison, perjury, or running away, also rank high. One aspect of murder convictions reveals the fears the justices experienced. In sixty-six prosecutions of slaves for murdering whites between 1706 and 1785, about 81 percent of the slaves received guilty verdicts and 4.6 percent had the charge reduced to a misdemeanor; about 52 percent of the slaves charged with murdering other slaves were convicted, of whom nearly 11 percent benefited from reduced charges. A partial cause for that difference in percentage was the perceived threat to white lives and domination as opposed to the endangering of slave property.[19]

18. Trial of Dick, November 15, 1802, Hanover County, C.S., box 2; Hening, *The Statutes at Large*, III, 459, VI, 110.
19. See A. Leon Higginbotham, Jr., *In the Matter of Color: Race and the American Legal Process: The Colonial Period* (New York, 1978), 289. Racism certainly encouraged the continuation of this pattern of convictions well after slavery ended. Gunnar Myrdal *et al., The American Dilemma: The Negro Problem and Modern Democracy* (New York, 1944), 969; and Hortense Powdermaker, *After Freedom: A Cultural Study of the Deep South* (New York, 1968), 173–74, are two among many perspectives on the problem. See also Samuel R. Gross and Robert Mauro, "Patterns of Death: An Analysis of Racial Disparities in Capital Sentencing and Homicide Victimization," *Stanford Law Review*, XXXVII (1984), 27–153; and Samuel R. Gross, "Race and Death: The Judicial Evaluation of Evidence of

The obvious anomalies in the conviction rates show, however, that antislave, proslavery bias was not the only factor in the process. Some kinds of behavior escaped detection more easily than others did. Hog stealers (89.9 percent) presented relatively little threat, but they could be readily discovered in the act or in possession of marked hogs. Arsonists (36.1 percent), on the other hand, could occasionally be caught in the act, but they would otherwise leave little or no incriminating physical evidence. Convictions for murder (70.3 percent) and poisoning/illegal medication (61.8 percent) represent the tension between the factors of danger and detectability. Even though both were particularly hostile acts, they were neither so easy to detect as hog stealing nor so difficult to discover as arson.

It was the legal status of slaves as property that influenced many judges to strive to identify accurately those responsible for actions defined as crimes. Indeed, this attempt helped to ensure, though it certainly did not guarantee, that slave courts would not necessarily be kangaroo courts. Because white owners had a substantial economic interest in the labor or fertility of slaves who appeared in criminal courts, they and their allies on the bench tried to balance the need for accurate identification and the conflicting desire to subdue the dangerous behavior of aggressive slaves. Just as it would threaten the safety or raise the fears of white society not to discover or to "let off too easily" the slave responsible for what they regarded as a major crime, so it would jeopardize a capital investment and labor productivity to convict and exile or execute the wrong slave. Moreover, the justices might feel compelled to try to protect the property rights of the slave's owner. The existing slave code and the circumstances of the case might work against this economic and legal motivation, but they could not always or entirely eliminate it. The percentage of *not* guilty verdicts reflects the effort of many judges to convict only those slaves whom they thought to have actually broken a law.

The crime of insurrection was a special case. The laws defining the offense and the harshness of the sanctions made convictions highly likely. However, in instances where no blood had been shed, they also increased the probability of accurate identification of slaves who had engaged in what owners called insurrectionary plotting or behavior.

Discrimination in Capital Sentencing," *University of California Davis Law Review*, XVIII (1985), 1275–1325, part of an entire issue devoted to a Death Penalty Symposium.

Virginia's lawmakers consistently classified numerous actions as conspiracy or insurrection simply because they were the actions—indeed, sometimes merely the expressions—of slaves. In other words, legislators created a status offense, one that could be committed almost only by slaves. They also thereby made available a weapon with which white authorities could "keep slaves in their place." Moreover, the vagueness of the legislation left county justices great latitude to make *ad hoc* or *ad hominem* applications of the definitions of slave conspiracy and insurrection.[20] Historians have frequently relied on insurrection trials as evidence of collective slave resistance because of their belief that the evidence in the trials was historically valid.[21]

The rough comparison of simple conviction rates for free white and slave trials provides yet another test of the reliability of slave trial records as evidence of certain kinds of slave behavior. Exact comparison is impossible. Different factors influenced the decisions to prosecute white and enslaved suspects.[22] The relatively greater difficulty of privately disciplining free whites, even when class differences made that seem appropriate to the disciplinarians, might have led authorities to rely more heavily on public prosecution to deal with whites suspected of minor crimes than was true for enslaved suspects. On the other hand, some white offenses against slaves might never reach the stage of prosecution, especially the legally defined crimes of manslaughter and murder.[23]

Conflicts in values figure in the different trials as well. Almost no

20. Hening, *The Statutes at Large*, II, 481, IV, 111–12; Shepherd, *Statutes at Large*, I, 122–26; Jordan, *White Over Black*, 115–28; Higginbotham, *In the Matter of Color*, 26–30, 39–40, 378, 382; Genovese, *Roll, Jordan, Roll*, 587–97; Herbert Aptheker, *American Negro Slave Revolts* (New ed.; New York, 1974). Authorities could also show restraint. Warwick County justices to Governor Andros, March 22, 1693/94, in Charles City County Records (1642–1842), VHS; *EJC*, I, 309.
21. The works of Jordan, Genovese, and Aptheker are three of the more obvious examples of such studies. For a note of caution, see Bertram Wyatt-Brown, *Southern Honor: Ethics and Behavior in the Old South* (New York, 1982), 402–34.
22. On procedures in criminal actions against free Virginians, see Scott, *Criminal Law in Colonial Virginia*. On the nature of offenses, see "Extract from Virginia Gazette, 1752 and 1755," *VMHB*, XXIV (October, 1916), 404–16; Dargan, "Crime and the Virginia Gazette"; Frederick Hall Schmidt, "British Convict Servant Labor in Colonial Virginia" (Ph.D. dissertation, College of William and Mary, 1976), 245–49; Saunders, "Crime and Punishment," 33–44; and Virginia General Court, Docket for October term, 1723, and Docket for October term, 1754, in Lee Family Papers, sec. 89, VHS.
23. John Brickell, *The Natural History of North Carolina* (Dublin, 1737), 272–73; Peter H. Wood, *Black Majority: Negroes in Colonial South Carolina from 1670 through the Stono Rebellion* (New York, 1974), 308–26; Accomack C.C.O.B. (1731–36), 191; *JHB*, 1727–40, p. 257.

whites were tried for insurrection; the trials of whites for rape some-times elicited different public responses than did trials of slaves for rape; and, in the counties surveyed for this study, almost no whites were tried for poisoning and none could be tried for illegally admin-istering medicine. Moreover, the justices who tried slaves were often not the same ones who tried free whites for felonies. All county justices could do in the case of many felony accusations was to examine ac-cused whites in order to determine whether they should later face trial before the General Court or the district or superior courts. Com-parison of the simple conviction rate in slave trials with the percent-age of free whites convicted in trials or deemed eligible for trial in higher courts will give us only a partial measurement of what dif-ference justices' antislave, proslavery bias made in the quality of evi-dence used and in their propensity to convict enslaved defendants.

Spotsylvania County, which had a large slave population and whose slaves made up a large percentage of the county's total population, provides a good source of the roughly comparable data I have de-scribed. Between 1786 and 1859, Spotsylvania justices convicted 62.3 percent of slave defendants, and they convicted or sent to a higher court 66.7 percent of free white defendants whom they examined or tried for offenses of which both slaves and free whites could be ac-cused. Moreover, the enslaved 60 percent of the county's population accounted for a proportionate 58.7 percent of convictions.[24] These figures do not add up to proof of anything; they only partially support the reliability of the trial records as evidence of certain interactions between slaves and whites or among slaves. Conviction rates for slave trials and the rates at which county justices convicted free whites or sent them to higher courts vary in other times and areas within Vir-ginia. They are sometimes higher and sometimes lower.[25] Antislave,

24. Spotsylvania C.C.O.B. and C.C.M.B. (1786–1859). In order to confine the test to the influence of slave status combined with race, I did not consider the few trials of free blacks.

25. The court records transcribed in Lyman Chalkley, *Chronicles of the Scotch-Irish Settlement in Virginia Extracted from the Original Court Records of Augusta County, 1745–1800* (3 vols.; Rosslyn, Va., 1912), I, 25–292, indicate that between 1747 and 1799, of those whites examined 70 percent were either found guilty or sent to a higher court. The records of Botetourt County for 1770 to 1789, Montgomery County for 1777 through 1787, and Washington County between 1777 and 1783—transcribed in Lewis Preston Summers, *Annals of Southwest Virginia, 1769–1800* (Abingdon, Va., 1929), 67–432, 687–817, and 956–1165—show convictions and transfers of cases to a higher court of, respec-tively, 72.7, 60, and 57.1 percent. Saunders, "Crime and Punishment," 41–42, reports for the city of Richmond (from 1780 to 1820), guilty verdicts of 43 percent for white males

proslavery bias did play some part in judges' identification of individual slaves and description, as opposed to evaluation, of slave behavior. Indeed, the data might show that judges held lower-class whites in as low esteem as they did black slaves. But the data from Spotsylvania and other counties do not show that animus toward or fear of slaves necessarily determined verdicts in courts of oyer and terminer. The rank discrimination of which white courts have been accused has often resulted as much or more from grossly unequal definitions of crimes, stipulation of different mandatory penalties for the same offense, or unjustly divergent discretionary sentences as from inaccurate identification of the person responsible. There is no reason, therefore, to reject any slave trial out of hand as historical evidence concerning the behavior of certain slaves.

The trial records meet another one of Stampp's standards reasonably well. That is, the testimony was often firsthand. Since slaves were allowed to testify in the capital trials of other slaves, the court records are clerks' accounts of the trials and reports of judicial decisions that judges made after evaluating firsthand testimony from both slaves and free people. Clerks did not regularly record testimony before the 1780s, but they did so in enough trials before then and in so many later trials that it is possible to discern judges' genuine efforts to elicit accurate testimony. The preceding comparison of slave trials and judicial actions against white suspects indicates that justices often employed similar canons of evidence when they heard black and white testimony. Moreover, a sufficiently high percentage of slave trials—30 percent—resulted in not guilty verdicts to demonstrate that judges frequently made a real, though obviously not perfect, attempt to differentiate credible and incredible firsthand testimony.[26] Nor did white testimony necessarily cancel out black testimony. Should a white person not trusted by the justices testify in conflict with a slave

---

and 43 percent for male slaves tried for crimes against property, 15 percent conviction of white males for "undefined felony" and 46 percent for male slaves. Several other Virginia county court records show similar conviction rates for whites.

26. Based on slave trials in Virginia, 1706–85. The percentage found not guilty in 751 trials in several representative counties between 1786 and 1865 was 42.7 (see Table 4). Clerks recorded the defendant's plea in 1,807 cases between 1706 and 1785. In only 123 cases (6.8 percent) did slaves plead guilty. In 751 trials in the counties listed in Table 4, only seven slaves (less than 1 percent) pleaded guilty; in the 1,499 trials recorded in C.S., there were only nine guilty pleas (again, less than 1 percent). It was obviously standard procedure for accused slaves to plead not guilty.

whom the justices had other reasons to believe, such as an owner's corroboration, the white person's testimony might not hold up. Sometimes a white person's testimony, such as that of an accused slave's owner, favored a slave defendant or at least conflicted with testimony given by other whites.

The most obvious weakness in the trial records is the absence of any testimony in some and the exclusion of a particular kind of testimony from all. Pre-1790s minute and order books contained indictments and verdicts, but rarely included testimony. The historian consequently has to rely on limited, yet still useful, evidence from that period. From the 1790s, however, courts conserved testimony in all capital trials, providing an even richer source for scholars. But slaves could not testify on their own behalf in court. While they often could speak in their own defense before a trial, to which jailers, owners, and other witnesses could attest in court, and their owners or owners' lawyers could defend them in court, their forced silence before the bench made true justice impossible. But exclusion of the defendant's testimony did not control identification of a slave as the one who broke the law. Instead, this unjust feature existed in tension with the forces that favored accuracy.

Judicial rules guaranteed that testimony would be close to the event, making the court records usually conform to another of Stampp's standards for "white sources." The procedural safeguards that legislators built into slave trials generally existed to maintain the integrity of the law or to benefit the slaveowner rather than the enslaved defendant. Such safeguards, however, could benefit slaves. The speed with which slave suspects stood trial in Virginia, for example, compares rather well with the delays that modern defendants regularly experience in spite of constitutional guarantees of a speedy trial.[27] In three groups of fifteen cases each from three periods (1760–1763, 1768–1771, and 1783–1785), the mean number of days between event and trial was, respectively, twenty-six, twenty-four, and nineteen, or about three weeks.

27. Thomas Church et al., Justice Delayed: The Pace of Litigation in Urban Trial Courts (Williamsburg, 1978); U.S. Law Enforcement Assistance Administration, Sourcebook of Criminal Justice Statistics—1977 (Washington, D.C., 1978), 542, 545. After 1786, Virginia law required trials of slaves to be held neither fewer than five days nor more than ten days after commitment (Hening, The Statutes at Large, XII, 345; Shepherd, Statutes at Large, I, 126).

Not only are slave trial records relatively accurate, firsthand, and close to the event; they also cover fairly well behavior classified as felonious crime. The "dark figure" of unreported and privately punished major crimes looms large, if only because so much of slavery was a secret matter, hidden from public view. Yet the record of slave trials for felonies may well serve as a good index, and an index only, of the scope of major slave crime in Virginia. It is changes over time and differences over space that the trial data show best. The relative number of convictions, not the absolute number, made all the difference. The data constitute an index since they show basic consistency over time. Differences in data sometimes derive from the diverse nature of the records used, the air of crisis surrounding some trials, or from idiosyncratic patterns in certain counties, towns, or cities.

Some considerations seem to militate against a claim for the comprehensiveness of evidence from slave trials. Private executions of rebellious slaves could have been numerous. It is indeed true that Virginian justices rarely found owners and overseers guilty of murder or even manslaughter of slaves, especially if defendants pleaded that they were "correcting" their slaves. Whites could kill their recalcitrant slaves—with legal impunity.[28] Moreover, planters might find other reasons to avoid public trials, which could consume a great deal of the taxpayers' time and money. Private condemnation apparently saved both, especially for slaveowners. Finally, some slaves simply ran away or committed suicide rather than face trial.[29]

It was, however, the interest of owners and judges in the economic health of slavery that increased the chance that slaves accused of major crimes would stand trial in a courtroom rather than suffer mutilation or perhaps death without being removed from their holder's domain. When planters believed that they could rely on the support of public institutions in their effort to control the most rebellious slaves, they would not resort to private retaliation. Slaveholders also were aware that Virginia's government would compensate them for the cost

28. For an example of the kind of private execution that could occur in Virginia, see John Davis, *Personal Adventures* (London, 1817), 89–92.
29. On fugitives, suicides, escapees, and those who died in jail, see *JHB*, 1742–49, p. 27; *Virginia Gazette*, April 22, 1737, (P), May 2, 1766, (R), June 15, July 20, 1769, (PD) September 22, 1768, March 7, 1771; Elizabeth City C.C.O.B. (1760–69), 591; Sussex County Court of Oyer and Terminer Minutes (1754–1807), 29, 33; *EJC*, VI, 503, 644–45; Petition of June 22, 1772, Legislative Petitions, Sussex County, VSL; Amelia C.C.O.B. (1751–55), 210–11; York C.C.O.B. (1752–54), 364–66; Mecklenburg C.C.O.B. (1765–68), 155–56; *Virginia Herald* (Fredericksburg), June 2, 1816.

of an executed slave. The murdered slave would yield no return. Tragically, the slaves who were publicly executed or banished almost paid their own way: masters received from the colony or state government nearly the full market value of executed or transported slaves, and they shared with all other taxpayers only a small fraction of the cost of that payment as well as of the trial and execution.[30]

Public trials also served the interest of white planters in maintaining social control. Whipping and other private punishments certainly deterred many slaves from committing lesser offenses. But public trials provided the final line of defense against the most threatening slaves. Only the most powerful institutions of white society could be expected to suppress some of those slaves who stole goods from people other than their owners, slaves who stole repeatedly, slaves who killed those men or women who would otherwise have controlled them, and male slaves who crossed over the subtle line drawn by whites concerning "proper" behavior toward white women. The justices' assumption that they must protect the moral and social order encouraged whites in the Old Dominion to insist upon public prosecution of the actions most in conflict with that order—i.e., the major crimes. White authorities could thereby use the majesty of the law and judiciary to coerce and intimidate slaves into outwardly accepting the primacy of white leaders' norms even when blacks rejected those standards. To be sure, this judicial oppression could easily lead to using torture to secure socially useful "confessions." Yet even this technique would meet opposition from owners determined to protect their human investment.[31]

The problem of torture should not be underrated, however. The nearly absolute power of white officials over slaves could lead to the

30. Carter, *Diary*, II, 676; Robert C. Nicholas to the Editor, *Virginia Gazette* (PD), July 16, 1773; Willie Lee Rose (ed.), *A Documentary History of Slavery in North America* (New York, 1976), 239–40; Accounts, 1754, in Sussex County Court Papers (1754–55); Accomack C.C.O.B. (1765–67), 220–21, 359; Marvin L. Michael Kay and Lorin Lee Carey, "'The Planters Suffer Little or Nothing': North Carolina Compensations for Executed Slaves, 1748–1772," *Science & Society*, XL (1976), 288–306. As a Virginia planter informed Frederick Law Olmsted (*A Journey in the Seaboard Slave States* [New York, 1856], 90–91), "a negro's life is too valuable to be risked at" ditchdigging. "If a negro dies, it is a considerable loss you know."
31. Kay and Carey, "'The Planters Suffer Little or Nothing,'" 288–306; Carter, *Diary*, I, 290; Philip Vickers Fithian, *The Journal and Letters of Philip Vickers Fithian*, ed. Hunter Dickinson Farish (Williamsburg, 1965), 185–87. A white store owner took it upon himself to whip another man's slave for allegedly stealing from his store. The slave's owner assaulted him and then sued him for the whipping. The storekeeper was humiliated by white justices who found the slave not guilty of the theft. See *Hoomes v. Kuhn* (1792), excerpted in Catterall, *Judicial Cases*, I, 99.

use of torture in order to "fix" a case, speed up the questioning process, find further evidence, or force suspects to reveal the identity of accomplices. In insurrection episodes, as in some regular cases, torture could yield the "confession" that anxious or angry whites wanted simply in order to satisfy their social and psychological needs. But, as the many not guilty verdicts indicate, torture did not necessarily occur, and when it did occur, it did not necessarily result in false confessions. Owners, defense lawyers, and the governor and the council all watched for evidence of torture and sometimes won pardons or reduced sentences for the few slaves they judged to have been tortured before or during the trial process.[32] In this respect, the problem of torture affects the historian's evaluation of the trial evidence in the same manner as do some other factors. That is to say, discriminatory laws, sentences, and means of extracting evidence give grim testimony to the injustice many slaves experienced in white courts. But one cannot therefore dismiss the trials as worthless evidence for slaves' interaction with whites and with other slaves. Similarly, all slaves faced intimidation because they were slaves, but not even this intimidation eliminates the worth of the trial records as evidence.

The most important question for historians who wish to use trials of slaves is, Which cases are reliable? Indeed, which trials are valid bases for statistical conclusions and which will support analysis of circumstances and even motivation? It is axiomatic that neither the number of trials nor the total of convictions will tell us exactly how many slaves engaged in major illegal behavior. One reason is that some of the convictions were bound to be inaccurate. Yet the status of some owners in relation to judges, the owners' ability to sell to Georgia some of the slaves accused of major crimes, the pattern of making examples of ringleaders rather than bothering to prosecute all accomplices, and the possibility that some of the not guilty verdicts were legally erroneous, that some slaves' illegal action escaped detection, and that some slaves themselves escaped, all suggest strongly that the total number of convictions is actually a conservative estimate, an undercount, of the amount of major illegal behavior by slaves.

32. On torture, see A. E. Keir Nash, "Fairness and Formalism in the Trials of Blacks in the State Supreme Courts of the Old South," *Virginia Law Review*, LVI (1970), 84–89; Petition of Sally Jones of Hanover County, Widow, September, 1786, in VEPLR; Opinion of Peter V. Daniel, Virginia Council Journals, 1832–33, pp. 157–58. Slaveowners' manipulation of the court system could easily lead to acquittal as well as to conviction. See, for example, Roeber, *Faithful Magistrates*, 157–58.

The statistical data from trials, then, are an indicator or benchmark of the minimum number of slaves involved in the minimum number of incidents. Given the many intervening variables and the relatively small number of cases in any given year, it is normally impossible to make reliable estimates of short-term changes unless they were dramatic. Since the number of trials and convictions remains fairly constant over time, however, it is safer to estimate long-term statistical changes, especially since they were bound to involve more slaves and incidents. Social historians of early America and the Old South are used to dealing with statistical universes of this magnitude and level of reliability. They use such data well when they remain aware of and compensate for the limitations of the data. The most satisfactory method is to make clear that any data represent an approximation, a minimum, or a maximum.

The mistakes of some historians of slavery when using such trials merely for statistical purposes indicate the caution required. Consider the three quantitative studies of convictions in Virginia as a whole, those by Phillips (1915), Johnston (1937), and Flanigan (1973). All three have the merit of trying to use comprehensive data, but they all fail to do so. Phillips employed only the Auditor's Office vouchers of condemned slaves. He made almost no distinctions over time and space, and his divisions according to circumstances were somewhat sketchy. Given his emphasis on the economics of slavery, he was particularly interested in the valuations of the condemned slaves. While relying only on the same records, Flanigan was more concerned with questions of legal history. He consequently did not try to fill in any of the gaps in the Auditor's Office records, such as the missing cases in the late 1850s through 1865 and the nature of the many convictions he had to classify as "undescribed." Nor did he analyze more than a handful of individual cases. Johnston successfully used numerous individual cases from the files of the governor and the council as a basis for explaining circumstances, behavior, and motivation. But when he tried to compile lists or tables of cases for several decades, his use of the executive papers became invalid. He regularly identified people or circumstances incorrectly, and he failed to provide a comprehensive survey of all extant trials in any year or longer period of time.[33]

33. Ulrich B. Phillips, "Slave Crime in Virginia," *AHR*, XX (1915), 336–40; Johnston, *Race Relations in Virginia*, 20–41, 75–94, 257–63, 317–21; Flanigan, "The Criminal Law of Slavery," 46–58, 404.

Those weaknesses have given rise to errors in other historians' treatment of slave crimes. Winthrop Jordan displayed most impressive scholarship in *White Over Black*, but mistakenly cited Johnston as the source for the statement that "from 1783 to 1814 the state recompensed owners of 434 executed slaves." Jordan said that that total did not include, among other things, slaves transported. Johnston did not offer an overall total in his study; Jordan's figure is much closer to the total of both executed and transported slaves for those years.[34] Jordan went on to use Johnston's totals for specific crimes, which were consistently well below the totals for slaves executed or transported for specific offenses. Yet how many readers have relied on Jordan's figures?

A recent example shows how easily an able historian can fall into the trap that Johnston unknowingly set. In the proceedings of an important national conference on slavery, Philip Morgan stated that only 66 slave executions were reported for Virginia between 1786 and 1815.[35] His source was Johnston, but his mistake, unlike Jordan's, was to count only Johnston's lists of slaves sentenced to hang for specific crimes, lists that not only are limited in themselves but that cannot support Morgan's statistical conclusion. (The actual figure is more than 212.)

Historians who wish to use selected trials of slaves in order to make certain points have also stepped into the quicksand of poor documentation and inadequate statistical support. The misuse of isolated trials can weaken an argument. In a useful article, "Slaves of the Chesapeake Bay Area and the War of 1812," Frank A. Cassell argued that the doubling of state appropriations for compensating owners of executed or transported slaves from 1812 to 1813 produced "grim figures" in which one can "read the personal tragedies suffered by slaves whose bid for freedom failed."[36] These figures are grim, and they do reflect personal tragedies. But to what degree do they reflect the failure of bids for freedom? Analysis of the convictions that led to transportation or execution of slaves between 1810 and 1814 reveals that convictions for attacks on whites remained much the same through those years. That would support Cassell's argument. What rose appreciably (266.67 percent) were convictions for burglary or robbery. It is not

34. Jordan, *White Over Black*, 392–93.

35. Philip D. Morgan, "Black Society in the Lowcountry, 1760–1810," in Ira Berlin and Ronald Hoffman (eds.), *Slavery and Freedom in the Age of the American Revolution* (Charlottesville, 1983), 117n45.

36. Frank A. Cassell, "Slaves of the Chesapeake Bay Area and the War of 1812," *JNH*, LVII (1972), 150.

clear to what extent a set of burglaries or robberies constituted a bid for freedom. Only examination of individual cases will answer that question.

But what about insurrection trials during the War of 1812? Convictions for conspiracy or insurrection did rise from one in 1810 and none in 1811 and 1812 to four in 1813. Cassell dealt with three of these, but once again was mistaken because his evidence was not comprehensive. According to Cassell's only source, the *National Intelligencer*, three slaves accused of plotting with the British to massacre Americans had been committed to the Williamsburg jail, but "the records are silent as to their final fate." In fact, the records show that numerous citizens pleaded for merciful treatment of the slaves, who, though convicted of conspiring to rebel and condemned to death, were more likely to have been the victims of entrapment. All three slaves were transported rather than executed.[37]

There are numerous other examples, but the main problem in all of them is the failure to use the available comprehensive evidence.[38] One needs to consult the Auditor's Office vouchers and accompanying documentation, Treasury Office records, the trial records filed with the state executive, petitions and letters also filed with the state executive, legislative petitions for some cases, trial records in the county court order and minute books, and newspapers, private papers, and correspondence. Only when these sources are combined to the greatest degree possible is the documentation sufficient to support conclusions. Complete coverage is impossible. It would be nonsensical to assert that available evidence can tell us everything we need to know about major slave crimes. But comprehensive evidence can provide a better basis for significant conclusions, hypotheses, and even speculation than can the limited, though often strong, evidence hitherto used

37. *Ibid.*, 148; trials of Anthony, Tassy, and Kit, James City, March 31, 1813, C.S., box 3, and VEPLR, and Petition signed by ninety-eight people, in VEPLR. The fourth insurrection trial of 1813 ended with a guilty verdict for conspiracy to commit murder and the final sentence of transportation. Trial of Sam, Fauquier, April 23, 1813, in C.S., box 3.

38. Much of Morgan, "Turmoil in an Orderly Society," 216–54, is based on a misuse of compensations noted in *JHB*. In "Dramatizing the Ideology of Revolution," 357, Isaac used a *Virginia Gazette* story about the trial of a slave to make an important point, but observed that the identity of the slave would never be known. "No other record of this court of oyer and terminer survives," he declared. However, the Lancaster C.C.O.B. (1778–83), 8, gives the particulars. For effective statistical use of the Auditor's Office records, see Peter Joseph Albert, "The Protean Institution: The Geography, Economy, and Ideology of Slavery in Post-Revolutionary Virginia" (Ph.D. dissertation, University of Maryland, 1976), 236.

by many able historians. Comprehensive evidence can also help us determine what we do not know.

My conclusions about the quality of the evidence do not assume that the quantity of convictions is the sole object of legitimate research and analysis. That is why a combination of diverse sources is the only valid basis for a study of slaves' behavior. Moreover, only the combining of different kinds of evidence will make it possible to compensate for the bias of the trial records. Historians cannot take these records on their own terms; they have to take into account the antagonistic behavior and points of view of all those involved in the trials. Historians must therefore be as clear as possible about the conflicting perceptions and values in slave crime. All criminal trials involve perceptions, values, and behavior that are at odds. But the trials of slaves are special since they reflect much deeper conflict than that which is present in normal criminal trials. That more profound conflict was cultural and histor-ical as well as procedural and behavioral; it developed over time and differed from place to place. That conflict is the focus of the remaining chapters of this book.

The strengths of the records of trials of Virginian slaves qualify them as satisfactory sources when individually tested and cautiously used. Weaknesses are there, but the strengths outweigh them. There is no way to eliminate every problem that these records present to the histo-rian. Surely some verdicts did result from a kangaroo court mentality. The limitations of this kind of evidence do necessitate careful exam-ination of the trials.[39] But if we remain sensitive to and compensate for the difficulties, we can better understand the nature of slaves' behavior in the slave society of Virginia.

39. Valuable studies of method include Hindus and Jones, "Quantitative and The-oretical Approaches to the History of Crime and Law"; J. M. Beattie, "Towards a Study of Crime in 18th Century England: A Note on Indictments," in Paul Fritz and David Williams (eds.), *The Triumph of Culture: 18th Century Perspectives* (Toronto, 1972), 299–314; and V. A. C. Gatrell and T. B. Hadden, "Criminal Statistics and Their Interpreta-tion," In E. A. Wrigley (ed.), *Nineteenth Century Society* (Cambridge, England, 1972), 336–96.

PART II

1619 to 1784

Introduction

In February, 1738/39, Leander, an Accomack County slave, was convicted of using a pass that a fellow bondsman had forged. As Leander
stood at the public pillory for an hour, he symbolized the many
changes through which fellow blacks and other residents of Virginia
had gone since the beginnings of slavery in that province. Leander was
not alone as a slave, as a slave convict, or as an acculturated person
who dared to use a pass forged by another Afro-American who could
read and write English. Nor were the trial and public punishment of
Leander unusual by that time. Accomack County, the colony of Virginia, the Chesapeake region, the colonial South, and parts of the
colonial North had become slave societies by 1739. Significant uprisings had taken place recently among the plantation slaves in the Caribbean. A major slave revolt had occurred that year in South Carolina,
and within two years numerous blacks would be transported, hanged,
or burned alive by white New York authorities who had accused them
of conspiring to revolt. That context, as well as socioeconomic and
other changes that had taken place or were in progress in 1739, contributed to the significance of Leander's conviction.[1]

The changes in the slave communities of late seventeenth-century
and early eighteenth-century Virginia crucially influenced the nature
of slaves' challenges to the criminal code during that period and there-

1. Trial of Leander, February 7, 1738/39, Accomack C.C.O.B. (1737–44), 131; Mullin,
Flight and Rebellion, 82–123; David Barry Gaspar, *Bondmen & Rebels: A Study of Master-
Slave Relations in Antigua With Implications for Colonial British America* (Baltimore,
1985); Peter H. Wood, *Black Majority: Negroes in Colonial South Carolina from 1670
through the Stono Rebellion* (New York, 1974), 308–26; Thomas J. Davis, *A Rumor of
Revolt: The "Great Negro Plot" in Colonial New York* (New York, 1985).

after. Population growth was the first important change. From approximately two or three thousand people in 1680 and six thousand in
1700, the number of slaves increased to about sixty thousand in 1740.
The sharpest change occurred in the 1730s. Not only did the importation of Africans more than double the numbers for the 1720s, but
births of Afro-Americans grew dramatically. Simultaneously the sex
ratio improved greatly, leading to less divisive competition among
men for available women as well as making possible a rise in the birth
rate.[2]

Between 1740 and 1785 the slave population grew less rapidly, but
still changed in a significant way. In 1740, slaves constituted about
one-third of the total population of Virginia. By 1790, they were about
44 percent of the state's people. Expressed in another way, the slave
sector of the colony was about half as large as the white in 1740, but
almost 80 percent as large by 1790. (These percentages do not even
take into account the free black population.) The change between 1740
and 1790 was a quantum leap in the relationship between the two
groups. Tithable figures tell more because they measure the size of the
adult slave population in relation to the adult white male population,
thus giving some idea of the balance of force. Table 6 shows the significant shift in the ratio of slaves sixteen years of age and older to white
males from the same age group in eight representative counties in
1755 and 1799. (Figures for the 1780s are not comparable since they
cover white males twenty-one years of age and older.) In 1755 the two
groups were nearly even; by 1799, slaves had become the numerically
dominant group within the most important socioeconomic age sector
of the population.[3]

I have found only a handful of trials of slaves for crimes in seventeenth-century Virginia records. Not even in the first two decades of

2. See Allan Kulikoff, "The Origins of Afro-American Society in Tidewater Maryland
and Virginia, 1700 to 1790," *WMQ*, 3rd ser., XXXV (1978), 226–59; Kulikoff, "A 'Prolifick'
People: Black Population Growth in the Chesapeake Colonies, 1700–1790," *Southern
Studies*, XVI (1977), 391–428; and Kulikoff, *Tobacco and Slaves: The Development of
Southern Cultures in the Chesapeake, 1680–1800* (Chapel Hill, 1986), 317–51. See also Ira
Berlin, "Time, Space, and the Evolution of Afro-American Society," *AHR*, LXXXV
(1980), 69–77; Walter Minchinton, Celia King, and Peter Waite (eds.), *Virginia Slave-
Trade Statistics, 1698–1775* (Richmond, 1985); and Susan Westbury, "Slaves of Colonial
Virginia: Where They Came From," *WMQ*, 3rd ser., XLII (1985), 228–37.
3. Besides the figures in Table 6, I have used Evarts B. Greene and Virginia D. Har-
rington, *American Population Before the Federal Census of 1790* (1932; rpr. Gloucester,
Mass., 1966), 134–55; and U.S. Census Office, *The Statistics of the Population of the United
States*, Vol. I, *Population and Social Statistics* (Washington, D.C., 1872), 68–70.

Table 6.   Tithable Slaves and Whites, 1755, 1799

| | 1755 | | | 1799 | | |
County	Slaves	Whites	Ratio	Slaves	Whites	Ratio
Accomack	1,135	1,506	0.75	2,239	1,940	1.2
Brunswick	976	1,299	0.75	3,614	1,319	2.7
Caroline	2,674	1,208	2.20	5,232	1,287	4.1
Dinwiddie	1,175	784	1.50	3,195	1,148	2.8
Fairfax	921	1,312	0.70	3,242	1,618	2.0
Henrico	898	529	1.70	2,141	859	2.5
Northampton	902	609	1.50	1,940	840	2.3
Spotsylvania	1,468	665	2.20	1,288[a]	350	3.7
Total	10,149	7,912	1.30	22,891	9,361	2.4

SOURCES: Robert E. Brown and B. Katherine Brown, *Virginia 1705–1786: Democracy or Aristocracy?* (East Lansing, Mich., 1964), 73; Greene and Harrington, *American Population Before the Federal Census*, 151; county personal property taxes, 1799.
NOTE: 1799 figures for Henrico County do not include the city of Richmond.
[a] One district only.

the eighteenth century did many trials occur. I could locate only forty-one for the years 1706 to 1719. But the planters had tested the trial system on the steadily expanding slave population and found it generally reliable by the 1730s. Thus I located nearly one hundred trials in documents for 1725 to 1739. The circumstances were set by 1740. They included the defiant or at least illegal behavior of a growing number of blacks, some African but many Afro-American, the increasing strength of the Anglo-American planter class as expressed in laws and institutions created by its leaders, and the conflict between the two groups of people, conflict that had become almost self-perpetuating because it was closely connected to conditions, needs, fears, and desires peculiar to the slave society called Virginia.

After 1740, Creole (native-born) blacks statistically dominated Tidewater Virginia and held their own in the newer Piedmont counties. Thus the conflict between slaves and the slave code entered a new phase after 1740. The five chapters in Part II cover the origins and development of slaves' conflict with Virginia's laws and courts. Chapter 3 explains the gradual process by which slaves accused of capital crimes became the subject of more and more formalized court procedures designed to "affright" other black bondspeople from endangering lives, property, or slavery. But an increasing number of slaves either knowingly challenged or violated for other reasons the norms upheld by white laws and courts. That this process had a great deal to do with the distinctive African and European origins of black and white Virginians after 1740 is the theme of Chapter 4, in which I explore the methods the colony's authorities used to combat poisoning, or the threat thereof, by Africans and Afro-Virginians as well as the patterns in that feared behavior. The subject of Chapter 5 is the most prevalent crime of stealing. Common though it was, it assumed different forms at different times and in different places. Because of its frequency, however, white authorities eventually recognized that harsh sanctions would not end stealing by slaves. The preference of blacks convicted of theft for such necessities as food and clothing reveals the purposefulness of their activity. White officials could do little more than try to check the major thefts. More troublesome, though less widespread, was arson, which by its nature often baffled prescientific methods of gathering incriminating evidence, thereby affording both male and female slaves the opportunity to attack their owners.

The most violent confrontations between white and black Virginians occurred in the open, when enraged men and women exploded with fury and assaulted owners or overseers, or when slaves bent on controlling slaveholders tried, sometimes succeeding, to destroy them. I analyze the nature of this deadly conflict in Chapter 6. I suggest that there was a political element in many killings of whites by their human property, though these mortal attacks were not widespread. Slaves killed other blacks as well, but not to a degree that seriously threatened the stability of the slave communities of eighteenth-century Virginia. Apparently the least dangerous threat from slaves was rape, at least during the mid-eighteenth century. It does not follow that the white judicial reaction to blacks accused of rape of white women was mild. Instead, sexual offenses were perceived as a particular threat to white dominance, and slaveholders responded accordingly to what they saw. Finally, Chapter 7 argues that the American revolutionaries were not alone in their effort to defy legal authority and overturn the old order. At least some black Virginians had their own notions of their rights and how they would defend them, making an increasingly severe problem for whites who would be masters and revolutionaries at the same time. The character of slaves' criminalized behavior reflected their Americanization. The late 1730s and the

1740s are a watershed period in which that process assumed great importance.

One historian who has provided invaluable measurements and estimates of the components of growth in Virginia's slave communities during the eighteenth century concludes that ethnic distinctions and differing experiences led Africans and Afro-Americans in the Tidewater to quarrel regularly during the early 1700s. From 1740 to 1790, however, "immigration declined and then stopped, plantation sizes increased, the proportion of blacks in the population grew, and divisions among slaves disappeared." The same historian poses the question whether this pattern repeated itself as white Virginians moved, and black Virginians were moved, toward the west.[4] Evidence from the trials of slaves indicates that one aspect of the Tidewater experience repeated itself: the initial pattern of division among slaves became an eventual coalescence of slave communities.

It was not, however, that divisions among slaves totally disappeared in the Old Dominion by the 1780s. Instead, the slave communities developed to the extent that their members' conflicts with whites overshadowed discord among themselves. The central fact of master-slave conflict is that during the middle decades of the eighteenth century, a socially visible number of slaves persistently challenged or strained white control over them. These slaves' actions were defined by white leaders as serious crimes. As a result, the record of the diverse and only somewhat successful methods at least one thousand slaves used to attack the conditions of their bondage or at least to survive within a slave society between 1740 and 1785 is quite full. That record also allows analysis of the development of a revolutionary mentality among a small number of slaves independent of the larger and more obvious movement toward the American Revolution. What derived from these movements—slave conspiracies and the Revolution— brought about still another fundamental change that affected the confrontation between slaves and the criminal code once again after the 1780s.

4. Kulikoff, "The Origins of Afro-American Society," 246, 259.

3. *Years of Adjustment, 1619–1739*

In August of 1706, five slaves stood before the Westmoreland County slave court for burglarizing and stealing goods worth more than twenty shillings from a white man's storehouse. All belonged to different people; three had absentee owners. Four out of the five collaborated once again to escape, only to be retaken and hanged with the one who had not tried to flee. Their hanging was a dramatic and deadly example of the special fate awaiting enslaved conspirators. Indeed, it is possible that a skeleton discovered during an archaeological dig at Pope's Creek Plantation is that of Dick, one of the condemned men. The body faced to the west instead of to the east—a position reserved for suicides and other social deviants in England.[1]

In 1723, Jacob, the property of Martha Flint of Lancaster County, stood trial for stealing tobacco and food from several whites. So did Martha Flint and another white woman, who received corporal and other kinds of punishment. Recognizing the nature of the case, the justices delayed proceedings against Jacob so that they could send someone to Williamsburg for an oyer and terminer commission. The situation looked rather grim for Jacob. The white women had received

1. Westmoreland C.C.O.B. (1705–21), 32a–b, 37a, 150; *EJC*, III, 128. Dick, one of the executed confederates, may have been the slave who was buried facing toward the west. A slave was in fact buried in this manner on Dick's owner's plantation at about the time of the trial and execution. It is impossible, however, to identify him with certainty as Dick. See Fraser D. Neiman, *The "Manner House" Before Stratford: (Discovering the Clifts Plantation)*, ed. Alonzo T. Dill (Stratford, Va., 1980), 28; Arthur C. Aufderheide *et al.,* "Lead in Bone II: Skeletal-Lead Content as an Indicator of Lifetime Lead Ingestion and the Social Correlates in an Archaeological Population," *American Journal of Physical Anthropology*, LV (1981), 285–91 (the slave buried irregularly is numbered 330 on pages 286 and 289); personal communication from Fraser D. Neiman, September 28, 1982.

severe sentences, but they would live through the punishments. For his part, Jacob might have to hang for the kind of collaboration most slaves appear to have deemed too risky. Whites could easily turn against slave accomplices, especially after the 1723 prohibition of black testimony concerning whites, and the slaves would probably get a smaller share of the take, especially in the instance of theft carried out in concert with a master or mistress such as Martha Flint. But the Lancaster justices fortunately realized what a compromising position Jacob was in. They found him guilty of stealing only six pence worth of goods and mitigated his sentence from execution to one hour at the pillory, having each ear nailed to the pillory and then cut off close to the head, and receiving, as had one of his white accomplices, a full whipping. They granted this "mercy," the judges said, because Jacob had acted in the company of "Christian White persons of the family wherein" he resided.[2]

These cases from 1706 and 1723 introduce the problems that slaves and slaveowners began to face more and more often. One was slave survival in their dependent status when their efforts to act for themselves were so fraught with risk and so often incurred the worst punishments that public authorities could impose. Conversely, another was slaveholder perpetuation of slavery and protection of their lives and property when the slave population of the Old Dominion was rapidly increasing and many of those slaves were, in spite of the risks, willing to act on their own behalf, thanks in part to the many opportunities available, such as Martha Flint's cooperation.

No matter how hard white Virginians labored during the seventeenth century to differentiate themselves from the people they regarded as heathen Africans and whom they had dragged onto their plantations, the wish to uphold slavery, keep order, and protect themselves from physical harm drove slaveholders into an increasingly rigid and formalized process of constant interaction with supposedly will-less slaves. Dual cultures—those of slaves and masters, Africans and Europeans, Afro-Americans and Euro-Americans, workers and owners, "heathen" and Christians, black Christians and white Christians—influenced that process. There was nothing static about it. As the slaves' tasks changed, as African "new Negroes" became Creoles, as some began to convert to Christianity, the Afro-American community

2. Trial of Jacob, October 31, 1723, Lancaster C.C.O.B. (1721–29), 104, 128.

changed. But white Virginians simultaneously sought to become self-sufficient planters. The behavior of each group profoundly influenced the other—as was especially true of white-defined slave crime, which was itself a cycle of interaction between whites and slaves.

One of the most basic legal definitions of *slave* is "one who has lost all power of resistance."[3] Any slave or group of slaves whose actions contradicted this definition presented at least a threat and at most a clear and present danger to the establishment and continuation of slavery in seventeenth-century Virginia. Since I have already examined the white response to these challenges, I shall now turn to the challenging behavior itself.

Much of what we know about the changing status of seventeenth-century black Virginians is based on court actions brought by black people against whites. Anthony Johnson of Northampton County showed his mastery of English common law when he held his own in civil cases before a county court. Elizabeth Key and Fernando brought famous freedom suits. Other slaves and free blacks established themselves as people with strong wills in a variety of court cases.[4] But the judicial actions that best illuminate the aggressiveness of certain blacks and how that behavior could alter the master-slave relationship were those in which white authorities brought criminal charges against black suspects.

The earliest known case was in 1640, when the General Court punished a runaway black servant with lifetime servitude, even though his accomplices, two white servants, received only one additional year of service to their masters and three more to the colony. Clearly, white authorities were willing to make racial distinctions. John Punch, the black servant, had performed the least-prosecuted but most effective single act of resistance to servitude of whatever kind. If servants killed their masters, someone else would rule over them. If they successfully ran away, however, they ended their bondage. John

---

3. *Corpus Juris Secundum. A Complete Restatement of the Entire American Law as Developed in All Reported Cases* (155 vols. to date; Brooklyn, 1936–), LXXX, 1316.

4. T. H. Breen and Stephen Innes, *"Myne Owne Ground": Race and Freedom on Virginia's Eastern Shore, 1640–1676* (New York, 1980), 12–15, 90–94; Warren M. Billings, "The Cases of Fernando and Elizabeth Key: A Note on the Status of Blacks in Seventeenth-Century Virginia," *WMQ*, 3rd ser., XXX (1973), 467–74; Catterall, *Judicial Cases,* I, 79–80; Joseph Douglas Deal, "Race and Class in Colonial Virginia: Indians, Englishmen, and Africans on the Eastern Shore During the Seventeenth Century" (Ph.D. dissertation, University of Rochester, 1981), 254–473.

Punch learned that if black servants ran away, they somehow presented a greater threat to their masters than did white runaways.[5]

Blacks in seventeenth-century Virginia also discovered that if they conspired to resist or "make insurrection" against their masters, they would normally appear to authorities to present a greater danger to white safety than did white servile conspirators. There are several instances in which officials tried to exercise more control over what they perceived to be black rebels. In 1644, but a few years after the adventurous John Punch had moved the General Court to action, the colony's council took note of the "riotous & rebellious conduct" of "Mrs. Wormleys negroes." This incomplete reference introduces the most salient fact about both rumors and reports of black conspiracies. The very hint of concerted aggressiveness among Afro-Americans could hardly fail to catch the attention of uneasy whites; "Mrs. Wormleys negroes" even attracted notice by the colony's highest governing body.[6]

Such people deserve as close attention as we can give them, for they prefigured the first perpetrators of what white Virginians called major slave crimes. In these early years, they showed a flexibility in their *modus operandi* that conformed to the contours of their environment. That is, in recognition of their common cause with white servants as well as of the handicap of being among a relatively small number of bondspeople, slave insurrectionaries sometimes allied with white servile rebels. In 1663, for example, a group of insurrectionaries discovered in Tidewater Gloucester County included black slaves and white servants. A similar interracial alliance occurred during Bacon's Rebellion, special case though that was.[7]

Some early slaves discovered that in order to become runaways, they would have to come close to, or actually carry out, insurrection. Becoming a member of a maroon community might require slaves to confederate and force their way out of the quarters or a plantation. Maintaining the maroon community could also necessitate violation

5. Breen and Innes, *"Myne Owne Ground,"* 28–30, and Deal, "Race and Class in Colonial Virginia," 260–62, contain discussions of this case, the documentation for which is most conveniently printed in Rose (ed.), *A Documentary History*, 22–23.

6. *MCGC*, 502; Aptheker, *American Negro Slave Revolts*, 165n12.

7. Aptheker, *American Negro Slave Revolts*, 164–65; T. H. Breen, "A Changing Labor Force and Race Relations in Virginia, 1660–1710," *Journal of Social History*, VII (1973), 22; Anthony S. Parent, Jr., " 'Either a Fool or a Fury': The Emergence of Paternalism in Colonial Virginia Slave Society" (Ph.D. dissertation, University of California, Los Angeles, 1982), 95–96, 163–65.

of Virginia's laws against insurrection. When in 1672 some unidentified fugitive slaves banded together to protect themselves, to attract more support, and to secure supplies, the House of Burgesses described them as "out in rebellion." In 1689, Mingo and Lawrence, two slaves of Ralph Wormeley, joined with a servant to begin a several-year episode of lying out. They eluded capture until their theft of firearms as well as food moved the colony's leaders to action.[8]

Such challenges to white supremacy would continue to provoke official responses. When the council discovered a plot in Westmoreland and other Northern Neck counties in October, 1687, they decided that three council members who lived in that area should sit as a special court there in order to have a "speedy trial." The governor and the council also felt it necessary to examine the March, 1693/94, report of "an Evil and Desperate design Contrived by the Negroes" in Charles City and New Kent counties. While the governor and the council agreed that Cussan, Frank, Robin, and Tom deserved severe punishment for violating the law against assemblies of slaves, and Governor Andros did issue a proclamation against such gatherings, they declined to commission an oyer and terminer court. The four bondsmen had attracted the leaders' attention, but they had not violated a capital statute.[9]

The next rumor of insurrection appears in the records of a county court. In February of 1702/03, an Accomack County slave named Tom stood trial for insurrection and having the "evil presume to lift up his hand in opposition to" his master. The justices found Tom guilty only of the second offense. He suffered thirty lashes as a punishment and then promptly escaped from the county jail, showing that he had not accepted the intended "lesson" of the whip, and that the court of oyer and terminer would not necessarily be able to control the most aggressive slaves.[10] The 1687 plot moved the government to create a special court and perhaps even helped to inspire the 1692 institution of the oyer and terminer courts. The 1694 episode came to the council's

8. Aptheker, *American Negro Slave Revolts*, 165–66; Middlesex C.C.O.B. (1680–94), 486–87, 535, 537, 546–47, 572–73; (Old) Rappahannock C.C.O.B. (1689–92), 335 (Transcript in VSL). Mingo received thirty-nine lashes; Lawrence was sent to the General Court; the servant had to serve for another five years and twelve days. See also Parent, "'Either a Fool or a Fury,'" 165–66.

9. Westmoreland C.C.O.B. (1676–89), 644; *EJC*, I, 86–87, 309; Dudley Digges and Warwick County Court to governor and council, March 22, 1693/94, Charles City County Records (1642–1842).

10. Trial of Tom, February 3, 1702/03, Accomack C.C.O.B. (1697–1703), 137.

attention because local justices asked for the power to try the four suspects. The 1703 trial conformed to the 1692 court statute as well. The lengths to which Virginia's officialdom went to suppress a few slaves between 1687 and 1703 show that those aggressive men exercised a great deal of power for people who were supposed to have lost all capacity to resist.

It was not just slave insurrectionaries who wielded unexpected power in the developing society of Virginia. The case of Jack Kecatan, black servant to Rice Hoe of Charles City County, is one more illustration of why many whites thought slavery was the best means not only of extracting labor from Africans and Afro-Americans but also of keeping them subordinate. This kind of thinking ensured that whites would make their definition and treatment of crime differ with respect to free and enslaved people. Crime control and the preservation of slavery and white supremacy became one and the same thing.

In 1653, Hoe thought he could control Kecatan's behavior by telling him that the promised termination of his servitude in 1664 depended upon good conduct. According to one deponent, however, Hoe had no intention of ever freeing Kecatan. In other words, he regarded Jack as his slave and was fraudulently promising freedom in order to trick him into docility. Several witnesses claimed that Kecatan had been anything but docile. Margaret Barker testified she had seen Jack attempt to rape one of Hoe's English servants and had stopped him by throwing an ax at his leg. Hoe's neighbors asserted that it was Kecatan's "common practice" to seduce or rape English servants. The same neighbors had also threatened to kill Jack if he did not stop killing their hogs. After responding to Hoe's promise of freedom with a short period of "good behavior," Jack supposedly further provoked Hoe by seducing or raping more of his English servants and by bringing a freedom suit against him in 1665.[11]

The repertoire of private sanctions against Jack was large: a thrown ax, death threats, a manipulative promise of freedom, and the denial of that freedom. Yet Jack Kecatan apparently acted just about as he wished to and finally, on his own terms, initiated a civil case against his supposed master. By the 1670s, however, blacks had less room to

---

11. Charles City C.C.O.B. (1664–65), 604–605, 617–18, also in *Charles City County Court Orders, 1664–1665, Fragments, 1650–1696*, ed. Beverley Fleet, Virginia Colonial Abstracts, XIII (Baltimore, 1961), 65–66.

maneuver. In 1673 the slave Will stood trial before the General Court judges themselves for aiding a prisoner's escape from the James City County jail. In 1678, Robin, a slave accused of raping a white woman, occasioned an order by the council that "strong measures" should be taken to apprehend him. One of the 1701 sessions of the Henrico County Court dealt with Daniel, the property of Henry Lewis. The slave was convicted of raping Dorothy Hatcher, wife of Henry Hatcher, after breaking and entering the couple's house. Daniel was hanged and his head placed on a pole near the James River "to Deter Negroes and other Slaves from Committing the Like Crymes and Offences"—a stark reminder of what awaited slaves accused of aggression.[12]

Concern that assertive slaves would steal their property led seventeenth-century whites to rely increasingly on statutes and courts as a deterrent. Even before becoming enslaved in North America in large numbers, Africans had the reputation among Europeans of being inveterate thieves. The irony of "man-stealers" accusing Africans of chronic stealing did not keep that image from gaining currency in the New World. In North American colonies, white authorities accused maroons and outlying slaves of extensive theft. The laws of late seventeenth-century Virginia gave some attention to the problem of stealing by Africans. Since certain kinds of crimes against property, such as burglary, were common law capital offenses, the 1692 creation of the oyer and terminer courts ensured that slaves suspected of major stealing would confront official Virginia in action. Among the earliest of cases tried in one of the new slave courts, then, occurred in James City County. In 1701, Tom was tried for aiding and abetting the theft of goods from a store.[13]

Before the eighteenth century, the challenge that aggressive African slaves presented to white Virginians was not totally clear, as indicated by the leaders' disparate and sometimes ineffectual responses. But by the time the new century began, several social and institutional changes meant that the interaction between criminalized slave behavior and official responses supported by law would become more reg-

12. Catterall, *Judicial Cases*, I, 79; *MCGC*, 520; Governor Nicholson to Board of Trade, December 1, 1701, in Colonial Office, Class 5, No. 1312, Pt. II, fols. 22–23, VCRP.
13. Nicholson to Board of Trade, December 1, 1701, in CO 5/1312, Pt. II, fols. 21–22; Hening, *The Statutes at Large*, III, 87; Surry and Middlesex counties' efforts to deter theft by slaves in 1672 and 1700, *VMHB*, VII (January, 1900), 314, and XII (January, 1905), 287; *JHB*, 1695–1702, p. 266. For prosecutions of free blacks for theft between 1679 and 1702, see Deal, "Race and Class in Colonial Virginia," 344–47, 355–58.

ularized and even rigid. As the number of slaves and their percentage of the total population had steadily increased and the Americanization of the slave population had begun, the developing legal and judicial systems had started to cover a broader range of slave behavior. The most structured manifestation of this social and institutional change was the House of Burgesses' passage of the province's first comprehensive slave code in October, 1705. From then until 1739, the judicially punished behavior of slaves would exhibit several distinct patterns as well as involve some significant social changes.[14]

Between 1706 and 1739, at least 105 Virginian slaves were convicted in oyer and terminer courts of violating the colony's criminal statutes. It is rather difficult to put this figure into demographic context since accurate, year-by-year, population statistics are so elusive and because we must be skeptical about the trust slaveholders then had for the oyer and terminer system. Were they willing to forgo private punishment in favor of public prosecution on a regular basis? The 1705 slave code had promised governmental compensation to owners of condemned slaves in order to encourage owners to hand over suspected malefactors, yet some masters decided to wait until the courts proved themselves.[15]

Even if we take into account the possibility that slaveholders were slow to prefer public punishment of slaves for even the most threatening behavior, it is still possible to detect some overall patterns in the convictions. As Table 7 indicates, convictions for crimes against property generally predominated, but guilty verdicts for crimes against persons accounted for two of the noticeable general increases—i.e., in the periods 1720 to 1724 and 1730 to 1734. The sharp rise in the total number of convictions, especially for crimes against property, between 1735 and 1739 represents the beginning of a long-term change that resulted from developments within the various slave communities and the entire slave society as well.

14. In "Forced Conformity: Puritan Criminal Justice and Indians," *Kansas Law Review*, XXV (1977), 361–73, Yasuhide Kawashima also gives extensive attention to prosecutions of slaves, thus providing an excellent comparative perspective on Virginia's experience. For the 1705 code, see Hening, *The Statutes at Large*, III, 447–62.
15. Berlin, "Time, Space, and the Evolution of Afro-American Society," 70–71, contains an excellent summary and citations of recent work on the demography of the early Chesapeake. In "Disorder and Deference: The Paradoxes of Criminal Justice in the Colonial Tidewater," in Bodenhamer and Ely (eds.), *Ambivalent Legacy*, 187–201, Peter C. Hoffer does attempt to place in demographic context recorded offenses for Richmond County from 1711 to 1754.

Table 7. Simple Conviction Rate in Courts of Oyer and Terminer, 1706–1739

Offense	1706– 1709	1710– 14	1715– 19	1720– 24	1725– 29	1730– 34	1735– 39	Total
Against Property								
Tried	6	13	10	10	18	11	30	98
Convicted	6	10	3	9	10	7	19	64
SCR	100.0	76.9	30.0	90.0	55.6	63.6	63.3	65.3
Against Persons								
Tried	1	3	0	8	6	14	4	36
Convicted	1	3	0	8	3	7	4	26
SCR	100.0	100.0	0.0	100.0	50.0	50.0	100.0	72.2
Against System								
Tried	0	0	5	0	2	0	1	8
Convicted	0	0	3	0	2	0	1	6
SCR	0.0	0.0	60.0	0.0	100.0	0.0	100.0	75.0
Unspecified								
Tried	2	1	3	0	1	0	4	11
Convicted	2	1	2	0	1	0	3	9
SCR	100.0	100.0	66.7	0.0	100.0	0.0	75.0	81.8

SOURCES: Miscellaneous county court order and minute books.
NOTE: "Simple conviction rate" is the percentage of persons tried who were convicted. This figure excludes persons against whom charges were dropped and therefore gives a better notion of the impact of trial testimony and judgment. See Hindus and Jones, "Quantitative and Theoretical Approaches to the History of Crime and Law," 20–21.

Most of the slaves convicted of any kind of crime against property, both capital and noncapital, in the early years of the period under review had been charged with stealing basic items. As the number of plantations and quarters grew, so did the opportunities for theft. What probably led slaves to desire hogs, other kinds of food, guns, axes, and clothes was necessity. The convicted slaves had a strong need for food and clothes in particular. The available testimony does not allow detailed analysis of that need, but the possibilities are obvious. Masters did not provide enough, both were scarce in bad years, or what was readily available was distasteful.[16] Yet between 1706 and 1739, only fundamental need would lead slaves to risk execution—and 83.3 percent of slaves convicted of major theft in this period were sentenced to

16. Mullin, *Flight and Rebellion,* 50–51.

hang. Further, convicted slaves' selection of guns along with axes, food, and clothing suggests that runaways needed security as well as sustenance. Security was a problem for all slaves who defied the laws against theft. They did not want to be caught, so many worked in pairs or groups. Of the twenty-nine slaves convicted of capital offenses and misdemeanors involving property between 1706 and 1724, twelve (more than two-fifths) had allegedly acted with accomplices who shared their need for basic items.

At first another pattern was that in spite of the continued presence of white servants in Virginia, and regardless of the continued possibility—not to be ended until 1723—that blacks could testify against free white accomplices who were either fences or instigators, it was not until 1723 that any slaves were convicted of stealing in confederation with whites. Slaves seem to have relied on fellow slaves. The five tried in the Westmoreland County slave court in 1706 for theft from a white man's storehouse were fairly typical. These early Virginian slaves had tried to exploit the relative lack of supervision occasioned by the absence of several of their owners. In January, 1716/17, Charles, Roger, and Toney of Middlesex County were convicted of burglarizing a white man's property, and they were put to death on the gallows. In this case and others, such as that of Jacob in 1723, some women were blamed as accessories.[17]

Before the 1740s, only one other slave would be convicted of collaboration with a white thief. Living in Northampton County on the Eastern Shore, he had responded to a distinctive aspect of the area's social composition, the unusually high number of free black residents. He had worked with a free black as well as a white accomplice. Other slaves from this period who collaborated in behavior that landed them in a slave court under suspicion of stealing fared better than had most of their predecessors. The reason was the 1731 and 1732 campaign by Lieutenant Governor Gooch and his London allies to extend benefit of

17. Westmoreland C.C.O.B. (1705–21), 32a–b, 37a, 150; *EJC*, III, 128; trial of Charles, Roger, and Toney, January 8, 1716/17, Middlesex C.C.O.B. (1710–21), 310; trial, December 20, 1722, Norfolk C.C.O.B. (1720–23), 58; trial of Jacob, October 31, 1723, Lancaster C.C.O.B. (1721–29), 104, 128. For an example of the cooperative effort of some outlying slaves who faced criminal prosecution, see *EJC*, III, 336–37; and trials, May 15, July 7, 1713, Middlesex C.C.O.B. (1710–21), 121–22, 127–28. Colony leaders perceived the very few cases of maroonage as military, not judicial, problems (*EJC*, III, 549–50; Lieutenant Governor Gooch to the Board of Trade, June 29, 1729, in CO 5/1322, fol. 10, VCRP).

clergy to slaves. In 1734, Harry, James, and Stepney of King George County on the thriving Northern Neck had hauled away four hundred pounds of tobacco, presumably to sell on the black market at that year's high prices. Instead of being hanged for one of the biggest larcenies between 1706 and 1739, these men successfully "pleaded their clergy." Now they could either try again—at the risk of not being able to plead their clergy a second time—or settle for a less dangerous means of attempting to participate in the free economy.[18]

The risk faced by enslaved aggressors against whites' property varied somewhat with time, place, mode of operation, the items involved, the victim, and who was willing and able to testify. The establishment of benefit of clergy for slaves made the temporal difference. Justices in various counties, then as now, handled similar cases in a variety of ways.[19] Slaves were also better off when convicted of stealing items from outside any building. Before the passage of special burglary legislation for slaves, common law could fall on slaves and free people alike with respect to burglary.[20] If a slave were convicted of breaking and entering a house or storehouse with the intention to steal at nighttime, or of burglarizing such places and stealing items worth more than five shillings, the court would have no choice but to sentence her or him to death. But slaves charged only with stealing items, especially those of lesser value, faced better odds in court. It is significant that throughout this period, including the years of "rising crime" in the late 1730s, not a single slave was convicted of stealing money or

18. Trial of "Caser," October 7, 1724, Northampton C.C.O.B. (1722–29), 145; trial of Harry, James, and Stepney, October 28, 1734, King George C.C.O.B. (1721–34), 678; Deal, "Race and Class in Colonial Virginia," 218–20; Breen and Innes, "*Myne Owne Ground*," 107–109. On economic conditions and tobacco prices on the Northern Neck and in 1734, see Marc Egnal, "The Origins of the Revolution in Virginia: A Reinterpretation," *WMQ*, 3rd ser., XXXVII (1980), 401–28; Carville V. Earle, *The Evolution of a Tidewater Settlement System: All Hallow's Parish, Maryland, 1650–1783* (Chicago, 1975), 16, 18, 228; and Melvin Herndon, *Tobacco in Colonial Virginia: "The Sovereign Remedy"* (Williamsburg, 1957), 48. It should be remembered that the many slaves who made away with a little here and a little there from their owners never appeared in the court records.

19. For example, in a December 9, 1724, trial, the Lancaster County oyer and terminer judges could not secure a guilty verdict on the first vote. Rather than record a verdict of not guilty, as most other justices would have done, those in favor simply delayed proceedings until the next day, when other hanging judges joined them to form a majority against Robin (Lancaster C.C.O.B. [1721–29], 162).

20. Webb, *The Office and Authority of a Justice of the Peace*, 63, 208–10. For the first special penalty for slaves convicted of burglary, see Hening, *The Statutes at Large*, IV, 326. There were always exceptions in trials of slaves. In his January 25, 1736–37, trial, George was convicted of stealing goods worth more than twenty-one shillings from an open boat. He was hanged (Goochland C.C.O.B. [1735–41], 127–29, 248).

of robbing—*i.e.*, stealing money from someone while threatening or using violence. The latter usually meant death for convicted whites as well as slaves, and the theft of money created severe problems of disposal since its mere possession by a slave would cause suspicion.

Hog stealing, a misdemeanor only and therefore tried in the regular county court sessions, was a relatively safe activity for slaves. Prosecution was somewhat irregular and punishment was a whipping and nothing more. The slave accused of stealing stored food, however, faced a great deal of risk if enough food had been taken. Horse stealing meant nearly certain execution for any offender, black or white, enslaved or free. It is not surprising that only one conviction of a slave for that threat to a primary means of personal mobility and sometimes status appears in available court records between 1706 and 1739. In 1723, Dick was hanged for stealing one horse. Liquor was sometimes sought by slaves. In 1737, John Brickell described what he saw as the typical behavior of slaves in North Carolina: "There are abundance of them given to theft, and frequently steal from each other, and sometimes from the Christians, especially Rum, with which they entertain their Wives and Mistresses at Night, but are often detected and punished for it." Whether rum was also popular among slaves in early eighteenth-century Virginia is not clear since most punishments for this sort of behavior were probably private. Only one Virginian slave was publicly punished upon being convicted of stealing any kind of alcoholic beverage before 1740.[21]

Virtually all the targets of the many slaves convicted of crimes against property were white. This preponderance of white victims by no means indicates that slaves did not steal from one another in Virginia as Brickell charged they did in North Carolina. When they did, however, they failed to take enough to attract their owners' attention, the owners did not care, or owners or slaves somehow dealt with such behavior on their own. In one instance, Jack received benefit of clergy after being convicted of breaking into the slave quarters of a master other than his own and stealing assorted goods. The salient fact of this

21. Schwarz, "Gabriel's Challenge," 296–97; trial of Dick, September 27, 1723, King George C.C.O.B. (1721–34), 137, 142; John Brickell, *The Natural History of North Carolina* (Dublin, 1737), 275. The one conviction for theft of liquor is singular in another way. Although Martin was also found guilty of burglary and stealing of ten shillings' worth of bacon and five shillings' worth of meat, he was not executed. Instead, he received thirty-nine lashes in Yorktown and another thirty-nine in Williamsburg. Trial, December 22, 1730, York C.C.O.B. (1729–32), 134.

1737 case is that the quarters belonged to a white. The legal offense was against the white property owner. One slave would have to kill another slave outright before the law would take notice. Even then, the interest at stake was that of the victim's owner.[22]

Even the trial process itself revealed how slaves and whites could confront one another. As might be expected, many of the witnesses against slaves accused of crimes concerning property were white. Some were slaves, though. Whites either forced or somehow managed to persuade some slaves to testify against fellow slaves. The examples of, and visible reminders provided by, Jane and Toney in Middlesex County undoubtedly scared some slaves into cooperating. Both received thirty-nine lashes, stood two hours at the pillory, and had their ears nailed to the pillory and cut off as punishment for committing perjury in a minor 1729 trial for hog stealing. The slaves found guilty received thirty-nine lashes.[23]

A possible source of increasing division among slaves appeared in the case of Tom, the property of George Tuberville of Westmoreland County, who in 1731 received the death sentence upon conviction for breaking into a storehouse and stealing goods valued at more than twenty shillings. One white person and two slaves provided enough testimony to satisfy the judges. The court clerk described one of the slave witnesses as a "Mulatto Christian." Given white authorities' growing doubts about court testimony by slaves, especially non-Christian ones, this identification of a material witness was not random. It was meant to indicate reliability. If that were indeed true, non-Christian slaves who planned to defy the criminal statutes had much to fear from some Christian slaves. And the latter may have faced danger from non-Christian slaves who survived punishment in court cases in which the Christians had given damaging testimony.[24]

At the same time, trials of bondspeople for property crimes revealed an increasing blending of cultures. Africans may have used aliases in their homelands, but if slaves planned to use aliases in order to cover up their illegal behavior in Virginia, they had to use names understandable to Euro-Americans. Thus when the York County court of

22. Trial of Jack, October 19, 1737, Richmond County Criminal Trials (1710–54), 243–45, VSL.
23. Hening, *The Statutes at Large*, IV, 127–28; trials, July 2, 1729, Richmond County Criminal Trials, 151.
24. Westmoreland C.C.O.B. (1721–31), 367a–68; Hening, *The Statutes at Large*, IV, 127, 326–27; *EJC*, IV, 20.

oyer and terminer tried a slave in 1737 for stealing an ax valued at five shillings, the clerk recorded his name as "Toney alias Dick alias Jack." Nevertheless, the justices somehow knew that the slave's absentee owner was William Fuller of Henrico County. "Toney alias Dick alias Jack" received a whipping, and the sheriff branded his left thumb with a *T* for thief, making an alias much less valuable.[25]

All the slave behavior that resulted in convictions for property crimes constituted a subterranean contact between two changing cultures. There were also numerous public encounters in the county courthouses in trials conducted by Euro-American officials against "new Negroes" and "country Negroes" alike for burglary or larceny. But the most dramatic conflict occurred when slaves engaged in face-to-face, violent interaction with white Virginians. Intracultural conflict also occurred when slaves attacked other slaves. The criminal code classified such behavior as crimes against persons. Africans and Afro-Americans in Virginia had to learn that violence in a North American slave society was sometimes useful or necessary and sometimes essentially self-destructive. Virginia was most instructive on this point. For example, early in the eighteenth century, at least one government official tried to prevent or punish white atrocities against slaves. Lieutenant Governor Spotswood's limited success only emphasized the vulnerability of slaves to violence. Sir William Gooch, who held that office after Spotswood, succumbed completely to local pressure in 1729. He asked King George II to pardon an overseer convicted of murdering a slave whom he was punishing. Execution would only make other slaves insolent, Gooch argued, and that would create an unacceptable danger.[26]

It is difficult to ascertain how much mortal violence whites inflicted on slaves in Virginia. Knowing how easily the attempt to prosecute a white person for killing a slave could end in an acquittal or with a pardon, officials may rarely have bothered to bring charges. We simply do not know how true this was, so we cannot rely on trial records as a measure of white homicides of slaves. Instances do appear, as in the case of slaves suspected of a crime. Prominent Eastern Shore resident Edmund Scarburgh made certain that Accomack County records con-

25. Trial, May 20, 1737, York C.C.O.B. (1732–40), 373.
26. The complaints, Spotswood's answer, and accompanying documents are in CO 5/1317, fol. 46, CO 5/1318, fols. 84v–85r, 95–98, VCRP. Gooch describes his experience in a letter to the Board of Trade, June 29, 1729, CO 5/1337, fols. 132–33.

tained his explanation of why his overseer had shot and killed one of his slaves in August, 1736. In Scarburgh's story, Jack hid in a cellar while being pursued for seriously wounding a female slave who belonged to a relative of Scarburgh's. When found, Jack rushed out of the cellar toward the overseer, who quickly shot the slave in the chest. Jack staggered, then dropped dead on the ground. Nearly two years later, the clerk of the House of Burgesses petitioned for compensation for his slave who he said had robbed someone while a runaway in North Carolina, had been chased and cornered, "presented a Gun against his Pursuers, and was by one of them shot dead on the Spot."[27]

The slave who wished, indeed had, to resist the tangible features of her or his own enslavement, much less slavery itself, labored under a severe, debilitating disadvantage. The power of any slave to control any white person through the use of violence paled before the overwhelming power of white people to use coercion and violence on slaves. It did not matter how strong or adept at physical combat individual slaves might be. If they had no place to hide after killing an overseer or an owner, they might as well "free themselves" by committing suicide, as some slaves did. Every single slave convicted of being the principal in a case of killing a white between 1706 and 1739 was sentenced to hang. The lesson was clear: intentionally kill a white person, and unless you escape by running away, you might as well have taken your own life.[28]

As is well known, masters possessed nearly unlimited legal authority to punish their slaves for misdemeanors and lesser offenses. The intervention of public officials could only strengthen this authority. This combination of private and public power appears starkly in Robert "King" Carter's action against two of his slaves, Bambara Harry and Dinah, in 1710. According to Carter, they were "incorrigible"—no punishment could control them. So Carter successfully petitioned the Lancaster County Court for permission to amputate their toes. Carter or his agent would perform the actual dismemberment,

27. Accomack C.C.O.B. (1731–36), 191–93; *JHB*, 1727–40, pp. 257, 338. See also Henrico C.C.O.B. (1719–24), 137–38.

28. Mullin, *Flight and Rebellion*, 58–60; *JHB*, 1727–40, pp. 254, 262; *Virginia Gazette*, December 9, 1737. One slave did escape a murder conviction, even though the dead man was white. The verdict was "homicide by misadventure," the trial was just after extension of benefit to slaves, and the slave received a brand on his hand as well as five lashes. Trial, October 17, 1733, Accomack C.C.O.B. (1731–36), 99.

leaving no doubt in the minds of Bambara Harry and Dinah who claimed to be in charge.[29]

Against this kind of day-to-day power, what could slaves do? One can partly answer that question by asking what some of them did do before 1740. The ultimate target for the slave committed to resistance or simply possessing a specific grievance was the owner. But it was not until 1732 that any slaves were convicted of murdering their master. Only one slave had previously been officially accused of anything resembling this offense. Charged in 1730 with murdering his master's daughter in Richmond County, James died in prison from an unrecorded cause. When the judges subsequently ordered that his body be quartered and that each quarter as well as his head be displayed at a different location in the county, it was obvious that they presumed him guilty. So may have a lynch party or a private executioner, though there is no positive evidence to support this speculation. The slaves who finally did stand trial for murdering their master had provided themselves with the only strength they could. Three of them had tried to create security in numbers. It did not work for Pompey, who hanged by the neck for killing Ambrose Madison. Turk and Dido, a man and a woman who were now part of Madison's estate, did receive lesser sentences of twenty-nine lashes for being accessories.[30]

Other principals in murder prosecutions themselves became victims. An unidentified female slave destroyed her Nansemond County mistress in February, 1736/37, with a broad ax. She reportedly confessed and then was burned to death as a perpetrator of "petit treason." If voluntary, her confession suggests either that she would rather die than tolerate her mistress any longer or perhaps that she subsequently regretted a moment of explosive passion. In nearby Orange County a few months later, Peter tried to get away on his master's horse after killing his master and another white man, but he did not succeed. The record of his trial contained the succinct order that his head be displayed in public after his hanging in order "to deter others from doing the like."[31]

29. Lancaster C.C.O.B. (1702–13), 185; Morgan, *American Slavery*, 313. For two other court-ordered amputations of Carter slaves' toes, see Parent, "'Either a Fool or a Fury,'" 292, 319n10.

30. Trial of James, November 3, 1730, Richmond County Criminal Trials, 167; trials, September 6, 1732, Spotsylvania C.C.O.B. (1730–38), 151.

31. *Virginia Gazette*, February 4, 25, 1736/37, June 10, 1737; Orange C.C.O.B. (1734–39), 181. Maryland judges ordered a similar display in 1739 for a slave woman con-

The authorities may have had some reason to believe in the deterrent effect of such public displays of official violence. Based on English practice, yet not used against whites in Virginia after the seventeenth century, the sanctions of burning and beheading completed a collection of increasingly severe penalties that slaves and, in Virginia after 1800, only slaves could incur. No doubt most blacks simply restrained themselves rather than risk certain death. Two slaves did stand trial in 1734 for "abusing" or assaulting their masters, but no other instances of slaves killing or otherwise attacking their owners have survived from the first four decades of the eighteenth century. There obviously could have been other cases that resulted in private retaliation, but the number of convictions is still quite low relative to the total slave population.[32] There can be no doubt, however, about the open, direct nature of these early violent encounters. When the record indicates the method of killing, it mentions a weapon of violence, such as an ax or a gun. Not one of the slaves convicted of murder before 1740 had used poison. Recognition of that secret and especially dangerous method would come after 1740.

In the matter of rape charges, we have little or no means of distinguishing between those cases in which a slave raped a white woman to avenge the honor of a black woman or indeed black women—if such motivation ever existed—and those in which rape resulted from other motives or from mental illness. Another problem is that the simple conviction rate in trials of slaves accused of raping a white woman was 100 percent between 1724 and 1739. (There are no rape trials in available records for the years 1706 to 1724.) There is reason to doubt some of these verdicts. Without additional evidence, it is impossible to determine whether this rate derived from fact or from a grim kind of practicality—judicial oversight when conviction was certain, and private punishment when the accuser refused to endure the shame of court testimony or evidence was otherwise legally weak.[33]

---

victed of an ax murder. Her head was to remain in public "Until she be Rotten" (Aubrey C. Land, *The Dulanys of Maryland* [Baltimore, 1968], 58). On "petit treason," see William Blackstone, *Commentaries on the Laws of England* (4 vols.; Philadelphia, 1771–72), IV, 204.

32. Trials of Sambo and Toby, March 5, 1733/34, and May 7, 1734, Accomack C.C.O.B. (1731–36), 114, 121.

33. John W. Blassingame, *The Slave Community: Plantation Life in the Antebellum South* (Rev. ed.; New York, 1979), 154–55, 172–73.

Several accusers did testify between 1724 and 1739. Janet Young, the white servant of Lancaster County resident Samuel Rain, incriminated Harry, William Rogers' property, in 1724. According to her, Harry came up behind her on the road and sexually assaulted her. The relatively low socioeconomic status of the servant and of the two masters appeared to make no difference in the credibility of Janet Young or in the willingness of the oyer and terminer judges to be as harsh as the law allowed. Rogers had one male and two female slaves as well as one servant woman when he died four years after the rape trial; he had had five tithables in 1720. Samuel Rain was young and had even less property than Rogers did. Two months before the trial, Rain had married the daughter of a man who had only one tithable—that is, himself—in 1720, and the obscure Rain never appeared by himself in any list of tithables or in the county court records from the period. The court accepted the evidence from a servant woman against the testimony of the relatively valuable slave of a man socially superior to both Janet Young and Rain. They then sentenced Harry to hang.[34]

The prominence of his master may have helped Caesar, Gawen Corbin's slave, when he faced the Spotsylvania County justices in November of 1724 on the charge of having attempted to rape and commit buggery of a four-year-old white girl. If Caesar did in fact do what his prosecutor claimed he had, then he may well have been mentally ill. Slavery was almost the only social condition experienced by any slave. Consequently it is difficult to discuss any slave's mental illness in a context other than the social pathology created by slavery. Caesar may once have been as much victim as he was later a victimizer, previously as brutalized as the four-year-old girl whom he later allegedly assaulted. There is no proof of this, yet the circumstances of bondage require careful weighing of the question of responsibility even in such a brutal instance as child abuse. This situation was tragic, but because of the dictates of slavery and white supremacy, the courts had only a limited range of responses to what the judges thought Caesar had done. Rather than going to his death, however,

34. Lancaster C.C.O.B. (1713–21), 334–36, (1721–29), 136, 141–42; Lancaster County Deeds and Wills (1726–36), 54, 65–66, 76–77, VSL; Lancaster County Register of Marriages (1715–1852), December 21, 1723, VSL; Lancaster County Marriage Bonds, I (1701, 1715–83), 30. The economic value—i.e., price—of the slave can be compared with other prices from the time in Richard Nelson Bean, *British Trans-Atlantic Slave Trade, 1650–1775* (New York, 1975), 199–200.

Caesar somehow got off with twenty-one lashes, standing at the pillory for one-half hour, and losing much of both ears.[35]

The only other rape trials from this period introduce the pattern that was dominant in all later cases. Slaves were convicted of overpowering and raping vulnerable white women. In 1736, Andrew received the death sentence from the Caroline County Court upon being convicted of raping a married woman. An economically valuable slave named Jemmy met the same fate in Goochland County two years later. The accusation was that he had violated Elizabeth Weaver, the daughter of Samuel Weaver. These two free women successfully claimed that the bondsman had "had carnal knowledge" of them without their consent. A typical aspect of these cases is that the slaves had apparently chosen women unknown to them, women not in the family or household of their owners. The unreported cases raise the important but probably unanswerable questions of whether owners simply refused to admit in public that they had failed to protect themselves and their families from their bondsmen, and whether slaves who did commit rape made sure not to attack members of their plantation "families."[36]

Rape would turn the relationship of slave and master upside down, to be sure, but insurrection openly threatened white domination of a slave society more than did any other action. In the early eighteenth century, there was no lack of Virginian slaves willing to choose insurrection as a means of intentional resistance to their enslavement. The initial response of white authorities indicates that they were not completely confident they could control such activity and also that they regarded insurrection as a special category of crime. Such a direct and open challenge to white authority might be expected to provoke as harsh a response as did behavior labeled as murder and rape. Yet only two-fifths of twenty convicts in the cases available before 1740 were sentenced to hang for this offense. It took many years for white authorities to decide just what judicial weapons they would use against slave rebels.

In one sense, slaves committed to collective rebellion regarded the criminal code for the enslaved as totally irrelevant. It was illegitimate and part of the system to be escaped from or destroyed. But planning

35. Trial of Caesar, November 18, 1724, Spotsylvania C.C.O.B. (1724–30), 37.
36. Trial of Andrew May 28, 1736, Caroline C.C.O.B. (1732–40), 349; trial of Jemmy, July 13, 1738, Goochland C.C.O.B. (1735–41), 327.

and recruiting for an insurrection had to take into account the official as well as unofficial responses that would occur. They would be based on the slave code's definition of insurrection, how seriously the authorities took the threat it presented, and the legal powers whites could use against rebels. Before 1723, alert slaves found an opening. Even after the various scares, plots, and uprisings during the seventeenth century, Virginia's white leaders still had not clearly defined collective insurrection. In the 1705 slave code, for instance, the burgesses merely repeated the 1680 penalty of thirty lashes for "any negro, mulatto, or Indian, bond or free" who should "at any time, lift his or her hand, in opposition against any christian, not being negro, mulatto, or Indian," a measure designed only to prevent insurrections. But they neither defined nor assigned penalties to actual conspiracies to rebel.[37]

A series of plots and uprisings between 1709 and 1723 provoked an uneven judicial response at first and a harsh and more effective legislative response after 1723. It will be useful here to review the criminal proceedings resulting from this series of laws. Table 8 summarizes available data, showing that the range of behavior to which colony authorities reacted with General Court prosecution before 1723 included planning of group escapes—much like forcible breakouts from prisoner-of-war camps or large prisons—threats and actual commissions of homicide by two or more slaves, and conspiracies to "possess themselves of the Country."[38]

Prosecution in special courts or in the General Court provided a centralized and authoritative response to slave conspiracies, especially in the case of plots that covered more than one county. But slaves would quickly learn of the relatively lenient nature of this response. Before May, 1723, only two slaves are known to have been executed for collectively plotting against or threatening white control. These odds made taking the risk, all other things being equal, somewhat worthwhile. The two men who were hanged were the chief conspirators, and the authorities wished to make an example of them. Hundreds more were reportedly involved. They came from different plantations and different counties. Free blacks participated as well. Clearly white leaders recognized that even though they might designate insurrection a crime, it was obviously not an ordinary crime.

37. Hening, *The Statutes at Large*, II, 481–82, 492, III, 459.
38. Dryden to Board of Trade, December 20, 1722, in CO 5/1319, fol. 83, VCRP.

Table 8. Slaves Tried for Illegal Assembly, Conspiracy, and Insurrection, 1709–1732

Trial date	Name	Owner	County	Verdict	Sentence or Punishment
Mar., 1709/10–	Manuell	John George	Isle of Wight	NG insurr.	40 lashes
Apr., 1710	James Booth	Free black		NG insurr.	29 lashes
	Salvadore	Jonathan Jackmans	Surry	Guilty	Hanged; quartered
	Scipio	William Edwards		Guilty	Hanged; quartered
	Tom Shaw	Samuel Thompson		Guilty	Unknown
	Peter			Charge dropped	Outlawed
Nov., 1722	Sam	Elizabeth (Carter) Burwell Nicholas	Middlesex	Guilty	Transport
	Sam	Mrs. Eliz. Richardson		Guilty	Transport
	Will	Gabriel Throckmorton		Guilty	Unknown
Apr., 1723	Dick	Mr. Kemp		NG insurr.	Transport
	Robin	John Rhodes		NG insurr.	Transport
	Tom (Jack, alias Bambara Tom)	Thomas Smith		NG insurr.	Transport
	Isaac	Armistead Churchill		NG insurr.	Transport
	Jeffrey			NG insurr.	Transport
	Sanco			NG insurr.	Transport
Oct., 1730	Unknown	Unknown	Norfolk or Prin-	Guilty	Hanged

Date	Name	Owner	County	Verdict	Sentence
	Unknown		cess Anne	Guilty	Hanged
	Unknown			Guilty	Hanged
	Unknown			Guilty	Hanged
	Unknown			Guilty	Hanged
May, 1732	Jack	Mildred Howell, infant	Spotsylvania	Guilty	Hanged

SOURCES: Mar., 1709/10–Apr., 1710: *EJC*, II, 234, 236, 242–43, 246; Edmund Jenings to Board of Trade, April 24, June 10, 1710, CO 5/1316, fols. 141–42, 144–45; Spotswood to Board of Trade, March 6, 1710/11, *ibid.*, no. 61; proclamations, reports, etc., of March, 1709/10–April, 1710, Colonial Papers, folder 20, nos. 11–14, VSL; Reward notice, April 21, 1710, CO 5/1316, fols. 166–69; Parent, "Either a Fool or a Fury," 167–71, who argues that there were two conspiracies, one in 1709 and one in 1710, as does Aptheker, *American Negro Slave Revolts*, 169–70; Tate, *Negro in Eighteenth-Century Williamsburg*, 109–11, argues for one conspiracy. The council minutes in particular and the lack of any discussion at all of a conspiracy in any record for March, 1708/09, to June, 1709, lead me to concur with Tate. Manuell was punished for knowing, but not revealing, the intentions of other slaves to run away.

Nov., 1722, and Apr., 1723: Drysdale to Board of Trade, December 20, 1722, CO 5/1319, fols. 83–84; Virginia General Court, Judgment in *King v. Sam, Sam, and Will*, November 2, 1722, copy of order concerning same, and valuation of slaves to be transported, in Virginia House of Burgesses, Committee of Propositions and Grievances, Papers, 1711–30, VHS; *LJC*, II, 690–91; *EJC*, IV, 20; *JHB, 1712–26*, p. 368; Winfree (ed.), *The Laws of Virginia*, 257–59; Aptheker, *American Negro Slave Revolts*, 176–77; Tate, *Negro in Eighteenth-Century Williamsburg*, 11–12. The council considered trying these slaves for treason, but rejected that alternative on the grounds that only slaves, some of them not Christian, could testify against them. They were finally tried only for the misdemeanor of threatening a white man's life. The sentence of transportation required a special act of the legislature.

Oct., 1730: Gooch to Board of Trade, September 14, 1730, February 12, 1730/31, and his Proclamation, October 28, 1730, all in CO 5/1322, fols. 158, 161–63, 212–13; Minutes of Dr. Bray's Associates, Society for the Propagation of the Gospel, October 2, November 12, 1730, I, 13, 15, VCRP; James Blair to Bishop of London, May 14, 1731, Correspondence of the Bishop of London, 110, Fulham Palace Papers, 15, VCRP; Gooch to Bishop of London, May 31, 1731, *ibid.*, 111; Aptheker, *American Negro Slave Revolts*, 179–80; Tate, *Negro in Eighteenth-Century Williamsburg*, 112.

May, 1732: Spotsylvania C.C.O.B. (1730–38), 106, 118.

NOTE: There was a law that expressly criminalized insurrection, that of 1680, as supplemented in 1683 (Hening, *The Statutes at Large*, II, 481–82, 492). It was understood, however, that the laws against assemblies of slaves and against "lifting the hand" against whites, as well as procedures for suppressing outlying slaves were also measures for preventing insurrection. Some of the slaves in Table 8 appear to have been punished even though found not guilty of insurrection.

That is one reason why the House of Burgesses decided to transport out of the colony rather than execute several convicts, just as the state of Virginia would begin to do to certain slave convicts in reaction to the involvement of Afro-Americans in Gabriel's Plot in 1800.[39]

The 1722 conspiracy showed the ultimate risk of continued plotting. "I can forsee no other consequence of this conspiracy," Lieutenant Governor Drysdale commented, "than the stirring upp the next Assembly to make more servere laws for keeping their slaves in greater subjection." Slaves were once again influencing the development of Virginia's criminal code. Drysdale himself stirred up the General Assembly's next session by telling the representatives that "your laws seem very deficient in the due punishing any Intended Insurrection of your Slaves: You have had a late Experience of the Lameness of them, I am persuaded you are too well acquainted with the Cruel dispositions of those Creatures when they have it in their power to destroy or distress, to let slip this fair Oppertunity of makeing more proper Laws against them." The representatives quickly obliged by making it a capital crime excluded from benefit of clergy for six or more slaves to "consult, advise, or conspire, to rebel or make insurrection, or . . . plot or conspire the murder of any person or persons whatever." They thereby established not only the ultimate penalty for but also a broad definition of conspiracy.[40]

The 1723 law was the basis on which the Norfolk and Princess Anne justices condemned the leaders of the 1730 plot. As if to show the flexibility of the statute in certain judges' hands, the Spotsylvania County oyer and terminer justices cited it when they condemned Jack for the attempted murder of three white men in 1732, even though they made no claim that he had plotted with five or more confederates. From this time, the insurrection legislation would favor masters rather than leave an opening for slaves. Until 1765, county courts would still have to communicate with the central government before trying any suspected rebel or conspirator, but local authorities would control the actual trials. Their knowledge of local conditions and their

39. Waverly K. Winfree (ed.), *The Laws of Virginia: Being a Supplement to Hening's The Statutes at Large, 1700–1750* (Richmond, 1971), 257–59.

40. Drysdale to Board of Trade, December 20, 1722, June 29, 1723, both in CO 5/1319, fols. 83–84, 114, VCRP; *JHB*, 1723–26, p. 360; Hening, *The Statutes at Large*, IV, 126; approval of British attorney general, even though there was nothing similar in English law, CO 5/1319, fols. 97–100, VCRP.

susceptibility to local fears and pressure would increase the chances of conviction. Their ability to use the conspiracy charge even when it did not apply, as in the 1732 Spotsylvania case, would make the law a rather potent weapon in their hands. Slaves would now take a very high risk even to talk about rebellion.[41]

Slaves committed to collective resistance needed to fear other slaves as well. If they had to be careful talking about rebellion, it was not just because whites would hear. Will, the slave of Robert Ruffin in Surry County, earned his freedom in 1710 for having informed on his fellow slaves' plans. If being an informer secured freedom more effectively than did insurrection, then the probability of betrayal could only grow. Divide-to-rule tactics brought about increased division among slaves at the very time their numbers had started to provide an adequate basis for collective action.[42]

Aspects of that division appear in the trials of slaves for offenses against other slaves. As might be expected, no slave stood trial before 1740 for fornication or adultery, or for theft or rape committed against a slave. But several murder cases reveal outlines of the conflicts within the slave population. Table 9 focuses on the key aspect of the trials. Before 1730, cases of major violence that masters would be less likely to bring to court—that is, one slave attacking another slave who belonged to the same owner—dominated the prosecutions. The one exception, the prosecution in January, 1725/26, of George for killing Harry with an ax and clubs, resulted only in a manslaughter conviction. In the two instances in which male slaves were convicted of murdering female slaves, the victims and their assailants had the same owners, suggesting, but by no means proving, jealousy as a motive. Slaves' attacks on slaves who belonged to another master were more likely to lead to court action since the victim's owner had no recourse in civil law. Such cases did not begin to appear until the late

41. Trial of Jack, May 1, 1732, Spotsylvania C.C.O.B. (1730–38), 106, 118. Authorities could also decide not to take judicial action against isolated incidents of rebelliousness. Lieutenant Governor Gooch informed the Board of Trade of a "riotous assembly" and the burning of a barn in retaliation against one of the white men who dispersed the gathering. Apparently no prosecutions resulted from the incident. Gooch to Board of Trade, March 26, 1729, in CO 5/1321, fols. 110–11, VCRP. On the Norfolk and Princess Anne plot, see Gooch to Board of Trade, September 14, 1730, February 12, 1730/31, both in CO 5/1322, fols. 158, 161–63; Proclamation, October 28, 1730, in CO 5/1322, fols. 212–13, and in *EJC*, IV, 228.
42. Tate, *Negro in Eighteenth-Century Williamsburg*, 110–11.

Table 9.   Slaves Convicted of Attacking Other Slaves, 1706–1739

	1706–1709	1710–14	1715–19	1720–24	1725–29	1730–34	1735–39	Total
Convicted	1	0	0	2	4	1	1	9
Sentenced to hang	1	0	0	2	2	0	1	6
Male victim	1	0	0	1	2	1	1	6
Female victim	0	0	0	1	1	0	0	2
Unidentified slave	0	0	0	0	1	0	0	1
Same owner	1	0	0	2	3	0	0	6
Different owner	0	0	0	0	1	1	1	3

SOURCES: Miscellaneous county court order and minute books.
NOTE: These statistics include only those trials for which the clerk identified the victim's status.

1720s, and then were the only kind with enslaved victims that occurred in the 1730s.[43]

The pattern of major conflict among slaves within Virginia plantations and quarters as well as among slaves who belonged to different owners reflects the development of the slave community in the Old Dominion at this time. As more and more slaves who lived under the same owner created or joined real families, the likelihood of deadly conflict on plantations may have decreased. While networks of kinship were still expanding beyond the confines of individual plantations, the likelihood of major conflicts grew among strangers or rivals from different plantations. This pattern would reappear as long as the slave population continued to move westward and follow the same development from small units of initially unrelated slaves to small groups of families generally unrelated to one another and at times from different ethnic groups.[44]

43. Trial of George, January 15, 1725/26, Lancaster C.C.O.B. (1721–29), 192–93 (George was able to receive benefit of clergy, even though no law expressly allowed judges to grant it to slaves until 1732); trial of Peter, February 28, 1721/22, Henrico C.C.O.B. (1719–24), 159; trial of Ben, August 16, 1726, Richmond County Criminal Trials, 111.
44. In "The Origins of Afro-American Society," 226–59, Kulikoff sees a steady waning of divisions within Tidewater Afro-American society. Even though trial records give

The axiom for the twentieth-century United States is that the most serious violence occurs among relatives and people who know one another. It would be fallacious to assume that this construct would hold true for major violence among slaves. The social contexts of statutory crime in these two periods differ too sharply. In the early eighteenth century the slave community appears to have been a collection of communities with similar goals rather than one large closely interrelated community. Those goals included survival in the face of oppression and the protection of such social institutions as the family. Slavery severely threatened the attainment of both goals, especially the latter, but so did major or deadly conflict among slaves. For their own sake, slaves consequently had to try to control killing and other violence among relatives and acquaintances. Slaves had a stronger interest in preventing such violence than did slaveowners who sought to maintain order, encourage productivity, and protect their property.

There was no time in the history of slavery in Virginia when slaves or whites could safely assume that the conditions of the past would prevail in the future. Many aspects of slavery were in constant flux. What changed between the 1600s and 1740 was particularly important. Those were the years in which slaves established themselves in their communities and whites formed the customs, conventions, and laws that were supposed to support their domination of the slave society. Between 1706 and 1739, however, at least one hundred slaves challenged or threatened that control in impressive ways, leading legislators to try to create new methods of slave domination. Many of the patterns of interaction present in Virginia between 1740 and 1865 began during those years.

---

slaves' names and similar information, they provide only minimal clues to the ethnic origins and identity of suspects. John C. Inscoe, "Carolina Slave Names: An Index to Acculturation," *JSH*, XLIX (1983), 527–54, is suggestive on this topic. We do, however, need a similar study of Virginian slaves' names.

4. *Poisoning in an Early American Slave Society*

In 1745 an enslaved Orange County woman demonstrated her power to inflict agonizing suffering and death on her master, proving that a supposedly weak woman who lacked legal volition could appropriate strength to herself beyond all expectations. In that instance, Eve mixed a poisonous substance into the milk Peter Montague, her owner, drank in late August of 1745. After an illness of several months, Montague died in late December. The local justices reacted fiercely, yet legally, to Eve's challenge, directing that she be carried "upon a Hurdle to the place of Execution and there to be Burnt." Tully Choice earned 225 pounds of tobacco for "finding a Sledge to draw Negro Eve to the Place of Execution" and for executing her. The oyer and terminer justices not only relied on common law, which classified servants' poisoning their masters as "petit treason." They also inflicted on Eve a form of execution reserved ordinarily for traitors and witches, both of whom presented an unusual threat to human power, traitors because they endangered government and witches because they supposedly had diabolical power. Eve died because of common law, her status as a slave, and her identity as a woman. The judges clearly hoped that the grim punishment would so terrorize other slaves that none would try to overturn the master-slave relationship by using the demonstrably powerful weapon of poison.[1]

---

1. Orange C.C.O.B. (1743–46), 454–55, (1746–47), 99, 103; Radzinowicz, *A History of the English Criminal Law*, I, 628–29. Blackstone, *Commentaries*, IV, 204, reported that drawing and burning had once been the punishment for English women found guilty of petit treason.

Map 1. Virginia Counties, 1750

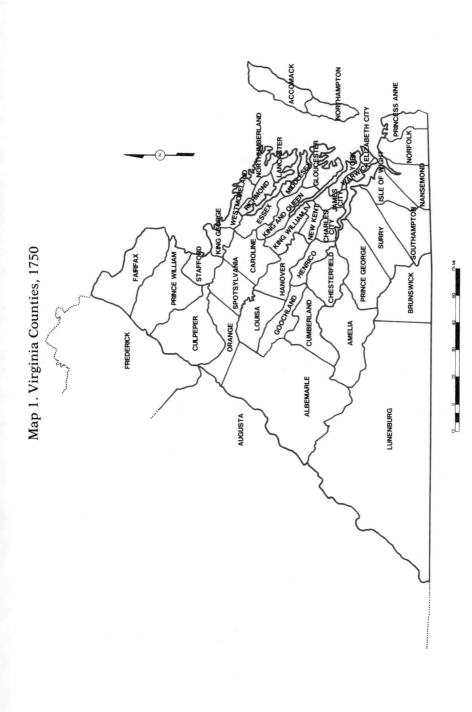

Insurrections periodically posed the greatest danger to white members of any slave society. Violent assaults and killings by bondsmen and bondswomen also made many whites fear for life and limb. Yet slaveholders and their allies in eighteenth-century Virginia thought that an equally great threat was that of being poisoned by slaves. Poisoning was more than another form of homicide or assault; it was also a secret attack against which there was no warning and little defense. It was by nature premeditated as well as efficacious.[2] More troubling still to whites, eighteenth-century white physicians, judges, and leaders had a particularly difficult time proving that it had occurred in specific cases, even though they suspected that it happened regularly.[3]

Hard to predict, hard to control, and hard to prove, poisoning was a weapon some slaves used against their primary enemies, white people who claimed absolute power over them, as well as against their secondary enemies, certain other slaves.[4] Poisoning by slaves and poison-

2. It is an axiom in modern criminology that poisoning is first-degree murder, or homicide with malice aforethought. The important historical consideration with reference to slaves charged with poisoning is that it required prior decision. It would rarely have been an impulsive act. See Jay M. Arena, M.D., *Poisoning: Toxicology, Symptoms, Treatments* (4th ed.; Springfield, Ill., 1979); Lester Adelson, *The Pathology of Homicide* (Springfield, Ill., 1974), 725–875; and Thomas A. Gonzales, M.D., *Legal Medicine: Pathology and Toxicology* (2nd ed.; New York, 1954), 690–888.

3. Jurgen Thorwald, *The Century of the Detective*, trans. Richard Winston and Clara Winston (New York, 1965), 267–316; Wyndham B. Blanton, M.D., *Medicine in Virginia in the Eighteenth Century* (Richmond, 1931), 4–11; Todd Savitt, *Medicine and Slavery in Virginia* (Urbana, 1978), 171–84; Gwendolyn M. Hall, *Social Control in Plantation Societies* (Baltimore, 1971), 69–74; Orlando Patterson, *The Sociology of Slavery* (Rutherford, N.J., 1970), 265–66; André João Antonil, report on Brazilian slaves, 1711, in Robert Edgar Conrad (ed.), *Children of God's Fire: A Documentary History of Black Slavery in Brazil* (Princeton, 1983), 57; Jordan, *White Over Black*, 113–14; Watson, "North Carolina Slave Courts," 24–36; Norman E. Whitten, "Contemporary Patterns for Malign Occultism Among Negroes in North Carolina," *Journal of American Folklore*, LXXV (1962), 311–25; Peter H. Wood, *Black Majority: Negroes in Colonial South Carolina from 1670 through the Stono Rebellion* (New York, 1974), 289–92; Philip D. Morgan, "Black Society in the Lowcountry, 1760–1810," in Berlin and Hoffman (eds.), *Slavery and Freedom in the Age of the American Revolution*, 138; Eugene D. Genovese, *Roll, Jordan, Roll: The World the Slaves Made* (New York, 1974), 616; Peter Kalm, *Peter Kalm's Travels in North America* (2 vols.; New York, 1937), I, 209–11. For the variety of substances that may have been available to Afro-Americans, see William Ed Grimé, *Botany of the Black Americans* (St. Clair Shores, Mich., 1976); Susan A. McClure, "Parallel Usage of Medicinal Plants by Africans and Their Caribbean Descendants," *Economic Botany*, XXXVI (1982), 291–301; and Edward S. Ayensu, *Medicinal Plants of West Africa* (Algonac, Mich., 1978).

4. White Virginians rarely stood trial for poisoning. A famous exception is George Wythe's murderer—who was found not guilty partly because the court could not legally hear a black woman's crucial testimony against him. Poisonings are also a very small percentage of known twentieth-century homicides. Julian P. Boyd and W. Edwin

ing trials held by whites were part of a struggle for power within any slave society. When legally impotent people used poison against those who asserted full control, they challenged the foundation of that society. When slaves resorted to poisoning in order to attack other slaves, they threatened not only those slaves but the economic interest of white slaveowners as well. In either instance, slaves attempted to make a dramatic change in their lives and also took special care to ensure that they would not be detected and severely punished or executed, as was so often the case when slaves openly and violently attacked their enemies.[5] White authorities in slave societies tried to counteract the threat in a variety of ways, among which were criminalization, judicial action, and corporal punishment or execution. Between 1740 and 1785, more enslaved Virginians stood trial for poisoning than for any other crime except stealing (see Table 10). Because of this level of prosecution and the degree to which poisoning trials of slaves reflected the development of the free and enslaved sections of the slave society of Virginia during the eighteenth century, such trials must be isolated and analyzed as symptomatic conflicts between slaves and white authorities.

The surviving records of 179 such trials in county courts of oyer and terminer reveal some significant patterns in the detected or feared use of poisoning by slaves. Spread over a period of more than fifty years, occurring in all regions of the Old Dominion, and involving many varieties of interaction between Afro-American slaves and Euro-American whites as well as among slaves, these cases are important and revealing examples of the fundamental conflict that lay hidden below the surface of an eighteenth-century slave society.

The charge of poisoning reflects Euro-Virginians adjusting to Afro-Virginians as much as it indicates Afro-Virginian initiative. Even though common law gave white authorities in the early eighteenth century strong weapons to employ against those slaves who used poi-

---

Hemphill, *The Murder of George Wythe: Two Essays* (Williamsburg, 1955); Gonzales, *Legal Medicine*, 701; Adelson, *The Pathology of Homicide*, 728; Marvin E. Wolfgang, *Patterns in Criminal Homicide* (Philadelphia, 1958), 95. For a trial of a free black Virginian for poisoning, see Spotsylvania C.C.O.B. (1849–58), 94, 99–100. (Held in 1851, this trial ended with an acquittal.) Records concerning the conviction of a white man for a chloroform murder are in the November, 1860, folder, VEPLR.

5. Between 1706 and 1785, at least eighty-five Virginian slaves received the death penalty when convicted of murder or attempted murder. Thirty-five others received the same sentence upon being convicted of poisoning.

Table 10. Slaves Tried for Poisoning Offenses, 1706–1784

	Tried	Sentenced to Hang			Granted Benefit			Misdemeanor Conviction			Not Guilty		
		White Victim	Slave Victim	Uniden. Victim	White Victim	Slave Victim	Uniden. Victim	White Victim	Slave Victim	Uniden. Victim	White Victim	Slave Victim	Uniden. Victim
1706–44	2	0	0	0	0	0	0	0	0	0	0	2	0
1745–49	3	1	0	0	0	0	0	0	0	0	1	1	0
1750–54	13	0	0	0	2	1	1	2	0	0	7	0	0
1755–59	17	2	0	1	6	2	2	2	0	0	1	1	0
1760–64	31	5	3	2	5	3	0	3	1	2	5	2	0
1765–69	25	3	1	0	6	2	2	1	1	2	2	3	2
1770–74	32	4	2	2	3	1	2	2	1	0	4	9	2
1775–79	33	4	0	0	1	0	1	3	1	10	6	1	6
1780–84	23	4ᵃ	1ᵇ	0	1	2	1	2	1	5	2ᶜ	4ᶜ	0
Totals	179	23	7	5	24	11	9	15	5	19	28	23	10

SOURCES: Miscellaneous county court order and minute books.
NOTE: The offenses were poisoning, administering poisonous medicine, and unlawfully administering medicine. The first known trial occurred in 1730 and the second in 1744.
ᵃIncludes two slaves known to have been pardoned by the governor and the council.
ᵇIncludes one slave known to have been pardoned by the governor and the council.
ᶜIncludes one slave against whom charges were dropped.

son and whom they thought they could detect, the first prosecution in available records is from 1730 and the first known conviction, that of Eve, did not occur until 1746. The problem was one of definition and detection. In October, 1748, the burgesses explained the necessity for a special law concerning one method of poisoning:

Whereas many negroes, under pretence of practising physic, have prepared and exhibited poisonous medicines, by which many persons have been murdered, and others have languished under long and tedious indispositions, and it will be difficult to detect such pernicious and dangerous practices, if they should be permitted to exhibit any sort of medicine, *Be it therefor enacted, by the authority aforesaid,* That if any negroe, or other slave, shall prepare, exhibit, or administer any medicine whatsoever, he, or she so offending, shall be adjudged guilty of felony, and suffer death without benefit of clergy.

The law excepted instances in which there was no ill intent or bad consequences or in which the slave acted with permission of a white authority. In the late 1740s, white leaders had learned from the actions of "many negroes" that it was expedient to keep tight control over even those slaves who could provide beneficial medical care.[6]

The 1748 law reflected the collision of three different historical experiences—European, African, and Virginian. English people had long regarded poisoning as a heinous crime. A statute passed during the reign of Henry VIII classified it as treason, punishable by boiling to death. Poisoning of a master by a servant was petit treason, a logical recognition of the rebellion implicit in a legal subordinate's use of such a weapon to destroy her or his superior. Africans also understood poisoning in accordance with the values of their societies. If witchcraft did not explain illnesses and sudden deaths, poisoning could. Shamans and tribal judicial authorities regularly took advantage of the reputation or genuine power of poison to maintain their position in tribal hierarchies. In Virginia, Euro-Americans primed to fear petit treason by servants confronted Africans and Afro-Americans whose background prepared them especially well to threaten or actually use

---

6. Radzinowicz, *A History of the English Criminal Law,* I, 628–29; trial of Eve, January 23, 1745/46, Orange C.C.O.B. (1743–46), 454–55; trial of Cuffey, January 19, 1729/30, Orange C.C.O.B. (1728–30), 196–97; Hening, *The Statutes at Large,* VI, 105. *Exhibit* presumably meant to display, perhaps as a threat or as a symbol of power. One slave complained of being poisoned "for his wife" in 1712 (Kulikoff, "The Origins of Afro-American Society," 244). The slave died in early 1713. In 1744 a slave supposedly drowned himself when suspected of poisoning his overseer (*JHB,* 1742–49, p. 94). In 1729, the governor and the council approved the emancipation of a New Kent slave as a reward for his many secret cures of various maladies, including poisoning (*EJC,* IV, 199).

poisoning. The result was a long series of threats and counterthreats and real poisonings. White authorities relied on court rituals, a special law, whippings, and the gallows to maintain their control. A significant group of slaves claimed to be able to control or destroy whites with poison. Some of them proved their claim, as indicated at first by the assertion in the 1748 law that "many persons have been murdered, and others have languished under long and tedious indispositions." Later deaths and illnesses of poisoning victims strengthened certain slaves' claims.[7]

Medicine was officially dangerous in the hands of some Virginian slaves. Many trial documents refer to the felonious or "evil and wicked" intent of the slave charged with illegal use of medicine. Other slaves so charged were said to have wanted to "destroy the lives" of, or to injure, their victims. One indictment in particular revealed why slaves who had used normally beneficial medicine could be feared, suspected, tried, and even hanged. In 1771, Loudoun County officials prosecuted Mill for having "prepared Poisonous Drugs and Medicines *with an Intent* to destroy her late Master." People with twentieth-century assumptions about medicine can more readily understand the charge of administering poisonous "drugs" than they can accept the possibility that "medicine" could be poisonous. One need only consider the harm medicine can do if malevolently, carelessly, or incompetently given, however, to grasp part of what eighteenth-century officials meant when they declared that slaves had been "guilty" of

7. Hening, *The Statutes at Large*, VI, 105; Blackstone, *Commentaries*, IV, 196, 199; Radzinowicz, *A History of the English Criminal Law*, I, 628–29. The literature on witchcraft in African societies is extensive. A standard, brilliant study is E. E. Evans-Pritchard, *Witchcraft, Oracles, and Magic Among the Azande* (New York, 1976). William Colbert, for example, reported that in "some Slave holding Countries it is thought that negroes can poison people by laying something in their way for them to walk over" (Journal, May 28, 1796, in Garrett Evangelical Theological Seminary Library, Evanston, Ill.). In *The Only Land They Knew: The Tragic Story of the American Indians in the Old South* (New York, 1981), 265–66, J. Leitch Wright, Jr., correctly suggests that American Indians might have shared their knowledge of local organic poisons with Afro-American slaves. Thus, in a handful of Virginia cases, the African background is irrelevant. (There could not have been a large number of contacts between the few remaining Native Americans and the growing number of blacks in eighteenth-century Virginia.) Two Tuscarora Indians poisoned themselves fatally (or were poisoned?) in 1709 before being tried for murder in New Kent County (Edmund Jenings to Secretary of State, June 24, 1708, Colonial Office, Class 5, No. 1341, fols. 16–17, VCRP). Note that even though the 1748 law singled out "many negroes," it also covered "any negroe, or other slave." *Other* referred to mulattoes or Native Americans, as in Hening, *The Statutes at Large*, IV, 132, 327, VI, 112.

administering medicine. Their main concern still was that slaves were administering the substances.[8]

The charge of administering medicine with ill intent, then, was really the accusation of poisoning under the cover of medicating. Ninety-five of the 119 slaves tried, not for "poisoning" as such, but for illegal use of medicine between 1748 and 1784 were explicitly charged with preparing and/or administering "poisonous" medicine. The charges assumed ill intent. White authorities took quite seriously the rationale of the 1748 law that slaves might try to poison "under pretence of practising physic." That law, the procedure of many a slave court, and the possibility that some poisoning by slaves remained undetected necessitate analysis of the overall pattern of trials and convictions for poisoning and for illegal use of medicine.

Some slaves may have killed their enemies with poison. We unfortunately have to settle for the results of the eighteenth-century trials as the best available evidence since so little testimony has survived. The most dramatic result was that some thirty-five persons were sentenced to hang for this offense. The courts identified as the victims at least twenty-three whites, seven slaves, and five people of unknown race and status. Those trials probably told slaveowners who knew about them to be on guard against poisoning. In addition, sixteen of the twenty-three condemned to hang for poisoning whites and four of the seven who received the same sentence for poisoning fellow slaves had apparently not worked alone. Their punishment was worse than that of their alleged accomplices because the judges believed they had acted with ill intent. The accomplices received benefit of clergy because the judges thought that the evidence was not sufficient to prove malicious intent. Yet the same judges regarded such slaves as sufficiently dangerous that they must be penalized.

8. Goochland C.C.O.B. (1765–66), 126–27 ("evil and wicked intent"); Northumberland C.C.O.B. (1762–66), 515–16 ("destroy the lives"); trial of Mill, August 20, 1771, Loudoun C.C.O.B. (1770–73), 211 (emphasis added). The third definition of *medicine* in the *Oxford English Dictionary* is "Applied to drugs used for other than remedial purposes," *e.g.*, poisons. One literary use is in Shakespeare's *Othello*, I, iii, 61. He juxtaposes "medicine," "poison," and "conjur'd" (I, iii, 60–112). Samuel Johnson's definition of medicine was exclusive: "Physick; any remedy administered by a physician" (*A Dictionary of the English Language* [2 vols.; 1755; New York, 1967]). Noah Webster's *American Dictionary of the English Language* (2 vols.; New York, 1828) explained under *medicine* that "even poisons used with judgment and in moderation, are safe and efficacious medicines."

Even slaves found not guilty worried planters. In 1754, Andrew, the property of Henry Anderson, deceased, and Beck, a woman who belonged to William Booker, Gentleman, jointly faced trial in the Amelia County slave court for giving poisonous medicine to Booker. Lacking evidence on which to convict the suspects, the oyer and terminer judges pronounced them not guilty and ordered them discharged. That was on October 30, 1754. On September 29, Booker had made his will, in which he declared that Beck should be given to his wife. A January 7, 1755, codicil tersely announced, however, that Booker had sold Beck. Booker probably was not about to allow any slave suspected of poisoning, especially of poisoning him, to stay in his possession or to become a danger to his wife.[9]

Even though owners tried to control much of their slaves' behavior, poison as threat or reality enabled some bondsmen and bondswomen, however briefly, to exercise extraordinary power over their legal superiors and their enemies of all kinds. Several cases illuminate this matter. Three that occurred in the 1740s may well have encouraged or hastened passage of the 1748 law. The case of Eve is the only known poisoning prosecution of the 1740s to end with a guilty verdict. The two other trials still highlight the socially visible threat of poisoning in a slave society. In Piedmont Caroline County, John Garnett's Tom escaped conviction in June, 1744, of killing Joe, the property of Richard Buckner, with poison. Yet the justices still suspected Tom of being a poisoner. Commenting that he had given "powder" to other slaves, the judges condemned Tom to be transported out of the colony. This penalty, not an established one at the time, was the expedient that slaveholders used to protect enslaved property from a real threat.[10]

In Orange County in 1748, the oyer and terminer judges tried to use the force of the law against Letty, a suspected poisoner who was supposed to have practiced her art in 1746 and in 1747 as well. This woman was indicted for putting poison in the water, bread, and meat of Richard Sims, a white man, and in food meant for Simon, the slave of John Grymes of Middlesex County. Witnesses testified that Sims consumed the substance in August, 1746, and died in January, 1747, and that Simon died in April, 1748, supposedly having been poisoned

9. Trials of Andrew and Beck, October 30, 1754, Amelia C.C.O.B. (1751–55), 195; Amelia County Wills (1734–61), 115–16.
10. Trial of Tom, June 9, 1744, Caroline C.C.O.B. (1741–46), 288–90.

at the end of the previous September. Even though the justices could have noticed that Simon and Sims, as had Montague, had languished for five or six months, indicating the use of the same kind of substance, they did not have the evidence to convict Letty, the slave of widow Hannah Potter of Middlesex County.[11]

Like the three cases from the 1740s, later suspected poisonings by slaves reflect the various struggles for power in which slaves were involved. For instance, 18 of the 118 slaves convicted of poisoning were women. Eight had acted with male accomplices, but 10 may have acted alone. Approximately 15 percent of all those convicted, the 18 constituted a small, comparatively inconsequential portion of slaves convicted of using poison or unlawfully practicing medicine. (Sixteen slave women were convicted of using other methods to kill an enemy.) Four of the 18 were sentenced to hang, however.[12]

The slave's official but by no means certain subordination to white people appears in a Westmoreland County case of 1774 in which a white man either convinced or forced some slaves to poison another white man.[13] In August, 1783, the Louisa County oyer and terminer justices convicted Peter of poisoning several white people. Upon reviewing Peter's death sentence, the governor and the council pardoned him. They observed that not only had his victims survived, but Peter himself had been victimized by some other slaves' attempt to "poison" his relationship with white authorities. According to the councillors, Peter "had no previous malice against those persons, nor sought their Death, but rather that it was an ostentatious Parade to Increase his Credit with those negroes who had Pressed him to Destroy those persons, their Enemies, for the purpose of Betraying him, as a person guilty of poisoning and Conjuring."[14]

If the councillors were correct, they had managed to uncover an unusually tangled relationship of power. Like the justices who reacted

11. Trial of Letty, May 26, 1748, Orange C.C.O.B. (1747–54), 113–14.

12. This use by women of poison may not be confined to eighteenth-century slaves. Some criminologists believe that contemporary Western women who wish to kill someone employ poison more often than men do (Wolfgang, *Patterns in Criminal Homicide*, 47, 56–57, 81, 90, 95).

13. Philip Vickers Fithian, *The Journal and Letters of Philip Vickers Fithian*, ed. Hunter Dickinson Farish (Williamsburg, 1965), 252. Westmoreland County court order books for 1774 are lost. Two slaves and a white man, tried for a poisoning conspiracy against a white couple, were acquitted (trials and examination of Myrtilla, Squire, and Frank Cousens, April 1, 1754, Goochland C.C.O.B. [1750–57], 380–81).

14. *CVSP*, III, 521; *EJCS*, III, 284.

so sharply to Eve and like the white conspirators who relied on slaves as accomplices in poisoning, the councillors understood what an effective weapon poisoning could be. Some slaves used their superior physical strength to control other people, but its open use would almost inevitably provoke a more powerful response. Poisoning, however, was secret and difficult to detect; at the same time, it was impressively frightening even when merely threatened.

It was to be expected that those slaves who were powerful within their own communities might use poisoning as a weapon, or the administration of needed medicine as a supportive means, by which to maintain their power. If some slaves indeed tried to frame Peter, they knew that conjurers made a claim to superiority that derived from their ability to use either beneficial or dangerous "medicine." The Piedmont Spotsylvania County oyer and terminer judges may have been dealing with a conjurer, or obeahman, when they convicted Obee of illegally administering medicine in 1778. The Afro-American Dr. Richard Nichols stood trial in the slave court of King George County in 1754 for using poisonous medicine, but was granted benefit of clergy when convicted. There is little evidence from other mid-eighteenth-century cases, however, to measure the extent of conjurers' actual reliance on medicine or poisoning. Passage of the 1748 law certainly indicates white authorities' concern about the intentions of slave doctors, who, like shamans in West Africa, could endanger as well as protect those on whom they practiced their arts.[15]

Slave doctors played an essential role in Virginia, as more than one historian has shown. There was no reason why whites would have wanted to suppress them as a group. Yet their value as physicians to other slaves and also to whites was precisely what allowed slaves bent on poisoning to camouflage their actions with relative ease. Slave-owners tried to maintain the benefits of letting slave doctors work and at the same time sought to keep conjurers under control. To whites concerned about their safety, the thirty-five slaves sentenced to hang, thirty-one between 1760 and 1784, were a constant reminder of the need for control. There were forty-four instances in which slaves found guilty of administering medicine without permission were granted benefit of clergy by judges who could neither prove ill intent nor perceive bad consequences. These convictions nevertheless reflected con-

15. Trial of Obee, July 29, 1778, Spotsylvania C.C.O.B. (1774–82), 94; trial of Dr. Richard Nichols, November 4, 1754, King George C.C.O.B. (1751–65), 373.

tinued suspicion of poisoning; they also kept slave doctors under supervision and gave them warning. The thirty-nine slaves given misdemeanor convictions also were subjects of suspicion. In fact, almost half of them may only have had medicine in their possession—they may not have tried to give it to a patient or a victim.[16]

There are some indications that those Virginian slaves who poisoned other people primarily attacked white enemies. Conjurers as well as other slaves who used poison adapted a West African practice to the circumstances of Virginia's racial slavery.[17] Africans had used poison to threaten, injure, or kill other Africans, but in Virginia, poisoning could not possibly have played the same role as it had in West African societies (enemies were usually other West Africans) or in West Indian slave societies (victims were mostly Afro-Americans because they so outnumbered Euro-Americans).[18] When male or female slaves

16. Blanton, *Medicine in Virginia in the Eighteenth Century*, 4–11; Savitt, *Medicine and Slavery*, 171–84; Kenneth F. Kiple and Virginia Himmelsteib King, *Another Dimension to the Black Diaspora: Diet, Disease, and Racism* (New York, 1982), 163–74; Robert Farris Thompson, "Icons of the Mind: Yoruba Herbalism Arts in Atlantic Perspective," *African Arts*, VIII (1975), 52–59, 89–90.

17. See Sidney W. Mintz and Richard Price, *An Anthropological Approach to the Afro-American Past: A Caribbean Perspective* (Philadelphia, 1976), 10, 27–42. See also McClure, "Parallel Usage of Medicinal Plants," 291–301, esp. 298 on poison and Obeah; Michael Mullin, "Slave Obeahmen and Slaveowning Patriarchs in an Era of War and Revolution (1776–1807)," in *Comparative Perspectives on Slavery in New World Plantation Societies*, ed. Vera Rubin and Arthur Tuden, *Annals of the New York Academy of Sciences*, CCXCII (1977), 481–90; Sobel, *Trabelin' On*, 41; and Monica Schuler, "Afro-American Slave Culture," *Historical Reflections/Réflexions Historiques*, VI (1979), 121–37. Schuler's argument that many West Indian slaves regarded slaveowners as sorcerers whom they could fight only with sorcery is, as Edward Kamau Brathwaite put it, "a metaphorical thunderbolt of immeasurable reverberations," but neither the trial records nor other available sources show whether Virginian slaves regarded their owners in the same way. Brathwaite's comment is in *Historical Reflections/Réflexions Historiques*, VI (1979), 151. See also Monica Schuler, *"Alas, Alas, Kongo": A Social History of Indentured African Immigration into Jamaica, 1841–1865* (Baltimore, 1980), 30–44.

18. On poisoning in West Africa, see John Barbot, *A Description of the Coasts of North and South Guinea* (London, 1732), 127, 372; Richard Jobson, "A Description and Historicall Declaration of the Golden Kingdome of Guinea," in Samuel Purchas, *Hakluytus Posthumus or Purchas His Pilgrimes* (20 vols.; Glasgow, 1905–1907), VI, 315–16; Sieur de Belefond Villaut, *A Relation of the Coasts of Africk Called Guinea* (2nd ed.; London, 1670), 250; John Atkins, *A Voyage to Guinea, Brasil, and the West Indies* (London, 1735), 52–53; William Bosman, *A New and Accurate Description of the Coast of Guinea* (London, 1705), 148; Great Britain, Board of Trade, *Report of the Lords of the Committee of Council . . . Submitting . . . the Evidence and Information . . . Concerning the Present State of the Trade to AFRICA* (London, 1789), *passim*; Wilfred D. Hambly, *The Ovimbundu of Angola* (Chicago, 1934), 202–203; Father Jerom Merolla da Sorrento, "A Voyage to the Congo," in A. and J. Churchill, *A Collection of Voyages and Travels* (4 vols.; London, 1704), I, 676; and Thomas Winterbottom, *An Account of the Native Africans in the Neighbourhood of Sierra Leone* (2 vols.; London, 1803), I, 128–29. Lievain Bonaventure Proyart, "Abbe Proyart's History of Loango, Kakongo, and Other Kingdoms in Africa," in John Pinkerton, *A*

in the Old Dominion turned to poison, they would logically have done so primarily in order to threaten, injure, or kill white people, their "status enemies." Twenty-three slaves received the death sentence for poisoning white people; only seven slaves were ordered to the gallows for poisoning other slaves between 1740 and 1784.

Such a wide disparity in sentencing occurred not only because the slave who poisoned a white person presented a greater threat to slaveowners than did a slave who poisoned a white person's human "property." Poisoning of slaves by slaves was another variety of anomalous behavior—either a consequence of aggression deflected away from whites or the results of ethnic discord, personal disputes, or efforts to stop a slave's collaboration with whites.[19]

In two Virginia counties, justices convicted more slaves of poisoning or of administering medicine than did judges in other counties whose records have survived. Slaves' poisoning or threatening of whites predominated in Brunswick County; slaves' poisoning or threatening of other slaves prevailed in Cumberland County. In Southside Brunswick, on the North Carolina border, at least six white people were judged to be the victims of poisoning or the recipients of illegally administered medicine between 1750 and 1785. During the same period, there was no recorded conviction of a slave for doing the same to another slave. (There were two unidentified victims.) In contrast, in the Piedmont county of Cumberland, located west of Richmond and just south of the James River, three enslaved black persons and one free white were thought to have been poisoned or given medicine illegally by slaves between 1750 and 1785. (One victim was unidentified.)[20]

General Collection of the Best and Most Interesting Voyages and Travels in All Parts of the World (17 vols.; London, 1808–14), XVI, 581, did not believe West Africans' ascription of widespread ills to poisoning.

19. John W. Blassingame, The Slave Community: Plantation Life in the Antebellum South (Rev. ed.; New York, 1979), 315; Earl E. Thorpe, The Mind of the Negro (Baton Rouge, 1961), 98–99; Leslie Howard Owens, This Species of Property: Slave Life and Culture in the Old South (New York, 1976), 93; Frantz Fanon, The Wretched of the Earth, trans. Constance Farrington (New York, 1966), 42; Charles A. Pinderhughes, "Questions of Content and Process in the Perception of Slavery," in Ann J. Lane (ed.), The Debate Over Slavery: Stanley Elkins and His Critics (Urbana, 1971), 105; Schuler, "Afro-American Slave Culture," 122–23, 128–29; Kalm, Peter Kalm's Travels, I, 209–11. It should be kept in mind that slaves may have been able to conceal poisonings of other slaves that they approved or that they wanted to judge on their own.

20. Trials of Webster and Sarah (July 25, 1758), Jenny and Tom (August 22, 1758), Dick (July 26, 1760), Judy, Bridger, and Jack (June 3, 1772), Senica and Dick (April 29, 1774), David (September 22, 1777), Charity and Andrew (March 10, 1780), Grace (November 26, 1781), Brunswick C.C.O.B. (1757–59), 233–34, 239, (1760–64), 90–91, (1772–74), 1–2,

Poisoning by slaves attained great social visibility in Brunswick County, no matter the actual number of incidents. The historical pattern of prosecuting slaves for poisoning whites in Brunswick began with convictions in 1758 and 1760 and developed over the years. Prosecutions reflected suspicion. White people would consequently have been more likely than slaves to stay on guard against being poisoned by slaves, remaining concerned even about slaves found not guilty, and wondering about other slaves who had attacked or shown overt hostility toward whites. Slaves who feared conjurers may have found themselves in a similar position in Cumberland County beginning with, perhaps, the 1756 and 1759 convictions. The Brunswick pattern was more likely to perpetuate itself, however, since the circumstances of slavery encouraged slaves' attacks on whites more than those on other slaves. So Brunswick whites ended up having more reason to fear their slaves than Cumberland slaves had to fear fellow slaves.

The earliest trials, which indicate the first time white authorities thought they knew poisoning had occurred, suggest some characteristics of the suspected poisoners. In Brunswick, a group of slaves was accused in 1758 of murdering Baxter Davis with poison. Sarah and Webster, two of Davis' slaves, were convicted of conspiring with William Edwards' Jenny as well as Tom, the property of George Carter. What stands out is the number of defendants. In only two other eighteenth-century poisoning cases—one in Brunswick in 1772 and one in Amelia in 1777—were more slaves prosecuted at one time. The only death sentence in the 1758 trial meant that the judges had singled out Webster as the conspirators' leader. With his accomplices, he presented a special kind of threat. They had either agreed to attack a particular white person, or Webster knew how to manipulate or force his accomplices into helping him. Three masters had clearly been unable to control their slaves; many others might be equally ineffective in spite of their best efforts.[21]

546, (1774–82), 168, 337, 408; trials of Dido and Okey (May 3, 1756), Quash and Isaac (May 29, 1759), Mingo and Peter (January 24, 1763), Toby (March 17, 1764), Peter and Bellon (May 23, 1765), Bellon (June 4, 1765), Ceasar (October 21, 1773), Cumberland C.C.O.B. (1752–58), 388–89, (1758–62), 56–57, (1762–64), 129–30, 394–95, (1764–67), 124–25, 133–34, (1772–74), 452–53.

21. Trials of Webster and Sarah, and of Davy, Bristol, Judy, Bridger, and Jack, July 25, 1758, June 3, 1772, Brunswick C.C.O.B. (1757–59), 233–34, (1772–74), 1–2; trials of Simon, Young Bristol, and Old Bristol, and of Harry, Fanny, and Freddy, December 27, 1777, February 20, 1778, Amelia C.C.O.B. (1776–80), 90–91, 101.

How many Brunswick people realized the danger or the opportunity this situation presented? If Webster acted with some fellow slaves in 1758, were they aware of how unsuccessful some other criminalized actions had been, such as the minor insurrection in 1752, the open killing of a white person in 1754, and the many thefts between 1747 and 1758? Dick, the slave of Richard Hill, received the death sentence for poisoning John Jones in 1760. Did he think he would be better at avoiding detection than Webster and his co-conspirators had been?[22] Important as these questions are, available evidence does not allow us to answer them. Other significant questions, however, do have some answers. Were there, for example, possible connections among the Brunswick cases? Also, what did the earlier cases have to do with the convictions of more than one dozen slaves for administering medicine to whites or attacking white enemies with poison in Brunswick County after the 1758 incident and before 1786?

Family connections, which figure in several of the Brunswick cases, increased the ability of slaves to use poisoning or the threat of poisoning. Three of the slaves tried for the 1772 conspiracy belonged to Nathaniel Harrison; Jemmy, who was found guilty in 1780 of poisoning two white people, but without ill intent, belonged to the estate of Robert Harrison; and Daniel Harrison's Grace was convicted in 1781 of administering medicine to an unidentified person. The Harrisons were probably related. Grace, Jemmy, and three other convicted poisoners or doctors may also have been related or simply members of the artificial, extended family created by their being owned by related individuals. (It is also possible that they had in common the capability to practice medicine.) All these slaves were part of a network that had the potential of bringing them into contact with one another at least occasionally and that allowed the transmission of knowledge about poison and medicine if not the distribution of the substances themselves.[23]

Similarly, many of the accused poisoners had allegedly dared to attack entire white families. This circumstance was sometimes un-

22. Trials of Peter, Harry, and James, June 25, 1752, Tony, July 24, 1754, and Dick, July 26, 1760, Brunswick C.C.O.B. (1751–53), 242–43, (1753–56), 262–64, (1760–64), 90–91.

23. Trials of Davy, Judy, and Jack, June 3, 1772, Jemmy, June 5, 1780, (Grace, November 11, 1781), Brunswick C.C.O.B. (1772–74), 1–2, (1774–82), 347, 408; Margaret Scott Harrison, *Sketch of the Family of Carter Henry Harrison (1736–1793) of "Clifton" in Cumberland County, Virginia* (Hampton, Va., 1959), 3, 7, 17; "Harrison of James River," *VMHB*, XXXII (January, 1924), 99; *Genealogies of Virginia Families from the Virginia Magazine of History and Biography* (5 vols.; Baltimore, 1981), III, 708–13.

avoidable.[24] In Cumberland County, a list of the accused slaves and their patients or targets looks at times like a family gathering. The Harris and Carrington families, for instance, as well as the extended families or small communities of several slaves, were some of the attackers and the attacked. In 1756, George Carrington's Dido received a guilty verdict and a capital sentence for poisoning an unidentified person. One of Carrington's other slaves died from poisoning in 1773, but Caesar, the property of George Carrington's son and heir, Nathaniel, escaped conviction for that killing. Suckey and Joe also survived their 1780 trial for poisoning the daughter of Benjamin Harris, their deceased master and a member of a family into which Nathaniel Carrington had married. Two years later, another of Benjamin Harris' slaves was sentenced to hang for murdering another slave by means not indicated. Finally, when Thomas Harris' slave Susannah died from poison in 1782, the county court of oyer and terminer tried but did not convict Harris' Frank and the slave of another owner. Unable to prove intentional poisoning, white officials still had reason to suspect that powerful networks existed among slaves who could use poison. The ties that bound the members of these networks doubtless frustrated the judicial process of gathering testimony.[25]

The Cumberland trials took place in the context of other Cumberland cases, of course, but also in the context of cases from nearby counties, such as Amelia, Chesterfield, and Goochland. Just as slaveholders' networks of various kinds reached across county boundaries, so did strong networks of kinship, friendship, and economics— i.e., fences, or the "black market"—among slaves. In 1764 and 1765 alone, the justices of oyer and terminer courts in adjacent Amelia, Chesterfield, Cumberland, and Goochland convicted fourteen different slaves of poisoning or illegally giving medicine to ten people.[26]

24. For example, Simon was accused of putting poison in a white family's water pail (trial, April 25, 1761, Orange C.C.O.B. [1754–63], 556–57).
25. Trials, May 3, 1756, October 21, 1773, February 25, 1780, July 11, August 28, 1782, Cumberland C.C.O.B. (1752–58), 388–89, (1772–74), 432–33, and Powhatan (created partly from Cumberland in 1777) C.C.O.B. (1777–84), 143, 226, 244–45. George Carrington came to Virginia from Barbados, so perhaps the slaves he brought had a West Indian connection (see "George Carrington of Cumberland County, [1711–1785]," Sons of the Revolution in State of Virginia, Semi-Annual Magazine, VI [1928], 16–25; and Garland Evans Hopkins, Colonel Carrington of Cumberland [Winchester, Va., 1942], 5, 87). On the Harris family, see Kathryn Wiggins, The Harris Papers: A Genealogical Notebook (2 vols.; Camarillo, Calif., 1968), I, 75, 79, 82, II, 90, 91, 93, 96, 99.
26. Trials of Harry and Boatswain, November 5, December 27, 1764, Amelia C.C.O.B. (1764–65), 247–48, 281–82, 327–28; trial of Bob, June 14, 1764, Chesterfield C.C.O.B. (1759–67), 542 (framed copy of the commission for this trial is in CWRD, no. 95); trials of

Perhaps there was no prior connection among these slaves, but knowledge of the nature and number of these trials would certainly have impressed both whites and blacks: aggressive slaves were more likely to use poison against their enemies, and slaves' practice of medicine was increasingly uncontrolled. These increases may not have had their basis in a conspiracy, but they certainly derived from some common causes other than the obvious one of slavery itself.

A Cumberland County administration of medicine conviction in 1759, the first in that county in which the court clerk identified the victim, raises the question whether trust between slaves, however misplaced in some instances, had something to do with the cycle of incidents that predominantly involved enslaved victims. Reuben Shelton's Quash had given medicine to Carter Henry Harrison's Quash and Peter. Since ill intent could not be proved and the medicine had had no bad consequences, Quash received benefit of clergy and thirty-nine lashes rather than the death sentence. The name "Quash" suggests that African birth may have led one slave to trust another as a "root doctor." One Quash attempted to practice medicine for good or ill while the other Quash may have been willing to accept the first as a practitioner. Whether Peter or the two men named Quash were African or not, two slaves apparently thought that there was good reason to trust another slave. Common origins or circumstances could not guarantee safety. An apparently African-born slave named Mustapha killed a Cumberland slave in 1762, and an African doctor could also use medicine as a cover for poisoning a slave.[27]

The idea of a historically connected sequence helps to explain the dramatic increases in poisoning and illegal medication cases. Such convictions indicated slaves' temporary power to threaten whites, yet also regularly led to strong assertions of the power by the judiciary. In Cumberland, for example, that increase took place in the 1760s. In January of 1763, Peter received the death sentence for poisoning a slave accomplice's master. A male slave and a female slave incurred

---

Toby, Peter, Bellon, and Tim, March 17, 1764, May 23, June 4, December 23, 1765, Cumberland C.C.O.B. (1762–64), 394–95, (1764–67), 124–25, 133–34, 249–50; trials of Tom, Judy, Margeray, Abraham, Will, Dick, and Taffy, June 20, 1764, February 9, September 20, October 11, 1765, Goochland C.C.O.B. (1761–65), 384–85, 451–52, (1765–66), 126–27.

27. Trials of Quash and Mustapha, May 29, 1759, and December 7, 1762, Cumberland C.C.O.B. (1758–62), 56–57, (1762–64), 114–15. From their African names one cannot assume that Quash and Mustapha were born in Africa.

the same penalty in 1765 for killing a slave with poison. Later the same year, judges determined that Tim, the property of William Macon, had threatened the life of Macon's Sue with poison. Three slaves were tried for attempting to poison two white men in 1769. Gloucester escaped a felony conviction for the attempted murder of Nicholas Speirs, but he did suffer thirty-nine lashes for allegedly using poison. Dick was found innocent of poisoning Thomas Wilburn, but Frank incurred twenty-five lashes and received benefit of clergy for his supposed participation in the same episode. There was also a slave named Toby who suffered thirty-nine lashes and successfully pleaded his clergy in 1764 because he was found guilty of administering medicine to three different slaves.[28]

The perceived use of poisoning could wane significantly at times. Although the 1760s were peak years for poisoning convictions in Cumberland County, they were also the last years for a long while in which such convictions would occur. Six slaves would be indicted for poisoning or giving medicine to other slaves in 1773, 1780, 1782, and 1785 in Cumberland and Powhatan, but the first five were found not guilty and charges were dropped against the sixth. There would be a few other poisoning cases in these two counties in later years.[29]

The Brunswick and Cumberland cases introduce another significant characteristic of poisoning and illegal dispensing of medicine by Afro-Virginian slaves. Just as there were temporal concentrations of cases and differing patterns of attack in these two counties, so there were diverse temporal and regional patterns throughout the Old Dominion. These patterns reflect other aspects of the connection between suspected poisoning by slaves and relationships of power in the slave society of Virginia.

While the 1748 legislation undoubtedly led to more prosecutions of slaves for poisoning, regional patterns provide the best explanation for the sharp increase in convictions during the 1750s (twenty-one) and

28. Trials, January 24, 1763, March 17, 1764, May 23, June 4, December 23, 1765, April 29, September 4, 1769, Cumberland C.C.O.B. (1762–64), 129–30, 394–95, (1764–67), 124–25, 133–34, 249–50, (1767–70), 347, 428.
29. Trial of Caesar, October 21, 1773, Cumberland C.C.O.B. (1772–74), 452–53; trials of Suckey (February 25, 1780), Joe (February 25, 1780), Frank and Harvey (July 11, 1782), charges (dropped) against Frank (August 18, 1785), Powhatan C.C.O.B. (1777–84), 226, 244–45, (1784–86), 211. Between 1786 and 1865, at least seventy-six enslaved Virginians were executed or transported for poisoning (C.S., boxes 1–10). Three of them were from Cumberland.

the 1760s (forty-two). That change began between the early and late 1750s, and is all the more remarkable because convictions of slaves for all types of crime declined in the war years of the late 1750s. The shift from Tidewater to Piedmont and Southside, which began in the 1750s, persisted in the 1760s, 1770s, and 1780s. Even though the majority of Virginian slaves lived in the Piedmont and Southside by the 1780s, convictions in the latter areas are generally more than proportionally higher than those in the Tidewater.[30]

Even the statistics of not guilty verdicts, which indicate at least the suspicion or fear of poisoning if not its prevalence, follow the same regional patterns as convictions. Only fifteen of the sixty-one persons found not guilty of poisoning or illegal use of medicine stood trial in Tidewater courts. African-born slaves, who were more likely than were Creoles to retain direct knowledge of West African poisoning and conjuring practices, predominated in the Piedmont and Southside counties in the 1750s and later. Yet this may not account entirely for the motives of the particular poisoners, who in any event may not have been African-born. Nor does demographic domination by the African-born in the Piedmont and Southside place the poisoners in the context of Virginia's slave society and the particular slave communities in which they lived.[31] What connection, then, did these divergent regional patterns have to relationships of power?

We cannot consider slaves in a vacuum, as if they controlled the Piedmont and Southside. They lived and struggled there with free white people, so poisoning incidents and trials were often but another kind of hostile interaction. Those slaves suspected of outright poisoning had acted primarily against whites. Moreover, the Piedmont and Southside white authorities who tried and convicted the people who have become historical statistics were hardly the self-confident, powerful gentry of the Tidewater. Somehow they became targets of or feared that they were under attack by poisoners. New to their status and insecure in their prerogatives, some masters could have acted in an especially provocative way against slaves, a portion of whom retaliated with poison. On the other hand, some owners may have been

30. Although records for such important Tidewater counties as James City and King and Queen are missing, so are the court documents for such Piedmont counties as Dinwiddie and Hanover. Thus, it is less likely that the availability of documents has skewed the data.
31. Kulikoff, "The Origins of Afro-American Society," 245.

somewhat vulnerable and erratic, exercising uneven control over their alleged possessions, and the challenge by aggressive slaves would be hard to prevent, detect, or remedy—except, perhaps, through the intercession of a slave doctor. Others were simply nervous about their hostile slaves and quick to accuse them of poisoning.

Until we know a great deal more about the diverse development of the Piedmont and Southside counties, however, we can identify only some of the factors influencing the high incidence of poisoning and administration of medicine convictions in that area.[32] Southside Lunenburg, for instance, was still inchoate in the 1760s. Its fledgling elite does appear to have been somewhat vulnerable to challenge. But there were few convictions for poisoning or illegal administration of medicine. In 1783 a slave did receive a guilty verdict in a trial for preparing medicine for someone unknown in Mecklenburg County (broken off from Lunenburg in 1764), and slaves in Charlotte County (created from Lunenburg in 1765) received five convictions for illegal administration of medicine in 1765, 1768, 1770, and 1782.[33] The preponderance of convictions in the newest sections of the original Lunenburg County indicates that the residents within the final boundaries of the county may have been able, for one reason or another, to hold their own against aggressive slaves who might otherwise have turned to poison.

Slaves charged with poisoning and unlawful medicating lived in relationship to free people with different degrees of power and alongside white communities at various stages of social development. So, too, did these slaves act in the context of slave communities at dramatically diverse levels of development and in possession of significantly different levels of power. Between the late 1740s, when the first known poisoning conviction was recorded in the Old Dominion, and the

32. The study of Virginia's regions is advancing. See Michael L. Nicholls, "Origins of the Virginia Southside, 1703–1753: A Social and Economic Study" (Ph.D. dissertation, College of William and Mary, 1972); Richard S. Dunn, "Black Society in the Chesapeake," in Berlin and Hoffman (eds.), *Slavery and Freedom in the Age of the American Revolution*, 49–82; Richard R. Beeman, *The Evolution of the Southern Backcountry: A Case Study of Lunenberg County, Virginia, 1746–1832* (Philadelphia, 1984); and Allan Kulikoff, *Tobacco and Slaves: The Development of Southern Cultures in the Chesapeake, 1680–1800* (Chapel Hill, 1986), 118–61.

33. Richard R. Beeman, "Social Change and Cultural Conflict in Virginia: Lunenburg County, 1746–1774," *WMQ*, 3rd ser., XXXV (1978), 455–76; trial of Cain, April 29, 1783, Mecklenburg C.C.O.B. (1779–84), 290; trials of Harry (September 24, 1765), Sue (September 24, 1765), Jacob (June 27, 1768), Hannibal (May 16, 1770), Jerry (May 4, 1782), Charlotte C.C.O.B. (1765–67), 81–83, (1767–71), 151, 349 (1780–84), 37.

1770s, when the American Revolution caused an artificial decrease in the number of slave trials, convictions of slaves for all major crimes increased steadily. One reason was a rise in the slave population. Another was a growth in tension between whites and slaves, both slaves' aggressiveness and whites' greater fear.[34]

Poisoning had a natural connection to insurrection, the most obvious example of an attempt by slaves to wield power over whites. As a hidden and real danger, poisoning had as great potential as did insurrection to disrupt, even to destroy, the relationship between aggressive slaves and white authorities, whether on plantations or in courts. At the planning stage, both poisoning and insurrection depended on secrecy. Like insurrection, poisoning involved an attack from within, an assault on the internal organs of the person and on the nerves and sinews of the system devoted to subordination and responsible for oppression. Even though far more slaves stood trial for stealing than for poisoning or insurrection, whites had much more to fear from the latter. Poisoning and insurrection trials had a historical relationship in Virginia. Some of the centers of prosecutions for insurrection in the early 1750s later became, at least temporarily, centers of cases involving slaves' poisoning and illegally administering medicine to whites. At the very least, some slaves were in communities that were capable of supporting open and collective challenges to white dominion and security and that were also capable of, and may have been driven to, using the hostile yet covert technique of poisoning. Even though insurrections had great potential for destruction, they had an equally great potential for failure. It was easier and less risky for slaves to attempt to poison white people. They could thereby threaten whites to almost the same degree as could slave insurrectionaries.[35]

34. The percentage change in total convictions of slaves for all crimes in every county with records extant was +70 percent (1745–49 to 1750–54); −21.4 percent (1750–54 to 1755–59; an artificial decrease due to the French and Indian War); +58.44 percent (1755–59 to 1760–64); +9.8 percent (1760–64 to 1765–69); +9.7 percent (1765–69 to 1770–74); +1 percent (1770–74 to 1775–1779); −9.3 percent (1775–79 to 1780–84).

35. Trials of Will, Venus, Simon, and Charlotte, August 4, 1752, August 19, 1761, February 29, August 27, 1764, Surry County Criminal Proceedings, Surry County Courthouse, Office of the Clerk, Surry, Va.; trials of Senner and Mingo, May 30, 1754, January 17, 1756, Sussex County Oyer and Terminer Minutes, 1–2 (Sussex was created from Surry in 1754); trials of Peter, Harry, and James, June 25, 1752, Brunswick C.C.O.B. (1751–53), 242–43; trials of Tom and Harry, April 4, 1753, May 28, 1763, York C.C.O.B. (1752–54), 204–205, (1759–63), 504–506; Tate, *Negro in Eighteenth-Century Williamsburg*, 101. The relationship was not inevitable, as the relative lack of poisoning convictions in Northampton County indicates. A free black and a slave were convicted on September 11 and November 13, 1750, of insurrection, but there was not even a trial of a

One reason why slaves' use of poison became so well established in reputation if not in fact in Virginia was that slaves there were African-born, of African descent, or, in a few cases, Native American. Perhaps more important, that technique of resistance was particularly appropriate for legally impotent slaves to use against free white people. Poisoning, arson, and stealing were the predominant secret methods some slaves used to try to control enemies and compensate for the deprivations imposed by those white people who thought they controlled the slave system. As were other labeled crimes—that is, assault, attempted murder, murder, attempted rape, and rape—poisoning was especially threatening to the safety of white people as well as to the authority and power of white leaders in a slave society. That is why county officials tried to find out as much as they could about the obscure practice, even though the work of conjurers or root doctors seemed to them to be part of an alien culture.[36]

Poisoning convictions reflected the tangled, hostile interaction between slaves and white authorities inherent in the slave society as it had developed by the eighteenth century. Some slaves relied on poisoning to try to change whites' attitudes or behavior toward them. Many white leaders reacted with hostility and fear, guaranteeing that they would perceive poisoning as a crime rather than as a means of self-defense or attack against the crime of slavery. Thus were many slaves and their masters locked into a basically dangerous relationship. The only certain way for white authorities to have prevented this occurrence, of course, would have been for them to reject or abolish racial slavery. Yet poisoning prosecutions would decrease in importance by 1800, as more slaves were convicted of violent murders and insurrection, and would continue to be of secondary importance after 1830, as many slaves attempted to use arson against their enemies.

---

suspected poisoner until December 19, 1778. It ended with a verdict of not guilty. Trials of Abimelech Webb, James, and Comfort, Northampton C.C.O.B. (1748–51), 271–72, 283–84, (1777–83), 134.

36. It is possible, of course, that African or Afro-American conjuring was only a variety of folk medicine or magic to Anglo-Americans, who had their kinds of folk medicine or magic. See Jon Butler, "Magic, Astrology, and the Early American Religious Heritage," *AHR*, LXXXIV (1979), 317–46. A white female servant was ordered whipped in 1730 for "takeing upon her by Inchantment, Charm, witchcraft or Conjuration, to tell where Treasure is, or where goods left may be found" (Richmond County Criminal Trials, 165).

5. *Property Against Property*

Judicial authorities first officially recognized the *modus operandi* of Guy, the slave of Lancaster County planter George Purcell, in 1742. Convicted of receiving stolen goods from Philip, another slave, Guy became a marked man—his ears were cropped. Two years later, Guy was sentenced to hang for breaking into a milk house and stealing thirty shillings' worth of hog meat. The career and life that were supposed to end did not, however. Somehow Guy avoided the hangman's noose and renewed his illegal behavior, making off with some property he had found in Landon Carter's slave quarters, which he had broken into in March, 1746. Guy received thirty-five lashes. Even with cropped ears, a reprieve from hanging, and lash scars on his back, Guy was not detected at his specialty until 1750. In neighboring Northumberland County, judges convicted him of burglarizing a storehouse and "taking and carrying away" goods valued at more than twenty shillings. Under sentence of death once more, Guy escaped from the Northumberland jail. A runaway notice published two years later identified Guy's characteristics that reflected his career of resisting the laws concerning theft. Guy was thought to be in Frederick County, passing as a free person under the name of Nicken and pursuing the occupation of fiddler. If he were, he had rejected his legal status as slave and was earning his own property.[1]

Like the majority of slaves convicted of crimes in the courts of Virginia between 1740 and 1785, Guy and other men and women had been

1. Trials of Guy, April 19, 1742, January 7, 1744, March 25, 1746, March 31, 1750, Lancaster C.C.O.B. (1729–43), 339–40, (1743–52), 7–8, 93, and Northumberland C.C.O.B. (1749–53), 3–4; *Virginia Gazette*, April 3, 1752.

accused of violating the property rights of white Virginians.[2] Thus was property pitted against property in a manner that negated slave-owners' definition of slaves as property without volition. It was not only by securing property that many slaves managed to threaten property. More and more slaves realized in the mid-eighteenth century that there was a powerful way to deprive whites of their property and injure their economic well-being at the same time. These were the slaves convicted of arson. Arson resembled poisoning in some ways. First and foremost, it was particularly effective. The first known conviction in a Virginia court brings out the point of just how damaging arson could be. In 1743, Phill burned the home, tobacco house, cornhouse (with contents), and dairy house of Thomas Emberson in Caroline County. Caroline slaves would long remember Phill and his attack. Phill's sentence was that he must hang, after which his head would be displayed on a pole in a public place. Nearly forty years later, the oyer and terminer court judges of Augusta County convicted Violet of burning her master's home. In 1780, Violet's severed head was to remain on display on a pole near Staunton. Every other slave known to have been convicted of burning a building in the Old Dominion between 1740 and 1785 received the death sentence. Both slave arsonists and white authorities meant business.[3]

Like poisoning, arson was a secret weapon and rather hard to detect. Only 42 percent of the slaves tried for arson received guilty verdicts.[4] Such convictions would depend not only on extracting damaging testimony from other slaves but also on the availability of reasonable evidence that fire had not resulted from any other causes. In the trial of Betty Downing's Synor, held in Northumberland County in 1776, an

---

2. For example, trials of Hannibal, March 8, 1774, April 17, 1780, York C.C.O.B. (1772–74), 529, (1774–84), 271–72. Also trials of Bacchus, January 15, 1771, January 1, 1772, March 17, 1773, Surry County Criminal Proceedings; trials, July 21, September 18, 1773, Chesterfield C.C.O.B. (1771–74), 305, 315; *Virginia Gazette* (PD), July 4, 1771, September 30, 1773, June 30, 1774; Ira Berlin, *Slaves Without Masters: The Free Negro in the Antebellum South* (New York, 1974), 11–12; Mullin, *Flight and Rebellion*, 120, 193n96, 131. The famous Somerset decision, which appeared to free all slaves in Great Britain, encouraged Bacchus and other slaves to run away, perhaps to Great Britain (see Mullin, *Flight and Rebellion*, 130–31; *Virginia Gazette* [PD], June 30, 1774; and David B. Davis, *The Problem of Slavery in the Age of Revolution* [Ithaca, 1975], 479–82).

3. Trial of Phill, December 10, 1743, Caroline C.C.O.B. (1741–46), 247–48; trial of Violet, February 18, 1780, Augusta C.C.O.B. (1779–82), 186, also in *VMHB*, XVI (1908), 94–95.

4. In the representative counties of Essex, Henry, Southampton, and Spotsylvania, the simple conviction rate in trials of slaves for arson between 1786 and 1865 was 24 percent.

unidentified witness testified that the defendant had set someone's house on fire by putting burning straw on the end of a pole. The judges found this testimony sufficiently specific and convincing to condemn her to hang.[5] Arson, as did poisoning, appealed to slaves who did not have the physical strength to confront their white enemies. Of the fourteen slaves known to have been convicted of felonious or lesser arson between 1740 and 1785, four (28.6 percent) were women. Further, six of the eighteen defendants found not guilty of arson were women. Compared to the percentage of women tried for or convicted of other crimes, except poisoning, these statistics were high. These figures cannot support general conclusions about how many female slaves used arson, but they do give some perspective on the method these women employed to counter the power of their masters. Even though some of the enslaved women who worked in the fields or were skilled in crafts may have been stronger than their masters, those who chose to attack owners relied mostly on arson and poisoning.

Arson lacked some of the distinctive characteristics of poisoning, however. Available evidence does not indicate that West Africans favored arson as a weapon against other West Africans.[6] But arson was significant to eighteenth-century Anglo-Virginians. English legislation classified most kinds of arson as a capital crime.[7] As an attack by Virginian slaves on their propertied owners, arson represents the eighteenth-century slave society's version of agrarian conflict: several of the convicted arsonists burned barns, mills, or storage houses. Even trials in which slaves were found not guilty revealed the distinct possibility that someone, and not something, was causing fires on many plantations.

Given the existence of comprehensive English statutes concerning arson, it was some time before Virginian legislators felt it necessary to

5. Trial of Synor, January 9, 1776, Northumberland C.C.O.B. (1773–83), 251–52.
6. None of the seventeenth-, eighteenth-, or nineteenth-century European observers describes Africans' using arson. Two twentieth-century anthropologists commented upon its appearance among the Yoruba: A. K. Ajisafe, *The Laws and Customs of the Yoruba People* (London, 1924), 30; and Cyrill Daryll Forde, *The Yoruba-Speaking Peoples of South-Western Nigeria* (London, 1951), 24. If one slave committed arson against another slave in Virginia, the criminal offense was technically against the owner of the victim. No extant trial indicates that any Virginian slave was even charged with using arson in this manner.
7. The last such statute, part of the infamous Waltham Black Act of the early 1720s, acknowledged that many propertyless English people either individually or collectively resorted to arson as a means of changing their socioeconomic relationship with the gentry. Radzinowicz, *A History of the English Criminal Law*, I, 654–55; E. P. Thompson, *Whigs and Hunters: The Origins of the Black Act* (New York, 1975).

develop special laws for arson by slaves. One element of uncertainty faced by some prosecutors and judges in arson cases resembles a problem connected with poisoning cases. If medicine administered by a slave turned out to be poisonous, how could one prove that the slave knowingly used it? The 1748 law was supposed to take care of that. If a slave set a building on fire and an occupant suffered injury or death as a result, how could it be proved that the slave intended the injury or the death in addition to the destruction of property? The laws of Virginia had long since provided white authorities with a solution to this problem. If a slave arsonist unknowingly killed a white person, that slave was by the slave code's definition guilty of murder in the first degree: almost any time a slave killed a white person, judges treated that act as homicide with malice aforethought. Injury would by the same standard be assault or attempted murder. Common law supported these notions, since any killing that results from the commission of a felony is always a murder, though not necessarily in the first degree.[8]

The patterns in arson convictions indicate slaves' motives as well as which kinds of arson provoked the strongest reaction from white authorities. Two slaves were sentenced to execution and to display of their heads on poles because they sought to destroy the victims' personal dwellings.[9] These slaves apparently aimed at white people and their property as well. Harry, Val and Bosen, Davy, Isaac, and Synor were convicted of burning white people's houses, but each of them except Isaac allegedly did so while in the process of, or in order to cover up, a burglary or theft. Burning of property was probably secondary to their intention of taking it for themselves. The oyer and terminer judges responded to the possible effect of their actions, namely, people being burned.[10] Finally, there were those slaves who burned mills,

---

8. William Blackstone, *Blackstone's Commentaries: . . . with . . . Reference to the . . . Commonwealth of Virginia*, ed. St. George Tucker (5 vols.; Richmond, 1803), V, 199–200, observes that death during the commission of a felony is murder. Authorities in certain towns and in some other colonies experienced much more fear of slaves' use of arson than did many of Virginia's officials. See Daniel Horsmanden, *The New York Conspiracy*, ed. T. J. Davis (Boston, 1971), 468–73; *Virginia Gazette* (P), March 3, 1775 (supp.), (PD), November 1, 1769; Brent Tarter (ed.), *The Order Book and Related Papers of the Common Hall of the Borough of Norfolk, 1736–1798* (Richmond, 1979), 56, 63.

9. Trial of Phill, December 10, 1743, Caroline C.C.O.B. (1741–46), 247–48; trial of Violet, February 18, 1780, Augusta C.C.O.B. (1779–82), 186, also in *VMHB*, XVI (1908), 94–95.

10. Trial of Harry, January 3, 1757, Cumberland C.C.O.B. (1752–58), 438–39; trial of Val and Bosen, May 12, 1763, Lunenburg C.C.O.B. (1763–64), 33–34; trial of Davy, Janu-

barns, or fodder and wheat stacks. Pompey, and Peter, and one woman (Alee) received mortal condemnation after attacking white people through their agricultural property. They meant for their actions to be taken as assaults.[11]

Arson by slaves could also serve the needs of a group. In 1782, Chastain Cocke's Peter stood trial and was convicted in Powhatan County both for unlawful assembly with "sundry" other slaves and for burning a barn that contained wheat, a carriage, and other items worth £100. If such a gathering became an occasion for a slave to commit arson, it was logical that white authorities would maintain the slave law against such congregations. When a slave committed arson with the approval of a group of slaves, white authorities were most likely to smell conspiracy as well as smoke. Thus the Old Dominion had come almost full circle from 1729, when the early eighteenth-century flurry of slave conspiracies was reaching a peak. Slaves had then burned down the barn of a public officer who had dispersed them for having "got together in a riotous manner." By 1782, individual slaves had begun to use arson regularly against white enemies and some slaves had taken it up again as a method of attacking in a group.[12]

However much satisfaction arson may have given slaves, it provided them nothing tangible to keep. Stealing white people's property—or "taking" it, as Virginian slaves defiantly called it by the nineteenth century—was something else. The property was useless to the victim, yet the slaves who had stolen the items possessed them as long as the act was not detected. The slaves could then consume what they had taken (food or drink) or use items as a medium of exchange. Arson might confer status when other slaves approved of the act. Stealing may have been more likely to improve the status of slaves since it made them economically indispensable as well as socially important. Arson

ary 31, 1765, Isle of Wight C.C.O.B. (1764–68), 115; trial of Isaac, January 23, 1770, York C.C.O.B. (1768–70), 419–20; trial of Synor, January 9, 1776, Northumberland C.C.O.B. (1773–83), 251–52. Many convictions occurred in winter—and perhaps the greater use of fire at that time made arson easier. There are no extant eighteenth-century cases of arson to cover up a killing.

11. Trial of Alee, August 16, 1766, Bedford C.C.O.B. (1763–71), 272–73; trial of Joe, December 17, 1773, Spotsylvania C.C.O.B. (1768–74), 296; trial of Pompey, June 29, 1781, Prince Edward C.C.O.B. (1773–81, Pt. 2), 96; trial of Peter, October 1, 1782, Powhatan C.C.O.B. (1777–84), 246–47.

12. Trial of Peter, October 1, 1782, Powhatan C.C.O.B. (1777–84), 246–47; Lieutenant Governor Gooch to Board of Trade, March 26, 1729, in Colonial Office, Class 5, No. 1321, fols. 110–12, VCRP.

increased the social power of many slaves; stealing enlarged both the social and economic power of many more.

Several white Virginians commented with dismay on the "proclivities" of Afro-Virginians to "steal whatever they could." According to Robert Williams, a Quaker, the conditions of slavery led blacks to "lying & thieving, Idleness & deceit." Deprived of free will and given a distorted understanding, Williams continued, slaves could be expected to behave that way. Warner Mifflin, a Friend who grew up in Virginia, remembered that when the question of total manumission came up at the time of the Revolution, "the prevailing opinion was, that negroes were such thieves, that they would not do to be free." At about the same time, however, an itinerant Methodist minister insisted that Maryland slaves on the Eastern Shore had given up pilferage after undergoing religious conversion. Religion stopped what owners and laws had been unable to control.[13]

All these theories served as support for other arguments. Widespread stealing proved that slavery was wicked because it was bondage that had made its victims immoral, said some people. Others almost agreed but then drew the opposite conclusion, that slavery made slaves so evil that they had to remain slaves. Slaves had to develop their own ethical viewpoint. I have found no direct evidence that eighteenth-century Afro-Virginian slaves shared the belief then prevalent in slave communities such as those in Jamaica that one could "take" property from white people but one could "steal" only from other slaves.[14] However, major theft by slaves was as widespread

13. Robert Williams, "Some Remarks on Slave Keeping Wrote in the 8 Mo. 1782," in Robert McColley, *Slavery and Jeffersonian Virginia* (2nd ed.; Urbana, 1973), 192; Hilda Justice, *Life and Ancestry of Warner Mifflin* (Philadelphia, 1905), 79; Thomas Rankin Journal, July 9, 1775, September 19, 1776 (MS in Garrett Evangelical Theological Seminary Library, Evanston, Ill.), 70, 114; Mullin, *Flight and Rebellion*, 60–61. According to an observer of North Carolina slaves in the mid-1770s, "they steal what ever they can come at, and even intercept the cows and milk them. They are indeed the constant plague of their tyrants, whose severity or mildness is equally regarded by them in these Matters" (Janet Schaw, *Journal of a Lady of Quality* [New Haven, 1923], 176–77).

14. *Minutes of the Baptist Association, in the District of Goshen: Held at Bethel Meeting-House, Caroline County, Virginia . . . 1816* (Fredericksburg, 1816), 7–8; Charles H. Nichols, Jr., "The Case of William Grimes, the Runaway Slave," *WMQ*, 3rd ser., VIII (1951), 556; Frederick Douglass, *The Life and Times of Frederick Douglass Written by Himself* (Rev. ed., 1892; London, 1962), 104–105; Mintz and Price, *An Anthropological Approach to the Afro-American Past*, 20; Rose (ed.), *A Documentary History*, 251, 278; Mullin (ed.), *American Negro Slavery*, 156; Charles Ball, *Slavery in the United States: A Narrative of the Life of Charles Ball* (Lewiston, Pa., 1836), 74; Eugene D. Genovese, *In Red and Black: Marxian Explorations in Southern and Afro-American History* (Knoxville, 1984), 135–36; Albert J.

in the mid-eighteenth century as it was in the early nineteenth, and there is firm evidence of the currency of that ethical distinction among Old Dominion bondspeople of the latter period. As early as the 1740s, many slaves probably already justified taking from whites. The important question is, then, What were mid-eighteenth-century slaves' motives and objectives in taking?

An essential aspect of any theft is that there be something that someone regards as worth stealing. Eighteenth-century white Virginians possessed many such items. Between 1740 and 1785 the Old Dominion was at the height of its economic growth. This was the golden age that produced political giants as well as large fortunes. There was, for the most part, internal stability for the colony and the state, which had such uneven years of growth in the 1600s and so great a decline in the early 1800s. Property was the basis of this prosperity and stability, and property in slaves was as relevant to the perpetuation of this state of affairs as was property in plantations and houses. Any slaves who reflected on these conditions had to realize that possession was one key to power for free people. Slaves too could participate occasionally in Virginia's golden age.[15]

Slaveholders, despite all their efforts, gave their human possessions excellent opportunities to share their other property. Complaints about thefts by slaves mostly concerned larceny from their owners. But of the 714 slaves convicted of stealing between 1740 and 1784, only 38, or 5 percent, had been operating on their owners' territory—*i.e.*, on

---

Raboteau, *Slave Religion: The "Invisible Institution" in the Antebellum South* (New York, 1978), 294–97; Michael Craton *et al.* (eds.), *Slavery, Abolition, and Emancipation: Black Slaves and the British Empire: A Thematic Documentary* (London, 1976), 141; Stanley Feldstein, *Once a Slave: The Slaves' View of Slavery* (New York, 1971), 175–77; Lawrence W. Levine, *Black Culture and Black Consciousness: Afro-American Thought from Slavery to Freedom* (New York, 1977), 121–25; "A Freeman" [Ezekiel Cooper] to Green, *Maryland Gazette*, 1791[?], in Cooper Collection, Vol. XX, MS. 4, Garrett. Comparison with the political dimension of endemic theft by a more modern group of workers is possible. Michael Grottner has concluded that constant pilferage by dockworkers in Hamburg, Germany, in the early twentieth century was "a form of social conflict, a form of struggle between workers and employers, which precipitated . . . certain changes on both sides in the configuration of power structures" ("Working Class Crime and the Labour Movement: Pilfering in the Hamburg Docks," in Richard J. Evans [ed.], *The German Working Class, 1888–1933: The Politics of Everyday Life* [Totowa, N.J., 1982], 54–79, esp. 61).

15. Consider Isaac, the property of John Carter, secretary of the colony. Although Isaac was not accused of stealing his owner's horse, he must have dealt with some of the best-bred horses available while in his owner's service. Perhaps tempted beyond the capacity to resist, Isaac was convicted of stealing someone else's horse and was hanged. Trial, March 18, 1740/41, Goochland C.C.O.B. (1735–41), 538–39, (1741–44), 15.

their own ground. Some 38 or more owners found it necessary—if in fact the slaves did not belong to absentee owners—to bring charges against their own slaves. Most did not, however. Lack of constant supervision could be a factor. Although 5 of Landon Carter's and 2 of Thomas Jefferson's bondsmen were found guilty of stealing offenses on outlying quarters, neither planter appears to have taken notice of the convictions.[16] It became normal for owners of property to go to court to counter those slaves they suspected of stealing who belonged to others. Such action was no sign of weakness. Of the 117 known victims of stealing by slaves between 1770 and 1774, for example, 94 can be identified. Eighty-five were men, several of them prominent. Nine were women, who successfully brought charges against another owner's slave in the same courts men used to protect themselves.

What opportunities, then, did slaves have to take goods from people other than their owners? Availability and risk were the two most important determinants of opportunity. For example, slaves confined to small geographical areas would often purloin their neighbors' property. Slaves also often stole goods in towns.[17] Not only were there unattended shops and warehouses all over Virginia, but towns provided other opportunities as well. The two known cases of pickpocketing took place in Williamsburg and Norfolk.[18] However, the risk could

16. Trials of Harry and Will, June 3, 1754, Richmond C.C.O.B. (1752–55), 10; trial of Kit, November 23, 1756, Prince William C.C.O.B. (1755–57), 252–54; trial of Sam, August 8, 1757, Northumberland C.C.O.B. (1756–58), 186–87; trial of Solomon, March 2, 1758, King George C.C.O.B. (1751–65), 781–82; trials of Jack and Will, July 28, 1781, Bedford C.C.O.B. (1774–82), 323.

17. Using the owners' and victims' names from trial records along with the tract maps and other references in Ralph T. Whitelaw, *Virginia's Eastern Shore: A History of Northampton and Accomack Counties* (2 vols.; Richmond, 1951), we can "match" the convicts with neighborhoods or with towns. For relevant cases, see the following (names of owners and victims and the tract numbers appear in parentheses): trials of Dick (John Kitson, William Drummond; A121), November 25, 1755, James (Naomi Ewell, William Nicholson; A145 and A144 or A145), June 1, 1757, Obadiah (Jonathan West, George Holden; A77, A71), June 29, 1757, Hannah (Agnes West, Tabitha Gray; A70, A109), July 26, 1758, Jacob (Elizabeth Warrington, Sacker Parker; A63, A121), April 27, 1779, and George (James Twisord, Edmund Custis; A64, A71), April 4, 1780, Accomack C.C.O.B. (1753–63), 115, 189, 194, 252–53, (1777–80), 334, (1780–83), 23. The case of Hannah involved the town of Accomac; those of Obadiah, Jacob, and George involved the town of Onancock. Several valuable discussions of black and white creation and perception of "neighborhood" are Carville V. Earle, *The Evolution of a Tidewater Settlement System: All Hallow's Parish, Maryland, 1650–1783* (Chicago, 1975); Isaac, *The Transformation of Virginia*, 52–55; Kulikoff, "The Origins of Afro-American Society," 250–51; Kulikoff, *Tobacco and Slaves*, 104–107, 123–27, 207, 209, 213, 215–17, 225–27, 323–24, 327–35, 339–45.

18. Trials of Nanny and Quash, June 2, 1742, York C.C.O.B. (1740–46), 102; trial of Hannah, January 1, 1774, Norfolk C.C.M.B. (1773–74), 156.

Table 11.   Slaves Sentenced to Hang for Theft, 1740–1784

	Condemned to Hang	% of Felons	% Slaves Tried for Theft
1740–44	12	33.3%	25.0%
1745–49	18	37.5	24.7
1750–54	27	48.2	29.3
1755–59	9	17.6	12.0
1760–64	26	33.3	23.0
1765–69	28	38.9	28.3
1770–74	48	48.0	28.7
1775–79	24	32.0	17.6
1780–84	27	27.0	18.6
Total	219	35.6	23.1

SOURCES: Miscellaneous county court order and minute books.
NOTE: Known pardons excluded; figure for actual executions is probably lower.

be high. The trend of amelioration in hanging sentences, which began in the 1730s, continued between 1740 and 1784, but many slaves still had to face the ultimate risk. Table 11 lists the sentences of execution for theft. By the 1780s, even sentences of hanging were decreasing as a percentage of sentences for slaves convicted of any kind of theft.[19]

A slight decrease in a percentage hardly removed the risk. Other circumstances maintained the overall danger of public punishment. Table 12 shows how many and what percentage of slaves tried for felonious theft were convicted. If slaves were prosecuted for felonious theft, their chances of being convicted of a felony did not change appreciably between the 1740s and the 1780s. What did change, however, were slaves' chances of being convicted of at least a misdemeanor. White people continued to rely on the courts to control other people's

19. In the representative counties of Brunswick, Essex, Henrico, Henry, Southampton, and Spotsylvania, as well as the city of Richmond, in the years 1785 through 1799, about one-fourth of the slaves found guilty of any kind of theft were sentenced to die, indicating that the trend in the two quinqennia between 1775 and 1784 was not anomalous. The figures are: Brunswick, one of five; Essex, three of ten; Henrico, six of eighteen; Henry, none; Southampton, two of five; Spotsylvania, two of eleven; and city of Richmond, nine of forty. Although only the Southampton execution from among these particular twenty-three appears in Condemned Slaves, box 1, one of the Richmond sentences was carried out. See Benjamin Henry Latrobe, *The Virginia Journals of Benjamin Henry Latrobe, 1795–1798,* ed. Edward C. Carter *et al.* (2 vols.; New Haven, 1977), II, 191–93.

Table 12.   Slaves Convicted of Theft in Oyer and Terminer Courts, 1740–1784

	Tried for Felonious Theft	*Felony Conviction*	*Granted Benefit*	*Misdemeanor Conviction*
1740–44	48	36 (75.0%)	14 (38.9%)	0 (0.00%)
1745–49	73	48 (65.8)	16 (33.4)	2 (0.03)
1750–54	92	56 (60.9)	18 (32.1)	6 (0.07)
1755–59	75	51 (68.0)	20 (39.2)	11 (14.70)
1760–64	113	78 (69.0)	36 (46.2)	14 (12.40)
1765–69	99	72 (72.7)	28 (38.9)	13 (13.10)
1770–74	167	100 (59.9)	40 (40.0)	22 (13.20)
1775–79	136	75 (55.1)	44 (58.7)	12 (8.80)
1780–84	145	100 (69.0)	44 (44.0)	8 (5.50)
Total	948	616 (65.0)	260 (42.2)	88 (9.30)

Sources: Miscellaneous county court order and minute books.

slaves through the 1770s and 1780s. Slaves taken to court for stealing still faced some kind of public punishment. In fact, the Old Dominion's slave courts began to concentrate on burglary in the 1770s. Among the many kinds of theft, burglary (breaking and entering with intent to steal, especially at night) was regarded by judges as one of the worst. That had been true for many years. But in the late eighteenth century, white Virginian leaders appear to have ranked burglary as the most serious crime against property, excluding arson, that slaves could commit. That ranking suggests that many whites also thought that burglary by slaves was increasing.

Whatever whites thought or did about major stealing by slaves, the trial records do indicate that slaves took large amounts of whites' property only after making a conscious choice. In a significant number of cases—from 21.1 percent of convicts between 1770 and 1779 to 43.5 percent between 1780 and 1784—such activity resulted from a group choice. Different slaves might have had varying degrees of commitment to the same action, but the data reflect practical unanimity. What all slaves in such a group had in common was the wish to appropriate property. The reasons why they wanted to do so were secondary. When in 1743 and 1744 the Orange County slave court justices convicted Deborah of receiving stolen goods from her husband and storing them in his chest, which was in her possession, they had uncovered familial cooperation. Along with Frank, Deborah's husband, the justices also found Coffy and Little Jack guilty of burglary and felonious stealing. Frank, labeled the ringleader, and Deborah may well have had similar intentions concerning the twenty-five yards of linen they took. Whether Coffy and Little Jack agreed does not matter. They, too, wanted the fabric and proceeded to secure it.[20]

It was obviously possible for owners to force slaves to do their stealing for them. An inconclusive series of prosecutions in Accomack County in 1748 and 1749 involved slaves of neighboring owners who wrecked fence rails, stole hogs, and otherwise harassed each other. The owners' animosity dictated the pattern, not a quarrel among the slaves. These circumstances make it rather hard to estimate how often owners did make their slaves do their illegal dirty work for them and take the punishment afterwards.[21] Yet we can learn something about collaboration in larceny between slaves and whites who were not their owners.

In the beginning of the eighteenth century, the larger number of white servants had made biracial cooperative theft more possible. The common economic interest of certain free whites and slaves, as well as Afro-Americans' increasing knowledge of Anglo-American culture, made such cooperation feasible again by the 1760s and 1770s. One of the first times a slave court took note of such collaboration was in 1774, when Pierce received the death sentence for stealing a horse in Southampton County. Pierce's owner sought a pardon at least partly on the grounds that William Parsons, a white man now in jail and soon to be tried by the General Court for a burglary, had induced Pierce to steal the horse. Had Pierce merely done Parsons' bidding, or had there been something in the transaction for him? About one year later, suspicion of inducement by a white saved Dick from conviction by the Northumberland County judges for burglary and theft of a large number of

20. Trials of Little Jack, November 23, 1743, Coffy, Deborah, and Frank, February 20, 1743/44, Orange C.C.O.B. (1743–46), 22–23, 47–48.

21. Judges who faced up to the implications of the criminal law had to deal with the problem of trying a slave for stealing while under the command of a white person. No intention was involved, so how could there be a crime, even under the slave code? There was a case in which slaves on adjacent plantations were harassing each other and vandalizing the property of their opponents' owners, both of whom were involved in litigation with each other (see trial, July 26, 1748, and accompanying material, Accomack C.C.O.B. [1744–53], 265, 283, 332–33, 339).

goods. Catherine Beckham, a free white woman, was examined on the same day for committing the same offense.[22]

Urban environments made cooperation in theft possible and fruitful for slaves. White Richmonders complained to the state legislature and to one another in 1782 about a large ring of thieves—some said as many as fifty slaves—under the leadership of some white men. The payoff for many of the slaves was that they could give their owners the amounts they were supposed to have earned from hiring themselves out and then keep the difference. Citizens of Petersburg also objected to the increasingly powerful conspiracies among slaves to steal from the town's shops and warehouses. Alarmed by the connection they perceived between a rise in stealing by slaves and the growing number of pardons the governor and the council had issued to slaves condemned to death for stealing, numerous residents of the Southside town petitioned the governor in 1781 to carry out the hanging of one convict in particular. The white people of Williamsburg also had their troubles with rings of slaves who stole their property. Even George Washington was not exempt. In 1765, he complained that some meal, tobacco, and an iron mill cock were missing from his Williamsburg millhouse and henhouse as of April 16. Four days later, the attorney for the king prosecuted Sam, the slave of John Brown of Charles City County, but could not prove Sam's guilt.[23]

22. Trial of Pierce, June 6, 1774, Southampton C.C.O.B. (1772–77), 370–71; trial of Dick, August 15, 1775, Northumberland C.C.O.B. (1773–83), 241–42. Beckham's case went to the grand jury, which never took it up because of the disruption caused by the American Revolution. In another case, a white man was examined and then sent to Williamsburg for trial for horse stealing and theft of sundry goods, and a slave was tried for the same but convicted only of stealing a pair of stockings (trial, May 17, 1768, Augusta C.C.O.B. [1768], 133–35). There was an instance of collaboration between a white man and a runaway slave (trial, April 17, 1780, Amherst C.C.O.B. [1773–82], 408–10, and *EJCS*, III, 310). John Harvie Creecy, *Princess Anne County Loose Papers, 1700–1789* (Richmond, 1954), 96–97, includes mention of a white man who was suspected of complicity in stealing goods with slaves.

23. Petition of some Henrico County citizens to Virginia House of Delegates, June 8, 1782, Legislative Petitions, Henrico County, VSL; Edmund Randolph to James Madison, August 30, 1782, in *The Papers of James Madison*, ed. William T. Hutchinson *et al.* (15 vols. to date; Chicago, 1962–), V, 91–92; *CVSP*, III, 632; *EJCS*, III, 329; trial of Charles, February 19, 1781, Goochland C.C.O.B. (1779–83), 70–71; trial of Simon, March 7, 1750/51, York C.C.O.B. (1746–52), 398–99; *Virginia Gazette*, March 7, 1751; Tate, *Negro in Eighteenth-Century Williamsburg*, 102. For the theft of goods from George Washington's Williamsburg house, see the trial of Sam, April 20, 1765, York C.C.O.B. (1763–65), 370–71. A month later, the same court found Sam guilty of participating in another burglary and felonious theft with two other slaves. The judges condemned all three to be hanged (York C.C.O.B. [1763–65], 372–73).

The slight decrease in sentences of hanging for theft as well as the small increase in the number of slaves being granted benefit of clergy had a consequence that oyer and terminer judges might have foreseen. The more slaves escaped the gallows, the more could become repeat offenders. The overwhelming majority of convicted slaves never appeared in the records again, but a significant number appeared twice, some even three or four times. Moreover, such reappearances happened more often in the 1760s and 1770s than in the 1740s and 1750s. In the 1740s, there were five slaves who stood trial more than once for theft; nine slaves had the same experience in the 1760s, and twelve in the 1770s. Population increases certainly had some effect, but missing records and name changes cover uncounted repeaters. None of these slaves stayed in jail after trial; none was hanged after the first trial. All were able to pursue property again if they were willing to take the risk.[24]

The property stolen gives some indication of slaves' motives. The figures in Table 13 show a pattern of preferences. Like a man named Peter, who stole a surplice from a church in Nottoway Parish, Amelia County, in 1773, the 136 other slaves convicted of taking clothes or fabric generally chose their targets carefully. It was most practical to appropriate commonly used fabrics, such as cotton cloth. In 1775, the year of the most trials and convictions of bondspeople for stealing clothes or fabric, court clerks listed the following items: cloth, gingham, linen, "clothes," a hat, a blanket, a coat, shoes, a gown, aprons, petticoats, shifts, sheets, a quilt, a counterpane, stockings, a cloak, a bonnet, buckles, and a pillow. (A slave might have been convicted of stealing several such items.) These things were almost all basics and if used wisely would not necessarily attract attention. These items were also recovered, though; otherwise they would not have appeared in the records. How many more articles of clothing changed hands as a result of undetected thefts?[25]

The best kind of food for slaves to take was anything that could be easily hidden and eaten quickly. It was impractical to haul away a

24. One cannot conclude that this was a continuous trend without data from after 1785.

25. Trial of Peter, October 9, 1773, Amelia C.C.O.B. (1772–78), 211. For the 1775 cases, see trials of Guy and Nimrod, January 7, 1775, Moll, January 30, 1775, Allego, January 31, 1775, Accomack C.C.O.B. (1774–77), 295–96, 309–15; trial of Ned, February 21, 1775, Cumberland C.C.O.B. (1774–78), 314–15; trial of Sam, May 16, 1775, Loudoun C.C.O.B. (1773–76), 550–52; trial of Gawin, September 25, 1775, Middlesex C.C.O.B. (1772–82), 419–20.

Table 13.   Items Stolen by Slaves Convicted of Theft, 1740–1784

	Clothes and Fabric			Food/Livestock[a]			Liquor			Money			Horses			Hogs[b]		
	T	G	C[c]	T	G	C	T	G	C	T	G	C	T	G	C	T	G	C
1740–49	20	15	33.3%	25	19	42.1%	6	1	0.0%	6	3	50.0%	12	6	50.0%	4	4	0.0%
1750–59	45	34	50.0	16	14	57.1	7	7	85.7	4	3	0.0	8	6	75.0	18	18	61.1
1760–69	45	37	29.0	43	35	40.0	17	15	46.7	22	17	41.2	4	2	50.0	15	14	28.6
1770–79	48	31	16.1	65	42	28.6	10	6	83.3	13	8	0.0	4	2	50.0	27	25	64.0
1780–84	22	20	45.0	31	22	31.8	9	9	77.8	2	2	100.0	2	0	0.0	3	3	0.0
Total	180	137	34.3	180	132	37.1	49	38	65.8	47	33		33	17	35.3	67	64	48.4

SOURCES: Miscellaneous county court order and minute books.
[a] Livestock excludes hogs
[b] All misdemeanor cases
[c] T = Tried, G = Guilty, C = Percentage of convicted slaves identified as collaborators with other slaves

large cache of food on the assumption that it would either last a long time or remain hidden. Since more than one-third of the men and women convicted of stealing food had worked with accomplices, they probably intended to share their take. When slaves stole cows or sheep, they had to be prepared to divide the animals quickly so as to disperse the incriminating evidence and to make the theft worthwhile to their slave community. What kinds of food did slaves take in major amounts? Hog stealing, a misdemeanor, was still widespread, and erratic prosecution continued to keep the risk low.[26] Other kinds of meat were popular as well. In 1770, the year in which the most people were convicted of stealing food, the following comestibles were mentioned in trial documents: a cow, two sheep, two turkeys, corn, unidentified meat, and bacon.[27] Slaves apparently concentrated on meat in 1780, the year in which the most slaves were tried for stealing food. Authorities caught slaves with four sheep, one cow, some bacon, an unidentified portion of meat, and a large quantity of sugar. Stealing food in that inflation-ridden war year may have been a response to shortages, but it involved a greater risk than usual. In August of 1780, court officials in Mecklenburg County valued a sheep at £10 rather than the usual 20 shillings or so. By December, Lancaster judges set the value of one sheep at £25. At those prices and with no statutory revisions, a slave who stole even the smallest article risked condemnation for a capital offense.[28]

26. Hening, *The Statutes at Large*, II, 129, 440–41, 481–82, III, 179, 276–79, VI, 121–24; "Commonwealth v. Isham," in "Negro Insurrection," September–October, 1800, folder, VEPLR; *CVSP*, IX, 141–42, 149. A slave stole three hogs; it was his third offense, the result of which was benefit of clergy rather than hanging (trial of David, April 14, 1769, Princess Anne C.C.O.B. [1762–69], 523). A sentence of hanging initially appeared to be the result of hog stealing, but it actually resulted from conviction of burglary (trials of Charles, Lettice, and Marjary, August 24, 1717, Middlesex C.C.O.B. [1710–21], 335–37). The generally low value of any hog is a clue to the inconsistent prosecution of suspected hog stealers. For prices, see Alice Hanson Jones, *American Colonial Wealth: Documents and Methods* (3 vols.; New York, 1977), II, 1295–1402, III, 2040, 2069–71; Earle, *The Evolution of a Tidewater Settlement System*, 122, 124–25; Lewis Cecil Gray, *History of Agriculture in the Southern United States to 1860* (2 vols.; New York, 1941), I, 140, 144, 206, 209–10, II, 918, 1042.
27. Trial of Jack, January 10, 1770, Fauquier C.C.O.B. (1768–73), 161–62; trial of Will, 1770, Charlotte C.C.O.B. (1766–71), 324; trial of David and Adam, April 23, 1770, Cumberland C.C.O.B. (1767–70), 510; trial of Mintus[?], May 11, 1770, Essex C.C.O.B. (1767–70), 334–35; trial of Sam, July 27, 1770, Amelia C.C.O.B. (1769–71), 107–108; trial of Cupid, November 21, 1770, Spotsylvania C.C.O.B. (1768–74), 141.
28. Trial of Jeffery, March 30, 1780, Chesterfield C.C.O.B. (1774–84), 277; trial of Isaac, Jacob, Thomas Hill, Shadrack, Jacob, George, Nim, and Joe, April 13, 1780, Accomack C.C.O.B. (1780–83), 21–24; trials of Abram, April 14, 1780, and Abraham, August 14, 1780, Mecklenburg C.C.O.B. (1779–84), 31–32, 68; trials of Abram, John, and Sambo, September 27, 1780, Sussex County Oyer and Terminer Proceedings (1754–1807), 37–39

What would slaves do with large amounts of liquor? White authorities in Richmond County had no trouble concluding that slaves broke into a storehouse and stole forty gallons of rum in the spring of 1745. They quickly tried two bondsmen, but failed to prove their guilt. In 1774 a Richmond County slaveowner conveyed his suspicions to Landon Carter: "My house was broken open last night and was robed of several gallons of Rum of different sorts. I suspect my groom to be the person and one of your servants who is at [?] at this present time. Should take it particularly kind in you if you would examine him immediately on his return and should you find any in his custody please acquaint me of it. I have been informed that he has a watch and that my groom was to pay him in Rum for it." Whether the amount was large or small, then, there could be a socioeconomic purpose to slaves' theft of liquor. Indeed, no known Virginia court ever successfully condemned a slave to death for stealing liquor. Judges and owners such as Carter surely understood that they could try to check, but not eliminate, this very functional kind of stealing.[29]

There is also a marked difference in cooperation among slaves convicted of stealing liquor and of stealing other items. In the first place, liquor had an economic function, as is apparent in the 1774 incident in which a slave was suspected of wanting to trade for a watch. Slaves could use it as a medium of exchange as easily as free people could. When liquor was simply one item among several carried off from a storehouse, as in a Middlesex County case of two slaves in 1751 taking brandy along with thimbles, pumps, and ribbon, the economic motive was paramount. On the other hand, when Sam, Cornelius, and Jack were tried by the justices of York County slave court in 1766 for stealing twenty gallons of rum and twenty gallons of brandy from a Yorktown warehouse, the judges' decision to convict them of a misdemeanor for having "misbehaved themselves" suggests that the trio jointly planned to reserve the liquor for themselves.[30]

(also Sussex County Court [Loose] Papers, 1779–81 [1780], microfilm in VSL); trial of Will, Goochland C.C.O.B. (1779–83), 65–66; trial of Will, December 8, 1780, Lancaster C.C.O.B. (1778–83), 70.

29. Trials of Janey and Scipio, May 22, 1745, Richmond County Criminal Trials, 317–19; Moore Fauntleroy Crandall to Landon Carter, July 10, 1774, Landon Carter Papers, Alderman Library, UVa. One slave was condemned to death for burglary as well as stealing liquor; another was pardoned after being convicted of the same offenses (trial of Harry, November 15, 1769, Essex C.C.O.B. [1767–70], 301; trial of James, November 29, 1782, Spotsylvania C.C.O.B. [1782–86], 8).

30. Trials of Peter and Robin, January 2, 1751, Middlesex C.C.O.B. (1745–52), 324–26; trials of Sam, Cornelius, and Jack, March 12, 1766, York C.C.O.B. (1765–68), 44–45.

As with the theft of liquor, not one slave whose trial for stealing money is in available documents received the death penalty for that alone. The York County oyer and terminer justices sentenced Thomas Smith's Matt to hang in May, 1766, for stealing a purse with four pieces of gold valued at £5 and ten pieces of silver valued at 20 shillings. The judges responded not only to the size of Matt's take but to his having entered a house to get the money.[31] No matter how much the thirty-three slaves convicted of theft of money in Virginia between 1740 and 1784 had taken, they faced only a limited risk. Nor did slaves usually appropriate large sums of money—four hundred Continental dollars was the most. One slave made away with £30, but he may have been somewhat desperate since he was a runaway. Twelve slaves took money with other items, perhaps sometimes doing so by mistake. Some slaves made another kind of error when they stole treasury bills. As slaves, they would have found it particularly hard to use such bills as a medium of exchange. By 1782, one slave had become sufficiently acculturated to be accused not only of stealing money but of using it to gamble, thereby "corrupting" other slaves in his neighborhood.[32]

Slaves had to have an even better explanation for their use of horses because judges sentenced to death more than one-third of the seventeen slaves convicted of stealing horses. The value of the animals in those cases was between £15 and £40 each, which was no more than the amount of money some slaves had stolen without incurring the death penalty. What explains this discrepancy? Although money was a prime medium of exchange in eighteenth-century Virginia, it was not so prevalent as were horses, which were on more than 90 percent of plantations by the 1750s. Not even that would explain why authorities regarded slaves' stealing of horses as so dangerous. Here, apparently, English common law strongly influenced the criminal code for slaves. Common law regarded horse stealing as more serious than the stealing of money, no matter who was responsible; so did Virginia's slave court justices. Another factor of which slaveowners may have been particu-

31. The royal governor and council pardoned Matt (trial, May 10, 1766, York C.C.O.B. [1765–68], 46–47).
32. Trial of Kitt, September 8, 1777, Louisa C.C.O.B. (1774–82), 174; trial of Cary, July 3, 1753, Spotsylvania C.C.O.B. (1749–55), 303–304, 375; trial of Ripon, October 4, 1760, York C.C.O.B. (1759–63), 184–85; trial of Frank, June 23, 1762, King George C.C.O.B. (1751–65), 1026–27; trial of Jacob, September 25, 1769, Cumberland C.C.O.B. (1767–70), 434; trial of Charles, April 29, 1782, Sussex County Oyer and Terminer Proceedings, 39–40.

larly aware was that horses could run faster than slaves, which would increase the chances of success for runaway slaves. Discrepancies in sentences for horse stealing indicate that justices did take circumstances into account.[33]

Stealing by slaves between 1740 and 1784 had a measurable impact. And that has to do with behavior. More than 700 slaves were convicted of stealing in any fashion. There were countless others hidden in the records of the 106 trials for which the county clerks listed only the charge of "felony." An untold number constitute the unknown or dark figure of slaves who remained undetected or who took only from their owners and thereafter had to deal only with their owners' responses. The 714 felony and misdemeanor convictions for stealing, as well as the 64 misdemeanor convictions for hog stealing, are fully 75 percent of all felony and misdemeanor convictions for any kind of crime in mid-eighteenth-century (1740–1784) Virginia slave courts whose records have survived.

In a different context, however, these cases seem to have less significance. The slave population of Virginia reached nearly 293,000 by 1790, so the 778 Afro-Virginians convicted of any kind of theft represent less than three-tenths of 1 percent of that figure, and therefore are a much smaller proportion of all the Afro-Americans who lived there between 1740 and 1784 than they are of all slaves convicted of crimes.[34] But it is the impact these people had on all Virginians that is most important. The 778 convicted people (some convicted more than once) were for the most part a self-selected population in spite of their having been the focus of court prosecutions initiated by whites. These slaves warrant close study simply because of their distinctive actions, their social visibility, and the response of white authorities to them.

These more than seven hundred people all had their own histories. Their identities derived in part from the status forced on them—that is, slave—but they shaped many elements of their careers as well.

33. On common law concerning horse stealing, see Radzinowicz, *A History of the English Criminal Law*, I, 633. For a runaway's theft of a horse, see trial of Matthew, August 6, 1740, Westmoreland C.C.O.B. (1739–43), 68–69; trial, May 15, 1750, Spotsylvania C.C.O.B. (1749–55), 57–59; trial, October 3, 1771, Essex C.C.O.B. (1770–72), 204; trial, June 6, 1774, Southampton C.C.O.B. (1772–77), 370–71. See also trial, February 15, 1745, Orange C.C.O.B. (1743–46), 262–63; and trial, November 23, 1756, Prince William C.C.O.B. (1755–57), 252–54. Still another slave convicted of horse stealing may have escaped hanging because his judges took official pity on his youth (trial of Scipio, May 20, 1773, Spotsylvania C.C.O.B. [1768–74], 245).
34. Greene and Harrington, *American Population Before the Federal Census*, 154–55.

Consider, for example, the stories of "recidivists," such as Guy. The more determined slaveowners were to keep their possessions from legally owning property, the more insistent some slaves would be on taking property. In response to such resistance, the authorities in a slave society would become somewhat harsh if they wished to protect their society. But that very harshness could in turn encourage such men as Guy to pursue their careers.[35]

There were certain types of careers in stealing as well. Runaways, for instance, sometimes had to run because they were suspected of stealing. More often, however, they had to steal so that they could run.[36] Charles Yates of Fredericksburg put Sam in the first category in his fugitive advertisement of March 7, 1771: "His thefts were certainly the Cause of his flight, to avoid the Gallows, for he was never punished whilst with me, nor ever complained, neither had he any Cause to be dissatisfied at his Treatment." Rather than trying to depict themselves as kind, county authorities evaluated another slave's behavior in a different manner, declaring that he must be captured "as it must be empossible for him to Subsist without purloining the property of some one of the Common Wealth to support himself during his outlying." Many a captured runaway would be jailed not just for return to her or his owner, but also in preparation for being tried for stealing.[37]

35. For the careers of other prosecuted slaves, see the trials of Davey, September 24, 1760, September 30, 1770, May 12, 1772, Lancaster C.C.O.B. (1756–64), 291–92, (1778–83), 1, 3–4; trial of Sambo, October 7, 1755, Lancaster C.C.O.B. (1752–56), 388; and trial of Dyah, August 29, 1766, Accomack C.C.O.B. (1765–67), 220–21, 359. Dyah's trial was expensive. The costs were as follows: to sheriff for riding to Williamsburg for the oyer and terminer commission, 540 pounds of tobacco; imprisoning Dyah for eighteen days, 18 pounds; executing Dyah, 225 pounds. The total was 783 pounds, which equaled £84 12d. (at two shillings per pound) or £169 4s. (at four shillings). For contemporary tobacco prices, see Melvin Herndon, *Tobacco in Colonial Virginia: "The Sovereign Remedy"* (Williamsburg, 1957), 49; Earle, *The Evolution of a Tidewater Settlement System*, 229. A slave convicted of stealing from nine people was executed (trial of Will, October 6, 1772, Charlotte C.C.O.B. [1771–73], unpaginated; Miscellaneous Petitions, Virginia Legislative, Alderman Library, UVa [CWRD microfilm]).

36. Leslie F. Manigat recognizes the distinction between running to avoid stealing trials and stealing to make running possible ("The Relationship between Marronage and Slave Revolts and Revolution in Saint Domingue-Haiti," in *Comparative Perspectives on Slavery*, ed. Rubin and Tuden, 429).

37. Mullin (ed.), *American Negro Slavery*, 108–109, 113; Mullin, *Flight and Rebellion*, 44. For examples of runaways tried for stealing, see trial of Cary, July 3, 1753, Spotsylvania C.C.O.B. (1749–55), 303–304; trial of Jack, May 6, 1766, Mecklenburg C.C.O.B. (1765–68), 155–56; *Virginia Gazette* (P), May 2, 1766, (R), April 8, 1773. For examples of runaways accused of stealing, see *Virginia Gazette*, May 15, 1746, November 7, 1754, October 3, December 10, 1755, March 26, 1767, (R), May 12, 1768, March 9, 1769, May 31, 1770, (PD), February 7, March 7, 1771, December 12, 1772, (R), January 7, 1773, (PD), June 30, November 17, 1774, (D), August 19, September 23, 1775, December 12, 1777, (P), January 3, May 9, 1777, (D), July 10, 1778, January 29, 1780.

Runaways were most ready to resort to violence in order to take property or to break away from their captors. In 1744, two slaves who belonged to John Triplett, "one of the Iron mine Company on Rappahannock" in Westmoreland County, arrived at the house of Richard Smith, whom they did not find at home. They asked Elizabeth, his wife, if she had any "powder" to sell. When she said she did not, Tom asked her if she wanted meal in exchange for gunpowder. Elizabeth held her ground, replying that her husband would deal with that question and that Tom and his companion should fetch her some firewood. According to Elizabeth, Tom started to do so, but then returned and knocked her down with a gun and beat her repeatedly. Once captured, Tom's companion was sentenced to severe corporal punishment. Tom was supposed to be hanged and his head was to be severed from his body and placed on a pole at an important crossroads in the county.[38]

The several instances of highway robbery may also have involved runaways. Following common law, Virginia oyer and terminer judges regarded such incidents in the harshest light. Putting people in fear of their lives was a more serious matter than threatening their property was. The slaves who resorted to such violence, or threatened it, would look to the law in vain for protection. John, for instance, received the sentence of hanging in 1764 for robbing a Sussex County man of some clothes as he traveled through Surry County. Frederick Parker's Mingo was supposed to suffer the same fate for robbing Mary Hawkins of £30 in Isle of Wight County. Simon managed to get off with thirty-nine lashes for robbing a white man of an unknown amount in Lunenburg County in 1770, but Alexander Spotswood's Ned was sentenced to hang in Spotsylvania County for highway robbery of Mary Ann Jones of Albemarle County in 1773. By definition, highway robbery was more likely to be a rural action. That slaves in a rural environment would take such a big risk probably resulted from their wish to sustain their independent status as runaways, come what might.[39]

The well-known existence of an extensive economic network managed by slaves in violation of slave codes testifies to a slave enterprise

38. Trials, June 6, August 8, 1744, Westmoreland C.C.O.B. (1737–43), 34a, 37a.
39. Trial of John, September 18, 1764, Surry County Criminal Proceedings; trial of Mingo, June 25, 1766, Isle of Wight C.C.O.B. (1764–68), 252; trial of Simon, December 4, 1770, Lunenburg C.C.O.B. (1769–77), 184–85; trial of Ned, June 7, 1773, Spotsylvania C.C.O.B. (1768–74), 256. There was a case of robbery and treason in which the judges ordered that Bob be hanged in a public place somehow "most Conspicuous, and least offensive" (trial of Negro Bob, August 5, 1778, Norfolk C.C.M.B. [1776–79], 87). See Radzinowicz, *A History of the English Criminal Law*, I, 637.

system. Sometimes this network was *ad hoc*, as when the slave Lemas offered some stolen goods for sale to "Ceaser" in Amelia County. At other times, especially in towns, slaves were essential parts of rings, taking property many times before only some of them were caught, and learning such techniques as pretending to inspect items in stores for their owners as a cover for casing the establishments. Slaves also knew that if they wanted to exchange goods for cash, there were white merchants who would deal with them.[40] Working with free blacks also eased the fencing problem.[41]

There were many other reasons why slaves might take property, some of which warrant examination. There was no such thing as a "joyride" for slaves who were trying to break out of their propertyless confines. Consider, for example, the fate of three slaves who were involved in May, 1751, in what at first appears to be an escapade. Joining with two white servants, the Eastern Shore trio went on a trip that netted one pail, one bucket, a dress, and bacon worth 24 shillings. Their travels required the appropriation of one canoe to reach an island in the Chesapeake Bay, one boat in which to return, and still another boat for purposes unknown. For this the three received a total of 119 lashes. That two of them broke out of the Accomack County jail and went into hiding for nearly a month testifies to their realization that they had entered the vicious circle of which slave trials formed a part. Tied to the rigors of slavery, some slaves acted as these three did. For doing so, however, they had to suffer some of the harshest rigors of the slave system.[42]

One case reveals a great deal about the mid-eighteenth-century de-

---

40. Trial of Lemas, November 15, 1750, Amelia C.C.M.B. (1746–51), unpaginated; Statement of William Rose, Henrico County and Virginia Jailer, June 8, 1785, in Col. Richard Morris Papers, Alderman Library, UVa; Henrico County citizens' petition to House of Delegates, June 8, 1782; Hening, *The Statutes at Large*, XI, 59; Randolph to Madison, August 30, 1782, in *Madison Papers*, ed. Hutchinson *et al.*, V, 91–95; Creecy, *Princess Anne County Loose Papers*, 96–97; Mullin, *Flight and Rebellion*, 61; trial of Frank, June 23, 1762, King George C.C.O.B. (1751–65), 1026–27; trial of Tom, September 25, 1784, Loudoun C.C.O.B. (1783–85), 404, and *CVSP*, III, 612; trial of Charles, February 19, 1781, Goochland C.C.O.B. (1779–83), 70–71, *CVSP*, III, 632, and *EJCS*, III, 329; *Virginia Gazette* (R), March 7, 1751, with trials of Simon, Matt, and Natt, March 7, 1751, and Joe, June 20, 1751, York C.C.O.B. (1746–52), 398–99, 428–30.
41. Trials of Adam and James, Norfolk C.C.M.B. (1774–75), 97. A free black, James Bailey, was tried and acquitted in Williamsburg (*Virginia Gazette* [P], April 21, 1775). A free black accomplice found guilty in Caroline County was ordered to pay the victim four times the $800 stolen. Failure to do so by mid-January would subject him to sale for a term of no more than seven years (trials of David and Robert Baker ["Mulatto"], December 1, 1778, Caroline C.C.O.B. [1777–80], 143).
42. Trials, May 29, June 27, 1751, Accomack C.C.O.B. (1744–53), 496–97, 511–12. It was also possible for slaves to steal food or clothes from one another. For rare examples,

velopment of the paradoxes and self-contradictions involved in property without will being tried for willfully stealing property against the will of "its" owner. In December, 1754, Colonel Wilson Cary's slaves Sam and Peter incurred the suspicion of Elizabeth City County authorities concerning their dealings with Colonel John Hunter's "mulatto slave woman." On December 12, both had to stand trial on the specific charge of stealing that woman. Even though Sam turned king's evidence and was discharged from further prosecution for doing so, the slave court judges could not convict Peter. Nineteenth-century Virginia prosecuting attorneys and judges would get such convictions as part of an intensive effort to counter northern states' personal liberty laws. This 1754 case is, however, the only such prosecution in extant records from the period prior to 1785. That any eighteenth-century slave court could bring such a case resulted from the willingness of white authorities to accept or ignore contradictions. If one slave tried to help another slave escape or in any way took her or him away from an owner, the law would classify that action as theft rather than kidnapping.[43]

What if the "mulatto slave woman" had been suspected of initiating the process by which Sam and Peter took her away from her owner? She would have been called a runaway. As Peter H. Wood has reminded us, runaways "stole themselves." Those eighteenth-century slaves who persisted in remaining runaways were often outlawed. Authorities thus categorized those who had broken the law against theft by stealing themselves. Outlawing gave designated white persons the legal right to kill the "outlaw," destroying "stolen property" and, in the event, eliminating a rather strong challenge to the right claimed by owners to hold people as property. It is important that the only time before 1785 that slave courts whose records have survived held a trial of slaves for running away was in March, 1776, when the oyer and terminer court of Northampton County tried and convicted eleven slaves for running away and for stealing the schooner they used to do so. The judges sentenced four of them to hang and inflicted thirty-nine lashes on each of the rest.[44]

see trial, November 15, 1753, Richmond County Criminal Trials, 346–47; trial, July 5, 1783, Lancaster C.C.O.B. (1783–85), 16; and *Virginia Gazette* (PD), March 26, 1767.

43. Trials of Sam and Peter, December 12, 1754, Elizabeth City C.C.O.B. (1747–55), 461.

44. Trials, March 14, 1776, Northampton C.C.O.B. (1771–77), 311–12, 318, 320. Relevant documents appear in *CVSP*, VIII, 158–59; and *VMHB*, XV (1907–1908), 406–407.

As Gerald W. Mullin and other historians have demonstrated, running away was a prevalent and powerful form of slave resistance. It was, according to the law, also another form of theft. That white authorities chose to prosecute it only in response to Governor Dunmore's limited emancipation proclamation supports the notion that stealing by slaves was not only an act of resistance, but in some instances could nearly be insurrectionary. But almost all slaves' criminalized actions had the same potential to be nearly insurrectionary. When American revolutionaries were being called insurrectionists and some slaves were looking for the opportunity to create their own revolution, these two groups would inevitably have diametrically opposed points of view about behavior regarded by the slave courts as criminal.[45]

45. Mullin, *Flight and Rebellion*, 56–58. There are few indications of what slaves themselves said about stealing before the nineteenth century. Hints about what some of them heard white spiritual leaders say are in Thomas Bacon, *Sermons Addressed to Masters and Servants, and Published in the Year 1743* (Winchester, Va., 1813), 104, 107–109, 161–62, 199, 215; Jupiter Hammon, *Address to the Negroes in the State of New York* (New York, 1787), 9; Luther P. Jackson, "The Religious Instruction of Negroes," *JNH*, XV (1930), 72–114. This chapter does not cover all kinds of stealing by slaves. Some of it may have had nothing to do with slavery; some cases are rather puzzling. For example, Princess Anne authorities attempted to try a slave for stealing a windmill's sails (Creecy, *Princess Anne County Loose Papers*, 55). The theft was supposed to have occurred in Norfolk County. That county's order books do not include trials of slaves, which appeared only in the court minute books. Since the book for 1757–70 has not survived, it is impossible to learn anything more about this case.

6. *Shattering Confrontations, 1740–1785*

In the late spring of 1767, Nan and Peter, the property of Robert Munford, Sr., as well as Jack, who belonged to the estate of John Ravenscroft, received guilty verdicts and death sentences in their Amelia County trials for murdering Moses Grant, a white man and possibly an overseer. One frustration with which Nan and Peter had had to contend in their adult years with Munford—Nan, at least twelve years; Peter, about seven—was the extraordinary turnover of male slaves on the plantation. The cause may have been resale, hiring out, or death. The detailed tithable lists that survive for eleven of the years between 1754 and 1769 show that twenty-three male slaves stayed on Munford's Piedmont plantation for an average of only 2.8 years each, while twelve female adult slaves stayed there an average of 6.4 years.[1] Whatever else these data suggest about the different functions of men and women on Munford's plantation, they do reveal a pattern that would have severely constrained male slaves, who could not know from year to year how long they would stay in the same place or under the same owner. The same conditions would have frustrated female slaves and children as well, since such a high turnover would cause jarring changes in work routines and preclude secure personal and familial relationships.

Nor were the reins of power firmly held. There was a rapid switching of overseers. Worst of all, Robert Munford appears to have been the

1. Trials of Nan, Peter, and Jack, May 29, 1767, Amelia C.C.O.B. (1765–67), 181; Amelia County Tithables, boxes 2–3, VSL; Sarah S. Hughes, "Slaves for Hire: The Allocation of Black Labor in Elizabeth City County, Virginia, 1782 to 1810," *WMQ*, 3rd ser., XXXV (1978), 263–67.

"R.M." whom an anonymous writer subjected to a violent verbal assault in the *Virginia Gazette* of December 23, 1773. The "correspondent" charged that R.M. had committed cruelties and atrocities against his slaves, having slaughtered no fewer than fifty of them and having castrated and cut off the legs and ears of one who had escaped to Charlotte County and tried to burn himself in jail. One does not have to determine whether a political enemy was employing hyperbole to discredit Munford, who had been a burgess for Amelia County between 1767 and 1771. What is most striking is that the correspondent had to assert that Munford had killed so many slaves and attacked one so savagely in order to convince white newspaper readers that R.M. was indeed guilty of cruelty.[2]

The only available evidence concerning the charges is circumstantial.[3] Some of the unstable conditions probably prevailed on the plantations and in the slave quarters of hundreds of other white Virginians. Nan and Peter's existence on Munford's land by no means determined their behavior. Nor could the atrocities of which Munford might have been guilty determine which kind of rebellious actions surviving slaves would have relied on to defend themselves against him. Nan and Peter had a choice, and they made it on the basis of numerous factors, some of which we shall never know, but at least one of which is clear. On the Munford plantation, female slaves and male slaves faced uncertainty. In response, some slaves might choose to run away; others might simply try to endure. Nan and Peter decided on direct resistance.

Nan and Peter were not alone among Virginian slaves. Whites could forge strong shackles, and many slaves might believe that discretion is the better part of valor, yet there would appear between the 1740s, the youth of the Afro-Virginian communities, and the 1780s, the in-

---

2. Amelia County Tithables; *Virginia Gazette* (PD), December 23, 1773.

3. The clause in Munford's will directing the way his executor was to "Sell any of my Slaves on Account of their ungovernable Disposition or any other cause" suggests, especially in light of the rapid turnover, that Munford regularly regarded some of his slaves as rebellious and relied on selling them and cancelling hiring arrangements to remove such people from his property (Amelia County Wills [1770–80], 315, VSL). Such clauses were means of protecting widows and avoiding trouble for executors (*M'Call* v. *Peachy*, 3 Munford 288 [December, 1812], excerpted in Catterall, *Judicial Cases*, I, 123–24). In 1775, two Munford slaves received guilty verdicts in hog stealing trials, but I have found no other convictions of Munford slaves (trials, November 1, 1775, Amelia C.C.O.B. [1772–78], 334). Slaves hired out to Munford might have been among the convicted and might not have been identified as his hirees.

fancy of the Commonwealth of Virginia, a significant number of slaves who, like Nan and Peter, either ignored or defied the shackles while acting on behalf of, in spite of, or occasionally against their own communities in a dramatic, partly successful, and sometimes ultimately suicidal fashion. These aggressive slaves would "shatter the concealing forms of the law" in face-to-face confrontations that, particularly in the case of attacks on whites but also in attacks on blacks, revealed a great deal about overt conflict in the Old Dominion in the mid-1700s.[4] Enslaved Virginians involved in these events went one step farther than those who mounted secret attacks such as poisoning or arson. In some cases enslaved Virginians were open threats rather than conscious aggressors.

These confrontations threatened white power and endangered the Afro-American communities. In 1937 an eighty-four-year-old former slave explained the practical problem faced by any slave who violently confronted white authorities: "Back in de slabery days dey didn't do somethin' and run. Dey run befo' dey did it, kaze dey knew dat if dey struck a white man dere want goin' to be no nigger. In dem days dey run to keep from doin' somethin'! Nowadays dey do it and den dey runs." The essential limitation that white power placed on slaves' choices stands out clearly. Arresting as this statement is, however, it does not explain those slaves who were exceptions. When bondspeople refused to run, they defied or ignored not only their oppressor but all conventions, rules, and laws of white society.[5]

In eighteenth-century Virginia, there were some slaves who openly attacked owners, overseers, and other whites, and then ran. Those who could successfully evade capture after killing a white person, or even another slave, had every reason to strike a blow and flee, once they decided to use violence. Their premeditation could include careful planning about running away, since there would be little question of attempting to secure a light sentence from a court of oyer and terminer. There are only rare instances of slaves who successfully eluded authorities after violently challenging the slave code. In 1752, for example, a "fellow" in Northumberland County tried to kill his sleeping master by hitting him with a broadax. The county court issued a "hue and cry" and placed a notice in the Virginia Gazette, but apparently did

---

4. John T. Noonan, Jr., *Persons and Masks of the Law* (New York, 1976), 60.
5. Rawick (ed.), *The American Slave*, VI, 232.

not find the assailant. Others fought hard, but failed. Jacob, the slave of William Womack of Prince Edward County, was apparently ready to do anything rather than return to slavery. When cornered in John Stanton's slave quarters by Womack and five neighbors in 1756, he defended himself with a broadax and "sharp pointed darts of a Sufficient lenght [sic] and Size to kill a man at a great distance." These weapons were no match, however, for the guns with which Jacob's pursuers eventually killed him. Many other slaves engaged in violent confrontations with whites in order to avoid recapture.[6]

Another kind of flight was available to slaves who could not or would not face trial or run away. That was to destroy the possession that their owners and white people were taking so much trouble to keep and control.[7] In 1742, Zachary Lewis convinced the legislators that Sacco had hanged himself "to avoid the punishment of the Law" for murdering an overseer. Two years later, Henry Wythe filed a claim for his slave who had drowned himself when accused of poisoning his overseer. An outlawed slave hanged himself in 1748 after attacking two white men. Not even this method of escape was foolproof, however. A Norfolk slave who was jailed for hog stealing in 1775 cut his own throat. He was not in as much legal danger as a person accused of a capital offense, but he clearly wanted to find a way out. However, an "eminent surgeon" successfully treated him.[8]

Many other slaves directed their violence toward the appropriate target—their oppressors. The important question for oyer and terminer justices was whether such violence arose from malice prepense. When the victim was white, Virginia's slave code, the dictates of white supremacy, and the image of blacks as "savages" combined to make it axiomatic that only malice prepense, or the "instigation of the Devil," could possibly explain a slave's killing her or his owner. That legal and judicial axiom, part of the indictment in all criminal cases in Virginia, obscured the diversity of circumstances and even of motives. Between

6. *Virginia Gazette*, August 21, 1752; Prince Edward C.C.O.B. (1754–58), 78; Legislative Petitions, Goochland, May 13, 1778, VSL.
7. A slave's suicide or attempted suicide would ordinarily not receive any attention from Virginia officials. But when persons accused of capital crimes escaped, denying their accusers the opportunity to condemn, execute, and gain compensation for them, owners quickly pointed this out to the House of Burgesses in hopes of receiving compensation anyway (Mullin, *Flight and Rebellion*, 60). Suicide was a form of escape for some slaves as early as their captivity in the Middle Passage (John W. Blassingame, *The Slave Community: Plantation Life in the Antebellum South* [Rev. ed.; New York, 1979], 7–10).
8. *JHB*, 1742–49, pp. 27, 94, 280; *Virginia Gazette* (Pi), September 14, 1775.

1740 and 1784, various people around the globe killed others for numerous reasons. It always made some difference to communities whether the killer was of a lower class or status than the killed. Consider three forms of homicide in English common law: parricide, regicide, and petit treason. When white leaders formulated special laws for and white courts gave distinctive sentences to slaves convicted of murdering whites, they were treating most such attacks as political as well as personal crimes of violence. Perhaps some slaves killed whites for reasons that had nothing to do with slavery.

Did this sort of violence result from decision or from psychological explosions? Black psychiatrist Frantz Fanon seems to suggest the latter when he declares in *Black Skin, White Masks,* "The Negro is a toy in the white man's hands; so, in order to shatter the hellish cycle, he explodes." Fanon's striking image parallels Noonan's shattering "the concealing forms of the law." Rage is the most appropriate response to oppression; unexpressed rage is as likely to lead to unpremeditated violence as consciously articulated rage is to support planned attacks. Fanon's explanation nevertheless raises serious problems for the historian.[9]

In the records, some slaves' challenges to slaveowners reveal people who simply burst under the external pressure of the slave system or the internal pressure of rage. When the authorities in Surry County hung Jemmy's head on a post near the fork of a road and burned his corpse to ashes, they were taking official revenge against him for killing not just his master, Benjamin Hyde, but Hyde's wife, Mary, and their three children on January 14, 1754. The provincial treasury made sure to pay £45 compensation to the Hyde estate after Jemmy's death. We do not know why Jemmy exploded, but it is fairly clear that his was an act of extraordinary violence, even for a slave forced to live in a society based on oppression.[10]

Fanon's image, lacking a political dimension, does not explain all those slaves who *chose* to employ violence against their oppressors. It is precisely this political implication that the historian must regard as crucial. The continuing debate on slave resistance has still not worked through an essential problem. There is little consensus on whether

9. Frantz Fanon, *Black Skin, White Masks,* trans. Charles Lam Markmann (New York, 1977), 140.
10. Trial of Jemmy, January 19, 1754, Surry County Criminal Court Proceedings, 39–41; Surry County Deeds, Wills (1738–54), 867, and (1754–68), 10 (Transcript in VSL).

resistance had to be political to be real or effective, and whether the actions of one or several slaves on a given Virginia plantation, for instance, could be political even though not collective as was the action of many thousands of slaves in Saint Domingue.[11]

Politics involves the distribution of power. On its simplest level, it is both the art of the possible and the means by which people within communities work out who gets what, when, and how. If, as has been suggested, the slave community was, and could only have been, a collection of mostly separate communities with shared features, then any conscious effort by a slave, or particularly a group of slaves, to change the relationship of power between a given slave community and the owner or owners who claimed sovereignty over slaves was in some sense political action. The clearest indication that some slave behavior that conflicted with capital statutes had a political dimension is not only the obvious objective of redistributing property or challenging the monopoly of force held by white authorities but also the formal manner in which owners sought the aid of slave courts as the most efficacious means with which to counter such challenges.[12]

Murder convictions of slaves in Virginia between 1740 and 1785 reflect the politics of slaves' opposition to the slave code. Of the twenty-four known white victims, most (58.3 percent) were free white men other than the convicted slaves' owners, many of them overseers and possibly some of them hirers of the convicted slaves. Moreover, about half of that majority lived in the newer Piedmont counties of Amelia, Chesterfield, Cumberland, Goochland, Mecklenburg, and Prince Edward. On the other hand, 41.7 percent, or ten, of the known white victims were masters, six of whom lived in older Tidewater counties and only three of whom resided in the Piedmont. The obvious inference is that resident planters were predominant in the Tidewater but not in the Piedmont, hence overseers were a usual target in the latter region. But there is also a political implication. The older a

---

11. Political considerations were obviously central to Fanon's writings (see *The Wretched of the Earth*, trans. Constance Farrington [New York, 1966], esp. 50–51). Elizabeth Fox-Genovese and Eugene D. Genovese, "The Political Crisis of Social History," in Fox-Genovese and Genovese, *Fruits of Merchant Capital: Slavery and Bourgeois Property in the Rise and Expansion of Capitalism* (New York, 1983), 179–212; Eugene D. Genovese, "The Legacy of Slavery and the Roots of Black Nationalism," Herbert Aptheker, "Comment," and C. Vann Woodward, "Comment," *Studies on the Left*, VI (1966), 3–24, 27–42.

12. This discussion of political action owes much to such studies as Harold D. Lasswell, *Politics: Who Gets What, When, How* (New York, 1936); and John Lukacs, "Polish Omens," *New Republic*, November 29, 1980, p. 14.

section of the slave society of Virginia grew, the more slaves who killed had to contend with their owners rather than with nonowners who merely acted as agents. Open slave-master conflict thus had the potential to become more prevalent as any area developed.[13]

A second political element appears in mid-eighteenth-century convictions of slaves for murder of whites. The choice of weapon and the timing or location of the killings, when known, indicate that in many cases slaves had clearly decided to attack their victims. In some instances, killing of whites resulted from a collective decision by slaves. Impulsive explosions occurred, to be sure, but they were secondary to intentional attacks. When a slave or slaves used agricultural implements to kill an overseer in a tobacco field, it was as possible for the attack to be premeditated as it was for it to be spontaneous. When a slave used a gun or a knife, however, it is highly probable that the assault was planned. Such weapons had to be secured and secreted at some risk.[14]

The convictions suggest the general growth of violent confrontations with whites. From the 1740s through the 1760s, the proportion of white victims to all known victims of slaves convicted of violent murder grew from three out of six (50 percent) in the 1740s, and five out of ten (50 percent) in the 1750s, to eight of twelve (66.7 percent) and seven out of eleven (63.6 percent) in, respectively, the 1760s and the 1770s. Whatever violent behavior developed within the Old Dominion's slave communities during the mid-eighteenth century came increasingly to focus on its pertinent object—white people, and white owners in particular.

Throughout mid-eighteenth-century Virginia, slaves took the extraordinary risk of openly attacking white people. For James, a Northumberland slave who was in the limbo of being owned by an infant whose guardian was Zachary Taylor, the 1743 attempt to kill an overseer was logical and perhaps even sensible since he was an outlawed runaway. Attack or be attacked; kill or risk being killed. It may even have been worth the danger of being punished, since James was not executed. He might still be able to escape from slavery. Fortune and

---

13. Mullin, *Flight and Rebellion*, 6, 47–48, 53, 128; Kulikoff, "The Origins of Afro-American Society," 240–42, 246–49.

14. See Virginia Research Center for Archaeology, *Colonial Plantation Hoes of Tidewater Virginia* (Williamsburg, 1980), for pictures and measurements of one example of tools used as weapons.

Ned were a couple who in January, 1745/46, apparently collaborated in their use of mortal violence against Joseph Pettway, their owner. Since their cooperation was successful, and they could not evade detection or escape a guilty verdict, they went to the gallows.[15] Seven years later, Plenna (or Pliny) and Solomon of Accomack County were sentenced to hang for the murder of Henry Jones, a farmer who had no slaves and who may have been employed by Plenna's and Solomon's master. When Plenna struck Jones on the back of his head with an ax, allegedly at Solomon's instigation, she committed herself and her accomplice not only to destroying a possible oppressor but to being destroyed by white authorities as well.[16]

Even though the lack of evidence frustrates further analysis of numerous eighteenth-century cases, there is a pattern in the totality of convictions of slaves for murdering white people—indeed, white or black people.[17] Between 1740 and 1785, at least twenty-four white people died violently at the hands of a slave or a group of slaves. If we assume that lost records would yield eight to sixteen more cases, and if we allow liberally for unrecorded cases, the number of which is relatively low for homicides, at least sixty-four to eighty whites in all were killed by slaves between 1740 and 1785. Since approximately fifty-three to sixty-eight slaves were convicted of murder upon being tried for these killings, perhaps less than one-tenth of 1 percent and probably less than 1 percent of Virginia's slave population in the mid-eighteenth century resorted to killing white people.[18]

15. Trial of James, May 9, 1743, Northumberland C.C.O.B. (1739–43), 342–43; trials of Fortune and Ned, January 21, 1745/46, Surry County Criminal Court Proceedings, 11–15. It was possible, but only remotely so, for a slave widely blamed for a killing to escape conviction. See the case of Dick, found not guilty of murdering a white man even though ten white witnesses testified against him (April 29, 1747, Louisa C.C.O.B. [1742–48], 225–26).

16. Trials of Plenna and Solomon, December 18, 1753, Accomack C.C.O.B. (1753–63), 28–29; Accomack Wills (1752–57), 270–71, 321; *Maryland Gazette*, December 6, 13, 1753; Mark J. Stegmaier, "Maryland's Fear of Insurrection at the Time of Braddock's Defeat," *Maryland Historian*, LXXI (1976), 476.

17. Trials, November 7, 1754, King George C.C.O.B. (1751–65), 379; trial, February 25, 1755, Amelia C.C.O.B. (1751–55), 210–11. These cases raise more questions than they can possibly answer.

18. These rough estimates are based on the assumption that I found 60 percent of all trials actually held. I allowed for the "dark figure" by *doubling* the totals I reached. Population was figured by taking the average of the 1740 and 1770 estimates from *Historical Statistics of the United States: Colonial Times to 1970* (2 vols.; Washington, D.C., 1975), II, 1172–73. I do not claim complete accuracy; I wish only to suggest the demographic context of convictions of slaves for killing white people. One can comprehend the profound significance of that small number of slaves if one remembers that fewer

A figure of this size raises all sorts of questions, but the most important implication is that slaves who actually killed white people in violent confrontations were rather unusual in mid-eighteenth-century Virginia. Their actions therefore take on great significance, especially in those instances in which the killing resulted from conscious choice. There are several possible explanations. Such actions may have had a causal life of their own, one that was almost unrelated to the reactions of white authorities. That is, the killing of one white person by one Virginian slave might have met the need of other slaves for retribution or vengeance. If so, such attacks were bound to occur on a regular but not a frequent basis. The risk of execution was undoubtedly sufficiently high to persuade numerous slaves to choose other means of protecting themselves.

It is difficult to determine what circumstances made such killings more likely to occur. In only five of the more than fifty counties whose records have survived were slaves convicted of murdering two or more white people between 1740 and 1785. In those counties, the mean number of years between convictions was about five. One way to try to place these figures in context is to compare them with convictions of whites for murdering other whites. Available figures suggest that slightly more whites were found guilty of murdering whites. But such comparisons must be weighed against demographic data; it is necessary to relate the number of convictions of slaves to population. This rough measure does initially indicate some correlation between the size of the adult black and white population and the number of killings of whites by slaves. But counties other than those in which more slaves were convicted of murdering whites had as many or more people yet fewer such killings. So some other variable than the size of the adult, income-producing population made the real difference.[19]

---

than 9 million people served in the Vietnam conflict—somewhat less than 5 percent of the population of the U.S. during the 1960s and 1970s. The nearly 58,000 people who died in battle, from wounds, or because of service-related accidents, etc., were .00029 percent of the U.S. population. Yet who would argue that the impact of that violence on the U.S. and the world as well was not profound? My figures are based on *Statistical Abstract of the United States, 1982–1983* (Washington, D.C., 1983), 361.

19. The comparison is by no means exact since it is based only on "examinations" of whites in the county courts that resulted in the defendant being sent to the General Court in Williamsburg for full trial. The General Court records burned in Richmond in 1865, so it is impossible to determine the verdict in all of these cases. Augusta County courts of examination sent eight white murder suspects to the General Court between 1745 and 1785; Spotsylvania sent five (see Lyman Chalkley, *Chronicles of the Scotch-Irish*

There was some causal relationship between the social development of an area and the character of mortal conflict between slaves and whites. Several episodes in the mid-eighteenth century shed light on such aspects of slaves' violent attacks on the whites. The 1760s opened, for instance, with an event that was unusual then but became increasingly regular thereafter. That was a collaborative killing of a master by several of his slaves. Ralph Justis of Accomack County was the victim; Stepney and George initiated the plot, Dick assisted, Harry concealed the killing, and James defied the laws against perjury when questioned at the other slaves' trials. A plot with so many involved was more likely to occur on a plantation where slaves were numerous, and those circumstances were likely to exist in the more developed Tidewater area at this time. Forty-three slaves lived on Justis' plantation at the time of his death. Cooperation between two of them could have led to other slaves learning about the plot. In this case, at least five appear to have known about it, if not actually participated.[20]

Justis was killed when much of northern Virginia, the Tidewater, and some of the Piedmont/Southside region were undergoing the shift from the dominant tobacco crop to a mixed-crop economy based mostly on grain.[21] Changes in the disposition of the labor force had to occur in adjustment to the new agronomy. Thus the seemingly settled, more rigid areas could experience fundamental change as easily as could the frontier regions. But only in the older counties could a planter have amassed as large a number of people in bondage as had Justis. But collective attacks did occur on smaller plantations.

A good example of both collective action on a smaller plantation and a killing affected by economic change is the next known murder of a plantation authority after Justis. In Loudoun County in 1767, Joe, Sam, and Pendoe mortally wounded Dennis Dallis, their overseer, with axes and hoes. All three were swiftly hanged. It was in Loudoun and the rest of northern Virginia that the colony's grain culture first developed, and one result was a further differentiation of function

---

Settlement in Virginia Extracted from the Original Court Records of Augusta County, 1745– 1800 (3 vols.; Rosslyn, Va., 1912), I, 47, 66, 94, 111, 154, 161, 197, 218; Spotsylvania C.C.O.B. [1749–55], 34, 108, 177; Spotsylvania C.C.M.B. [1755–65], 190–91). From 1762 through 1785, the Spotsylvania justices sent no whites to Williamsburg on the charge of murder.

20. Trials of Stepney, George, Dick, Harry, and James, January 15, 1760, Accomack C.C.O.B. (1753–63), 317–18, 371; Accomack Wills (1757–61), 169, 339, 400.

21. See Albert, "The Protean Institution," *passim.*

within the slave labor force. The valuations of the three condemned men were £70 for Sam, £50 for Joe, and £35 for Pendoe. Thus slaves of markedly different worth, and therefore probably having different roles on the plantation, were willing to cooperate in killing the man charged with directing their varied occupations. There were two other male slaves and one female adult slave on George West's 460-acre plantation.[22]

By the 1760s, certain slaves were capable of subtle behavior because they had a thorough knowledge of white culture. In 1769, Phill and Winney were hanged soon after being convicted of murdering their master near Fredericksburg. The victim's brothers reported that the killing had been carried out "most barbarously" near John Knox's house and that the slaves had been lying out because they were suspected of a felony. There was nothing unusual about this part of the description. It is exactly what one might expect from enraged relatives of a person killed by blacks in the 1760s. But the brothers also claimed that Phill and Winney had tried to "pass for free Negroes, and have shewn some forged indentures, and certificates thereon of their freedom" and had been using assumed names. These slaves were definitely assimilated, and probably skilled—the kind that Mullin argues were prevalent among runaways. This type of slave was also more likely to live in the Old Dominion in 1769 than in 1739.[23]

A changing white society confronted a developing slave culture in a violent and tragic manner in the summer of 1772. Like several other veterans of Colonel Simon Fraser's Highland Regiment, which had fought in Quebec during the Seven Years' War, Daniel MacPherson had settled in Virginia. MacPherson quickly secured a share of the property in the Old Dominion, buying farm equipment, a James River schooner and flatboat, and several slaves. He also acquired a not untypically direct approach to controlling slaves. When he thought a bondsman had stolen from him, MacPherson whipped the man without taking him to court. The unidentified slave demonstrated the risks for both slaves and whites of nonjudicial punishment. Seemingly safe on the shore of the James River, he yelled "scurrilous language" at

22. Trials of Joe, Sam, and Pendoe, February 27, 1767, Loudoun C.C.O.B. (1765–67), 236–37, (1767–70), 149; Leven Powell's list, Loudoun County Tithables, 1767, VSL. See trial, March 30, 1768, Mecklenburg C.C.O.B. (1765–68), 480. West's moderately sized plantation was in Virginia's most fundamentally changed economic region at the time.
23. *Virginia Gazette* (R), June 15, July 20, 1769. Stafford court records for these years have not survived. (Much of the Quantico Marine Reservation is in Stafford County.)

MacPherson, who was on the *St. Andrew*, his schooner. But MacPherson hurried ashore to attack the slave. When the slave jumped into the river to evade the assault, MacPherson followed, the two men fought, and both drowned. The Scotsman left a widow; his five slaves, the farm equipment, and the schooner were all worth £300. The slave left no legally recognized property behind and may not have had a family, but he certainly had created a memory for both black and white Virginians of what could happen when a slave challenged a white man. The risk for both was real.[24]

Another kind of connection between Afro-American slaves and Virginia's white culture is apparent in the collaboration of a man and a woman in the 1773 killing of Jeremiah Skidmore, the man's master. They returned to an early eighteenth-century phenomenon, namely, black and white cooperation in a violent attack. When Harry was convicted and sentenced to death, the white female servant was examined and then sent to the General Court in Williamsburg for trial. There is almost no parallel in all the records of slave trials in the Old Dominion for this sort of combination. Not much is known about Skidmore, except that he was a landless farmer who owned one female slave in addition to Harry. Was Skidmore an overseer? Had he tried to break a personal relationship between the black man and the white woman? These and other questions can only be raised.[25]

What is particularly significant about the shattering confrontations during the American Revolution, the most important political change in eighteenth-century Virginia, is that they were not fundamentally different from earlier attacks. The few violent and mortal attacks known to have been made by slaves on whites between 1776 and 1785 show the same variety the earlier confrontations did. In one case, a group of slaves killed their master; in the other two, individual slaves killed whites who were not their owners. The earliest instance demonstrates the willingness of some slaves to cooperate in killing their owner. Eight slaves in Elizabeth City County were of the same mind in their assault on Lockey Collier, their master. In late October, 1778, they strangled Collier in his bed and were reportedly "about two hours about it." Most of them reportedly confessed. There had been difficul-

24. *Virginia Gazette* (PD), August 6, 1772; Chesterfield C.C.O.B. (1771–74), 153, 159; Chesterfield Will Book (1765–74), 148–49.
25. Trial of Harry, December 27, 1773, Bedford C.C.O.B. (1772–74), 243–44; Bedford Wills (1763–87), 203–205.

ties between Collier and his slaves. In 1773, he had placed two adver-tisements for runaways, and in 1775, another man filed a notice for runaway "Billy Barber," who was well known to many gentlemen, and who was apt to be somewhat resourceful in his own behalf, since the advertiser warned readers against harboring Billy. The advertiser also warned "a certain Lockey Collier . . . whose Property he is," perhaps because Collier had been no more just and honorable in his dealings with whites than with blacks. What brought on the final conflict is not at all obvious, but the sustained, conscious unity of the slaves involved is.[26]

The same purposefulness motivated Will, the slave of George Kessel, when he fatally fractured the skull of Hans Cloverfield, a Rockingham County miller, in 1778. Not only did Will use whatever was at hand as a weapon—a stave from a hogshead—but he managed to escape from jail after being condemned to hang and to having his head displayed on a pole. Five years later, another frontier slave, Henry Garrett's Philip, killed a white man and wounded a white woman during a robbery in Augusta County. Whether the killing preceded or followed the robbery, it definitely was part of an intentional confrontation meant to gain something for a slave. At some time before the Revolu-tion, a slave who lived near the Rappahannock River was drunk when he killed his owner's son. But there seems to have been conscious intent, since the son, known to have victimized slave women, became "over ficious" with the slave's wife.[27]

Between 1740 and 1785, there were probably many other violent clashes between slaves and whites. Some received public notice of one sort or other, but some—how many we shall never learn—were known only to those involved. In addition, the question remains of how often whites used violence against slaves and those slaves managed to con-trol the powerful urge to strike back. Reciprocity was an essential element in the continuation of slaves' challenges to the slave code. There were, however, instances in which slaves violently attacked

26. *Virginia Gazette* (DH), July 15, 1775, November 6, 1778, (PD), August 12, October 21, 1773. For a similar killing in North Carolina, see Marvin L. Michael Kay and Lorin Lee Cary, "Albion's Fatal Tree Transplanted: Crime, Society, and Slavery in North Car-olina, 1748–1772" (Paper presented to the annual meeting of the Southern Historical Association, November, 1978, St. Louis), 14–15.
27. Trial of Will, June 7, 1778, Rockingham C.C.O.B. (1778–86), 11, 23, and in *VMHB*, VII (1900), 303–304; trial of Philip, March 18, 1783, Augusta C.C.O.B. (1783–85), 5; John Davis, *Personal Adventures* (London, 1817), 89–92. See also New Kent County trial, November 24, 1783 (C.S., box 1).

other people but could not have been attempting to change the relationship between themselves and their owners. These anomalous attacks were made by slaves against other slaves, as well as the sexual assaults some male slaves allegedly made against white women. They warrant discussion on their own.

Some slave behavior makes sense only when seen in context. Motives are rather hard to fathom, especially when many eighteenth-century records contain little testimony. Consider, for example, the behavior of Davy, the slave of Goochland County resident Joseph Anthony, in 1741. When Davy killed Nanny, who belonged to the same master, he also threatened Pendor, Anthony's only other "income-producing" slave. Pendor met her death from starvation and exposure because she was lying out in order to escape from Davy. Anthony's response was not only to accept £40 in compensation for Davy's hanging but also to petition the House of Burgesses "praying such Relief, as to this House shall seem fit" for the loss of all his working slaves.[28] Why would Davy have become so aggressive toward fellow slaves?

The experience of an Eastern Shore slave forty years later raises the same question. Consider how little we can learn about the motivations of Peter, the possession of John Parke Custis and the object of a Northampton County trial on January 5, 1782, for "feloniously Attempting to ravish Mary Cooper a white woman." Peter was convicted. The court further ordered that he be castrated and "be bound to his good behaviour in the penalty of £400 specie the space of twenty years, with good and sufficient security; or untile [sic] he be removed out of the County and not to return."[29]

The trial record does not prove that Peter actually did attempt to rape Mary Cooper. But it does establish that the justices as well as Mary Cooper thought he had. Assuming for the sake of analysis that Peter had in fact done something illegal, can we find out enough about the circumstances to shed any light on Peter's motivation? We do know

28. Trial of Davy, December 15, 1741, Goochland C.C.O.B. (1741–44), 17–18, 153; *JHB*, 1742–47, p. 8. The house rejected the petition, as if reinforcing the notion that court trials were the only, and therefore the indispensable, public power that would protect slaves from other slaves.
29. Trial of Peter, January 5, 1782, Northampton C.C.M.B. (1777–83), 334–35. The county levy allotted funds to the jailer for forty-nine days' imprisonment of Peter (*ibid.*, 339). Lloyd E. Warren, "The Warrens of Northampton County, Va.," *WMQ*, 2nd ser., VIII (1918), 188–89, is the only reference in available genealogies or local histories to Mary Cooper.

that Peter lived with fourteen tithable slaves at Arlington, a 4,650-acre Northampton County plantation.[30] Did the size of this slave community mean that aggressive tendencies would inevitably be directed toward relatively defenseless objects outside the plantation?[31] Mary Cooper, Peter's accuser, seems to have been vulnerable to aggression because of her low social status. It is worth speculating whether the increased vulnerability of whites in 1780 and 1781 left an opening for aggressive slaves. Like many of her fellow Virginians, Mary Cooper had endured a bad year of intensive warfare from 1780 to 1781 that tested the state's military and psychological defenses. The conviction figures for 1780 to 1782 mirror the uneasiness of white Virginians. The rate of sentences of execution rose significantly during 1780 and 1781.[32]

There is still another sign of instability in Peter's environment, namely, the insecurity of Peter's own position at Arlington. John Parke Custis' plantation had not been profitable. Custis' death in November, 1781, probably worsened Peter's situation. It raised the rather threatening question of what would happen to him.[33] But why would such circumstances lead to behavior that whites would call attempted rape? We can speculate at length on this question. We can also surmise

30. There were five nontithable slaves at Arlington (Inventory of John Parke Custis estate, Fairfax County Inventories, Book E, p. 17; Northampton County Personal Property Tax Book, 1782, VSL). On Arlington, the Custis plantation to which Governor Berkeley retreated during Bacon's Rebellion, see Whitelaw, *Virginia's Eastern Shore*, I, 109, 114.
31. There were constraints on aggression in the compact houses of seventeenth-century Plymouth. See John Demos, *A Little Commonwealth: Family Life in Plymouth Colony* (New York, 1970), 49, 135–39.
32. See Elizabeth Cometti, "Depredations in Virginia During the Revolution," in Darrett B. Rutman (ed.), *The Old Dominion: Essays for Thomas Perkins Abernethy* (Charlottesville, 1964), 135–51. The total sentenced to hang was twenty-three of seventy-six (30.3 percent) tried in 1780; eight of twenty-nine (27.6 percent) tried in 1781; and eleven of fifty-four (20.4 percent) tried in 1782.
33. George Washington to John Parke Custis, August 24, 1779, in John C. Fitzpatrick (ed.), *The Writings of George Washington from the Original Manuscript Sources, 1745–1799* (39 vols.; Washington, D.C., 1931–44), XVI, 164–68; Charles B. Clark, *The Eastern Shore of Maryland and Virginia* (3 vols.; New York, 1950), I, 84; James Thomas Flexner, *George Washington in the American Revolution (1775–1783)* (Boston, 1968), 470–72. The inventory of the estate was not taken until April, 1782. The slaves had to be removed and Arlington rented until the heir came of age. These actions apparently were taken (Fairfax County Inventories, Book E, p. 17; *Writings of George Washington*, ed. Fitzpatrick, XXIV, 387; John Hooe, Accounts with the Estate of John Parke Custis, in George Bolling Lee Papers, VHS). Herbert Gutman and Richard Sutch discuss the significance of forced movement of slaves from plantation to plantation in Paul A. David *et al.*, *Reckoning With Slavery: A Critical Study in the Quantitative History of American Negro Slavery* (New York, 1976), 132–33.

that Peter's punishment had high social visibility, even though it was one of only four officially ordered emasculations since the 1769 Virginia law confined this penalty to slaves convicted of attempting to rape a white woman. News of the event undoubtedly traveled fast among Northampton slaves, and Peter's transfer to another Custis plantation in either Fairfax or New Kent County, which had occurred by April, 1782, would spread the news among the slaves in Peter's new community.[34]

The primary characteristic of the preceding analysis is that it proves nothing about Peter's motivation. Like the sparse record of Davy's attack on Nanny and threatening behavior toward Pendor, the short account of Peter's trial serves only to raise questions. Nevertheless, we can successfully delineate the circumstantial patterns present in the trials of slaves for attacks that apparently had nothing to do with resistance to slaveowners or other white authorities. For example, available court records indicate that between 1740 and 1785, at least seventeen slaves as well as twenty-four whites were the victims of slaves' mortal attacks. Such homicides could have been reprisals against informers. They certainly could have resulted from deflected aggression.[35] Moreover, slaves faced slightly less risk of execution if convicted of murdering a fellow slave rather than a white.[36] Jealousy and other personal considerations undoubtedly figured in some cases.

The actual convictions of slaves for killing slaves between 1740 and

34. On the physiological effects of castration, see George K. Sturup, *Treatment of Sexual Offenders in Herstedvester, Denmark—The Rapists, Acta Psychiatrica Scandinavica*, Supp. 204 (Copenhagen, 1968). In *Slavery and the Numbers Game: A Critique of Time on the Cross* (Urbana, 1975), 19–20, Herbert Gutman discusses the social visibility of whippings as a punishment for slaves. His argument, which can be applied also to castration, is that one use of corporal punishment would have an impact quite beyond its simple quantitative value. The 1769 law is in Hening, *The Statutes at Large*, VIII, 358. That Peter had been transferred is apparent in the inventory of Custis' estate (Fairfax County Inventories, Book E, pp. 14, 17). The other officially ordered emasculations are in Goochland C.C.O.B. (1779–83), 140; Southampton C.C.O.B. (1778–84), 336; and Accomack C.C.O.B. (1774–77), 214.

35. "Deflected aggression" refers to aggressive behavior transferred to inappropriate but available victims who hold less power. See Charles A. Pinderhughes, "Questions of Content and Process in the Perception of Slavery," in Ann J. Lane (ed.), *The Debate Over Slavery: Stanley Elkins and His Critics* (Urbana, 1971), 105; Earl E. Thorpe, *The Mind of the Negro* (Baton Rouge, 1961), 98–99; Blassingame, *The Slave Community*, 315; Leslie Howard Owens, *This Species of Property: Slave Life and Culture in the Old South* (New York, 1976), 93; Fanon, *The Wretched of the Earth*, 42–43, 247, 250; Rollo May, *Power and Innocence: A Search for the Sources of Violence* (New York, 1972), 94–95.

36. Trials of Pompey and James, June 21, 1762, Spotsylvania C.C.O.B. (1755–65), 266; *EJCS*, I, 488; trial of Will, December 21, 1785, Henrico C.C.O.B. (1784–87), 380; Hening, *The Statutes at Large*, VIII, 137.

1785 reveal the diverse patterns of deflected aggression and personal conflicts. Fighting among slaves regularly led to murder convictions. In 1760 and 1785, convicted killers had used a knife; in 1742 and 1777, assailant and victim had been fighting; and in 1752 the slaves had probably been fighting since the convicted man had struck two slaves with a hominy pestle.[37] Personal relationships were at stake in some of the killings. In two cases reported in newspaper notices, white observers cited jealousy as the cause. In an accidental death, a male slave's jealousy led him to unintentionally destructive behavior; in a Williamsburg stabbing, the aggression appears to have been purposeful.[38] No other observer cites jealousy as a motive, but the circumstances of available cases as well as voluminous testimony from trials in later years strongly suggest that a portion—exactly what proportion will never be known—of the slaves who killed other slaves in the mid-eighteenth century did so out of jealousy.

The pattern of convictions of slaves for murdering other slaves suggests the importance of that factor. In the seventeen cases from the years 1740 to 1785 in which the identity of the victim is known, there are three instances of a male slave killing a female and one example of a female killing a male. Other motives were possible, but jealousy could easily have figured in these cases. To a lesser extent, it might have influenced the twelve cases of men killing men and the one case of a woman killing a woman.[39] In the context of the pattern of convictions, the 1746 trial of Boatswain in Louisa County demonstrates how circumstances can suggest the motive of jealousy. The group of slaves connected with the case appeared to be part of a love triangle. Boatswain lived in Louisa but his master was from Hanover County. Will and Rachel, his two victims, were the property, respectively, of Hanover and Louisa owners. A plausible reconstruction is that Boatswain was taking revenge against Rachel for rejecting him and

37. Trial of Jenny, October 10, 1760, King George C.C.O.B. (1751–65), 923–24 (commission is in Oversize Photo and Miscellaneous Manuscripts Vault, CWRD); trial of Daniel, October 8, 1785, York C.C.O.B. (1784–87), 233; trial of Philip, March 17, 1742/43, Elizabeth City C.C.O.B. (1731–47), 270; trials of Lewis and Will, September 4, 1777, mentioned in *EJCS*, I, 488; trial of Cudjo, September 10, 1752, Cumberland C.C.O.B. (1752–58), 19. The presence of a hominy pestle south of the James River as early as 1752 is a limited indication of the grain culture there.

38. *Virginia Gazette* (R), July 14, 1768, (PD), October 20, 1774.

39. On October 11, 1751, Sue was sentenced to hang for murdering Ben, the only known case of a woman killing a man (Norfolk C.C.M.B. [1749–53], unpaginated). It is possible that some of the slaves who used poison to kill other slaves acted out of jealousy.

against Will for alienation of Rachel's affections. Slavery made all three live where they did and prevented Boatswain from taking civil or ecclesiastical action; the personal relationship among the three led to tragedy.[40]

Some of the division in slave communities may have resulted from continued interethnic conflict. In 1752, for example, a Piedmont slave named Cudjo used a hominy pestle to kill Iris and Beck. The rare (for Virginia) white acknowledgment of an African name and Cudjo's location in an area that experienced a large influx of "new Negroes" at that time indicate that ethnicity may have figured in this episode. The factor of ethnic hostility may have figured in a 1762 case, when Mustapha killed Bob in the same Piedmont county. On the other hand, when compared with cases involving white victims, killings of slaves by slaves appear to have been much more the actions of individuals than of groups. Individual slaves may have had grievances against other slaves, but it was more probable that groups of slaves would work together against white enemies. In only one instance between 1740 and 1785 was more than one slave convicted of murdering the same slave. In that case, the council pardoned both convicted men because the deceased had "given provocation of the highest Nature" and "the killing happened in the course of a mutual Fighting."[41]

The pattern of convictions also suggests that a trend of the 1720s and 1730s later continued. In tried cases between 1740 and 1784, more (fifteen, compared with eight) enslaved victims of slaves' mortal attacks and their assailants had separate owners. Incomplete as these figures probably are, they suggest that slave communities may have suffered from relatively little internal division because of mortal violence. If they had, owners would have had to rely heavily on the courts. Their economic interest was clear. The courts refused to grant damages to the owner of a slave killed by another slave, necessitating use of the criminal courts to protect one investment from another.[42]

---

40. Trial of Boatswain, March 19, 1745/46, Louisa C.C.O.B. (1742–48), 180–81. See also trial of Cudjo, September 10, 1752, Cumberland C.C.O.B. (1752–58), 19.

41. Trial of Cudjo, September 10, 1752, Cumberland C.C.O.B. (1752–58), 19; trial of Mustapha, December 7, 1762, Cumberland C.C.O.B. (1762–64), 114–15; trials of Pompey and James, June 21, 1762, Spotsylvania C.C.O.B. (1755–65), 266; trials of Lewis and Will, September 4, 1777, mentioned in *EJCS*, I, 488.

42. Catterall, *Judicial Cases*, I, 84; *American Digest*, XLIV, cols. 1054–58, para. 1325. A few states, such as Louisiana, allowed limited liability (Thomas D. Morris, "'As If Injury was Effected by the Natural Elements of Air, or Fire': Slave Wrong and the

Some postslavery commentators claimed that black violence increased, once the restraints of slavery disappeared.[43] This impressionistic and self-serving estimate cannot be substantiated, but it also ignored the significant difference between violence directed by slaves toward white people and violence among slaves. The latter was more likely than was the former to occur when slaves were not under the surveillance of white authorities. Each kind of violence was subject to subsequent judicial sanctions, though mortal violence among slaves sometimes drew less harsh penalties. Yet slaves probably did not kill slaves more often than they killed whites. Where there was more contact and less external restraint, there was either less or no more deadly violence. The "unrestrained savage" simply did not exist. Slaves sometimes chose killing whites or even other slaves, but for specific reasons and in specific circumstances.

At the core of white fears of the "black rapist" is the legend of the violent "black savage."[44] Even after the high simple conviction rate of slaves for sexual offenses is taken into account, patterns in convictions for rape and attempted rape of white women between 1740 and 1785 show such generalized fears as groundless. Yet the aggregate trial statistics yield only some of the information that an individual trial such as that of Peter cannot. The obstacles are great. Besides there

---

Liability of Masters," *Law & Society Review,* XVI [1982], 569–99). Only one female slave was convicted of murdering her child—not yet called infanticide—in a court whose records have survived (trial of Sall, January 11, 1773, Brunswick C.C.O.B. [1772–74], 184–85; execution verified in *LJC,* III, 1598). The Accomack County Court of Oyer and Terminer tried the Indian slave Jenny for murdering her child on November 20, 1694, but found her not guilty because of insufficient evidence (Accomack C.C.O.B. [1690–97], 195–96). For a good example of how seriously white authorities could take convicting a slave for the murder of another slave, see the trial of Will, June 15, 1747, Amelia C.C.O.B. (1746–51), 42; Amelia C.C.M.B. (1746–51), 14. Will's severed head was displayed on a roadside pole. Preoccupation with economic consequences of slaves' deaths appears in some commentary on killings. The case involving Joseph Anthony's Davy is but one example (trial, December 15, 1741, Goochland C.C.O.B. [1741–44], 17–18, 153; *JHB,* 1742–47, p. 8). See also *Virginia Gazette* (R), July 14, 1768, (PD), October 20, 1774.

43. Joseph A. Tillinghast, *The Negro in Africa and America* (New York, 1902), 68–71, 162–63, 201–203; Thomas Manson Norwood, *Address on the Negro, by Judge Thomas Manson Norwood, on his retiring from the bench* (Savannah, 1908), 17–18, 21. See also George M. Fredrickson, *The Black Image in the White Mind: the Debate on Afro-American Character and Destiny, 1817–1914* (New York, 1971), 52–55, 253–54, 271–82; and Kenneth Paul O'Brien, "The Savage and the Child in Historical Perspective: Images of Blacks in Southern White Thought, 1830–1915" (Ph.D. dissertation, Northwestern University, 1974), 37–39, 54–56, 93–126, 184–226.

44. See also Lawrence J. Friedman's entry "Rape Complex, Southern" in *The Encyclopedia of Southern History* (Baton Rouge, 1979), 1029.

being some reason to question the accuracy of the courts' description of slaves' behavior in rape cases, there is no basis for comparison of slaves' sexual assaults against whites and against slaves or those of whites against any victim. No eighteenth-century Virginia court whose records have survived ever convicted a slave of raping another slave or a white man of raping a female slave.[45] Nor is there more than the most indirect evidence of regular reprisals, such as lynchings and castrations, against slaves for alleged sexual assaults against white women. Such factors make it difficult to analyze convictions of slaves for sexual offenses as anything other than part of the maelstrom into which slavery threw its victims.

But the results of rape trials between 1740 and 1785 show sufficient diversity that we can learn about some aspects of male slaves' alleged sexual attacks on white women and white fears of and responses to such attacks. There are four reasons why it is possible to conclude that such behavior did sometimes actually occur and therefore merits analysis in itself. First, the judiciary rejected more accusations as the years went by. The proportion of not guilty verdicts between 1740 and 1785 was higher than it had been before 1740. The simple conviction rate for felonious rape fell from 100 percent between 1724 and 1739 to 69.2 percent between 1740 and 1785. For felonious attempted rape, the decline was from 100 to 75 percent. (Table 14 tells the rest of the statistical story.) Second, judges gave capital sentences to slaves convicted of sexual offenses less often as time passed, indicating that hysterical reactions were not necessarily the rule. (Some 56.4 percent of those tried for rape were found guilty, sentenced to hang, and not recommended by the judges for a pardon.) Third, trials occurred in many different places at random times, suggesting that busy judges could react to perceived events and not just to self-perpetuating fears. Fourth, the low absolute number of convictions shows that, no matter how much whites had exploited and brutalized defenseless slave women, bondsmen rarely engaged in overt sexual aggression against whites who subsequently were willing to prosecute those men in public.

45. Charges were brought in 1783 against two slaves. One defendant was found guilty of an accompanying burglary and theft charge, but he was not convicted of the rape. Charges against the other slave were dropped when no witnesses appeared against him (trial of Toby, December 2, 1783, Norfolk C.C.M.B. [1782–83], 222; cancelled trial of Kitt, July 29, 1783, Westmoreland C.C.O.B. [1776–86], 148).

Table 14.   Slaves Tried for Rape or Attempted Rape, 1740–1785

| | | | Sentence for Felony | | | | |
Charge	Tried	Convicted of Felony	Hang (No Pardon)	Hang (Pardoned)	Corporal Punishment	Castration	Whipped for Misdemeanor
Rape	39	27 (69.2%)	22	2	2	1	4
Attempted Rape	12	9 (75.0)	3	0	3	3	2
Total	51	36 (70.6)	25	2	5	4	6

SOURCES: Miscellaneous county court order and minute books.

Still, the motivation in such cases may remain forever hidden.[46] Only one case for the period 1740 to 1785 stands out because of the personal circumstances involved. The summer of 1775, like that of 1781, was a time of special vulnerability for Virginia. The white population of Tidewater Lancaster County witnessed the conviction of one slave for raping a white woman and another for attempting to rape a white woman. The conviction of Tom for attempting to rape Cloe Carter was unique in that the court sentenced him only to corporal punishment, and not to castration. The Carter family had high standing in Lancaster; Cloe Carter may have shared that high rank. But the oyer and terminer justices had some reason for not using the severe penalty. The same justices had not held back when dealing with Natt, the slave of Walter James. When they met on September 6, 1775, to try Natt for raping Sarah James on August 21, they heard the testimony of four white people and then convicted and sentenced Natt to hang on September 18. One reason for this grim result can be found in a salient aspect of the case. This incident was one of only two recorded convictions for rape or attempted rape in which a slave was accused of attacking a member of his owner's family.[47]

Sarah James was Walter James's daughter-in-law, and a special one at that. In James's will, which he had written about a year earlier, he had promised two loans to Sarah that indicated his affection for her and the support he wished to provide his grandchildren and her after the 1774 death of Benjamin James, who was his son, Sarah's husband, and the children's father. Sarah was to have the use of the James land and plantation, and she was also to have the use of Walter's slave Natt until her son became twenty-one. Should she remarry before that time, all four of her children would share Natt. Walter James did not die until 1779; Natt died in late 1775, however. Natt certainly knew about Benjamin's death in 1774 and he could easily have been told what was in store for him should Walter die. Like Peter in North-

---

46. In "Rape Complex, Southern," Friedman concludes that there needs to be considerably more study of interracial sexual contact before we can advance beyond hypotheses. The controversy of the 1960s and later decades over the nature and prevalence of rape reinforces Friedman's statement. Agreement concerning convictions of slaves for rape of white women seems rather distant in face of the depth of disagreement concerning rape. A full discussion is Susan Brownmiller, *Against Our Will: Men, Women, and Rape* (New York, 1975), esp. 115–21, 128–43, 170–73, 210–55.

47. Mullin, *Flight and Rebellion*, 130–36; Benjamin Quarles, *The Negro in the American Revolution* (Chapel Hill, 1961), 19–32; trials of Tom, September 14, 1775, Natt, September 6, 1775, Lancaster C.C.O.B. (1778–83), 8, 7.

ampton County, Natt faced an uncertain future. As with Peter's case, the evidence is insufficient to support any more conclusions, though this case is unusual.[48]

In the only other recorded mid-eighteenth-century conviction of a slave for raping or attempting to rape a white woman in his owner's family, the factor of vulnerable widowhood again appears. In June of 1783, the oyer and terminer justices of Southampton County found Bob, the property of Williams Vick, guilty of raping Elizabeth Vick, Williams Vick's mother. The apparent victim had become a widow in 1778 and would herself die in 1786. She held two slaves—a man and a woman—two horses, and ten cattle as part of her husband's estate. Bob lived with six or seven other adult slaves on the property.[49] Several kinds of relative defenselessness figure in such rape cases. The general vulnerability of the victims created an opportunity for sexual aggression that contradicted the white assumption of supremacy. The almost complete inability of all female slaves to prevent being raped by white men had some influence on the conviction of slaves for rape of white women.

Whatever their personal morals, no masters would or could have ever taken the slightest legal—and therefore socially effective and significant—action to defend enslaved women against sexual assault by other white men. The law simply did not criminalize the rape of slave women. And for a law to have been efficacious, it would have had to deal specifically with such rapes partly because the enslaved victim would have to testify. Such a provision was unthinkable to most whites. No Virginia judge heard a case against any white man for violating common law when the victim was a slave. Legal silence, custom, and judges defined bondswomen as beyond the protection of common law whenever the accused was white.[50]

48. Elizabeth Hogg Ironmonger, *Thomas James (Clerk of Kingston Parish, 1783–1796). Ancestry and Descendants, 1653–1961* (Crozet, Va., 1961), 58–61; Lancaster County Wills (1770–83), 156, 158, 195.

49. Trial of Bob, June 13, 1783, Southampton C.C.O.B. (1778–84), 336; Southampton County Personal Property Taxes, 1782–90; Southampton County Wills (1772–82), 231–32, 244–45.

50. In 1767, Maryland jurist Daniel Dulany put the case succinctly: "A slave has never maintained an action against the violator of his bed" (1 [Maryland] Harris and McHenry 563). Even a Virginia case heard as late as 1769 cited the origins of rape prosecution in English law, charging Joe with violating Rachel Sutton "against the Statute of the 13th. 14th. 15th. & 18th. of Elizabeth" (Westmoreland C.C.O.B. [1776–86], 84; petition of John Lawson, October 31, 1787, Legislative Petitions, Westmoreland County, VSL).

Therefore, no matter what private measures some owners might take to protect their female slaves from sexual assault by white men, their inability or unwillingness to take legal action or to allow slaves to go to court to protect slave women created a situation that allowed, perhaps even encouraged, some slaves to rape white women. The vulnerability of slave women made some slave men more aware of those white women who were vulnerable. Among the many thousands of slave men who knew that slave women's vulnerability made them subject to rape by white men were the few who would for whatever reason select those white women who were most available as targets of sexual assault. The total legal weakness of slave women made their physical vulnerability inevitable. Those white women who were either legally or socially weak—widows, "spinsters," etc.—became more visibly vulnerable to some slaves.

The pattern of convictions between 1740 and 1785 supports this

Women Identified as Victims of Slaves Convicted of Rape or Attempted Rape, 1741–1784

Sarah Sparks
Catherine Hansford, spinster
Frances Lipscomb
Judith Watson, wife of Edward
Sarah Leland, wife of John
Jane Evans, wife of John
Elizabeth Woolridge, spinster
Comfort Heath, wife of John
Delilah Houston
Elizabeth Holton, wife of John
Martha Ceely
Martha Gibson
Peggy Dorey
Dorothy Hudgins
Sarah Russell
Frances Whitlock
Sarah Hamrick, widow
Mary Richardson ("a white young woman")
Elizabeth Gray, wife of Walter
Frankey Davis
Mary Johnson
Ann Evans

Mary Coleman, wife of Nath.
Margaret Andrews, widow
Sarah James, widow
Cloe Carter
Frances Daniel
Catherine Minimy
Elizabeth Childers
Mary Ann Hogan
Susannah Barrett, widow
Rachel Sutton, spinster
William Carwile's daughter
Edith Fowler
Keziah Puckett
Mary Cooper
Anne Stap, spinster
Christian Hooton and her daughter Elizabeth
Rebecca Hoffman
Elizabeth Vick, widow
Anne Crump
Winifred Waller
Mary Deen
Sarah Glenn, wife of John

analysis of the relationship between white men's unprosecuted rapes of slaves and slaves' punished rapes of white women. The first indicator of vulnerability is in the available names of the victims. Legal procedure required warrants in rape cases to state whether the alleged victim was single or someone's wife.[51] Of the forty-four women, more than 20 percent (or ten) are listed as young, widows, or spinsters. More than half (twenty-three) appear with no identification concerning their relationship to a man—*i.e.*, "wife" or "daughter"—an ordinarily important legal omission in an eighteenth-century record, but not one to be pushed too far as evidence concerning the women's status since some clerks were careless. Only about 18 percent (or eight) of the victims were identified as the wives of named men. Without statistics concerning the percentage of adult, white females in Virginia who were spinsters, widowed, or divorced, it is difficult even to estimate whether 20 percent is a disproportionate number of "unattached" women in the population of victims.[52] What is clear, however, is that even if only half of the women whose status is not specified were actually unattached, they, combined with the ten identified women, would constitute a disproportionate 48 percent of the victims who were legally and socially vulnerable as well as physically vulnerable.

The list of names reveals another weakness. Most of the family names are somewhat nondescript. An effort to identify the background

51. Starke, *The Office and Authority of a Justice of the Peace*, 292. The 1890 U.S. census, the earliest to distinguish among married, single, widowed, and divorced women, shows that 32 percent of women over fifteen were single, 10.5 percent were widowed, and less than 1 percent were divorced. The U.S. census of 1790 for Virginia (including Kentucky) shows 70,825 families in the state and a total of 215,046 free white women (not broken down by age). Since slightly less than half the free white males were over sixteen, roughly 107,500 free white women over sixteen years of age lived in Virginia. One can only guess how many of them were married women living within the 70,825 families, etc. Irene B. Taeuber and Conrad Taeuber, *People of the United States in the 20th Century* (Washington, D.C., 1971), 288; Greene and Harrington, *American Population Before the Federal Census*, 142–43. In *Liberty, a Better Husband: Single Women in America: The Generations of 1780–1840* (New Haven, 1984), 3, Lee Virginia Chambers-Schiller states that spinsters were "never more than a few percent" of the population of colonial America and that among women born between 1835 and 1838, the percentage was 7.3.

52. I have used only those names that appear in the records of convictions. Even though clerks based their record of trials on the warrant or indictment as well as on the trial proceedings, the absence of "single woman" or "wife of" from many of the records of slave trials leaves room for doubt. Starke, *The Office and Authority of a Justice of the Peace*, 292. For a note on the case that involved Mary Richardson, see Peter H. Wood, *Black Majority: Negroes in Colonial South Carolina from 1670 through the Stono Rebellion* (New York, 1974), 236n60.

of ten randomly selected women met with minimal success. Elite white women apparently escaped from the few slaves who were tried for rape or else they secured retribution in private. The trial and conviction of slaves for raping or sexually assaulting even those white women of low status occurred because those women had at least some status. They were white and they were women, which was enough to move judges into action against accused slaves. Had these women enjoyed higher status, they might never have had to resort to public action against slaves who had allegedly threatened, assaulted, raped, or, as may have happened in some instances, merely displeased them. Indeed, being unattached may have led some women to turn to the courts instead of depending on men they knew.

The pattern of convictions of slaves for raping or attempting to rape white women is one more indication of the dangers some slaves could create, or seem to create, for white society. Although not so severe a danger as that to which slaves were subjected, it was nonetheless real at times and led to tension within the slave society of Virginia. Mary Gray, the wife of George Gray, experienced this tension in 1783. The law, the courts, and her husband could not protect her from Patrick Davis' Jame, who attempted to rape her in her Greenbrier County house. Jame broke the law, the courts acted after the fact, and George Gray was absent. All that saved her was her own resistance. Yet the attack had apparently occurred, and not all women could successfully defend themselves. Presumably, Mary Gray would neither forget it nor ever thereafter be able to feel secure around supposedly docile slaves.[53]

It is particularly difficult to conclude that we know much more about how many times male slaves sexually assaulted white women than we do about why such attacks occurred. While the trials do illuminate some aspects of what the fifty convicted men apparently did, they do not reveal the extent of private retaliation for unprosecuted rapes. There were examinations of a York County white man in 1783 and a Mecklenburg County white man in 1784 for castrating slaves. The first man was found not guilty. Even though the Mecklenburg justices heard him admit that he had "Ordered his Negro man Ned to Castrate . . . Will," they discharged the second man because they be-

53. Trials of July 21, 26, 1783, and Petition of Patrick Davis, December 6, 1783, both in Legislative Petitions, Greenbrier County (now West Virginia).

lieved his action was not a felony. How many undetected or unprosecuted castrations occurred? Were these castrations performed as
a punishment for sexual aggression? We can only guess.[54]

Often spurious evaluations of behavior, the trials are also relatively
poor descriptions of events. Rape trials have less validity as evidence
than do other kinds of trials of slaves. Even eighteenth-century whites
had a notion of the weakness of some convictions. In September, 1753,
the justices of Chesterfield County condemned John Brummall's
Daniel to death for having raped a white woman. After Daniel broke
out of jail and was recaptured, the justices decided to ask the governor
to pardon him since they now had "the strongest Reasons to suspect
the Veracity of the Witness." Lieutenant Governor Dinwiddie agreed.
The same consideration may have persuaded Governor Harrison to
pardon a Brunswick County slave who was convicted of rape in 1784.
These cases, like some of the upheld convictions, could also have resulted from liaisons initiated by white women. When discovered, such
women could charge rape to try to protect themselves. Once having
established that reversals and injustices occurred, however, we can
conclude that those responsible were perhaps suffering from another
prejudice, one against the testimony given by female rape victims.[55]

Another problem about eighteenth-century trials for sexual offenses
is that attempted rape was subject to interpretation. A Southampton
County slave who stood trial in 1784 for attempted rape escaped castration because the justices convicted him only of a misdemeanor.
Their strained, convoluted, and weak attempt to justify themselves
was that the evidence included "several instances of misbehaviour
from which some intention of the attempt might be infer'd." This
reasoning may reflect fear that derived from the same justices' convicting a slave for raping his master's mother fourteen months earlier. Yet
it reveals somewhat strikingly the lengths to which authorities could
go to suppress even the hint of slaves' sexual aggression against
whites.[56]

It is consequently necessary to use the rape convictions culled from

54. Trials, November 18, 1773, York C.C.O.B. (1774–84), 411; April 9, 1784, Mecklenburg C.C.O.B. (1779–84), 530.

55. Trial of Daniel, September 23, 1753, Chesterfield C.C.O.B. (1767–71), 1–2, 12;
JHB, 1752–55, *passim*, 1756–58, pp. 115, 270; trial of James, September 24, 1784,
Brunswick C.C.O.B. (1784–88), 12; *EJCS*, III, 384.

56. Trial of unidentified slave of William Millars, August 3, 1784, Southampton
C.C.O.B. (1778–84), 469–70. The earlier case, June 13, 1783, is *ibid.*, 336.

available eighteenth-century records as a good indicator of sexual attacks and as a rough index, and an index only, of the number of such incidents. The records certainly do not reveal the existence of "the slave rapist"—that is, the prevalence of slaves who raped white women. Nor do other sources show a pronounced fear among whites that any such thing as "the slave rapist" existed.

7. *Two Revolutions*

The record of the trial of James, the possession of James Gordon of Lancaster County, for stealing and killing a sheep tells us little more than that he was found guilty and "burned in the hand" for the offense. We can, however, catch a glimpse of his personality in a *Virginia Gazette* report of his extraordinary response to being granted benefit of clergy. Instead of saying the expected "God save the King," James "roared out, with the greatest seeming sincerity, 'God d——n the K——g and the Governor too.' " As Rhys Isaac has observed in a provocative analysis of this newspaper report, James shared with many another Virginian the necessity of acting out his part in the high drama of revolution. The trial may have been act one, scene one.[1]

The year 1775 was a dangerous time for assertive slaves such as James because the responses of their masters could not be predicted— as seen in the great increase in slaves prosecuted for felonies in Virginia's county courts of oyer and terminer during that year.[2] In James's own Lancaster County, several assertive slaves had managed to create a disturbing year for authorities. Another Gordon slave was convicted of stealing; one slave had been found guilty of rape and another of

1. Trial of James, December 21, 1775, Lancaster C.C.O.B. (1778–83), 8; *Virginia Gazette* (DH), January 6, 1776; Rhys Isaac, "Dramatizing the Ideology of Revolution: Popular Mobilization in Virginia, 1774 to 1776," *WMQ*, 3rd ser., XXXIII (1976), 357.

2. The number found guilty and the simple conviction rate for each year was thirty-two (64 percent) in 1774; forty-seven (58 percent) in 1775; and thirty (76.9 percent) in 1776. Extant records indicate that fifty trials occurred in 1774 and thirty-nine in 1776, but eighty-one trials appear in the order books for 1775. The percentage of slaves exonerated during 1775, however, was unusually high at 42 percent, reflecting a state of some uncertainty as much as deliberation and procedural caution.

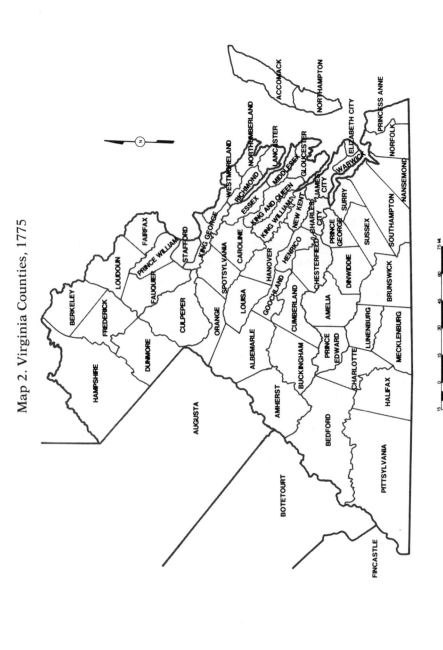

Map 2. Virginia Counties, 1775

attempted rape; and the first offense for which oyer and terminer judges tried a slave in Lancaster County after December, 1775, was attempted murder. When James stole and killed a sheep in late 1775, he was that much more threatening. James faced special circumstances. His private world had, like the wider public world, recently undergone a drastic modification similar to that suffered by Peter, the slave convicted of attempted rape of a white woman in 1782. James had either reached the tithable (income-producing) age of sixteen between June, 1775, and 1777, or else he had become Colonel Gordon's possession during the latter half of 1775, a difficult time indeed for a bondsman to be transferred from one owner to another.[3]

James's trial presented him with a real opportunity to shape fellow Virginians' perception of him. He could convince white Virginians that even though he had violated their laws against stealing, he meant nothing rebellious. To accomplish this, he could publicly side with the currently acceptable rebellion of the white population against Governor Dunmore and the king. That would simultaneously indicate that he did not plan to support Dunmore in combat. He next could try to convince his master that he was safe, that he need not be sold—or resold. In that way, James could restore his good standing with a powerful master. James the slave also knew the obvious method of flattering James the master, who had committed himself to the American Revolution.[4] Finally, James might also be able to impress his fellow slaves with his ability to survive in the white man's court.

The more than seventeen slaves known to have been convicted of crimes of confrontation—assault, attempted murder, murder, at-

3. Lancaster C.C.O.B. (1778–83), 7–9; Lancaster County Tithables (1775), 32, (1777), 44, VSL. Both lists were taken by Colonel Gordon, the first being dated June, 1775. James also appears in the Lancaster County Personal Property Tax Book, 1782, VSL. In all instances he is the only James enumerated and his name appears near the beginning of the roster of slaves. Will, the slave tried for stealing in late 1774, appears in none of the tax records that James does. Will might have been overage or underage, but he might also have been sold after his conviction.

4. Northern Neck Proprietary of Virginia, Tax Book, 1772, in Louise (Anderson) Patten Papers, VHS; Lancaster County Tax Book, 1773 (apparently the 1773 tax book for the Northern Neck Proprietary), VHS; Lancaster County Tithables (1775), 32, (1777), 44; Will and Inventory of Colonel James Gordon, Lancaster County Records, no. 18 (1764–70), 105, 108–109, 127, and no. 20 (Wills, 1770–83), 45 (Microfilm in VSL); Wesley M. Gewehr, *The Great Awakening in Virginia, 1740–1790* (Durham, 1930), 37–38, 94, 103; Robert E. Brown and B. Katherine Brown, *Virginia 1705–1786: Democracy or Aristocracy?* (East Lansing, Mich., 1964), 253; Daniel Blake Smith, *Inside the Great House: Planter Family Life in Eighteenth-Century Chesapeake Society* (Ithaca, 1980), 210–16; Armistead C. Gordon, *The Gordons in Virginia* (Hackensack, N.J., 1918), 45.

tempted rape, and rape—the more than eighteen found guilty of poisoning, illegal medication, or arson, and the three or more convicted insurrectionaries from the years 1770 through 1775 show that people either challenged more dramatically or constituted a greater threat to slaveholders than did James. The Lancaster justices, in order to think of someone more threatening to their safety than James was, needed only to remember the hundreds or thousands of bondspeople who had joined Dunmore. Those convicted of crimes by the courts of oyer and terminer played an ambiguous role. Having acted independently, they faced judgment by people who themselves had sought independence in an act of legal treason that they nonetheless justified as an honorable defense of their natural rights.

White patriots in rebellion against King George III and slaves who challenged or ignored the slave code, "criminals" alike in that they had violated existing laws, still acted in rather different contexts. The patriots broke off from the society and government that denied them freedom or, as some insisted, that had attempted to enslave them. Convicted slaves had confronted the society and government that had already truly enslaved them. Patriots freely used violence, especially deadly violence, to achieve their objectives of freedom and independence. But they would rarely have to live with their enemies, once the revolution succeeded. They could instead transform their illegal bid for independence into the creation of new governments and laws. Slave rebels who stayed in Virginia, however, would often still have to deal with the people they had challenged. They had a somewhat more subtle set of strategic and tactical problems.[5]

What would happen, for instance, if slaves somehow became more than an embarrassment to the revolutionaries and actually got in the way of the American Revolution? What if slaves' actions of the type that whites already regarded as dangerous seemed now to threaten the Revolution? Worst of all for whites, what if some slaves decided to effect a revolution of their own, one that worked at cross-purposes to

---

5. For divergent discussions of some of the issues raised here, see Richard M. Brown, "Violence and the American Revolution," in his *Strain of Violence: Historical Studies of American Violence and Vigilantism* (New York, 1975), 41–66; Louis Hartz, "A Comparative Study of Fragment Cultures," in U.S. National Commission on the Causes and Prevention of Violence, Task Force on Historical and Comparative Perspectives, *Violence in America: Historical and Comparative Perspectives,* ed. Hugh Davis Graham and Ted Robert Gurr (New York, 1969), 115–17; and F. Nwabueze Okoye, "Chattel Slavery as the Nightmare of the American Revolutionaries," *WMQ*, 3rd ser., XXXVII (1980), 3–28.

the patriots'? As Duncan MacLeod has convincingly argued, leading white southerners decided by the 1790s that black people in bondage presented less of a threat to republican virtue than they would as free people. White authorities in Virginia could still try "troublesome property" under laws that, with several modifications, went all the way back to 1692. Using extraordinary powers, local judges could try those blacks whose behavior not only endangered people and property but also attacked the very institution of slavery on whose continuation so many white people believed their freedom now depended.[6]

The most important question, then, is whether slaves' behavior actually became more aggressive, even revolutionary, during the American Revolution. White authorities appear to have believed that slaves presented a greater than usual threat to white people. An Englishman explained the problem to Richard Henry Lee in the dramatic spring of 1776. According to General Charles Lee, "Your dominion over the Blacks is founded on opinion; if this opinion falls your authority is lost." As a result, he continued, that authority must have armed support. In military instructions written to another Virginian at about the same time, Charles Lee stated that "the opinion which the slaves will entertain of our superiority or inferiority will naturally keep pace with our maintaining or giving ground." Lee well understood the symbiotic relationship between various kinds of weakness that whites might show and the rising aggressiveness of slaves.[7]

Many oyer and terminer judges seem to have comprehended the relationship of power that developed between slaves and whites during the prerevolutionary and revolutionary periods. How else would

---

6. Duncan J. MacLeod, *Slavery, Race, and the American Revolution* (Cambridge, England, 1974); Garry Wills, *Inventing America: Jefferson's Declaration of Independence* (Garden City, N.Y., 1978), 71–75. Some slaves could literally be caught in the crossfire: in Mecklenburg in 1769 a slave was shot as the result of a quarrel, an election dispute, and a court case that involved whites only (*Virginia Gazette* [R], June 29, 1769). The concept of just punishment (*Virginia Gazette* [Pi], July 20, 1775) and the discussions in *Virginia Gazette* (PD), July 18, 1771, December 23, 1773, are indicative of American revolutionaries' attitudes toward slaves.

7. Charles Lee to Richard Henry Lee, April 5, 1776, quoted in Benjamin Quarles, *The Negro in the American Revolution* (Chapel Hill, 1961), 122, but corrected according to copy in Lee Family Papers, 1742–1795, microfilm reel 2, frame 576, Alderman Library, UVa (original at American Philosophical Society); Charles Lee to Brigadier General Armstrong, April 10, 1776, quoted in Quarles, *The Negro in the American Revolution*, 122. Both are also printed in *The Lee Papers* (4 vols.; New-York Historical Society *Collections*, 1872–75), I, 379–80, 409–10. For Lee's repetition of this opinion, see *The Lee Papers*, I, 369, 372, 378. See also Aptheker, *American Negro Slave Revolts*, 21–22.

James's anti-Tory outburst have appeared in the *Virginia Gazette*? White judges were responding to slaves' actions as much as to their own anxieties when they tried more and more slaves in prewar years. Whites had good reason to believe that they would have something to fear if preoccupation with armed conflict with external enemies made them more vulnerable to attack from within.[8]

The many convictions indicate how some aggressive slaves attempted to deal with the new society. They resembled those slaves who made other responses to the "new order." Historians are finding more and more evidence that black Americans played an active role in the changes that accompanied the American Revolution.[9] Fighting for the British or the Americans, slaves actually fought for themselves. Those slaves who stayed in Virginia were just as important for its future as were those who left. Like James in Lancaster County, they had to find the limits of the new social and political environment. Whites would be using both old and new ways to "keep blacks in their place," as might be expected, but blacks would be at work carving out a place for themselves and doing so, when possible, on their own terms.[10]

The American Revolution provided many new opportunities for black Americans to seek freedom. It would be a mistake, however, to assume that they thereby were merely acting imitatively. It is equally likely that some slaves were actively fomenting their own Afro-American Revolution. Their efforts existed in the American context, to be sure, but the slaves took the initiative. If the American revolutionaries of 1776, in John Adams' famous estimation, had experienced a revolution in their "hearts and minds" long before, the slaves who fought for their own freedom had also undergone that transformation. Slaves on

8. There were peaks and troughs in prosecutions. Anxiety preceded wars, as in the mid-1750s, the mid-1770s, and 1780. The peaks of 1762 and 1782 appear to have resulted from efforts to "catch up" on cases deferred from the war years.

9. Benjamin Quarles helped to lead the way in *The Negro in the American Revolution*. See also Gary B. Nash, "The Forgotten Experience; Indians, Blacks, and the American Revolution," in William Fowler, Jr., and Wallace Coyle (eds.), *The American Revolution: Changing Perspectives* (Boston, 1979), 31–46; Willie Lee Rose, "The Impact of the American Revolution on the Black Population," in Larry R. Gerlach (ed.), *Legacies of the American Revolution* (Logan, Utah, 1978), 183–97; Ira Berlin, "The Revolution in Black Life," in Alfred Young (ed.), *The American Revolution: Explorations in the History of American Radicalism* (De Kalb, Ill., 1976), 349–82; and the valuable essays in Berlin and Hoffman (eds.), *Slavery and Freedom in the Age of the American Revolution*.

10. During the 1760s and the early 1770s, white authorities feared intensive use of poisoning by those Virginian slaves who claimed to know the art. The 1760s and 1770s saw an especially high number of convictions for crimes of confrontation. Attacks on property also increased. More than simple population growth was at work.

plantations could not create the formal committees of correspondence and new governments to unify and strengthen their revolution, but many separate slaves may have simultaneously decided to try to change the slave societies of which they were a part.

Evidence from the trials of slaves supports, though it does not prove, the argument that a significant number of Virginian slaves wished to bring about their own revolution between the 1750s and the 1780s. Even though the 1730s and the 1740s were a time of major growth in the slave population, and hence of significant change in Virginia as a slave society, there is not a single insurrection prosecution of any slave in extant records from those years. There were insurrection scares and even some activity in other colonies during the same decades, but the Old Dominion apparently escaped the experience of New York and South Carolina. Tightening Virginia's laws against conspiracy and insurrection may well have had its intended effect. After all, a Spotsylvania slave was hanged for conspiracy to murder a white man in 1732, even though his actions did not conform to statutory specification of collaboration with five or more persons. But not even this kind of terror could suppress slaves in the early 1750s, when a cycle of insurrectionary thinking emerged.

On September 11, 1750, the justices of the Northampton County Court sentenced Abimelech Webb, a free black man, to receive thirty-nine lashes and required him to post a bond of £100 for his good behavior. The charge was "suspicion of his combining with sundry Negros in a Conspiracy against the white People of this County." In early November the county authorities sentenced James, the slave of Katherine Robins, to twenty lashes for the same reason. This first instance of a new series of rebellious confederacies was not especially noteworthy. Neither Webb nor James received as harsh a punishment as was possible, since they appear to have been suspected because of speech alone. The distinctive aspects of this episode, however, are the timing, location, and participants. No imperial war was in progress. The long administration of the royal lieutenant governor was coming to a peaceful end. So Abimelech Webb and James verbally confronted slavery itself without being able to take advantage of a temporary vulnerability in the society at large. The two men's circumstances were important. The property of a woman who owned only one female slave at her death in 1754, James had to operate outside his own plantation. Both men and their unknown allies lived in Northampton

County, the scene of notable accomplishments by free blacks in the seventeenth century and the residence of a relatively large number of free blacks in the late eighteenth century. Northampton was also adjacent to Accomack County, which had the largest free black population in the Old Dominion in 1790.[11]

Perhaps most telling is that the collaborators included a free black man. Northampton was one of the oldest counties in the colony, so the slave community had had a long time to develop. When some slaves in Northampton began to think of insurrection as the solution to their problem of lifetime bondage, they worked in alliance with a free black man who had his own battle to fight with white society. The case of Abimelech Webb presented just one of the many dilemmas that resulted from free people living in the same society as slaves. White people thought they knew how to make the existence of slaves support their own freedom. They had a harder time dealing with the presence of free blacks. Recognizing his status as a "slave without a master," Webb probably understood his commonality of interest with James. They both sought their own definition of freedom.[12]

Against the odds, Virginian slaves had hopes of rising against whites in their own behalf. In 1736, William Byrd II assured a correspondent that "our negroes are not so numerous or so enterprizeing as to give us any apprehension or uneasiness." Relying on this quotation and on the fact that "no white person was killed in a slave rebellion in colonial Virginia," historian Edmund S. Morgan concludes that, in Virginia,

11. Trials of Abimelech Webb, September 11, 1750, James, November 13, 1750, Northampton C.C.O.B. (1748–51), 271–72, 283–84; Deal, "Race and Class in Colonial Virginia," 470–71. The dramatic killing of an overseer took place two years later in Accomack County. Northampton County Wills (1740–50), 516–17, (1750–54), 1–7; Breen and Innes, "Myne Owne Ground." Northampton County secured state legislation in 1832 authorizing expulsion of all free blacks because whites feared they would foment insurrection of the type experienced the year before in Southampton, another rural Virginia county that had a large free black population (Supplement to the Revised Code of the Laws, 248–49). The law was only partially effective. The free black population of Northampton was 1,333 in 1830; in 1840 it was 754 and climbed back to 962 by 1860. The free black population of Accomack County grew steadily in the same years. For these and other population figures, see U.S. Census Office, The Statistics of the Population of the United States, Vol. I, Population and Social Statistics (Washington, D.C., 1872), 68–70.

12. Ira Berlin, Slaves Without Masters: The Free Negro in the Antebellum South (New York, 1974). In available cases, only one free black was convicted of collaboration with a slave between 1740 and 1785 (Caroline C.C.O.B. [1777–80], 143). See also March 17, 1750, Norfolk C.C.M.B. (1749–53), unpaginated; York C.C.O.B. (1759–63), 504–506, (1763–65), 30; Tate, Negro in Eighteenth-Century Williamsburg, 101, 108; Isle of Wight C.C.O.B. (1768–69), 70–71, 78; Norfolk C.C.M.B. (1773–74), 46, (1774–75), 97; and Virginia Gazette (P), April 21, 1775.

"slaves proved, in fact, less dangerous than free or semi-free laborers. They had none of the rising expectations that have so often prompted rebellion in human history. They were not armed and did not have to be armed. They were without hope and did not have to be given hope." More white than black Americans would support first a resistance movement and then a successful revolution. Nevertheless, the existence of even a few insurrectionary slaves among Afro-Virginians—especially in several different areas of the province—would demonstrate to other slaves the possibility of their using force to try, even with the expectation of almost certain failure, to define freedom for themselves. The conviction of James in isolated Northampton on the Eastern Shore was, in fact, the first of a series of convictions for conspiracy. Most slaves were not dangerous, but some were.[13]

Three slaves in Brunswick County showed in 1752 that the aid of free blacks was not essential and that members of a relatively young slave community were also capable of spreading ideas of freedom and rebellion. Peter, Harry Cain, and James stood trial for insurrection and conspiracy to commit murder. The judges identified Peter as the leader, sentencing him to hang on July 6, and let Harry Cain and James off with misdemeanor convictions and punishments of thirty-nine lashes each. The clerk of Brunswick County reported that the misdemeanor was "being privy to an Opinion entertained among many Negroes of their having a Right to their Freedom and not making a Discovery thereof." St. George Tucker would declare in 1801 that slaves in 1775 fought for freedom "merely as a good." In 1800, however, "they also claim it as a right." But if the Brunswick clerk was saying anything about the blacks tried there in 1752, it was that they, as well as many Negroes, claimed freedom as a right. If this was true of some slaves in the newly developed Southside, was it also true of some slaves in other areas of the Old Dominion?[14]

There is evidence of insurrectionary thinking elsewhere. Two months after the Brunswick trials and seventy miles closer to the Atlantic, the Surry County justices found Nicholas Thompson's Will

13. William Byrd to Peter Beckford, December, 1736, quoted in Morgan, *American Slavery*, 309.

14. Trials of Peter, Harry, and James, June 25, 1752, Brunswick C.C.O.B. (1751–53), 242–43; [St. George Tucker], *Letter to a Member of the General Assembly of Virginia on the Subject of the Late Conspiracy of the Slaves, with a Proposal for their Colonization* (Richmond, 1801), 7, also quoted in Mullin (ed.), *American Negro Slavery*, 117.

guilty of insurrection and conspiracy, but only at the level of a misde-meanor. Like the Brunswick slaves, Will appears to have incurred a penalty for rebellious talk. The authorities suspected that Will had had two accomplices—Sharper, who was absent (perhaps dead), and Abraham, a Christian slave who ended up testifying against Will. The witnesses gave only enough evidence to support a misdemeanor con-viction, yet the fact that three slaves were under suspicion and six were able to testify concerning Will's intentions suggests that many Negroes in Surry, as in Brunswick, believed they had a right to their freedom.[15]

There may even have been open expression of such beliefs in Wil-liamsburg, the capital. On March 28, 1753, someone in Yorkhampton Parish detected Tom and perhaps Harry engaging in rebellious speech or actions. Harry escaped conviction in his trial on April 4, but Tom was found guilty of a misdemeanor and given twenty-five lashes. The reduction suggests that Tom had engaged only in insurrectionary talk. Thus the town of Williamsburg ensured that Tom's words would reach the highly placed. With the other convicted insurrectionaries or plot-ters in Northampton, Brunswick, and Surry counties, Tom would go into the court records as evidence of what was in some slaves' hearts and minds as early as the 1750s.[16]

After the York County cases in 1753, a period began in which few such trials were recorded. Nevertheless, rebellious thinking was oc-curring, and white leaders were wary of and taking preventive mea-sures against possible uprisings. Unrecorded cases clearly did exist. In July, 1755, after George Washington's first expedition into the country claimed by the French, one year after Washington's capitulation at Fort Necessity, and about a week after General Braddock's defeat, Virginia's lieutenant governor Robert Dinwiddie responded to Colonel Charles Carter's report of slave discontent in Lancaster County: "The Villainy of the Negroes in any Emergency of Gov't is w't I always fear'd. I greatly approve of your send'g the Sheriffs with proper Strength to take up those y't appear'd in a Body at Y'r Son's House, and if found Guilty of the Expressions mention'd I expect You will send for

15. Trials of Will and Abraham, August 4, 1752, Surry County Criminal Court Pro-ceedings, 29–32.
16. Trials of Tom and Harry, March 28, 1753, York C.C.O.B. (1752–54), 204–205; York County Deeds, Orders, Wills (1745–59), 72–73, 118–20, wherein a "Tom" was appraised at £30.

a Com'o. to try them, and an example of one or two at first may prevent those Creatures enter'g into Combinat's and wicked Designs ag'st the Subjects." Dinwiddie told the Earl of Halifax a few days later that slaves had been "very audacious on the Defeat of the Ohio." "These poor Creatures," he added, "imagine the Fr. will give them their Freedom." Once again, some slaves had seized an opportunity to express collectively their hope for freedom, provoking a nervous response from Dinwiddie, who frankly informed the Earl of Halifax that the slave threat could limit the militia that might be spared for action against the imperial enemy.[17]

The aggressiveness of Old Dominion slaves found outlets at times when foreign enemies threatened control of imperial possessions. Virginia officials fell back on the "villainy," "outside agitator," and "poor creatures" arguments in order to explain away some slaves' active pursuit of the same freedom that King George's subjects thought was the British birthright. But the British quest for empire had conflicted with the spread of British liberty, a circumstance of which slaves, Native Americans, Acadians (Cajuns), and other exploited or conquered peoples in the New World and elsewhere were quite aware. Not surprisingly, Dinwiddie's version of the "outside agitator" argument fastened on the Acadians, whose diaspora at the hands of the British had begun in earnest in 1755. Many of them had gone to Virginia, where the royal governor suspected them of having "frequent Cabals with our Negroes." Outside the law and mistaken about the French nation's wish to free them, insurrectionary slaves in the Old Dominion during the 1750s prefigured the dramatic changes in parts of the slave population that would occur in the 1770s.[18]

Insurrectionary expressions and perhaps actions by slaves took

17. Robert Dinwiddie to Charles Carter, July 18, 1755, and Dinwiddie to Secretary Halifax, July 23, 1755, both in *The Official Records of Robert Dinwiddie, Lieutenant-Governor of Virginia, 1751–1758* (2 vols.; Richmond, 1884), II, 102, 114. Other colonists perceived the same threat. Earl of Morton to Duke of Newcastle, January 15, 1760, in Newcastle Papers, CCXVI, fol. 296, British Library Add. MSS. 32,901, VCRP; Petition of Glasgow Merchants trading to Virginia, 1756[?], MSS. North a.6, Bodleian Library, Oxford, VCRP; A. Roger Ekirch (ed.), " 'A New Government of Liberty': Herman Husband's Vision of Backcountry North Carolina, 1755," *WMQ*, 3rd ser., XXXIV (1977), 642.

18. Dinwiddie to Massachusetts Governor William Shirley, April 28, 1756, in *The Official Records of Dinwiddie*, II, 396. James Oglethorpe helped to spread the "outside agitator" argument in the early 1740s (Daniel Horsmanden, *The New York Conspiracy*, ed. T. J. Davis [Boston, 1971], 350–51; Oglethorpe to Georgia Trustees, May 28, 1742, Colonial Office, Class 5, No. 641, fol. 145, VCRP).

place, then, in a far wider temporal and circumstantial context than that of the imperial wars or the War for Independence. That slaves were prosecuted for such thinking and behavior reflects the most important situation in which some slaves began to pursue freedom after 1750. Trials of slaves for insurrection were more numerous in the mid-1770s than in the early 1750s, to be sure, but were sufficiently frequent in the years before the French and Indian War that the explanation of the 1770s cases had to be extended back at least twenty-five years. The temporal context of those cases is the 1750s through the 1770s—and perhaps even the decades before the 1750s in some instances. Some slaves' active quest for freedom in the 1770s was not simply mimetic behavior prompted by white revolutionaries' resistance to Great Britain. Some slaves were involved in a resistance movement that derived from their own thinking and circumstances as well as from the more well known prerevolutionary and revolutionary movements.[19]

Some slaves exhibited other kinds of rebelliousness in the same regions as those in which some expressed insurrectionary thoughts. Surry and Sussex had no fewer than seven trials of slaves for poisoning between 1754 and 1764, two of which resulted in convictions for giving medication illegally. Brunswick County, in which three slaves stood trial for insurrection in 1752, experienced an epidemic of poisoning trials from 1758 through 1777 at least. Northampton County had only one poisoning trial, that being in 1778, while York County officials sentenced one slave to hang in 1763 for poisoning and discharged two suspected accomplices. Thus two of the centers of insurrectionary thought or activity in the early 1750s later became, at least temporarily, centers of white suspicion concerning poisoning by slaves. In view of this correlation, we can ask whether the same communities that supported open, collective challenges to white dominion and security later undertook (or even turned by necessity to) poisoning. In-

19. Peter H. Wood discusses the motives of slaves involved in open resistance during this period in " 'Taking Care of Business' in Revolutionary South Carolina: Republicanism and the Slave Society," in Jeffrey J. Crow and Larry E. Tise (eds.), *The Southern Experience in the American Revolution* (Chapel Hill, 1978), 268–93, esp. 275–87. See also his " 'Impatient of Oppression': Black Freedom Struggles on the Eve of White Independence," *Southern Exposure*, XII (November/December, 1984), 10–16; Wood, " 'The Dream Deferred': Black Freedom Struggles on the Eve of White Independence," in Gary Y. Okihiro (ed.), *Resistance: Studies in African, Caribbean, and Afro-American History* (Amherst, 1986), 166–87.

surrection and poisoning were both "intestine" crimes in the eyes of white authorities. They were assaults by the "enemy within."[20]

White leaders already had problems with slaves who defiantly threw the rhetoric of freedom back at the protectors of British America's largest slave society. But in the 1760s the first clear signs appeared that other slaves were going to appeal to a higher justification for their self-assertion. In 1770, Landon Carter characterized evangelistic slaves as "so much worse" as a result of their conversion. They, like many other dispossessed people, had found in a revised version of Christianity a new and rebellious light.[21] By the 1760s, the Great Awakening was more than a private episode to a significant number of slaves. Slaves had been baptized before the 1760s, but a new breed began to make themselves known as preachers in the 1760s, and not all of them preached what nervous whites would call the good news.

Some masters understood part of the threat some of these slave preachers presented. Charles, who ran away in early 1765 and was still out in April, 1771, was "a great preacher," declared his owner, "from which I imagine he will endeavour to pass as a freeman." According to owner Seth Ward in Chesterfield County, Primus "has been a Preacher ever since he was sixteen [*i.e.*, since 1768 or 1769] . . . and has done much Mischief in the Neighbourhood." Nat, who escaped even though in irons with another slave, "pretends to be very religious, and is a Baptist teacher." He had been the property of the Reverend John Dixon of the College of William and Mary.[22]

In spite of many white leaders' best efforts, the Great Awakening sometimes brought the sword, and not peace, to the slave society of Virginia. They initially characterized all New Light preachers, whether white or black, as artful, cunning pretenders and, worse, rabble-rousing troublemakers. White New Light leaders had no more

20. In "Turmoil in an Orderly Society," 252, 289–90, Timothy Morgan argues that individual resistance by slaves increased after the suppression of collective resistance. The notion that the many poisoning cases in the 1760s were in part complementary to the insurrection cases in the 1750s helps to explain the complete absence of insurrection trials from the extant records of the 1760s. (Carelessness or a cover-up was also possible. At least one insurrection trial, which reportedly took place in Sussex County in 1767, is missing from that jurisdiction's comprehensive compilation of criminal trials. *Virginia Gazette* [PD], October 1, 1767; Surry County Proceedings of the Courts of Oyer and Terminer, 1754–1807.) There is one further explanation: Virginia's authorities changed their way of responding to the danger of revolt. That adjustment was itself a response to a change in slaves' tactics.

21. Isaac, *The Transformation of Virginia*; Carter, *Diary*, I, 378.

22. *Virginia Gazette* (R), October 27, 1768, (PD), February 27, 1772, (P), May 1, 1778.

wish to encourage rebelliousness among New Light slaves than did Old Lights. Smarting under the charge that the Great Awakening was making slaves disobedient and was creating a social chaos that was especially dangerous in a slave society, white New Light authorities, like some Anglican clergy in the early part of the century, had more than theological reasons for employing ecclesiastical institutions as a means of disciplining slaves. At the Meherrin Baptist Church in Lunenburg County, for example, someone raised the question in 1772 whether it was a matter of church discipline for a member "to suffer any of his Domesticks in Open sin uncorrected." The unanimous answer of the members, a handful of whom were black, was affirmative. The same church members made some effort to prevent owners from acting cruelly toward their slaves, but they consistently took it upon themselves to admonish, discipline, or excommunicate slave members for everything from "little falcities" to fighting, running away, and stealing. Half a dozen slaves were excommunicated from Morattico Baptist Church in Lancaster County by the 1780s for the offense of adultery as well as for stealing a hog and lying.[23] Baptist churches would later excommunicate many slaves.

The efforts of white church leaders produced divergent results. Advocates of slave conversion had always been able to fall back on the argument that Christianity would make slaves more obedient. One clergyman was proud to note that stealing had markedly decreased among converted slaves in a Maryland county. Another gratefully repeated the testimony of a Brunswick County justice that the level of violence there among both whites and slaves had dropped significantly since the Methodists had come into their midst in the 1770s. Secular officials could more easily control New Light slaves if sacred institutions would help. But two difficulties would plague this approach. First, Christianity would prove to have a revolutionary effect on one group of slaves at the same time that it helped keep another group in bondage. Second, white ecclesiastical leaders, such as those in the Baptist churches, would prohibit slaves from occupying the

23. Meherrin (Lunenburg County) Baptist Church Minute Book (1771–1837), 1, 3, 5, 10, 27, 28, 34, 64, VSL; Morattico (Lancaster County) Baptist Church Minute Book (1778–1844), 7, 10–13, VSL; James David Essig, "A Very Wintry Season: Virginia Baptists and Slavery, 1785–1797," *VMHB*, LXXXVIII (1980), 176; W. Harrison Daniel, "Virginia Baptists and the Negro in the Early Republic," *VMHB*, LXXX (1972), 60–69; Albert J. Raboteau, *Slave Religion: The "Invisible Institution" in the Antebellum South* (New York, 1978), 145, 180; Isaac, *The Transformation of Virginia*, 171–72.

pulpits of established congregations, thus encouraging, even forcing, slave preachers, the very ones who might have fostered the most dynamic and fruitful interaction with black converts, to become ecclesiastical outlaws. Moreover, it was but one step from being an ecclesiastical outlaw to being a civil one.[24]

One of the few insurrection trials to which any Virginian refers in the 1760s would be revealing, were its record available. It involved Jupiter, alias Gibb, a thirty-five-year-old slave who stood about six feet tall and who had scars on his back from the "severe" whipping he had sustained at the Sussex County courthouse after being tried there in 1767 "for stirring up the Negroes to an insurrection, being a great New light preacher." Jupiter had already sought to declare his independence from Virginia but had failed. Now he was at least going to attempt to establish his physical independence. A brief runaway advertisement cannot tell us how many slaves Jupiter had been stirring up. It pointedly demonstrates how both Jupiter and his master, George Noble of Prince George County, connected New Light preaching and slave insurrection, and how Sussex County officials thought it necessary to use the whip to try to accomplish what white preachers had been unable to do.[25]

Jupiter and other converts were by no means the only insurrectionary slaves whom white authorities tried to suppress in the 1760s. According to Robert Munford of Mecklenburg County, his bondsman Jack not only was distinguished by the faint brands R and M on his cheeks and a career of many robberies for which he supposedly feared prosecution, but "it appears he has been principally concerned in promoting the late disorderly meetings among the Negroes." Neither Munford's advertisement in April, 1766, nor any official record sheds light on what those meetings were about. Yet Jack stands out from almost all other slaves suspected of stealing because he was also accused of conscious rebelliousness. Whether Mecklenburg County officers trumped up the charge in order to get rid of Jack is not known, but in 1772 he was back in custody and convicted of raping Mary Johnson. Identified as insurrectionary, robber, and rapist, Jack be-

24. Rankin Journal, July 9, 1775, September 19, 1776, pp. 70, 114; Richard Whatcoat Journal, September 5, 1797, December 20, 1799 (MS in Garrett Evangelical Theological Seminary Library, Evanston, Ill.); Tate, *Negro in Eighteenth-Century Williamsburg*, 89; Raboteau, *Slave Religion*, 146–47, 180, 238; Jordan, *White Over Black*, 179–215.

25. *Virginia Gazette* (PD), October 1, 1767.

came the complete outlaw, and the gallows his only rostrum. Near Williamsburg in June, 1769, Mrs. Samuel Ashley overheard several slaves discussing a plot "against the white people, which they intended putting in execution very soon." Five bondsmen received twenty-five lashes each at James City County Court, another suffered thirty-nine lashes, and a seventh plotter was hanged.[26]

The only other insurrectionary activity reported in Virginia in the 1760s was in Hanover County at Christmas, 1769. The basic cause of the localized and apparently spontaneous uprising, according to an informant of the *Virginia Gazette*, was that slaves who had "long been treated with too much lenity and indulgence, were grown insolent and unruly." Even if the Hanover records were available, they probably would not touch on this event, since whites killed the ringleader and some of his allies on the spot. The incident occurred when a white steward attempted to correct a slave who had failed to do an assigned task and had given "most insolent and provoking answers" when questioned. A pitched battle followed, and some forty to fifty slaves fought against the whites. Having firearms was all that allowed the white men to gain the upper hand. These slaves also had a low opinion of white control.[27]

A demographic factor was at work in the 1769 uprising as well as in other incidents and scares of the 1760s. As the proportion of slaves to whites changed through the 1750s, the 1760s, and the 1770s, the possibility of insurrection grew accordingly. Should enough slaves decide to rebel, it became more likely by the time of the American Revolution that they could. Anthony Benezet, the Pennsylvania Quaker who struggled so passionately to end the slave trade and to abolish slavery, consciously chose to omit from his polemical pamphlets any mention of the "continual Danger the southern Colonies are exposed to, from the vast disproportion between the Negroes & the whites." He feared that it was a "Subject of too tender a nature to be exposed to view, in places where it might fall into the Hands of the Negroes," especially those who could read. Virginian Arthur Lee and royal governor Dun-

---

26. *Virginia Gazette* (PD), May 2, 1766; trial of Jack, June 12, 1772, Mecklenburg C.C.O.B. (1771–73), 257; *Virginia Gazette*, June 22, 1769, quoted in *Pennsylvania Gazette*, facsimile edition, XVII (1769–71), 132.

27. *Virginia Gazette* (R), January 25, 1770, also in Mullin (ed.), *American Negro Slavery*, 94–95. Some slaves of Charles Carter were involved, suggesting a possible connection between this plot and Gabriel's Plot. Carter's Hanover slaves figured in the latter (*JHB*, May 28, 1770, p. 28).

more would both notice the same disproportion, but for somewhat different reasons.[28]

When Dunmore first understood the danger that slaves presented to white Virginians, he supported the whites' "cause." That much might be expected of a royal governor who, for the time being at least, expected the support of white Virginians. What is interesting is the manner in which the supreme legal authority in the royal province of Virginia thought he and other officials should respond to the threat posed by the slave population, which would increase through continued importation and births. Dunmore mistakenly or designedly overstated that population as "double the Number of white people." Then he said that slaves might be held down in peacetime through "unremitted observance of their conduct, a rigorous exertion of the Laws relating to them, and the most exemplary punishment of all the refractory (a lamentable necessity for a Country to be under)."[29]

To what extent did the actions of county and colony officials contribute to the successful accomplishment of Dunmore's other remedy for the insurrection problem, namely, the stringent use of the slave code and courts to hold down "malefactors"?[30] Prosecutions of slaves for various felonies and misdemeanors rose to a record high in 1775—a reaction to rising slave resistance rather than its prevention. Dunmore did not create rebelliousness among slaves and then exploit it for royal purposes. Instead, he tried to turn it to his objectives. Dunmore could count on slaves running away and taking up arms against white patriots, but he had to have some reason to believe that the runaways would materialize when he needed them. On April 21, 1775, the mem-

28. Anthony Benezet to Joseph Phipps, May 28, 1763, Benezet to David Barclay, April 29, 1767, Benezet to Granville Sharp, March 29, 1773, all in Roger Bruns (ed.), *Am I Not a Man and a Brother: The Antislavery Crusade of Revolutionary America, 1688–1788* (New York, 1977), 98, 140, 264; Arthur Lee, "Address on Slavery," *Virginia Gazette* (R), March 19, 1767, also in Bruns (ed.), *Am I Not a Man,* 107–11. See also Richard K. MacMaster, "Arthur Lee's 'Address on Slavery': An Aspect of Virginia's Struggle to End the Slave Trade, 1765–1774," *VMHB,* LXXX (1972), 141–57; and Lee, *An Essay in Vindication of the Continental Colonies of America,* quoted in Jordan, *White Over Black,* 309.

29. Not even these measures would prevent slaves from siding with a foreign enemy, however, in order to take revenge on their masters. Dunmore concluded that it was "a matter of the greatest concern, to find proper means of averting a calamity so alarming" (Dunmore to Board of Trade, May 4, 1772, Dunmore to Lord Hillsborough, May 15, 1772, both in CO 5/1530, fols. 46–47, 5/1333, fols. 187–88, VCRP).

30. Dunmore also sought to reduce slave importations through raising the duties on such trade into Virginia. It is well known that this measure failed. Darold D. Wax, "Negro Import Duties in Colonial Virginia: A Study of British Commercial Policy and Local Public Policy," *VMHB,* LXXIX (1971), 29–44.

bers of the Municipal Common Hall of Williamsburg assumed that Dunmore had created the unrest. "We have too much reason to believe," they "humbly" reported to the governor, "that some wicked and designing persons have instilled the most diabolical notions into the minds of our slaves." In reply, Dunmore insisted that he had received a report of an insurrection in Surry County on the basis of which he had taken appropriate action. Both statements referred, of course, to Dunmore's removing the gunpowder from the powder magazine in Williamsburg.[31]

We have reason to suspect both statements. The Common Hall members failed to admit that they were concerned about royal forces and about slaves' use of force. And Dunmore did not mention the possibility of white rebellion against the Crown. There is no record of a contemporary trial in Surry County for conspiracy or insurrection among slaves. Yet news of a Georgia insurrection made slave rebellion look quite possible in the context of the patriots' resistance. Three white people had been killed and several slaves executed by being burned to death in Darien, Georgia, just half a year earlier. Virginians who remembered the uneasy years of the French and Indian War and the political crises of the 1760s would not fail to take note. James Madison reported a plot in Virginia in November, 1774, in which slaves planned to side with British troops, expecting that the British would free them. How many more such plots developed is unclear, especially since Madison told his correspondent that they should be concealed as well as suppressed. Insurrection became more of a reality in Virginia by early April. One conviction of a slave occurred in Prince Edward County on April 15, and two more took place in Norfolk County, near Surry County, on April 21, the same day the Williamsburg officials and Dunmore had exchanged charges and explanations.[32]

31. William James Van Schreeven et al. (eds.), Revolutionary Virginia: The Road to Independence (7 vols.; Charlottesville, 1973–83), III, 54–55; Quarles, The Negro in the American Revolution, 21; Mullin, Flight and Rebellion, 131.

32. Virginia Gazette (P), April 28, 1775 (supp.), June 16, 1775; James Madison to William Bradford, November 26, 1774, in The Papers of James Madison, ed. William T. Hutchinson et al. (15 vols. to date; Chicago, 1962), I, 129–30; Harvey H. Jackson, " 'American Slavery, American Freedom' and the Revolution in the Lower South: The Case of Lachlan McIntosh," Southern Studies, XIX (1980), 86; trial, April 15, 1775, Prince Edward C.C.O.B. (1773–81), 468; trials, April 21, 1775, Norfolk C.C.M.B. (1774–75), 109–10. Peter H. Wood discusses other contemporary signs of black rebelliousness in " 'Impatient of Oppression,' " 10–16; and " 'The Dream Deferred,' " in Okihiro (ed.), Resistance, 166–87. Dunmore's "cover story" produces echoes of New York governor Andros' 1675

Dunmore now encouraged the slaves' momentum. At the end of April, he let some white Virginians know that he was considering calling slaves to arms. In early June, he took asylum aboard a man-of-war at Yorktown, after which he began to accept fugitive slaves. Spring and summer, 1775, were predictably filled with insurrections and rumors of insurrection. In July, the lower Tidewater area was somewhat unstable. Two slaves received guilty verdicts in Southampton County conspiracy trials. In nearby North Carolina, white officials were convinced they had foiled a plot. In Williamsburg itself, the York County justices examined Thomas Gay, a white man, for trying to raise a rebellion among York's slaves; they found him guilty, however, only of a breach of the peace. By August, reports of impending insurrections had spread up and down the Atlantic Coast as well as across the ocean to imperial offices in London. In September, a tutor in Caroline County had to publish a denial that he had tried to foment a slave uprising.[33]

A distinctive group of blacks were willing to confront white people during the revolutionary period in a way not even the many slaves convicted of murder and other crimes against the person were. These challenged slaveowners' collective authority at a time when white leaders were increasingly able to back up their claim to hegemony with firepower and growing numbers of trained troops. Who were these men?[34] Table 15 indicates how the names of some slaves convicted of participating in insurrection or insurrectionary plotting reflect the Tidewater domination of the prosecutions. The Southampton and Essex slaves belonged to the same owners or to owners who were

---

appearance at the mouth of the Connecticut River ostensibly to defend colonists against Indians. His real intention all along was to defend the west bank of the river against Connecticut's claim (Philip J. Schwarz, *The Jarring Interests: New York's Boundary Makers, 1664–1776* [Albany, 1979], 26).

33. Van Schreeven *et al.* (eds.), *Revolutionary Virginia*, III, 141, 144n19; trials, July 15, 1775, Southampton C.C.O.B. (1772–77), 414; Jeffrey J. Crow, *The Black Experience in Revolutionary North Carolina*, North Carolina Bicentennial Pamphlet Series, XVI (Raleigh, 1977), 57–58; examination of Thomas Gay, July 17, 1775, York C.C.O.B. (1774–84), 95; *Virginia Gazette* (P), June 16, 1775, (D), September 23, 1775; James Dunlop to Alexander Dunlop, July 20, 1775, in James Dunlop Manuscripts, Scottish Record Office, GD 1/151, no. 1 (abstracted in VCRP Survey Report 8619); May 26, 1775, newspaper clipping from London, copied in *Virginia Gazette* (Pi), August 10, 1775, attached to Matthew Pope to John Jacob, August 25, 1775, in British Library Add. MSS., 34,813, fol. 90, VCRP; W. P. W. Curll to [?], November 16, 1775, in *Richmond College Historical Papers*, Vol. I, No. 1 (June, 1915), 101; Sylvia R. Frey, "Between Slavery and Freedom: Virginia Blacks in the American Revolution," *JSH*, XLIX (1983), 377.

34. Only men were ever tried for conspiracy or insurrection throughout Virginia's history.

Table 15. Slaves Convicted of Conspiracy or Insurrection, 1775, 1777

Date	Slave	Owner	County	Charge	Verdict	Sentence
Apr., 1775	Toney	John Baulding	Pr. Edward	Insurrection, Conspiracy to Murder	Misdemeanor	15 lashes
	Emanuel	Matthew Phripp	Norfolk	Insurrection	Insurrection	Hang
	Emanuel de Antonio	James Campbell & Co.				
July, 1775	Phil	John Bailey	Southampton	Conspiracy	Disorderly	15 lashes
	Mial					39 lashes
Mar., 1777	Ben	Marg. Hawkins	Essex	Insurrection	Insurrection	Hang
	John	Wm. Hawkins				
	Jack	Muscoe Garnett				
	Toney	James Garnett				
	Alick	Leah Edmondon			Unlawful	20 lashes

		Meeting	
Harry	James Gatewood		39 lashes; pillory $\frac{1}{2}$ hour; ears nailed and cut off.
Sam	Wm. Gatewood		20 lashes
Titus	Caleb Gatewood	& aid & abet Harry in enlisting	39 lashes
George	Ambrose Hord	aid & abet	39 lashes; pillory $\frac{1}{2}$ hour; ears nailed and cut off.
Will			39 lashes; pillory $\frac{1}{2}$ hour; ear nailed and cut off.
Roger	Wm. Barten		Not Guilty

SOURCES: Prince Edward C.C.O.B. (1773–81), 468; Norfolk C.C.M.B. (1774–75), 109–10; *Virginia Gazette* (P), April 28, 1775 (supp.), June 16, 1775; Essex C.C.O.B. (1773–82), 316.

part of the same social group. Regarded as less serious than the Norfolk plot, the Southampton episode may have been confined to John Bailey's plantation. The Essex events involved several pairs of slaves who had identical owners or owners in the same family. All these owners were from the Essex elite—two Edmondons sat on the county court, and the Garnett name was synonymous with high status. This slave conspiracy went well beyond the confines of a single plantation.[35]

The Essex plot was the most daring of known plots during the war years. First, it involved more defendants than did other episodes. More important, the slaves were tried for "being present at an unlawfull meeting of Slaves and recruiting Men to be employed for purposes unknown and training them to arms and instructing them in Military Discipline." In other words, the conspiracy's leaders tried to raise a guerrilla force to battle against the county militia. Contemporary events make it apparent that Ben, Jack, John, Toney, and the others wished to be prepared to seize an opportunity. One of James Garnett's slaves had successfully escaped to the British in 1776. A month before the Essex trials, British ships had received three hundred or more slaves from plantations in nearby Gloucester, Lancaster, and Northumberland counties. Whether the slaves prosecuted in 1777 knew about the Stono Rebellion of 1739 in South Carolina, they did not want to have the same relative disadvantage those runaways may have had, which was lack of military training. Here was a shrewd realization that desire and strength were not enough, yet even this attempt failed.[36]

35. Both Emanuel and Tony are names that turn up almost always in Tidewater records. The name Emanuel at least coincidentally appears in an insurrection trial in Isle of Wight in 1709 and in two others in Norfolk in 1775. Both an Antonio and an Emanuel were convicted in the New York Conspiracy of 1741 (Charlotte C.C.O.B. [1774–80], 106; Richmond County Criminal Trials, 334; Carter, *Diary*, II, 1075; Horsmanden, *The New York Conspiracy*, 468–69). An Emanuel hanged in the Boxley plot, 1816 (Spotsylvania C.C.M.B. [1815–19], 62, and C.S., box 3). Phripp and James Campbell & Co. were involved in extensive trade networks, suggesting diverse origins of their slaves (Van Schreeven *et al.* [eds.], *Revolutionary Virginia*, V, 335, 339; Norfolk County Loose Wills [1778–1845], no. 26, VSL).

36. Trials, March, 1777, Essex C.C.O.B. (1773–82), 311–12, 316; "Inspection rolls of Negroes . . . Nov. 30, 1783" (British embarkation papers), Papers of the Continental Congress, no. 53, 278, microfilm M-247, reel 66, National Archives ("Bristow Garritt," formerly property of "James Garrit" [a common misspelling of Garnett], left Virginia with Dunmore in 1776); Richard Graham to Leven Powell, February 20, 1777, in "The Leven Powell Correspondence," *John P. Branch Historical Papers of Randolph-Macon College*, Vol. I, No. 2 (1902), 123; Peter H. Wood, *Black Majority: Negroes in Colonial South*

In only one case is the history of a conspirator available. James Garnett's Toney had been corporally punished and granted benefit for stealing in 1767. Toney knew the enormous risk he was taking in 1777, testimony to the firmness of his resolve and the height of his hopes. Moreover, a slave found guilty with Toney in 1767 was apparently not involved in the 1777 episode, which may single Toney out as a bold individual who would chart his own course.[37]

As before, the legal status of a slave during the revolutionary struggle of 1775 to 1783 was, in the words of Arthur Lee, that of an "outlaw, . . . since neither consenting to nor aiding the Laws of ye Society, in which he lives, he is neither bound to obey them, nor entitled to their protection." Fugitives and rebels faced new threats during the Revolution, however. Those who fought for King George relied on Dunmore's and Clinton's promises to free them, and well they might have. Old Dominion officials quickly upgraded running away in a group to a conspiracy and classified military service for the Crown as insurrection, punishable with death without benefit of clergy. Those slaves who fought covertly or openly on the American side did not incur quite the same risk if captured by the British. They were supposed to be treated according to the laws of war. But the reality was that slaves were plunder, no matter whether they were in combat or not. That danger faced Virginian slaves, since British raiding parties regularly carried off bondspeople during the war. Under these legal circumstances, the best defense for slaves was to take the offensive. As in peacetime, slaves who successfully "stole themselves" outsmarted the slave code.[38]

Carolina from 1670 through the Stono Rebellion (New York, 1974), 308–26; Frey, "Between Slavery and Freedom," 378–79. The two Emanuels did hang for their leadership of the 1775 Norfolk conspiracy, but the Virginia Gazette (P), April 28, 1775 (supp.), labeled that conspiracy "the late disturbances."

37. John, who belonged to William Hawkins, the owner of Toney's 1767 accomplice, was convicted of participating in the 1777 conspiracy (trial of John, March 17, 1777, Essex C.C.O.B. [1773–82], 311). In October, 1795, James Gatewood's Henry (Harry) was found not guilty when tried for preparation and administration of medicine (trials, November 16, 1767, October, 1795, Essex C.C.O.B. [1767–70], 29, [1795–97], 126).

38. Lee, "Address on Slavery"; Lee, An Essay, quoted in Jordan, White Over Black, 309. Van Schreeven et al. (eds.), Revolutionary Virginia, V, 64n20, contains a valuable discussion of how white Virginians applied the laws of war and the slave code to runaway slaves during the Revolution. See also Quarles, The Negro in the American Revolution, 19–32, 51–181; and Mullin, Flight and Rebellion, 130–36. A Loyalist commented that he was "extremely sorry" that Dunmore had promised freedom to slaves who would support him "as without serving his cause it may subject many of those poor Wretches to the Loss of Life, & most severe punishments" (W. P. W. Curll to [?], November 16, 1775, in Richmond College Historical Papers, 100–101). Slaves who ran away to Cornwallis' troops

But legal and judicial actions during the Revolution made successful slave rebellions difficult. Runaways became outlawed almost automatically without the previously required announcement. Also, county courts took the trouble to prosecute suspected runaways. Once again, however, it was too late. The Convention waited until January, 1776, to make running away to Dunmore a conspiracy. Convicted slaves received death sentences or benefit of clergy.[39] Some even spent the rest of the war working in the colony's lead and salt mines.[40] In 1785 the English governor of Nova Scotia accused some runaways who had taken refuge there of being "desperate villains," but he did not indicate whether any were Virginians. Moreover, none of the valuable lists of slaves who survived disease and warfare, who successfully eluded capture by those who claimed to own them, and who finally escaped to Canada mentions any Virginian slave convicted in a court whose records have survived. Slaveowners may not have been able to predict on the basis of a "prior criminal record" just which slaves would defy them so dramatically during the Revolution.[41]

Desperate authorities resorted to unusual measures in order to control aggressive slaves during the war. Accused of robbery in Norfolk in 1778, Bob was also charged with treason. When convicted of both, he received the death sentence, including the requirement that his corpse be displayed in public. Sancho was court-martialed in 1781 for giving

---

apparently took "plunder" with them in the form of their owners' clothes (Johann von Evald, *Diary of the American War*, trans. and ed. Joseph P. Tustin [New Haven, 1979], 305–306).

39. Trials, March 14, 1776, Northampton C.C.O.B. (1771–77), 311–12, 318; Van Schreeven et al. (eds.), *Revolutionary Virginia*, V, 64n20; *CVSP*, VIII, 158–59; owners' petition, *VMHB*, XV (1907–1908), 406–407. The *Virginia Gazette* (D), April 13, 1776, reported that two of the slaves "who mistook one of our armed vessels at Jamestown for a [royal] tender, and expressed their inclination to serve Lord Dunmore" were to be executed as an "example."

40. *VMHB*, XV (1907–1908), 295–96, 406–407; *Proceedings of the Convention of Delegates Held at the Capitol, . . . On Monday, the 6th of May, 1776* (Richmond, 1816), 8. Another slave was accused of a felony and sent to Williamsburg to be tried by the Committee of Safety in December, but he died (*ibid.*, 10). See also *Virginia House Journal, 1776*, p. 44; Quarles, *The Negro in the American Revolution*, 25–26; Northampton C.C.O.B. (1771–77), 318, 320; *VMHB*, LXXXVIII (1980), 325–26; *CVSP*, VIII, 158–59; and Mullin, *Flight and Rebellion*, 133.

41. Governor John Parr to Lord Shelburne, May 1, 1785, quoted in Carole W. Troxler, *The Loyalist Experience in North Carolina* (Raleigh, 1976), 48; "Inspection Rolls of Negroes . . . Nov. 30, 1783"; "Book of Negroes Registered & Certified . . . [to] 31 July 1783," and "Book of Negroes Registered and Certified . . . [to] November 30, 1783," both in Miscellaneous Papers of the Continental Congress, 1770–89, microfilm M-332, reel 7, National Archives.

intelligence to and acting as a pilot for the British invasion force. He hanged by the neck.[42] Four out of six Prince William County oyer and terminer judges tried to convict and hang Billy for treason in 1781, but two dissenting judges and influential planter Mann Page, who was executor of the estate of Billy's owner, went straight to Governor Jefferson with the successful argument for mercy that a slave, being a noncitizen, could not commit treason. In the same year, angry Botetourt County citizens complained about the reprieve of a slave sentenced to hang for not only committing a robbery and attempting to poison someone but for recruiting slaves to join Cornwallis.[43]

By the late years of the war, many slaves had freed themselves and many slaves had attacked whites in various ways—despite all the legal threats made and actions taken against them. Some people would still insist on executions and harsh corporal punishment, but others would see some practical sense in easing up. Slaves already had several reasons to want to aid the enemy of white patriots. According to powerful Northern Neck planter John Francis Mercer, for example, it had become prudent to improve the conditions of slaves during wartime, lest there be no slaves who would remain.[44]

Some of the ambiguities in the legacy of the American Revolution for the slave society of Virginia appear in the next recorded insurrection case to occur in the new Commonwealth. In August, 1785, a slave named Will stood before the oyer and terminer judges of Southside Mecklenburg County on the charge of "plotting, advising and consulting" a slave insurrection. The judges' decision was that Edward Dodson's slave was guilty of the offense officially defined as dangerous, antisocial, and capital, and the court, they declared, was "taking into

42. Trial of Negro Bob, August 5, 1778, Norfolk C.C.M.B. (1776–79), 87; Petition of William Evans, November 22, 1785, Legislative Petitions, Caroline County, VSL. Sancho's execution occurred as planned. In 1781, another time of invasion, and in Halifax County, Virginia, where a British-American clash had occurred, a colonel reported that the owners of the few available guns had secreted them "for their own Defence against Insurrections of Slaves or Tories—Reasons that seem to carry weight (with me at least)" (*CVSP*, II, 233).

43. Perhaps all the skill Billy had gained as the well-known waitingman of John Tayloe of Mount Airy and from repeatedly running away helped him figure out how to save himself. Tayloe's opinion was that Billy had "a surprising Knack . . . of gaining the good Graces of almost every Body who will listen to his bewitching and deceitful Tongue, which seldom or ever speaks the truth" (Quarles, *The Negro in the American Revolution*, 129; Mullin, *Flight and Rebellion*, 73, 75 [quoting Tayloe], 94, 107, 111; *VMHB*, XV [1907–1908], 407; *CVSP*, II, 90–91).

44. John Francis Mercer to Battaille Muse, August 9, 1782, quoted in Mullin, *Flight and Rebellion*, 132.

consideration the extream youth of . . . Will." According to an August, 1785, report, the news of a slaveowner's emancipating his nearly 170 slaves in an unidentified county may have caused "2 or 3 combats between Slaves and their Owners, now struggling for the Liberty to which they conceive themselves entitled." There would be an insurrection scare in Cumberland County in 1786, but it would come to nothing. What neither the Mecklenburg nor the Cumberland officials could know was that in the ninth and tenth years of the youthful Commonwealth, the extremely young Will and the anonymous slaves in Cumberland and elsewhere probably had been well educated, having witnessed both kinds of resisters and revolutionaries at one time or another between the 1750s and the 1780s. Aggressive slaves and concerned owners would continue to learn how their revolutionary objectives conflicted, even if they did derive from similar concepts of the value of freedom.[45]

45. Trial of Will, August 19, 1785, Mecklenburg C.C.O.B. (1784–87), 392; James Currie to Thomas Jefferson, August 5, 1785, in *The Papers of Thomas Jefferson*, ed. Julian Boyd *et al.* (21 vols. to date; Princeton, 1950–), VIII, 342–43; W. T. Moulson to Governor Henry, May 6, 1786, in VEPLR.

PART III

1785 to 1865

Introduction

The Revolution produced at least some change in the situation of Afro-Virginians. In the first place, northern states gradually decided in favor of general abolition, giving mobile Virginia slaves a slightly greater opportunity for finding sanctuary. Quakers and their associates provided an even better method of escape for some slaves in 1782 when they successfully lobbied in the Old Dominion's legislature for the law that thereafter allowed white emancipators to free any slaves they wanted to by deed without having to petition the state government for a private law. As Quakers, Methodists, and others began to take advantage of this legislation, they created one more ambiguous situation for slaves. The increasing number of individual manumissions encouraged early abolitionists to put more effort into advocating a general emancipation of the state's slaves. That seemed to present an opportunity for which the Commonwealth's young slaves could hope. But white people began to realize that such an emancipation would destroy the slave society they knew and would leave a biracial society about whose character they had deep anxieties.[1]

Ambiguous at first, the legacy of the American Revolution for Virginian slaves eventually became obvious and ominous. The importation

1. Jordan, *White Over Black*, 367–68, 375; Arthur Zilversmit, *The First Emancipation: The Abolition of Slavery in the North* (Chicago, 1967); Albert, "The Protean Institution," 116–204, 267–307; Philip J. Schwarz, "Clark T. Moorman, Quaker Emancipator," *Quaker History*, LXIX (1980), 27–35; Quarles, *The Negro in the American Revolution*, 162. A slave ran away from Virginia to the French, unfortunately without success (materials concerning Bob, in *Letters and Papers of Edmund Pendleton, 1721–1803*, ed. David J. Mays [2 vols.; Charlottesville, 1967], II, 402–409, 444n14, 445; and *The Papers of James Madison*, ed. William T. Hutchinson *et al.* [15 vols. to date; Chicago, 1962–], V, 27–28, 96–98, 101–103, 110n2, 111, 157–59).

of slaves stopped before the war and became illegal in 1778, but the prices as well as the number of slaves in the Old Dominion grew steadily in the 1780s. Virginian slavery was still an expanding institution.[2] But slaveholders knew that slaves could threaten that expansion. The short debate among white Virginians over general emancipation established that one reason many whites recoiled from the thought was their anxious prediction that it would inevitably result in an uncontrollable crime problem. When some Amelia County citizens petitioned the legislature in 1785 not to end bondage, they cited "the Horrors of all the Rapes, Murder, and Outrages, which a vast Multitude of unprincipled, unpropertied, revengeful, and remorseless Banditti are capable of perpetrating." The proslavery argument would become more familiar and insistent down the years. Emancipation would liberate a criminal class, according to many white people.[3]

The American Revolution thus created a new problem for Virginia's slaves. The fears of the many new republicans for their lives and fortunes, planned or already possessed, led them to pronounce slaves guilty before they were even charged. As long as proslavery apologists could not use the free blacks of Saint Domingue, the British West Indies, or the northern United States as polemical "whipping boys," the prediction that emancipated black people would unleash a severe crime problem rested partially on the assumption that slavery itself had kept them from aggressively antisocial behavior. Slavery would be these proslavery apologists' constables, sheriffs, judges, and execu-

2. Jordan, *White Over Black*, 342–426; Albert, "The Protean Institution"; David B. Davis, *The Problem of Slavery in the Age of Revolution* (Ithaca, 1975), 39–163, 255–62; Robert William Fogel and Stanley L. Engerman, *Time on the Cross: The Economics of American Negro Slavery* (Boston, 1974), 86–89.

3. Amelia County petition, November 10, 1785, Frederick County petition, November 8, 1785, Legislative Petitions, VSL; Duncan J. MacLeod, *Slavery, Race, and the American Revolution* (Cambridge, England, 1974); François Dupont to Etienne Claviere, January 10, 1789, in Charles T. Nall (ed.), "A Letter from Petersburg, Virginia," *VMHB*, LXXXII (1974), 147; Albert, "The Protean Institution," 116–48; Ira Berlin, *Slaves Without Masters: The Free Negro in the Antebellum South* (New York, 1974), 82; "A Freeman" [Ezekiel Cooper] to Green, *Maryland Gazette*, 1791[?], in Ezekiel Cooper Collection, Vol. XX, MS. 4, Garrett Evangelical Theological Seminary Library, Evanston, Ill., wherein Cooper argued that gradual emancipation as well as governmental action "will easily Suppress the gross, flagrant, Idleness either of Whites or Blacks"; Carter, *Diary*, II, 1148–49; *Virginia Gazette* (P), June 16, 1775; trial, December 1, 1778, Caroline C.C.O.B. (1777–80), 143. Even though Pennsylvania's liberal abolition law of 1780 declared that blacks convicted of crimes should be treated the same as white criminals, much of the strength of that stipulation was lost in the exception that "a slave shall not be admitted to bear witness against a freeman" (Roger Bruns [ed.], *Am I Not a Man and a Brother: The Antislavery Crusade of Revolutionary America, 1688–1788* [New York, 1977], 448–49).

tioners. Attempts to reenslave free black convicts reflected this thinking.

Given the importance of criminal prosecutions to the ultimate control of slaves, the interaction between slaves accused of crime and the whites who charged, tried, convicted or exonerated, and punished them took on new importance. Only when slaves themselves as well as changing economic and political conditions threatened the welfare of Virginia would the public debate over general emancipation reopen. The analysis of slaves and crime necessarily includes some discussion of the manner in which the changing conditions of all Virginians, both black and white, influenced and in turn were influenced by the behavior of slaves labeled by whites as criminal.

In spite of humanitarian, republican, or even self-interested reforms, 628 slaves would still be hanged from government-owned ropes between 1785 and 1865 for a variety of offenses. Nearly 900 other slaves would go into forced exile either outside the United States in Florida, Cuba, the Dry Tortugas, or some other deadly location, or else traders would smuggle them into such slave marts as New Orleans and sell them under circumstances that were more suspicious than usual. Many public petitions would vigorously support the executions and even lament what they called the leniency of transportation. Some enraged citizens would even swear to shoot exonerated slaves on sight; others would simply do so and remain anonymous and silent. As often as not, whites tried under the 1788 law for killing their slaves would be found not guilty, and others would successfully flee prosecution or even be rescued by groups of their friends. Some slaves suffered torture while in the custody of public officials. Others did not even get that far. As before the American Revolution, white authorities could shoot down outlawed slaves, after which the state auditor would remit the value of the dead slave to the owner of record. Patrollers remained active, sometimes more efficient in harassment or brutality than in their efforts to prevent the kind of behavior that concerned the authorities. Finally, the same events in Saint Domingue, Charleston, and Virginia that enabled some Virginian slaves to perceive rebellion in a new context also scared whites so badly that they began to search for and even enact new ways to suppress dangerous slaves in the Old Dominion.[4]

4. Supporting execution: Memorial concerning slave Hanover, received August 18, 1809, D. Jameson *et al.* to Governor Tyler, June 27, 1810, and Henry E. Watkins to William

It was by no means simply the declining economic welfare of the Commonwealth and its isolation in national politics that threatened slavery in the Old Dominion between the 1780s and the 1860s. The growing strength of abolitionism as well as the militancy of blacks elsewhere in the United States and the Western Hemisphere constituted a direct challenge to the increasingly peculiar institution. What was worse, as far as proslavery whites were concerned, was that some slaves, and even some white allies, mounted direct attacks on slaveholders in Virginia, the most dramatic of which were the Gabriel and Boxley plots and the devastating Nat Turner Revolt. When nervous whites debated in 1831 and 1832 whether their slave society could continue to be safe, the danger facing them was not just the ability of other Nat Turners to rebel collectively. There was also the proved willingness of many other slaves to attack whites in ways that the criminal justice system, much less individual owners, was having a difficult time suppressing.[5]

Slaves in Virginia had to be conscious of postrevolutionary changes in their lives and in the world around them. Tidewater slaves learned firsthand from the slaves of French refugees from Saint Domingue about the massive rebellion there. The "example of the West Indies" was one reason for servile unrest in Norfolk and Northampton County in 1792, Governor Lee indicated in May of 1792.[6] The slave grapevine undoubtedly conveyed news of such plots as Gabriel's all over Virginia; accounts of individual acts of defiance and resistance probably spread locally. Ironically, however, something was happening to the slave communities that would decrease their ability to threaten whites. The overwhelming and destructive demographic change that was so obvious after 1830 in fact began somewhat before that time.

Untold thousands of slaves fled with Dunmore and Cornwallis, and uncountable other Africans never got to Virginia because of the 1778 cessation of importation. By the 1820s, black Virginians had to endure

---

Richardson, Clerk of the Council, March 24, 1826, all in VEPLR. Shooting of exonerated slave: Affidavit of John Wilson, February 19, 1819, and Mayor of Norfolk to Governor Preston, February, 1819, both in VEPLR. Threat to shoot on sight: letters and petitions about Davie, September, 1794, in VEPLR.

5. Joseph C. Robert, *The Road from Monticello* (Durham, 1941); Alison Goodyear Freehling, *Drift Toward Dissolution: The Virginia Slavery Debate of 1831–1832* (Baton Rouge, 1982); Jack P. Maddex, Jr., *The Virginia Conservatives, 1865–1879* (Chapel Hill, 1970), 7–8.

6. Governor Henry Lee to Robert Goode, May 17, 1792, in Virginia Executive Letter Books, 1792–94, pp. 5–7, VSL.

Table 16.   Virginia's Slave Population, 1790–1830

Region	Slave Population (1790)	% of All Virginia Slaves	Slave Population (1830)	% of All Virginia Slaves	% Increase (1790–1830)	Annual Growth Rate (1790–1830)
Tidewater counties	109,697	37.5%	121,027	25.7%	10.3%	0.25%
Piedmont/Southside counties	178,262	60.9	320,604	68.0	79.8	1.50
Western counties	4,668	1.6	29,740	6.3	537.1	4.70
Virginia	292,627	100.0	471,371	100.0	61.1	1.20

SOURCES: U.S. Census Office, *The Statistics of the Population of the United States*, Vol. I, *Population and Social Statistics* (Washington, D.C., 1872), 68–72; and author's calculations.

Table 17.   Decennial Population Growth Rates, 1790–1830

	1790–1800	*1800–1810*	*1810–20*	*1820–30*
Slaves	1.7	1.3	0.8	1.0
Whites	1.5	0.7	0.9	1.4
Free blacks	6.8	4.1	1.8	2.1

SOURCES: U.S. Census Office, *The Statistics of the Population of the United States*, Vol. I, *Population and Social Statistics*, 68–72; *The Statistical History of the United States from Colonial Times to the Present* (Stamford, Conn., 1965), 756; author's calculations.

more partings—Tidewater slaves had to say "fare thee well" to the many Afro-Americans being carried into the Piedmont, Southside, and western regions. Slaves everywhere in Virginia had to watch more and more coffles of chained men and women, boys and girls, turn toward the new cotton states and territories in the Deep South. As Tables 16 and 17 indicate, the Tidewater slave population declined from nearly two-fifths of the state's enslaved population to a little more than one-quarter; the Piedmont and Southside population grew steadily on its own and as a portion of the Commonwealth's people in bondage. Several Tidewater counties were already losing slave population in the 1790s. This loss encompassed the other reason cited by Governor Lee for the unrest in 1792, namely, the "practice of severing husband, wife and children in sales."[7] Moreover, the entire state's slave population was growing at a slower annual rate than was the white population by the decade between 1810 and 1820. An already intolerable situation, then, grew worse after 1831.

In the midst of these developments, slaves continued to stand trial for a variety of major offenses. Chapters 8 through 10 explore the changing patterns in these trials between 1785 and 1831. From the mid-1780s, the recording of trials of slaves for felonies improved steadily. Trial records had to be sent to the state executive in capital cases, so the file is nearly complete. The increasing professionalization of court clerks, the initially voluntary and eventually mandatory providing of counsel for enslaved defendants in capital cases, and a gradual improvement in the standards of proof required for conviction all enhanced the quality of the testimony and cross-examination. This generally better record of evidence makes it possible to reach several valid

7. *Ibid.*

conclusions about the changing nature of the motives and behavior of slaves convicted of major crimes.[8]

The analysis in Chapters 8 through 10 stops at 1831 in order to make clear the context in which Nat Turner's Revolt occurred and to highlight the relationship between that momentous event and the last years of slave crime in the Old Dominion, a period to which Chapter 11 is devoted. The connection between bondspeople's major illegal behavior between the 1830s and the 1860s and the national conflict that led to the death of slavery is a subject too large to consider here. Chapter 11 only suggests the connection while exploring changes in slave crime between 1830 and the Civil War, as a consequence of which various governments finally recognized slavery itself as a crime throughout the United States.

8. Providing counsel and sending the trial record to the executive in capital cases are in Shepherd, *Statutes at Large*, I, 126, II, 280. Other improvements are apparent from inspection of many county records.

8. The Internal Enemy, 1785–1831

The post–War of 1812 cases of Old Matt and Matthew indicate the hidden dangers to which members of the slave society of Virginia continued to be subject between 1785 and 1831. They also illustrate the permanence of the conjurer's role in that society. These two men, nearly one hundred years of age and sixty, were convicted of poisoning some white people in Piedmont Cumberland County in 1816. "Old Mat, the Conjuror" was born about 1717. As such he was a direct link, either by African birth or by association with the high percentage of Africans in the colony in the early 1700s, to the African and early eighteenth-century past. His Afro-American son was a potential agent of cultural transmission from prerevolutionary times through the Revolution and to the new nation. But Old Matt died in prison, and Matthew was transported outside the United States. He would be only a historical example of cultural transmission in Piedmont Virginia.[1]

Numerous citizens of Cumberland were acutely aware that Matthew and Old Matt (and Daniel) allegedly had in 1816 poisoned white people. Their petition to the state governor and the council urged that the convicted poisoners be executed as examples: "The slaves in many parts of the United States have made attempt to make themselves

---

1. Slaves' testimony in trials of Matthew, Old Matt, Daniel, and Nancy, December, 1816, and January, 1817, Cumberland County, C.S., box 3, and VEPLR; "A List of Slaves and Free Persons of Color received into the Penitentiary . . . 1816 to . . . 1842," C.S., box 10. For Old Matt and Matthew's background, see Cumberland County Deed Book (1752–60), 30; Cumberland County Wills (1769–92), 378–80, (1792–1810), 97; Amelia C.C.O.B. (1751–55), 195; Amelia County Wills (1734–61), 115–16; Cumberland C.C.O.B. (1764–67), 133–34; "Macon Family," *WMQ*, 1st ser., X (April, 1902), 277; and Van Schreeven *et al.* (eds.), *Revolutionary Virginia*, VI, 394–95n11.

Map 3. Virginia Counties, 1800

Masters of our Country by rising in arms against us. That course failing, there [*sic*] resource now it appears in our neighborhood and Country to be by secretly taking the lives of whole familys by Poison and several of our Most Valuable Citizens have fallen Victims to that Nefarious practice lately, for which these three wretches above named were condemned." The petitioners saw the relationship between slave insurrections and poisoning, the secrecy inherent in the use of poisoning, the threat to white citizens (especially those who were powerful and those with families), the regional character of poisoning, and the way in which poisoning by slaves had become a tradition, a "Nefarious practice." The tradition would survive in the United States, being remembered by many Afro-Americans in the 1980s.[2]

Prosecutions for poisoning, sexual assault, and arson led many white Virginians to insist, as had old indictments, that all criminals were inspired by the Devil.[3] But white Virginians continued to have trouble detecting the "work of the Devil." The difficulty of uncovering poisoning and arson and the problem of defense against poisoning, sexual assault, arson, and stealing were conditions of which aggressive slaves could take advantage. Some had already been using poison for some years with great effect. Between 1785 and 1831, poisoning became somewhat more familiar to white Americans. Prosecutions for rape were less frequent than for poisonings, yet whites had become sufficiently anxious after 1785 that they pushed evidence beyond its limits and convicted slave men of rape who had done nothing illegal or who were "guilty" only of responding to invitations of one sort or another. By the 1820s, the perceived instances of rape were so many, the decade constitutes the peak of official white concern about sexual assault by slaves between the seventeenth century and the end of slavery. Arson increased definitely but not dramatically between 1785 and 1831. It would not become a primary weapon until the 1850s. For the time being, slaves were learning that it was a somewhat useful technique of resistance. Most of the felony convictions of slaves continued to be for theft.

The circumstances of slavery and the nature of the Old Dominion's

2. Petition of February 12, 1817, VEPLR; John Gwaltney, *Drylongso: A Self-Portrait of Black America* (New York, 1980), 43; John W. Blassingame, *The Slave Community: Plantation Life in the Antebellum South* (Rev. ed.; New York, 1979), 109–10, 113.

3. Jordan, *White Over Black*, 24, 39n80.

slave code maintained rape and arson by slaves as prosecuted crimes whose victims all were white.[4] Slaves were regularly prosecuted for poisoning other slaves. But only one-fifth (23 of 117) of the slaves convicted of poisoning or administering medicine between 1750 and 1784 had given substances to other slaves. The similar figures for 1785 to 1831 confirm that trend. Only 2 slaves were sentenced to death and none were transported for poisoning other blacks—a mere 5.7 percent of the 35 slaves so convicted and sentenced. At the very least, poisoning caused county and state officials less and less concern.[5]

Prosecutions of slaves for poisoning or administering medicine illegally to whites in several representative jurisdictions of Virginia remained rather steady yet low in frequency from 1785 to 1831. The cutoff date obscures the importance of the entire period, however. In the same locations, there were twenty-eight prosecutions for poisoning or illegal administration of medicine between 1785 and 1824 and only six in the next forty years. The transitional decade was the 1820s; there were three prosecutions from 1820 to 1824 and none between 1825 and 1829 or in 1830 and 1831. Convictions followed an even more revealing pattern in these representative places. From 1785 through 1799, five slaves received guilty verdicts; none did thereafter until three were convicted in the same incident in 1859.

The fear of poisoning had clearly outstripped its officially detected occurrence. The extreme public reaction becomes apparent when Old Matt's use of poison is related to the number of major poisoning convictions at the time. These convictions did not represent all incidences of slaves' poisoning of whites. Moreover, even one incident of successful poisoning had an impact beyond its statistical value. Yet Virginian prosecutors obtained only eight capital convictions of slaves for poisoning of whites between 1810 and 1819.[6] Those who petitioned the

4. Not a single conviction of a slave for raping a slave appears in state records for 1785 to 1831, nor did any such prosecutions take place in several representative counties and a city. The same is true of arson. Surveyed are Brunswick (1786–99), Essex (1786–1831), Henrico (1786–1802), Henry (1786–1831), Southampton (1786–1831), and Spotsylvania (1786–1831), and the city of Richmond (1786–99).
5. Between 1750 and 1784, known courts sentenced seven slaves to execution for poisoning of or administering medicine to other slaves. See also James L. Smith, *Autobiography of James L. Smith* (Norwich, Conn., 1881; New York, 1969), 4–7.
6. During the same years in Essex, Henry, Southampton, and Spotsylvania counties, there were eight prosecutions but no convictions of slaves for poisoning or illegal administration of medicine.

authorities about Old Matt and his accomplices perceived a widespread conspiracy at work. Other people were able to be somewhat more specific about the kinds of poison being used—somewhat more so than were eighteenth-century white observers. Tales of poisoning spread even when no trials occurred. And the reputation of some slave conjurers grew well before a court conviction gave substantiation.

Some whites and many slaves cooperated in ascribing great powers to certain slaves. Pleading for protection, a slave informer in Virginia put the case simply in 1802. "The white men will only whip me openly, and the blk man will kill slyly and that I had rather be hanged than poisoned." If whites did not call an Old Matt or someone else a conjurer, they named him "Dr. Billy" or "Dr. Jim." A white Nottoway County doctor acknowledged the power held by Dr. Billy in 1807. He had a reputation as "a preparer, adviser and exhibitor of poisons," which he made a "trade" of selling. The physician said that his practice showed him that many more cases of poisoning occurred in Dr. Billy's neighborhood than elsewhere. Indeed, he added, "I doubt not but what we have many such Characters among us as Billy who are said to make an income by retailing such preparations to our negroes." Another physician discounted the reputation of a contemporary Pittsylvania County conjurer. Named in a slave's testimony as a conjurer who had poisoned two white children, Tom was sentenced to death for the illegal preparation and exhibition of medicine. At the trial of his alleged accessory, however, Dr. James D. Patton of Danville resolutely denied that the children in question had died from poisoning. But Tom's reputation was still somewhat intact.[7]

Thus had the phenomenon of poisoning become an expected part of the slave society of Virginia. It remained closely connected to fundamental relationships of power, yet it had become somewhat less mysterious and foreign, and many white authorities understood it a bit

7. Informer in VEPLR, May 5, 1802, interview at Nottoway County jail, and quoted—in a reading somewhat at variance with mine—in Johnston, *Race Relations in Virginia*, 68; Dr. James Jones to Governor Cabell, May 19, 1807, in VEPLR; trial of Mingo Jackson, alias Dr. Jackson, August 15, 1809, Henrico C.C.O.B. (1808–1809), 475; Thomas Massie to Dr. William B. Hare, January 1, 1818, in U. B. Phillips Papers, Sterling Memorial Library, Yale University; trials of Tom and Amy, January 20, 1806, Pittsylvania County, both in VEPLR. For other statements about conjurers, see trial of George, June 1, 1791, Fauquier County, *CVSP*, V, 333–39; trial of Paul, May 17, 1794, Powhatan County, C.S., box 1, and VEPLR; trial of Delphy, June 10, 1816, Louisa County, VEPLR. There were even accusations that some conjurers used their arts to seduce white women (Wyatt-Brown, *Southern Honor*, 315–16).

better. Poisoning was an Afro-American practice and reflected changing social contexts. Legal importation of Africans into Virginia ended in 1778. Slaves used poison primarily against whites, relying on domestic American substances such as Jamestown weed, arsenic, roots, and ground glass. Further, poisoning was closely defined by white lawmakers.[8]

Between 1785 and 1831, slaves in the Old Dominion continued to learn how to deal with whites' fear of sexual assault by slaves. Bondsmen apparently did not depend on sexual assault to frighten whites occasionally or retaliate against them, as slaves did use poisoning. What made slaves' learning efforts so difficult was that whites had conflicting perceptions of slaves' behavior. One thing that some blacks understood stands out in the expression of moral guilt by several accused or convicted men. These statements may have been made to throw whites off balance or for self-interested reasons, yet the context was apparently well understood. For example, when a Westmoreland County white man caught Mooklar, whom a "spinster" and her companion had identified as a rapist, he asked the imperiled slave about being condemned to death. Rather than make any excuses, keep silent, or act defiant, Mooklar simply said that he did deserve execution. A slave in Cumberland County who was later executed for rape and murder of a ten-year-old child asked another slave to pray for him because "he had done that, which he was afraid he should never get over." This statement was not surprising from a man later convicted of killing a child, but he also had a reputation as consistently defiant. According to two white witnesses, he "had been roguish and frequently offended the neighbours," "he had been a rogue and would steal any little thing," and he was the "vilest negro in the neighbourhood." In 1817 a Franklin County slave went one step farther than Mooklar and Charles. Charged with having raped a young woman, Anthony told the jailer that "he was overpowered by the Devil which induced him to commit the said offence."[9]

Although rape of white females by male slaves was a familiar charge

8. As an indication of the degree to which an Afro-American could be cut off from the African past, testimony in one trial indicated that the accused had heard a white doctor, and not a conjurer, identify the poison (trial of Kesiah, February 3, 1829, Henrico County, C.S., box 5, and VEPLR).

9. Trial of Mooklar, August 22, 1808, Westmoreland County, C.S., box 2; trial of Charles, July 15, 1826, Cumberland County, C.S., box 5, and VEPLR; trials of Anthony, September 15, 1817, October 1, 1818, Franklin County, C.S., box 3, and VEPLR.

in nineteenth-century Virginia, it still had not provoked the level of fear that the threat of poisoning did. Attempted rape and rape convictions of slaves were in fact likely to lead to collective petitions for mercy and pardons rather than to the insistence on castration, transportation, or execution.[10] Yet convictions occurred regularly. The laws of the Commonwealth help to show what kinds of sexual assault by slaves were criminalized and punished when officially detected after 1785. The 1792 revision of the slave code left intact the old sanctions of hanging for rape and castration for attempted rape of a white woman. An 1805 act said that attempted rape of a white female would be considered a felony and punished "as heretofore," thus perpetuating the old penalties. It was in 1823, however, that the legislature attached the death penalty to the offense of attempted rape of a white female, a punishment that was retained as long as there was a slave code.[11]

In this legal context, slaves charged with sexual crimes seem to have been in grave peril. But confusion or ignorance could work in favor of an accused slave. In Cumberland County, a commonwealth's attorney labored mightily in an 1819 rape trial to elicit from the white accuser the information needed to establish that a common law rape had occurred, that is, force, penetration, and emission. Elizabeth Smith testified that William Bosher's Dennis had thrown her on a bed and gotten on top of her, then acted "violently." He did not force his way inside her, she added, but "he done as he pleased Rogered her and got off: after satisfying himself." Rapidly losing his case for a rape, the prosecuting attorney asked, "In plain english, did he fuck you?" She answered, "Yes he did." But immediately upon being questioned about the meaning of the entering of her body, she declared she did not understand. She later asserted that she was still a virgin, even though she maintained that penetration and emission had occurred.[12]

The peril was, however, real. When hearing attempted rape and rape cases, judges faced the fundamental difficulty of how to determine whether the accuser was actually taking advantage of slaves' legal

10. See, for example, case papers for a Westmoreland County trial on September 22, 1800, VEPLR. The state executive pardoned the two slaves convicted in this trial. See also Johnston, *Race Relations in Virginia*, 258–62.

11. Convicted slaves could still receive benefit of clergy. Shepherd, *Statutes at Large*, I, 125, III, 119; James Curtis Ballagh, *A History of Slavery in Virginia* (Baltimore, 1902), 86; *Supplement to the Revised Code of the Laws*, 280–81.

12. Officials remarked in a message to the governor and the council that Elizabeth Smith appeared "to be a very simple weak woman." Dennis ended the confusion by escaping from jail. Trial, June 10, 1819, and accompanying documents, VEPLR.

disabilities in order to escape the public opprobrium attendant upon bearing a mulatto child or to harm the charged slave in some other way. However, a Mecklenburg County slave learned in 1829 that even the testimony of white witnesses could not protect him, once the court believed a free black woman's story that he had broken into her house and violated her brutally. According to Amey Baker's testimony, Lewis had stated that "he came for *cunt* and *cunt* he would have, that he had been told there was a plenty of it there and he would have his satisfaction before he left the house or kill" her and her companion. After two whites stated that various white and black men regularly visited Amey Baker's house to have sex with her and her companion, five other men gave her a good character report. The judges accepted the word of the victim, even though she was a free black, and of those witnesses whose testimony supported her good reputation. Lewis hanged.[13]

Like the evidence from eighteenth-century trials of slaves for rape, that from nineteenth-century trials leaves some room for doubt about the extent to which any slaves used rape as a means of resistance to slavery. There are some suggestive cases, but they are only that—suggestive.[14] Other trials reflect Brownmiller's theory that rape is aggression against vulnerable targets. Of fifty-one adult women named as victims in trials that resulted in conviction, seven were labeled "spinsters," three were widows, and twenty-two were named without being identified as someone's wife. Only nineteen were listed as "Mrs." or as someone's wife. Moreover, even the married victims sometimes testified that they had unsuccessfully used various stratagems to try to convince the would-be rapists that their husbands were nearby. Almost all the testimony included clear assertions that, by definition and as might be expected, the rapes happened only after the male slaves used their greater strength or a weapon to overpower or intimidate the victims.[15]

13. Trial of Lewis, June 15, 1829, C.S., box 5, and VEPLR. In some cases, the supposed victim was accused of being a whore or "person of bad character" (trials of Jerry, May 25, 1807, Henry County, Peter, October, 1808, Hanover County, and Ben, August 7, 1810, Prince William County, VEPLR; trial of Fern, May 12, 1792, Spotsylvania C.C.O.B. [1787–92], 646–47, [1792–95], 60). See also Johnston, *Race Relations in Virginia*, 258–62.

14. See trial of Armistead, alias John Tyree, May 1, 1823, Caroline County, C.S., box 4, and Court of Quarterly Sessions, Caroline County, August 13, 1821, and accompanying documents, Caroline County Historical Papers, box 3, VSL; *Commonwealth v. Tyree*, 2 Va. Cases 262 (1821), excerpted in Catterall, *Judicial Cases*, I, 134–35; trial of Joseph, October 6, 1829, Shenandoah County, C.S., box 5, and VEPLR.

15. Susan Brownmiller, *Against Our Will: Men, Women, and Rape* (New York, 1975), esp. 210–55; trials of Tom, January 11, 1810, New Kent County, and Gabriel, June 12,

The factor of aggression also appears in those cases in which the rape was supposed to have occurred during the commission of another aggressive crime, such as burglary during the night in a dwelling. The few cases of child molestation certainly exhibit aggression, but they may also be evidence of pathological behavior.[16] Other cases, such as those involving free black victims, definitely exclude conscious resistance as a motive. The relatively lenient sentences given most of the slaves convicted for raping free black women suggest that white perceptions of the racial factor in sex crimes were critical between 1785 and 1831 just as they would be in the more well known period from the Civil War into the twentieth century.[17]

The laws concerning, and the trials of slaves for, rape of white females between 1785 and 1829 do reveal that white leaders perceived more danger to white women from slave rapists at some times than at others. In Figure 1, though the number of major convictions remained fairly constant through most of these years, there were distinct peaks, some of which relate to a change in the law. One obvious peak was between 1820 and 1824. The real change in the number of rape trials occurred after the 1823 raising of the penalty for attempted rape from castration to hanging.[18] Thus the modification was as much a response to a perceived increase in the danger of rape as it was an effort to deal with conduct construed as attempted rape. Figure 1 also highlights the temporary increase in sentences of death or transportation for slaves'

1829, Patrick County, VEPLR; trials of Mooklar, August 22, 1808, Westmoreland County, David, April 18, 1808, Amherst County, and Jack, August 25, 1818, Orange County, VEPLR. See also Norfolk (Va.) *Herald,* May 16, 1822, quoted in Savannah *Daily Georgian,* May 25, 1822.

16. Trials of Harry and Nelson, September 9, 1788, Nelson County, and Jamey, June 9, 1803, Jefferson County, VEPLR; trial of Dick, November 19, 1808, Southampton County, VEPLR; trials of Peter for rape of an "infant" (under twelve), Patrick County, and Jack for rape of a six-year-old, November 6, 1822, Wood County (now West Virginia), VEPLR.

17. Trial of Ned, July 20, 1790, Essex C.C.O.B. (1788–90), 298; trial of Tom, June 27, 1797, Surry County Criminal Court Proceedings, unpaginated, and C.S., box 1; trial of Tom, January 11, 1810, New Kent County, C.S., box 2, and VEPLR; trial of Tasco Thompson, October 18, 1833, VEPLR, as quoted in Johnston, *Race Relations in Virginia,* 262–63. It is historically appropriate that white citizens of Southampton County were particularly conscious of the implications of free black status in a slave society. The free black population of that county was distinctive for its size and independence, a subject that needs detailed study.

18. There was once a legend of the absence of rapes by slaves. See Johnston, *Race Relations in Virginia,* 257; Phillips, "Slave Crime in Virginia," 337; Brownmiller, *Against Our Will,* 128. In *From Rebellion to Revolution,* 104–105, 109–10, Genovese discusses the absence of evidence concerning rapes by slaves involved in North American insurrection plots or outbreaks.

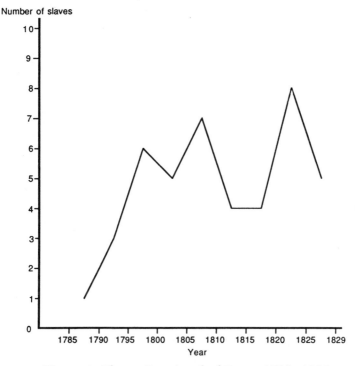

Figure 1. Slaves Convicted of Rape, 1785–1829

attempted rapes of white women after the change in the law.

Although the tightening of the slave code provisions concerning sexual assault continued until slavery ended, the concern of white judicial authorities about such aggressive and dangerous behavior was definitely higher before 1831 than after.[19] From 1785 to 1831, there were thirty-nine slaves who were executed for raping white women; between 1832 and 1865, the number was nineteen. The use of capital punishment against slaves convicted of rape decreased from 0.85 instances per year in the first period to 0.58 instances per year in the second. Measured specifically in relation to the year in which the penalty for attempted rape changed, the use of capital punishment for rape decreased from an annual occurrence of 0.78 to 0.67. The comparable figures for attempted rape, however, were 0.17 (1785–1831), 0.24 (1832–65), and 0.08 (1785–1822), and 0.45 (1823–65), showing a real rise in the use of capital punishment for attempted rape. Of even

19. *Acts of the General Assembly*, 1836–37, p. 49.

greater importance is the degree of change in the separate periods beginning in 1823 and 1832. The transitional years were clearly those between 1823 and 1831, close to the transitional years for poisoning trials and convictions.

This significant increase in white authorities' fear concerning slaves' sexual aggressiveness against white females during the 1820s resembles the fears about assault, attempted murder, and murder of whites by slaves during the same period. In fact, there is also a similarity among the conviction statistics for rape, attempted rape, murder, attempted murder, assault, and, to some degree, poisoning of whites by slaves in the period from 1795 to 1799. Those years and the years from 1820 to 1829 preceded the times of greatest fear of insurrection and, in the cases of Gabriel and Nat Turner, of the greatest insurrectionary planning or activity. The aggression against white people caused the most anxiety about all these kinds of slave behavior, both individual and collective. That aggression presented two real dangers to white people, the loss of life or physical safety and the loss of slavery.

Whites perceived rape by slaves of white women as resistance to slavery, but only in relationship to their perception that such rape was a danger to the safety of white women and the honor of white men and women. Proslavery whites understood slave resistance as behavior that threatened slavery, not as political action or heroic opposition to oppression. This understanding strongly reinforced their determination to punish slaves for sexual assault as defined by common law and by the preservers of slavery. Common law recognized rape as an offense against the person; the slave code and the slave courts regarded it also as an intolerable attack against slavery and white supremacy.

After the American Revolution, the fear white people expressed about arson by slaves resembled their fear of poisoning and rape. By the 1790s, Virginians had grown more defensive about fire.[20] When Frederick County planter Rawleigh Colston lost his home in a fire, a thirteen- or fourteen-year-old slave he had purchased as a house servant less than a year before faced execution. Colston was stunned, he

---

20. During the 1790s, prominent men such as John Marshall and William Foushee of Richmond helped to found the Mutual Assurance Society of Virginia, which would provide the first fire insurance to many of the Old Dominion's businesses and showplace plantation homes. *Papers of John Marshall*, ed. Herbert A. Johnson and Charles T. Cullen (5 vols. to date; Chapel Hill, 1974–), II, 296–97, III, 43–44; Shepherd, *Statutes at Large*, I, 307–10, 405–406. See also Thomas Armstrong, " 'Have We No Police?' The Evolution of Ante-Bellum Police Systems in Virginia" (Typescript, 1976, courtesy of the author), 4, 8.

wrote to John Marshall, that ninety-two Frederick County citizens had petitioned the governor and the council to pardon William "under the false pretext of humanity." Not only did this seem to Colston a selective application of a "benign principle" to "those who had been guilty of the most atrocious crimes," but it flew in the face of the "many *horrid* acts of the same kind which had lately passed with impunity, for the want of proof—regardless of the future security of individuals, whose families may be involved in utter ruin, if not involved in the flames." Colston went on to describe to Marshall several unpunished instances of houses or barns (with grain or corn) destroyed or nearly so. All these fires were of suspicious origin.[21]

As in previous years, it was hard to convict arsonists. Only one-third of the slaves tried for arson in Essex, Henry, Southampton, and Spotsylvania counties between 1785 and 1831 received guilty verdicts. But the whole number of slaves convicted did rise after 1785. The available records of trials between 1706 and 1784 contain only thirteen arson convictions; the centralized state records of execution and transportation for arson include thirty-nine slaves for the years from 1785 to 1831. (This figure does not, of course, include slaves convicted but granted benefit of clergy.) The number per year for the earlier period was 0.12. For 1785 to 1831, it was 0.85. Even if we double the figure for earlier years to account for lost records, the annual number rises only to nearly 0.23. This rise outstripped population growth.

When the Old Dominion reached the peak of its development in the eighteenth century and more and more planters sought to build finished, rather than cheap and temporary, dwellings and outbuildings, slaves who resorted to arson could do much more damage. A fragment of the returns for the United States direct tax of 1798 in one parish of Spotsylvania County confirms the notion that semipermanent and permanent structures abounded and were within easy reach of many slaves. Opportunity was only one factor. Slave arsonists had to deal with a practical condition: fear of fire kept people on the lookout for it. Only an effective, fast-burning fire had the potential to do damage, sufficient to satisfy the wish for revenge, before the owner could try to extinguish it. The court records are often silent about what was burned, but in the twenty-four cases in which that informa-

21. *Papers of John Marshall,* III, 36–38; trial of William, August 3, 1796, Frederick County, C.S., box 1, and VEPLR. William was executed.

tion is given, the presence of grain or hay was prominent, particularly in the northern Virginia incidents. Other kinds of burnings occurred, such as jails and a shop, but agricultural buildings suffered the most damage from slave arsonists.[22]

The slaves convicted of arson resembled other bondspeople found guilty of crimes in some ways.[23] A key similarity was their ages.[24] Of those slaves found guilty of arson, however, a smaller percentage (32.3 percent) used arson as a weapon against their owners than did slaves convicted of poisoning (51.5 percent) or violently killing white people (48.6 percent). Problems of detection no doubt had something to do with this discrepancy. The simple conviction rate for poisoning in Essex, Henry, Southampton, and Spotsylvania counties between 1785 and 1831 was 7 percent; the rate for arson was 33.3 percent. What seems to be at work as well is a lower level of personal hostility in arson incidents than in poisonings and killings. Arsonists almost always wanted to destroy a white enemy's property but not the person. A few such cases existed but were a distinct minority.[25]

The other atypical characteristic of slave arsonists is the relatively large number of women among them. Some 23.1 percent of all ex-

22. Cary Carson, "Homestead Architecture in the Chesapeake Colonies" (Paper presented to the Forty-first Conference of the Institute of Early American History and Culture, April 30, 1981, Millersville [Pa.] State College); U.S. Treasury Department, Bureau of Internal Revenue, Virginia, Spotsylvania County Tax Book, 1798, in Holladay Family Papers, 1728–1931, sec. 86, VHS; trials of Claiborne, January 13, 1798, Petersburg, and Eldred, March 9, 1830, Caroline County, C.S., boxes 1, 5; trials of Billy and Caesar, November 29, 1811, Elizabeth City C.C.O.B. (1808–16), 220–21, and C.S., box 3.

23. Motives for arson resembled those for many other kinds of attacks on whites. See, for example, *Papers of John Marshall*, III, 36–38; trial of William, August 3, 1796, Frederick County, C.S., box 1, and VEPLR; trials of Sarah, June 11, 1806, King George County, Winney, May 5, 1806, Frederick County, Winney, December 23, 1818, Greenbrier County (now West Virginia), Tom, November 4, 1819, Nottoway County, and Ann, April 21, 1826, Spotsylvania County, C.S., boxes 1–5, and VEPLR.

24. The average age of men transported for all offenses in the years from 1816 to 1842 was 25.5; that of the women was 21.5. The thirty-five women were 10.2 percent of all the transported bondspeople. Of the fifteen slaves deported for arson between 1801 and 1831, two were women, and the mean ages for the men and the women were, respectively, 26.8 and 26.5. The small size of the group makes it difficult to draw firm statistical conclusions, but they do appear to have been fairly typical of other convicted slaves. "A List of Slaves and Free Persons of Color received into the Penitentiary . . . 1816 to . . . 1842," C.S., box 10.

25. In one case the death of the inhabitants was supposed to have been the slave arsonist's objective (trials of John Fox and Nelson, May 21, 1816, Gloucester County, C.S., box 3, and VEPLR). In another, arsonists were charged with having burned the corpses of two white people whom they had already killed (trials of Abel and Celia, June 28, 1821, Southampton C.C.O.B. [1819–21], 321–27, and C.S., box 4).

ecuted as well as banished slave arsonists during those years were women. The only major crime with a higher rate was poisoning or administering medicine, for which 27.3 percent of the convicts were women. Since 28.6 percent of the slaves convicted of felony or misdemeanor arson in known slave courts of the Old Dominion between 1740 and 1785 were women, it is apparent that arson, like poisoning, continued to appeal to the physically weaker sex as a weapon against white people. In some instances, whites were victimizing other whites by means of slave arsonists, since whites knew that the slaves could never testify against them.[26]

That the Frederick County authorities, with the consent of the governor and the council, executed a teenaged boy for arson is but one indication of how seriously white leaders took the threat of arson, especially against members of the elite. A 1799 resolution of the Norfolk Common Council concerning a recent danger of fire reveals a real concern about arson and also about the possible identity of the arsonists. In March, 1799, the city officials offered a reward of $500, or emancipation in the case of a slave, for apprehension and conviction of "the person or persons who attempted to set fire to this Borough the last evening." That emancipation was available ensured that the legal meaning of "person or persons" encompassed slaves as well as free people. Later the same year, Absalom Johnson of Henrico assumed that an angry Solomon would resort to fire or some other means to carry out a personal threat. Little did Johnson know, of course, that less than a year later Gabriel and his allies would plan to burn buildings on a large scale as the first step in taking over Richmond.[27]

Arson by slaves was thus one more indication that whites simultaneously feared that slaves would attack or damage them in some way and generally had little idea whether any particular slave presented a clear and present danger. Slave narratives of various kinds are replete with testimony of their knowledge that fear and ignorance about intentions made ordinarily powerful whites somewhat vulnerable to

26. Trial of Jim, December 4, 1811, Buckingham County, C.S., box 3; trial of George, April 29, 1791, Fauquier C.C.M.B. (1791–93), 416–17, and C.S., box 1, and VEPLR, and CVSP, V, 333–39; trial, June 1, 1807, Henrico C.C.O.B. (1807–1808), 155–56; Representation of Robert Preston, Washington County, May 22, 1809, VEPLR.

27. Norfolk Borough MS. Common Council Order Book, no. 2, March 15, 1799, p. 3, Office of the City Clerk, Norfolk, Va. See also Henrico C.C.O.B. (1799–1801), 94; Mullin, Flight and Rebellion, 150–51; and Tommy Lee Bogger, "The Slave and Free Black Community in Norfolk, 1775–1865" (Ph.D. dissertation, University of Virginia, 1976), 123–26.

ordinarily less powerful slaves' attacks.[28] Slaves feared harsh reprisal and suffered from ignorance of white people's intentions. They undoubtedly missed many a chance to take the offensive.

Reciprocal fear and mutual ignorance would take form with respect to arson by slaves as many Virginians settled into a relatively new way of life in a predominantly plantation society. Arson threatened to become an urban crime as well. Only 10 percent of the convictions of slaves for major arson between 1785 and 1831 were in town or city slave courts. That figure rose only to 15.8 percent between 1832 and 1865, but more than 80 percent of those (ten of twelve) were in the city of Richmond alone. In 1828, two slaves stood trial for burning the barns of William Jarvis and Judge John Marshall in Henrico County, at the edge of the city of Richmond. Both were found guilty. Insured or not by the Mutual Assurance Society, not even John Marshall, Chief Justice of the United States, was safe from a slave arsonist, *if* a slave in fact burned his barn.[29] We remain ignorant. Other town and city dwellers were equally vulnerable to arson, just as they were to burglary and theft.

One difference between arson and theft is that traditions had grown concerning the various forms of larceny and burglary before the Revolution. The conflicting perceptions and behavior of whites and slaves concerning stealing became somewhat entrenched between the 1780s and the 1820s. Often believing slaves were generally thieves, white authorities in slave societies such as Virginia nevertheless knew better than to think that they could eliminate stealing by slaves.[30] But it was not just white authorities who had developed a characteristic attitude. The slaves themselves, like slaves throughout the Western Hemisphere, had formulated an ideological distinction between taking and stealing.[31]

28. White Virginians would regret not prosecuting slaves suspected of arson (trial of Mary, August 7, 1819, Prince William County, C.S., box 4, and VEPLR; William A. G. Dade to council members James E. Heath and P. V. Daniel, August 11, 1819, in VEPLR; trials of Ben, Joe, Bob, Lewis, Bob, and Dick, December 10, 1819, Albemarle County, C.S., box 4, and VEPLR; Robert Davis to [?], December 13, 1819, in VEPLR; trial of Pat, March 31, 1820, Charlotte C.C.O.B. [1818–20], 232–35, and C.S., box 4). See Rawick (ed.), *The American Slave, passim; Weevils in the Wheat.*

29. Aptheker, *American Negro Slave Revolts,* 23, 144, 146, 266; trials, June 2, 1828, Henrico C.C.M.B. (1827–29), 237; *Papers of John Marshall,* III, 16–18 (Marshall's 1796 Mutual Assurance Society policy for his home and stable shows that the latter was just over the boundary between the city of Richmond and Henrico County).

30. For a Virginia example, see Elijah Fletcher to Jesse Fletcher, January 11, 1811, in *The Letters of Elijah Fletcher,* ed. Martha von Briesen (Charlottesville, 1965), 25–26.

31. *Minutes of the Baptist Association, in the District of Goshen: Held at Bethel Meeting-*

THE INTERNAL ENEMY 215

Private and public authorities created another important aspect of the context in which taking by slaves occurred. The oyer and terminer court records give two clear indications of whites' reactions to major thefts by slaves. First, between 1785 and 1831, only seven slaves were executed or transported for major stealing from their owners. Between 1740 and 1784, however at least three dozen slaves received guilty verdicts for the same crime, and masters almost exclusively dealt with their property's attack on their property. Second, when slaves did appear before oyer and terminer justices, the punishments became less harsh as time passed. In Essex, Henry, Southampton, and Spotsylvania counties, 62.8 percent (fifty-four of eighty-six) of all slaves found guilty of felonious, capital stealing were granted benefit of clergy between 1785 and 1831. Twenty-two others received only misdemeanor convictions. A total of ten were sentenced to hang or be transported, but several of them received pardons. Between 1785 and 1799 in Virginia, thirty-one slaves were executed for stealing. That number included all the slaves convicted of capital stealing, burglary, or robbery and not pardoned by the governor and the council. From 1801 to 1831, however, the availability of the penalty of transportation made a sort of amelioration possible. One hundred eighty-seven slaves were transported for stealing in those years; twenty-two were executed.[32]

House, Caroline County, Virginia . . . 1816 (Fredericksburg, 1816), 7–8; Charles H. Nichols, Jr., "The Case of William Grimes, the Runaway Slave," *WMQ*, 3rd ser., VIII (1951), 556; Frederick Douglass, *The Life and Times of Frederick Douglass Written by Himself* (Rev. ed., 1892; London, 1962), 104–105; Mintz and Price, *An Anthropological Approach to the Afro-American Past*, 20; Rose (ed.), *A Documentary History*, 251, 278; Mullin (ed.), *American Negro Slavery*, 156; Charles Ball, *Slavery in the United States: A Narrative of the Life of Charles Ball* (Lewiston, Pa., 1836), 74; Eugene D. Genovese, *In Red and Black: Marxian Explorations in Southern and Afro-American History* (Knoxville, 1984), 135–36; Albert J. Raboteau, *Slave Religion: The "Invisible Institution" in the Antebellum South* (New York, 1978), 294–97; Michael Craton et al. (eds.), *Slavery, Abolition, and Emancipation: Black Slaves and the British Empire: A Thematic Documentary* (London, 1976), 141; Stanley Feldstein, *Once a Slave: The Slaves' View of Slavery* (New York, 1971), 175–77; Lawrence W. Levine, *Black Culture and Black Consciousness: Afro-American Thought from Slavery to Freedom* (New York, 1977), 121–25; "A Freeman" [Ezekiel Cooper] to Green, *Maryland Gazette*, 1791[?], in Cooper Collection, Vol. XX, MS. 4, Garrett. Comparison with the political dimension of endemic theft by a more modern group of workers is possible. Michael Grottner has concluded that constant pilferage by dockworkers in Hamburg, Germany, in the early twentieth century was "a form of social conflict, a form of struggle between workers and employers, which precipitated . . . certain changes on both sides in the configuration of power structures" ("Working Class Crime and the Labour Movement: Pilfering in the Hamburg Docks," in Richard J. Evans [ed.], *The German Working Class, 1888–1933: The Politics of Everyday Life* [Totowa, N.J., 1982], 54–79, esp. 61).

32. Only eight slaves would be executed for stealing between 1832 and 1865, so the figures for 1800 to 1831 were definitely part of an ameliorative trend. Moreover, most of

Slaves involved in major thefts faced less and less risk during the 1780s and through the 1820s. Whenever white authorities chose not to execute slaves for crimes other than first-degree murder, they were in fact moving the penal code for slaves closer and closer to that for free people.[33] The increasingly smaller number of hangings of slaves convicted of property crimes between 1785 and 1831 shows that white authorities came to regard major stealing by slaves as less reprehensible and dangerous as time passed. "I have always been Averst to taking away the Life of a Slave for the Crime of Stealing," a slaveowner wrote to Governor Cabell in 1806. This change in attitude could not have escaped the slaves. Few would know the overall figures for Virginia, to be sure, but slaves in Essex, Henry, Southampton, and Spotsylvania counties, for example, certainly had some idea of the decline in executions in their counties for such convictions—a decline we can measure fairly exactly. From 1785 to 1801, there were ten slaves in those counties sentenced to hang for stealing; only one did go to the gallows, and he was in Southampton County in 1789.[34]

But enslaved Virginians still had to be aware of the special risks they were taking. For example, of the five white men in the Virginia Penitentiary in July, 1810, convicted of burglary, four had five-year terms and one had ten years. During the same years in which these five white men were sentenced to prison terms (May, 1806, to July, 1810), eighteen slaves were transported and two executed upon being convicted of burglary. In spite of the lack of statistics as to the respective numbers of free whites and slaves tried for burglary, it is still apparent that even though locks were picked or doors and windows forced and property taken in both instances, slave burglars faced a higher risk than did free white ones.[35]

---

the executions for property crimes between 1800 and 1865 were for robbery. It was the use of force and violence that led to executions of slaves also found guilty of crimes against property.

33. In the 1790s, legislators removed from the penal code for free Virginians the death penalty for all crimes except murder in the first degree (Shepherd, *Statutes at Large*, II, 8). I have developed this argument in "Slaves and Capital Punishment" (Paper presented at the Southern Historical Association convention, November, 1985, Houston).

34. John Caruthers to Governor Cabell, June 10, 1806, VEPLR; trial of Ned, December 4, 1789, Southampton C.C.M.B. (1786–90), unpaginated, and C.S., box 1. Ned was convicted of nighttime burglary and theft of goods worth £50.

35. "List of Prisoners in the Penitentiary on 1st July 1810," VEPLR. The same list includes four free blacks in prison for burglary—two had five-year terms, one had a seven-year term, and one had a ten-year term.

Which slaves took the big risks in order to steal? It is obvious that they were the most aggressive ones. We also know the ages of nearly 80 percent of the 124 slaves convicted of and transported for stealing in Virginia between mid-1816 and mid-1842. Their mean age was just over twenty-six. The average age of all 344 slaves transported during that period was just over twenty-five. Most of the slaves deported for theft were between the ages of twenty and thirty-four; twenty others were fifteen to nineteen; and fifteen more were between thirty-five and fifty. There was none younger than fifteen or older than fifty.[36]

Major stealing was very much the activity of enslaved men. A striking characteristic of the slaves transported or executed for theft between 1785 and 1831 is that only one of them was a woman. Thirty-five women were banished from the Commonwealth for other crimes between 1816 and 1842, a little more than 10 percent of the slaves deported. One woman was exiled in early 1816 for stealing; about one hundred slaves were transported for stealing between mid-1816 and December, 1831.[37] The low numbers did not necessarily result from slaveowners' hesitation to part with a slave whose child-bearing capacity increased her ability to return the owner's original investment. First, judges regularly sentenced women to transportation when they were convicted of arson, poisoning, or violent crimes. Second, other factors than owners' wishes may have led slave women to decide against committing major thefts. Third, the trial records from the slave courts of seven representative jurisdictions show that few slave women were even tried for stealing, much less convicted.[38]

36. Three Southampton County cases exemplify the aggressiveness of some slaves. Trials of Tom, April 26, 1820, Dred, May 16, 1821, and Sam, July 16, 1821, Southampton C.C.O.B. (1819–22), 305–306, 329–30, 332–33, and C.S., box 4; Henry Irving Tragle (ed.), *The Southampton Slave Revolt of 1831: A Compilation of Source Material* (New York, 1971), 446; trial of Tom (property of Robert Ricks), April 26, 1820, Southampton C.C.O.B. (1819–22), 135; Thomas C. Parramore, *Southampton County, Virginia* (Charlottesville, 1978), 70–71. A Tom, property of Robert Ricks, stood trial for conspiracy to murder the whites of Southampton County in 1801 but was found not guilty (Southampton C.C.M.B. [1799–1803], 152). "A List of Slaves and Free Persons of Color received into the Penitentiary . . . 1816 to . . . 1842," C.S., box 10.

37. Trial of Betty, January 24, 1816, Norfolk city, C.S., box 3, and VEPLR. She was convicted of stealing blankets, quilts, pillowcases, a sheet, two goblets, and a one-pint tumbler, the whole being worth $22.

38. The jurisdictions were Essex, Henry, Southampton, and Spotsylvania (1785–1831), Brunswick and Henrico (1785–1800), and city of Richmond (1785–1800). Of the twelve women tried for major stealing—six in Richmond alone—four were convicted, three of whom were in Richmond. Six women were tried for hog stealing, three convicted.

Did many slaves "make a career" out of major stealing between 1785 and 1831?[39] The court documents of seven representative jurisdictions do contain some indication that certain slaves successfully continued to bring valuable items into their possession—for a while. Runaways almost had to continue stealing. They might take horses in order to effect their escapes; then they would also need food and clothing again and again.[40] But slaves who lived on their owners' plantations while they also continued to steal from other people are intrinsically more interesting. Their stealing was a matter of conscious choice.[41]

Slaves caught once, as well as those who stood trial repeatedly, concentrated on somewhat the same items as those that slaves took throughout the eighteenth century—clothes and fabric, food and livestock, liquor, money, horses, and hogs.[42] Tables 18 and 19 indicate how many slaves were convicted and punished for major thefts in Essex, Henry, Southampton, and Spotsylvania counties from 1785 to 1831 as well as the number sentenced to transportation or execution through-

39. The records of slaves transported or executed for stealing do not provide good answers to this question for the simple reason that those sentences almost always ended such careers in Virginia. The same records rarely have much to say about previous behavior either. One case, however, involved five different thefts for which the accused hanged (trial of Ben, March 16, 1796, Northumberland C.C.O.B. [1796–97], 19, and C.S., box 1).

40. Runaways convicted of horse stealing: trial of George, November 29, 1819, Culpeper, VEPLR; trial of Stephen, June 7, 1826, King George County, C.S., box 5, and VEPLR; trials of James and Albert, October 23, 1826, Greenbrier County (now West Virginia), C.S., box 5, and VEPLR, at date and at December 11, 1826.

41. White instigation or compulsion was always possible (trials of Fox and Isaac, July 21, 1817, October 20, 1817, Southampton C.C.O.B. [1816–19], 199). There had been a bad crop in the area the year before, so Isaac's owner may have thought it necessary to instigate the stealing of food to feed himself or his slaves (see Nathaniel Cargill to Reuben Grigsby, June 19, 1817, in Grigsby Family Papers, VHS). There are other examples of white instigation: trial, July 6, 1792, Richmond city Hustings C.O.B. (1792–97), 25; trials of Jack and Jerry, July 5, 1805, Berkeley County (now West Virginia), C.S., box 2; trial of John, February 22, 1808, Brunswick County, C.S., box 2, and VEPLR; Warrant for arrest of Joseph Dickinson, laborer, August 2, 1826, "Suits Involving Slaves," Caroline County Historical Papers, box 3, VSL; William Grimes, *Life of William Grimes the Runaway Slave* (New York, 1825), 20.

42. For "careers," see trials of Will and Billy Harris, January 16, 1795, January 26, 1797, August 18, 1796, Richmond city Hustings C.O.B. (1792–97), 287–88, 492, 550–51, and C.S., box 1; Benjamin Henry Latrobe, *The Virginia Journals of Benjamin Latrobe, 1795–1798*, ed. Edward C. Carter *et al.* (2 vols.; New Haven, 1977), II, 191–93; trials of Isaac, Bob, and Nelson, May 27, 1797, Richmond city Hustings C.O.B. (1792–97), 599–601; trials of Isaac, Jacob, and Charles, October 26, 1797, Richmond city Hustings C.O.B. (1797–1801), 46–48; trials of Isaac, Phill, and Tom, February 7, 1799, Richmond city Hustings C.O.B. (1797–1801), 244–47, and C.S., box 1. One Richmond slave was caught but, in the opinion of the Richmond *Recorder* (January 30, 1802), inadequately punished (Rose [ed.], *A Documentary History*, 241–43).

Table 18. Items Stolen by Slaves, 1785–1831

	Clothes/Fabric			Food/Livestock[a]			Liquor			Money			Hogs		
	T	G	C[b]	T	G	C	T	G	C	T	G	C	T	G	C
Essex	13	7	0%	19	8	37.5%	3	1	0%	1	1	0%	18	13	30.8%
Henry	4	2	0	0	0	0	0	0	0	1	1	0	3	3	66.7
Southampton	19	8	25	24	7	14.3	7	6	0	0	0	0	0	0	0
Spotsylvania	15	12	0	11	5	0	0	0	0	2	0	0	3	2	0

SOURCES: County court minute and order books, Essex, Henry, Southampton, and Spotsylvania counties, 1785–1831.
NOTE: There were so few trials of slaves for horse stealing in these counties that no figures have been given for them.
[a] Livestock excludes hogs
[b] T = Tried, G = Guilty, C = Percentage of convicted slaves identified as collaborators with other slaves

Table 19. Items Stolen by Slaves Transported or Executed, 1785–1829

	Clothes/ Fabric	Food/ Livestock[a]	Liquor	Money	Horses	Total
1785–89	3	2	0	1	0	6
1790–99	7	4	1	5	2	19
1800–1809	2	4	1	1	0	8
1810–19	15	11	3	3	4	36
1820–29	11	12	1	5	5	34
Total	38	33	6	15	11	103
% tranported or executed for theft	36.9%	32.0%	5.8%	14.6%	10.7%	100%

SOURCES: C.S., boxes 1–10; miscellaneous county court order and minute books.
NOTE: These 103 cases represent only part of the slaves transported or executed for theft. Court clerks did not always record items stolen. Some slaves were convicted of stealing items in more than one category.
[a]Hog stealing excluded.

out Virginia during those years for stealing the same items. Food and clothing remained as important to slaves who stole as they had been in the eighteenth century. Liquor, money, and horses kept their secondary importance. Collaboration appears to have declined, if our measure is the statistics of slaves convicted for the same incidents. But there are other indications that collaboration was still essential in some instances.

Few of the transported or executed slaves took money, but some managed to carry away a great deal of it. The confederates in an 1821 Southampton County case got $8,000 to $16,000. Eight slaves in Tidewater Mathews County had several years previously managed to cart away $1,900 in silver.[43] Few other slaves would dare to steal amounts this large at any time in Virginia's history. When a slave in Rock-

43. Trials of Tom, April 26, 1820, Dred, May 16, 1821, and Sam, July 16, 1821, Southampton C.C.O.B. (1819–22), 305–306, 329–30, 332–33, and C.S., box 4; "A List of Slaves and Free Persons of Color received into the Penitentiary . . . 1816 to . . . 1842," C.S., box 10; Tragle (ed.), *The Southampton Slave Revolt*, 446; trials of Humphrey, Harry, Abram, Yeoro (?), Billy Good Child, James, Wharton, and Hugh, March 18, 1813, Mathews County, C.S., box 3. Since Humphrey and Harry were also accused of putting John Ripley in fear of injury during the nighttime burglary of his home, they hanged. The other six men were transported.

ingham County stole goods worth $500 from a store, he set what may have been a record for one slave's single burglary and theft of goods in Virginia between 1785 and 1831.[44]

Court clerks sometimes recorded the value of goods taken—there are ten instances in which the value exceeded $100. A Hampshire slave stole ninety-three pairs of stockings, six greatcoats, and seventeen watches worth $300 in 1817. Other amounts ranged between $120 and $260. In cases with detailed records, almost all slaves transported or executed for theft had been accused of stealing goods worth $50 or less, and most of them had been found guilty of stealing articles worth less than $25. These figures do not include horses, which cost $50 or so. A slave who stole one was feared not only because he or she might have been running away but because horses were valuable. That price also serves as a benchmark for the general value of goods stolen by slaves whose punishment was transportation or execution. Because the value of hogs remained relatively low and the slave code made hog stealing a misdemeanor, prosecution of this offense continued to be inconsistent—that is, frequent—in a county such as Essex and nonexistent in one such as Southampton.[45]

There were nearly two dozen slaves who were executed for property crimes after the institution of transportation. Clearly, certain methods used by slaves who stole could still provoke a harsh judicial response. Seven of the executed men had used violence in the course of highway

44. Trials of Davy, March 27, 1797, Isle of Wight County ($514, including $497 cash, taken from a Smithfield store), and of Caesar, February 3, 1798, Petersburg city (£97 cash), C.S., box 1; trial of Amos, October 15, 1829, Rockingham County, C.S., box 5.
45. Trial of Jim (age 24), September 15, 1817, Hampshire County (now West Virginia), C.S., box 3; "A List of Slaves and Free Persons of Color received into the Penitentiary . . . 1816 to . . . 1842," C.S., box 10, and VEPLR; trial of Ned, December 4, 1789, Southampton County (£50 value), C.S., box 1; trials of Frank and James, June 29, 1801, Mathews County (clothes, blankets, etc., $260), C.S., box 2; trial of George (age 19), December 20, 1810 (clothes, etc., $133), Accomack C.C.O.B. (1809–11), 259, 262, and C.S., box 3; trial of Wonder, October 26, 1813 (watch, $100), Richmond city Hustings C.M.B. (1810–14), 368, and C.S., box 3; trial of Adam, April 20, 1815, Fauquier County (diverse goods, $240), C.S., box 3; trials of Solomon and Charles (ages 46 and 35), August 30, 1824, Lancaster County (goods, $200), C.S., box 4; trial of Smith Anderson (age 19), July 17, 1826, Prince Edward County (oranges, sugar, candies, and calicoes, $100), C.S., box 5; trial of Willis, June 29, 1831, Culpeper County (fabric, hats, knives, and shoes, $120.75), C.S., box 6; trial of Randolph (age 22), November 19, 1831, Lynchburg city (clothes, $200), C.S., box 6; trial of James, May 1, 1815 (horse valued at $50), Fauquier C.C.M.B. (1815–16), unpaginated, and C.S., box 3; trial of George, November 30, 1815 ($106 for horse and saddle), Fauquier C.C.M.B. (1815–16), unpaginated, and C.S., box 3; trial of Albert, August 4, 1827 (horse worth $50), Greenbrier County (now West Virginia), C.S., box 5.

robberies.[46] Others had broken into people's homes at night and either terrified or injured them.[47] Another category of slaves had taken particularly large amounts, such as the $8,000 or more attributed to a group in Southampton.[48]

Slaves tried to minimize their risks and to steal what they wanted to, using the means that anyone might who would engage in larceny. In towns and cities, accomplices kept careful track of watchmen or constables. In rural areas, they watched for patrollers. In any instance, one slave might serve as lookout while another did the actual breaking in. Some men relied on false or stolen keys to get into storehouses; others broke or pried doors open, even using a fence rail to do so. Given the earthen floors in many smokehouses, one could even dig under the foundations and up into the building. Prior inspection and the setting of a diversionary fire could make entrance possible.[49]

Once the theft had taken place, slaves faced what for them was a singularly difficult task—hiding, using, fencing, or otherwise transferring the items out of their possession. A Culpeper County slave learned the risks involved in eating stolen meat right after it had been removed from the larder of an accomplice's master. Grease had gotten on his legs and he had tried to rub dust on the grease, but his overseer noticed since he knew about the break-in and was searching for evidence. Other kinds of material could be secreted in slave cabins, but searches by whites could easily turn up such hidden articles. Buried goods were

46. Trials of Jack and Jerry, July 5, 1805, Berkeley County (now West Virginia), C.S., box 2; trial of Ned, October 8, 1810, Chesterfield County, C.S., box 3; trial of Tom, July 21, 1818, Norfolk County, C.S., box 4, and VEPLR; trials of Jack and George, August 23, 1826, Princess Anne County, C.S., box 5, and VEPLR.

47. Trial of Mike, July 22, 1813, Amelia County, C.S., box 3; trial of Robin, August 5, 1813, Sussex C.C.O.B. (1813–18), unpaginated, and C.S., box 3; trials of Burwell and Jeff, October 4, 1820, Surry County, C.S., box 4; trial of Lewis, August 23, 1826, Accomack County, C.S., box 5, and VEPLR.

48. See also trials of John and Jacob, February 5, 1818, Sussex County, C.S., box 3, and VEPLR.

49. Trial of Billy, March 29, 1806, Richmond city, C.S., box 2, and VEPLR at date and at April, 1807; trial of John (age 36), August 20, 1829, Richmond city, C.S., box 5, and VEPLR; trial of Caleb, June 1, 1826, Amherst County, C.S., box 5, and VEPLR at April 22, 1826; trials of John Johnson, Jack, and Billy Muse (ages 40, 30, and 30), November 20, December 16, 1818, Fredericksburg city, C.S., box 3, and VEPLR, with "A List of Slaves and Free Persons of Color received into the Penitentiary . . . 1816 to . . . 1842," C.S., box 10; trial of Hembry (age 27), March 14, 1826, Louisa C.C.M.B. (1822–26), 464–67, and C.S., box 5; trial of Henry, February 11, 1802, Southampton C.C.M.B. (1799–1803), 253–54, and C.S., box 2; trial of Peter, July 29, 1809, King William County, C.S., box 3, and VEPLR; trials of Peter and Isaac, July 15, 1816, October 20, 1817, Southampton C.C.O.B. (1814–16), 424, (1816–19), 226, and C.S., box 3, and VEPLR.

the safest. Some slaves saw the utility of fencing articles in order to obtain easily hidden cash in exchange for less easily hidden objects. It sometimes became necessary to use part of the take to buy the silence of another slave who threatened to turn informer.[50]

Given what some slaves wanted to steal and the problems involved, there were certain places in which those slaves who engaged in major thefts were particularly active. One might expect that to be true in rural areas. There were patrollers in the countryside, but they were not out every night, as were urban constables and watchmen.[51] On plantations, slave quarters were sometimes at sufficient distance from the owner's house to allow unsupervised activity at night. But Table 20 reflects the age-old fact of life in urban areas. When we include Fredericksburg, Petersburg, Richmond, and other towns clearly identified in the records, 39 of the 240 slaves executed or transported for stealing between 1785 and 1831, or more than 16 percent, operated in towns or cities. If it were possible to identify and add to that figure the number of slaves convicted of stealing items in the many towns not listed in county records, the percentage would probably be higher. Put another way, Fredericksburg, Petersburg, and Richmond slaves alone in 1830 were 2.2 percent of all slaves in the Old Dominion, yet the 24 slaves from those towns and cities who were convicted of major stealing between 1785 and 1831 were exactly 10 percent of all Virginian slaves so convicted.[52]

50. Trials of Billy and Lewis (alias Reubin), August 2, 1808, Culpeper C.C.M.B. (1807–1809), 272–76, and C.S., box 2; trials of Isaac and Sam, October 20, 1817, July 16, 1821, Southampton C.C.O.B. (1816–19), 226, (1819–21), 332–33, and C.S., box 4; trial, July 6, 1792, Richmond city Hustings C.O.B. (1792–97), 25; trial of Robin, November 25, 1816, King William County, C.S., box 3, and VEPLR; trial of Jack, December 16, 1818, Fredericksburg city, C.S., box 4, and VEPLR; Russell, *The Free Negro in Virginia*, 162–63; trials of Jack and Aby, January 9, 1809, Chesterfield County, C.S., box 2, and VEPLR.

51. Trial of Caleb, June 1, 1826, Amherst County, C.S., box 5, and VEPLR at April 22, 1826. Account papers and records on patrollers in various counties show clearly that patrollers operated periodically rather than regularly, on weekends rather than on weekdays. The exceptions were times of insurrection scares or after Nat Turner's Revolt. See "Patrollers, 1806–1835," Caroline County Historical Papers, box 3, VSL; and Patrollers' Papers, 1813, 1814, 1815, Sussex County Court [Loose] Papers, box 195, bundle 12, box 196, bundle 3, and box 202, bundle 12, VSL. On constables and watchmen, see trials of Billy and Jeff, March 29, 1806, Richmond city Hustings C.O.B. (1804–1806), 397–98, and C.S., box 2, and VEPLR, at date and at April, 1807. See also Armstrong, "'Have We No Police?'"; Louis B. Cei, "Law Enforcement in Richmond: A History of Police-Community Relations, 1737–1974" (Ph.D. dissertation, Florida State University, 1975).

52. Rose (ed.), *A Documentary History*, 241–43, contains an interesting newspaper evaluation of the difficulties of averting urban thefts by slaves in 1802.

The next ten jurisdictions ranked in Table 20 reflect the salient factor in stealing by slaves in rural areas. Unlike poisoning and arson, stealing prevailed in both the Tidewater and Piedmont/Southside regions. The counties following Mathews and Gloucester shift from Piedmont (Cumberland) to Tidewater–Northern Neck (King George) to Tidewater–Eastern Shore (Northampton) back to Piedmont (Chesterfield) and so on. Although Fauquier County had the highest slave population, it ranks twelfth, suggesting that the number of slaves by itself had much less influence than did concentration of slaves and historical factors. Southampton County's low rank suggests that areas where the tension between slaves and white people was high did not necessarily also experience a great deal of major stealing.

Motive is also an important cause of theft by slaves. White observers occasionally cited the role of "temptation." Anthony, a Buckingham County bondsman, won a pardon in 1793 partly on the basis of a petition on his behalf that pointed out that he had been "induced and tempted from the very careless and unsafe manner in which one John

Table 20.   Major Stealing Incidents per 1,000 Slaves, 1785–1831

Jurisdiction	Incidents, 1785–1831	Mean slave population, 1790–1830	Incidents per 1,000 Slaves
1. Fredericksburg	6	938	6.39
2. Petersburg	8	2,041	3.92
3. Richmond city	10	3,651	2.71
4. Mathews County	5	2,885	1.73
5. Gloucester County	9	5,734	1.57
6. Cumberland County	8	6,074	1.31
7. King George County	5	3,832	1.30
8. Northampton County	4	3,366	1.19
9. Chesterfield	9	8,241	1.09
10. King William County	6	5,801	1.03
11. Isle of Wight County	4	4,101	0.98
12. Fauquier County	9	9,889	0.91
13. Southampton County	4	6,703	0.59
14. Sussex County	3	6,500	0.46

SOURCES: C.S., boxes 1–10; miscellaneous county court order and minute books; U.S. Census Office, *The Statistics of the Population of the United States,* Vol. I, *Population and Social Statistics,* 68–72.

Buckhannon had built and secured his storehouse." But temptation alone does not explain the decision to steal. The prevalence of slaves' distinction between taking and stealing reflects the conscious decision involved in slaves' appropriation of articles such as food and clothing, but some evidence is available that slaves consciously linked the taking of food and the failure of owners to provide an adequate diet.[53] According to the testimony of King, against whom the Southampton County oyer and terminer justices dropped charges of burglary and theft of flour and bacon worth $4.50, Jacob had told King early in the evening of April 23, 1830, that William Blow, to whom Jacob was hired out, "did not give him enough to eat." The pair consequently broke into Blow's smokehouse and stole a barrel of flour and the meat.[54]

The actions of various runaways between 1785 and 1831 indicate that they still had to take food, clothing, and other articles in order to run. Gangs of maroons lived along the North Carolina–Virginia border. Although their force never equaled that of West Indian maroons, they were active and resourceful. They were also rather determined, aggressive, and sometimes desperate, consequently becoming involved in trials for murder as well as theft.[55] Naturally, stealing horses directly aided runaways.[56] There were slaves who "stole themselves" by running away permanently, and that became increasingly frequent. Slaves in some cases acted on their own and in others with

53. Trial of Anthony, September 9, 1793, Buckingham County, VEPLR, and CVSP, VI, 522–23. See also trial of John, April 17, 1813, Pittsylvania County, C.S., box 3, and VEPLR; trial of Jim (age 24), September 15, 1817, Hampshire County (now West Virginia), C.S., box 3, and VEPLR. The debate on the amount of food and clothing supplied to slaves has concentrated on averages. The debaters have never doubted that supplies were inadequate on some plantations or at some times. Obviously they were. See, for example, Nichols, "The Case of William Grimes," 555–56.

54. Trials of Jacob and King, May 17, 1830, Southampton C.C.M.B. (1824–30), 327–28. Just over a year earlier, Jacob was convicted of stealing a great deal of brandy in confederation with several other slaves (ibid., 256–57).

55. Herbert Aptheker, "Maroons Within the Present Limits of the United States," in Richard Price (ed.), Maroon Societies: Rebel Slave Communities in the Americas (Garden City, N.Y., 1973), 157–59; Petition of Mecklenburg County citizens, October 21, 1790, Legislative Petitions, Mecklenburg County, VSL; trial of Sutton, February 10, 1810, Gloucester County, C.S., box 3, and VEPLR; trial of Mingo, January 4, 1819, Princess Anne County, C.S., box 4, and VEPLR; Parramore, Southampton County, 70–71; trials of Lewis and Jasper, May 31, 1823, Norfolk County, C.S., box 4.

56. See, for example, trial of Lewis, September 28, 1816, Washington County, C.S., box 3, and VEPLR; trial of George, November 29, 1819, Culpeper County, VEPLR; trial of Stephen, June 7, 1826, King George County, C.S., box 5, and VEPLR; trials of James and Albert, October 23, 1826, Greenbrier County (now West Virginia), C.S., box 5, and VEPLR; trials of Nelson and Cooper, August 23, 1819, Rockingham County, C.S., box 4, and VEPLR.

free blacks or sympathetic whites.[57] Virginia authorities occasionally indicted such slaves in order to extradite them from neighboring states, but the charge of horse stealing in one such case revealed how the slave in question had moved outside Virginia's jurisdiction.[58]

The cooperation among many of the slaves who stole, as well as between them and the beneficiaries of their taking, reflects the role stealing played in slave communities. An undetermined number of slaves acted with accomplices. Some were even in gangs, as in the case of some runaways, and others were involved in a statewide horse-stealing ring. Although some slaves apparently stole for their own benefit only, many others shared the proceeds of their work with fellow slaves. One gave muslin to his wife; two Richmond slaves shared candles and soap with family members. Stolen flour served another slave as the means to pay a debt. Bacon and meat would regularly be distributed among slaves. Tom, a Madison County slave, even arranged to treat his fellow slaves to liquor he planned to appropriate.[59]

Some slaves turned in or helped to capture other slaves suspected of theft.[60] But those many slaves who supported bondsmen who stole

57. Statement of Thomas Myers, 1801, Lancaster County, VEPLR, and *CVSP*, IX, 227; George Carter to Thomas Maund, September 25, 1817, in George Carter of Oatlands Letterbook (1807–19), 100–101, VHS; *Report of the Joint Committee on the Penitentiary* (*Virginia House Journal*, 1839, doc. 41), 9, lists five persons incarcerated, during the period from 1800 to 1838, for persuading slaves to "abscond." One of the charges against white George Boxley in his attempt to lead a slave insurrection in 1816 was that he had stolen two slaves. Boxley claimed he had only helped them to escape (Spotsylvania C.C.M.B. [1815–19], 85–87; *CVSP*, X, 435; Louisa C.C.M.B. [1815–18], 38). John W. Green to Governor Nicholas, March 10, 1816, VEPLR; Augustus Finch Shirts, *A History of the Formation, Settlement and Development of Hamilton County, Indiana* (N.p., 1901), 165.

58. Indictment of Sarah and James Pindall, August 9, 1808, Harrison County (now West Virginia), plus actions of December 15, 1809, and February 3, 1810, VEPLR. A similar case was that of Jacob Beeson's Jane, Wood County, actions of February–June, 1810, and January, 1811, VEPLR. Jane was extradited from Ohio, but Marietta sympathizers detained her newborn child on the grounds that the child's birth in Ohio meant freedom. Jane was soon sold by her master.

59. Deposition of August 15, 1786, VEPLR; trial of Meritt, September 23, 1819, Isle of Wight County (muslin), C.S., box 4, and VEPLR; trial of Billy, March 29, 1806, Richmond city (candles and soap), C.S., box 2, and VEPLR; trial of Edward Parker, July 7, 1829, Fredericksburg city (flour), C.S., box 5, and VEPLR; trial of James Hogan, November 13, 1819, Loudoun County, C.S., box 4 (he used firewood he cut illegally in order to pay a debt to another slave); trials of Kitt, August 12, 1806, and Jack and Aby, January 9, 1809, Chesterfield County (meat), C.S., box 2, and VEPLR; trial of Billy, August 2, 1808, Culpeper County (meat), C.S., box 2; trial of Tom, May 30, 1829, Madison County (liquor), C.S., box 6, and VEPLR.

60. Trial of Hurricane, September 19, 1806, Southampton C.C.M.B. (1804–1807), 221–25, and C.S., box 2, and VEPLR, at date and October, 1811; trial of Robin, November 10, 1807, King and Queen County, C.S., box 2, and VEPLR; trial of Jordan, November 2, 1819, Isle of Wight County, C.S., box 4. There were even a few convictions of slaves for robbing other slaves (trial of Bob, May 2, 1786, Frederick County, C.S., box 1; trial of Peyton, February 9, 1818, Chesterfield County, C.S., box 3, and VEPLR).

Table 21.   Slaves' Crimes and the Virginia Penitentiary
             Population, 1800–1829

	Stealing Incidents	Slaves Convicted	Slaves Convicted (Other Major Crimes)	Free Blacks	Whites
1800–1804	5	6	41	25	169
1805–1809	22	27	33	47	174
1810–14	29	37	38	70	123
1815–19	36	52	46	83	253
1820–24	28	35	69	92	331
1825–29	34	42	87	23	211

SOURCES: C.S., boxes 2–6; county and city court order and minute books; *Annual Report of the Board of Directors of the Penitentiary Institution, 1847/8* (*Virginia House Journal*, 1848, 15), 32, 34.
NOTE: Between 1825 and 1828, Virginia sold thirty free blacks out of the state and into slavery when they were convicted of major crimes. Thus the total for 1825–29 could be expressed as 53 rather than 23.

suggests that stealing continued to be a form of resistance against the conditions of slavery.[61] There was even a statistical correlation between taking by slaves and other behavior that can be classified as resistance. When the years in which there were ten or more incidents of major stealing for which a larger number of slaves went to the gallows or into exile are related to other sets of data—long-term trends of stealing incidents and convictions, slaves' convictions for every kind of crime, and convictions of free people for major crimes (in Table 21)—it is possible to compare the peak years for two groups of Virginians.

These data point to simple conclusions. Taking by slaves only sometimes involved a response to the same conditions that stealing by free people did. The peak years for whites were not the same as those for slaves, with only two exceptions.[62] But stealing by slaves exhibited singular patterns, and its context included the conditions of slavery and the motivations of slaves. The patterns were behavioral as well as temporal and regional. Stealing and aggressive behavior sometimes

61. For example, see trial of Lighty, July 5, 1808, Henrico C.C.O.B. (1808–1809), 20–21, and VEPLR; trial of Billy, October 29, 1810, Henrico C.C.O.B. (1810–11), 310–11.
62. Well over two-thirds of the free people in the Virginia Penitentiary were there as punishment for property crimes (*Report of the Joint Committee on the Penitentiary*, 9).

Table 22.   Stealing Incidents, 1785–1829

	Incidents Resulting in Execution or Transportation		
	Northern Neck/ Middle Peninsula	Central Piedmont	Southeastern Tidewater
1785–89	1	3	3
1790–94	0	2	2
1795–99	3	3	3
1800–1804	3	0	0
1805–1809	4	5	3
1810–14	7	5	1
1815–19	5	6	9
1820–24	7	5	7
1825–29	5	7	5
Totals	35	36	33
Average Slave Population, 1790–1830	41,939	49,942	44,482
Incidents per 1,000 Slaves	0.83	0.72	0.74

SOURCES: C.S., boxes 1–10; miscellaneous county court order and minute books; U.S. Census Office, *The Statistics of the Population of the United States*, Vol. I, *Population and Social Statistics*, 68–72.

NOTE: Northern Neck/Middle Peninsula: Essex, Gloucester, King and Queen, King George, King William, Lancaster, Mathews, Middlesex, Richmond, and Westmoreland counties. Central Piedmont/Upper Tidewater: Charles City, Chesterfield, Goochland, Hanover, Henrico, New Kent, Petersburg, Powhatan, and Prince George counties, and Richmond city. Southeastern Tidewater: Elizabeth City, Isle of Wight, James City, Nansemond, Norfolk, Princess Anne, Southampton, Surry, Sussex, Warwick, and York counties, and Norfolk city.

occurred simultaneously. When crimes by free people decreased during the War of 1812, for the obvious reason that soldiers were under stricter discipline than were civilians, taking by slaves continued at the same pace as before and after the war period.

The war did, however, affect slaves who stole, as illustrated by Table 22. In the 1810 to 1814 quinquennium, there was only one major stealing incident in the southeastern Tidewater region. This period of quiet was presumably due to local troops' heightened state of military readiness as well as the increased opportunity for slaves to run away, since the British navy was offshore.[63] But in the less endangered Northern

63. Cassell, "Slaves of the Chesapeake Bay Area," 144–55. On the one incident in the southeastern Tidewater, see trial of Robin, August 5, 1813, Sussex C.C.O.B. (1813–18),

Neck and Middle Peninsula area and the safe Piedmont, the war seemed to have no impact on major stealing convictions. Once the war ended and the danger of large numbers of slaves running away passed, major stealing incidents in the southeastern Tidewater area increased markedly.

Besides the twenty incidents of major stealing that took place between 1815 and 1819 in the three targeted regions, seventeen occurred elsewhere in the Old Dominion. They were neither so violent nor so distinctive as the incidents in the southeastern Tidewater counties. But all the convictions do help us to understand why some Princess Anne citizens could call the depredations of Mingo, a well-known maroon, and his accomplices an "open war against the property and even lives of our Citizens."[64] It was between 1815 and 1819 that more slaves were sentenced to execution or transportation for property crimes than in any other quinquennium between 1785 and 1829. The level of such convictions rose significantly between the 1800 to 1804 and 1805 to 1809 quinquennia. This rise may be attributed at least partially to judges getting used to the penalty of transportation. The level of convictions continued to rise through the 1815 to 1819 period, then dipped slightly to a level at which it stayed through the 1830 to 1834 quinquennium.

Major stealing did not by itself constitute an open war against Virginian slaveholders. It was the interrelationship of violence and theft that was so threatening. Table 21 shows that as slaves were increasingly convicted of major thefts between 1785 and 1831, so were more and more slaves being convicted of several violent crimes and threatening crimes against property such as arson. Rape, arson, assault, and homicide sent tremors through certain areas when they occurred. Slaves could resist bondage in a pitched battle and be called insurrectionaries. If they engaged in less collective forms of resistance to white authorities, they were called thieves, criminals, or banditti.

---

unpaginated, and C.S., box 3. For later activity in the area, see trials of Jacob and John, February 5, 1818, Sussex County, C.S., box 3, and VEPLR; trials of Shadrack and Wilson, May 5, 1818, Isle of Wight County, C.S., box 3, and VEPLR; trial of Tom, July 21, 1818, Norfolk city, C.S., box 4, and VEPLR; trial of Mingo, January 4, 1819, Princess Anne County, C.S., box 4, and VEPLR, and related materials in VEPLR, at December 7, 1818, February 19, 1819; trial of Betty, January 24, 1816, Norfolk city, C.S., box 3, and VEPLR; trial of Lewis, April 13, 1815, Warwick County, C.S., box 3; trial of Isaac, October 20, 1817, Southampton C.C.O.B. (1816–19), 226, and C.S., box 3, and VEPLR; trial of Jordan, November 2, 1819, Isle of Wight County, C.S., box 4; trial of Lawrence, November 20, 1815, York County, C.S., box 3.
64. Petition of Princess Anne County citizens, December 1–11, 1818, VEPLR.

9. *Deadly Relationships, 1785–1831*

In the autumn of 1826, two Essex County slaves had been drinking, and Peter killed John in a knife fight. Liquor had apparently reduced John's ability to refrain from insulting comments about the relationship between Peter's wife and John's master. Undoubtedly smarting under the pain of what may have been sexual exploitation of Peter's wife by his master, Peter struck out at John rather than at John's owner, the appropriate but legally well protected violator of Peter's marriage. These circumstances of slavery impressed the Essex County justices, who unanimously recommended mercy. But the governor and the council summarily rejected it, and Peter hanged shortly thereafter.[1]

Peter's case reflects some of the circumstances in which many slaves continued to confront one another and white people in Virginia between 1785 and 1831. One of the most important questions for the historian is whether more or fewer killings by slaves occurred after 1785 than before. In 1795, St. George Tucker claimed that among slaves, "murder is not very uncommon; and not unfrequently their victims have been their overseers, and sometimes, though very rarely, their own masters and mistresses, by means of poison. In most of these cases, the most humane persons have been the sufferers. They occur, however, so very seldom, that I am inclined to believe as many cases happen in England of masters or mistresses murdered by their servants, as in Virginia."[2] Tucker was essentially correct, since between

1. Trial of Peter, October 16, 1826, Essex C.C.O.B. (1823–26), 511–14, and C.S., box 5, and VEPLR. See also Tragle (ed.), *The Southampton Slave Revolt*, 450.

2. St. George Tucker to Rev. Jeremy Belknap, June 29, 1795, in *Collections of the Massachusetts Historical Society*, 5th ser., III (1877), 409.

1785 and 1794, only two slaves had been executed for murder of an owner in Virginia, both for killing the same master. Thirteen more had gone to the gallows after being convicted of murdering six white people. A distinct rise in the number of such incidents in 1795 and later, however, revealed that there were increasingly severe tensions within the slave society of Virginia. The "relations between the races," as so many later would put it, were outwardly harmonious. That relationship was, after all, between slaveowner and slave as much as or more than between black and white. The price of external harmony was repression, to which some slaves responded with killing and other attacks. Other slaves attacked fellow bondspeople. These actions were so frequent that slaves' behavior became distinctly revealing about slavery in Virginia between 1785 and 1831. Only insurrection had as great an impact on black and white Virginians as did these deadly assaults.

For slaves who lived in Virginia during those years, dealing daily with the constraints of bondage was one of their greatest challenges. Killing or assault was a way some of them responded—more than 148 were convicted of murder of whites, more than 24 were found guilty of attempted murder, and nearly 10 were executed or transported for assault. The most important aspect of almost all these cases is that slaves had acted primarily against conditions unique to slavery. Killing of other slaves was generally anomalous, though occasionally related more to the circumstances of slavery than to other factors. Slaves' attacks on white people, however, mostly derived from motives of resistance to specific oppressive features of the institution.

The violent deaths of white people must dominate consideration of killing by slaves. Tables 23 and 24 reveal two distinct trends. In the first place, white people constituted nearly two-thirds of the victims of slaves convicted of first-degree murder between 1785 and 1829. (They were at least 50 percent of the victims in 1830 and 1831.) Similarly, 71.5 percent of the slaves executed or transported for murder between 1785 and 1831 had mortally attacked whites. Between 1785 and 1829, judges in four representative counties—Essex, Henry, Southampton, and Spotsylvania—convicted eighteen slaves of murdering white people and fourteen slaves of killing other slaves. All the former received the death sentence; only half of the latter did so. The others were granted benefit of clergy on the grounds that they were guilty only of manslaughter. In other words, the risk of capital punishment was still

Table 23. Persons Violently Killed by Slaves, 1785–1864

	Owners, owners' family	Other Authorities	Other Whites	White Victims	% of Victims	Slaves, same owner	Slaves, other owner	Infanticide Victims	Free Blacks	Black Victims	% of Victims	Total Victims
1785–89	1	0	1	2	66.6%	1	0	0	0	1	33.3%	3
1790–94	0	2	3	5	41.7	3	4	0	0	7	58.3	12
1795–99	11	0	6	17	77.3	1	2	2	0	5	22.7	22
1800–1804	6	2	4	12	70.6	1	4	0	0	5	29.4	17
1805–1809	2	3	3	8	72.7	1	0	0	2	3	27.3	11
1810–14	4	0	2	6	60.0	3	0	0	1	4	40.0	10
1815–19	2	3	2	7	41.2	2	3	5	0	10	58.8	17
1820–24	7	3	9	19	55.9	3	9	2	1	15	44.1	34
1825–29	8	2	8	18	75.0	0	4	2	0	6	25.0	24
1830–34	2	1	4	7	46.7	2	3	2	1	8	53.3	15
1835–39	5	2	9	16	88.9	0	2	0	0	2	11.1	18
1840–44	4	0	1	5	41.7	3	4	0	0	7	58.3	12
1845–49	2	2	2	6	42.9	1	6	0	1	8	57.1	14
1850–54	4	0	8	12	41.4	2	9	4	2	17	58.6	29
1855–59	5	1	13	19	39.6	4	13	6	6	29	60.4	48
1860–64	6	0	6	12	60.0	4	4	0	0	8	40.0	20
Total	69	21	81	171	55.9	31	67	23	14	135	44.1	306

SOURCES: C.S., boxes 1–10; miscellaneous county court order and minute books; VEPLR.
NOTE: Categorized by relationship to convicted slave or by type of homicide. Unidentified victims do not appear in this table. Moreover, some of the victims in the category "Other Whites" might have been such authorities as overseers, hirers, constables, etc., but full identification was impossible in many cases.

Table 24. Slaves Convicted of Violent Murder, 1785–1864

	Owners, owners' family	Other Authorities	Other Whites	White Victims	% of Victims	Slaves, same owner	Slaves, other owner	Infanticide Victims	Free Blacks	Black Victims	% of Convicts	Total Convicts
1785–89	2	0	1	3	75.0%	1	0	0	0	1	25.0%	4
1790–94	0	6	4	10	58.8	3	4	0	0	7	41.2	17
1795–99	12	0	7	19	76.0	3	2	1	0	6	24.0	25
1800–1804	7	4	5	16	76.2	1	4	0	0	5	23.8	21
1805–1809	3	7	6	16	84.2	1	0	0	2	3	15.8	19
1810–14	5	0	3	8	66.7	3	0	0	1	4	33.3	12
1815–19	8	3	2	13	61.9	2	3	3	0	8	38.1	21
1820–24	8	4	11	23	60.5	3	9	2	1	15	39.5	38
1825–29	20	2	8	30	83.3	0	4	2	0	6	16.7	36
1830–34	8	1	6	15	65.2	2	3	2	1	8	34.8	23
1835–39	9	2	10	21	91.3	0	2	0	0	2	8.7	23
1840–44	5	0	1	6	46.2	3	4	0	0	7	53.8	13
1845–49	4	2	4	10	55.6	1	6	0	1	8	44.4	18
1850–54	4	0	9	13	41.9	2	10	4	2	18	58.1	31
1855–59	10	1	8	19	40.4	5	13	5	5	28	59.6	47
1860–64	14	0	5	19	67.9	4	5	0	0	9	32.1	28
Total	119	32	90	241	64.1	34	69	19	13	135	35.9	376

SOURCES: C.S., boxes 1–10; miscellaneous county court order and minute books; VEPLR.
NOTE: Categorized by relationship of convicted slave to victim or by type of homicide. Unidentified victims do not appear in this table. Moreover, some of the victims in the category "Other Whites" might have been such authorities as overseers, hirers, constables, etc., but full identification was impossible in many cases.

much higher for a slave who fought with, and ended up killing, a white person than for one who fought with, and ended up killing, another slave. How many slaves would fight a white person under these conditions without a strong motivation to resist that person's authority? The judges' presupposition of premeditation by slaves who killed whites was not necessarily inaccurate, in spite of the assumptions on which it may have been based.

Killing always results from a relationship. The connection can be accidental or casual; it can be long-standing and tense. But the general subordination of blacks to whites figured in almost all killings of whites by slaves. A particular form of this subordination influenced the timing and characteristics of such killings. The counties with the proportionally largest number of slaves found guilty of murdering whites between 1785 and 1831 were Bedford, Prince Edward, and Southampton, with, respectively, six, four, and five slaves so convicted, making the minimal killing rate in each county—the number of blacks found guilty of murdering their owners or other whites in ratio to each one thousand persons in the mean total population of each county from 1790 to 1830—0.37 for Bedford, 0.34 for Prince Edward, and 0.35 for Southampton. There is no correlation between the ratio of slaves to whites and a high number of murder convictions of slaves. (That percentage of slaves in the population of each county was: Bedford, 26.2 in 1790 and 43.4 in 1830; Prince Edward, 49.2 and 60.9 in the same years; and the percentages for Southampton were 46.6 and 48.3.) Other similar counties had no convictions of slaves for murdering whites. Nor is there a correlation between the indicated counties' convictions and dramatic changes in demography. (The growth rates, 1790–1830, for each county were 2.9 percent for Bedford, 1.9 for Prince Edward, and 0.6 percent for Southampton.)

It is Southampton County's general history, one small and bloody part of which Nat Turner and his enemies made so well known, that best begins to explain why more killings of whites by slaves could occur in one county as opposed to another. Between the American Revolution and 1831, the date of the Southampton revolt, the small Tidewater county experienced a relatively high level of violence overall. In a county with highly visible Baptists, Methodists, and Quakers, there lived a relatively large number of violent people to whom the converted may have been eager to deliver a message of love and peace. Free whites, free blacks, and even a handful of Indians, as well as black

Table 25.   Slaves Tried in Southampton County for Attacks, 1785–1827

Year	White Victims		Free Black Victims		Slave Victims	
	Tried	Convicted	Tried	Convicted	Tried	Convicted
1794	2	1	0	0	0	0
1796	1	1	0	0	0	0
1799	5	5	0	0	0	0
1801	11	2	0	0	0	0
1802	2	2	0	0	1	1
1806	2	0	0	0	0	0
1814	2	0	0	0	0	0
1815	1	1	0	0	0	0
1817	0	0	2	2	1	1
1818	2	0	0	0	0	0
1821	4	2	0	0	0	0
1822	0	0	0	0	1	1
1824	0	0	0	0	1	1
1826	0	0	0	0	1	1
1827	2	2	0	0	1	1
Total	34	16	2	2	6	6

SOURCES: Southampton County Court order and minute books; C.S., boxes 1–5; VEPLR.
NOTE: Attacks include assault, attempted murder, murder, and poisoning or illegal administration of medicine. No slaves were convicted of homicide between 1828 and 1831. The obvious exception is the convicted insurrectionaries of 1831, but they were convicted of insurrection only.

slaves, exhibited a pronounced tendency to fight with, assault, or kill their fellow residents. Suits for breach of the peace fill the county court records; trials of free whites, an occasional Meherrin Indian, and free blacks for acts of violence appear regularly in the order and minute books; the court of oyer and terminer met frequently in order to judge slaves accused of assault, attempted murder, and murder. Table 25 provides a quantitative measure of these trials.[3]

Violence was a prevalent response to various kinds of provocation in Southampton County. Slavery was one kind of provocation by itself, to be sure, but whites offered any number of others to slaves, including violence directed toward them. By the beginning of the nineteenth

3. Parramore, *Southampton County*, 50–52, 144–48, and *passim*, contains a good general treatment of the county's early social history.

century, most Southampton slaves were probably well aware that several slaves had made visible use of violence as a means of dealing with both free and enslaved enemies. As a result, more slaves than elsewhere chose to attack their enemies in a way that was bound to attract judicial attention. The same pattern prevailed in other counties, such as Bedford and Prince Edward. Slaves could act violently toward whites anywhere in Virginia simply because slavery was their lot and they all could choose how to respond to it. As in the cycles of poisoning in the eighteenth century, however, slaves violently attacked their enemies more often during the late eighteenth and early nineteenth century in those areas in which certain aggressive slaves had earlier begun a progression of attacks.

Violent attacks of slaves on their enemies came in waves as well. There were periods of calm and episodes of sustained violence. Table 25 illustrates that point for Southampton County as Table 26 does for Virginia in general. The tangled, often hostile relationship between slaves and white people was a constant, but individuals acted in a variety of ways in separate contexts and for diverse purposes. The number of slaves executed or transported for violently killing other people fluctuated significantly between 1785 and 1829 partly because of the intervening variables such as poor record keeping between 1785 and 1789 and the exigencies of war between 1812 and 1814. But periods of heightened activity such as 1795 to 1799 and the 1820s reveal the force of individuals making history.

Table 26.   Slaves Executed or Transported for Murder, 1785–1829

	Convicted, Condemned	Executed	% Convicted	Transported	% Convicted
1785–89	6	6	100.0%	0	0.0%
1790–94	17	17	100.0	0	0.0
1795–99	28	27	96.4	1	3.6
1800–1804	20	15	75.0	5	25.0
1805–1809	17	15	88.2	2	11.8
1810–14	14	9	64.3	5	35.7
1815–19	24	15	62.5	9	37.5
1820–24	40	29	72.5	11	27.5
1825–29	43	32	74.4	11	25.6

SOURCES: C.S., boxes 1–5; miscellaneous county court order and minute books; VEPLR.

It was not just that more attacks began to occur. Some were highly visible because of the methods used or because of the victim. The status of Dr. Robert Berkeley of Frederick County gave him no protection when his slaves attacked him in 1818. After beating Berkeley to death, the five or more confederates discussed where to hide the corpse. They rejected leaving it by a road or putting it in a pond; instead, they favored incineration, which they promptly effected in the fireplace of a cabin. They then buried the bones in a hole at one end of the cabin. Celia and Abel, young Southampton slaves, also resorted to cremation of their two victims, a man and his wife to whom Abel was hired out. In 1821 the pair used an ax to slay Mr. and Mrs. James Powell, then burned their house with them in it. (Yet they spared the couple's infant.) A group of slaves belonging to John Hamlin of Lunenburg County, in early 1827, clubbed and strangled their master, then cut him into pieces, placed the pieces in a basket, burned the pieces and the basket, and buried the remains in the middle of a field. When Princess Anne County resident Daniel Stone's Parker mortally wounded his overseer with an ax at the beginning of autumn, 1829, he not only expressed no remorse but affirmed the justice of what he had done. "They may hang me," he declared to the white men who apprehended him, "but I shall go to heaven."[4]

The Richmond *Enquirer* branded the 1818 killing an act of "savage barbarity." But it was slavery that helped to create these homicidal episodes. One of Berkeley's killers dramatically insisted that "the devil is dead," and another had told a free black friend a few months before that "his master was a bad master and he would sooner die than serve him." Abel had informed another slave that if the man to whom he was hired whipped him again, "he would be damned if he . . . did not kill him." The owner of the Lunenburg slaves had a general reputation for brutality, and Parker's overseer had threatened him with another whipping.[5]

There are tragic and fatalistic aspects of these killings. The day after he had slain his master with an ax, Bill calmly went to a neighbor's

4. Trials of Randolph, Robert (Robin), Sarah, Barnaby, and London, May 25, 26, 1818, Frederick County, trials of Celia and Abel, June 28, 1821, Southampton County, trials of David, Archer, Billy, Nathan, Big Stephen, Tom, Sam, Little Stephen, and Robin, March 19, 1827, Lunenburg County, trial of Parker, September 28, 1829, Princess Anne County, C.S., boxes 3–5, and VEPLR.
5. Richmond *Enquirer*, May 29, 1818, p. 3. See also "An act authorising a sale of certain slaves belonging to the estate of Doctor Robert Beverley, deceased," January 13, 1820, *Acts of the General Assembly*, 1819, pp. 98–99.

house to borrow a spade for digging Elijah Powell's grave. The neighbor later testified that "in a kind of jocular way without any suspicion" he asked Bill about the killing, which everyone in the area already had learned about. "Bill, God-dam your Soul how came you to kill your master last night?" Bill's laconic reply was, "He has lived long enough, he has got to die some, I have expected it before now, for it was appointed as a meeting." Bill was soon in jail, where he confessed to a jailer's wife. She told him that "he was doing right to be praying and that he had better confess his crime at once" to the authorities, which Bill did. He was tried, found guilty, and hanged by the neck in the spring of 1826. Bill's description of a "meeting," his praying, and his confession indicate that no matter how necessary he thought the killing had been, he had not cast it in a grandly heroic light. It happened because it had to, and that was all.[6]

Yet slaves convicted of murdering white people had deliberately selected their victims. The act required a combination of general factors, specific causes or grievances and circumstances, and a slave willing to risk everything. Why some slaves took such risks while others did not is unclear and will likely remain so. We can nevertheless know some things about the circumstances of slaves' killings of white people.

Court records from the period 1785 to 1831 often contain some discussion of motivation, if only because establishing motive would help convict many slaves on trial for murder. Perhaps most prevalent was the wish to retaliate for physical cruelty, such as repeated whippings, or to prevent future mistreatment. In December, 1807, overseer William Firth was trying to distribute the work force for the day's tasks on John W. Cocke's farm in Campbell County. Jim, one of Cocke's slaves, told Firth that some slaves were needed to shell corn. Firth angrily replied that he was in charge of such matters and that he would have to teach Jim some "manners." Firth broke a tobacco stick over Jim's head. Jim fought back, the two men scuffled, and Jim declared that "he would not be whipped for nothing." Yet he went back to work in response to Firth's order. Soon thereafter, the ill-fated overseer directed Jim and some other slaves to shell corn. Jim now would not do what he had earlier insisted needed doing. Clearly this was a test of wills, but one in which the overseer thought the rules all favored him.

6. Trial of Bill, April 1, 1826, Madison County, C.S., box 5, and folder for March 20–31, 1826, VEPLR.

Firth went to "correct" Jim, but the equally ill-fated slave picked up a thick-handled, six-foot tobacco fork and fatally fractured Firth's skull. Jim hanged in early 1808.[7]

Jim's paramount consideration was keeping Firth from dominating, injuring, or whipping him. Such concerns were commonplace in slaves' killings of masters and overseers. Two years before Jim's case, Creese had killed her mistress because Mrs. Morrisett had hit her and told her to do something that Creese believed to be impossible. Male and female slaves would regularly declare their intention to kill any white who tried to whip them again. Sometimes slaves would directly threaten their future victims; usually they kept their incriminating talk within the hearing of other slaves.[8] The wish to retaliate was important. Although he said he knew he would "go to Hell," Dick claimed that mistreatment led him to try to kill his master in 1802. At a Brunswick County trial in 1817, a white witness testified that he had known Caty from her childhood as "well disposed" and from "a peaceable family," but Caty was found guilty of murdering Linah Harwell, her former mistress. A slave's testimony shed more light on the incident. Cherry testified Caty had once told her that Harwell had called Caty "a bitch and a strumpet." "If she did not quit fooling with her," Caty continued, "she would some time or other take an Iron and split her Brains out." Shocked, Cherry asked Caty "if she was not afraid to talk so, and what sort of a Conscience she had." Caty replied, "Never mind that" and then repeated her threat.[9]

Some convicted slaves had chosen violent methods to defend their honor and rights as husbands or members of families. In 1818 a Tidewater slave killed a white man at the fork of a road near a tavern. Manuel had thrust a bayonet or three-sided dirk into Langford Harrison's head. There was evidence that would convince any white Virginian judge of prior intention. Spurning a warning from another

7. Trial of Jim, January 14, 1808, C.S., box 2, and VEPLR.

8. Trial of Creese, April 14, 1806, Chesterfield C.C.O.B. (1805–1809), 204–205, and C.S., box 2, and VEPLR, and Johnston, *Race Relations in Virginia*, 20–22. For other examples, see Johnston, *Race Relations in Virginia*, 20–29, 317–19; and trials of Sam, September 22, 1809, Montgomery County, George, April 27, 1818, Goochland County, and Henry, February 8, 1819, Botetourt County, C.S., boxes 3–4, and VEPLR.

9. Trial of Dick, March 8, 1802, Mecklenburg County, trial of Caty, December 23, 1817, Brunswick County, C.S., boxes 2, 4, and VEPLR. See also trials of Humphrey and Thornton, February 26, 1824, Hanover County, C.S., box 4, and discussed in Johnston, *Race Relations in Virginia*, 79–82.

slave that Harrison would beat him, Manuel had vowed that "he had often given him the road, but would not do it again." The reason was fundamental. According to Manuel, Harrison "had had connection with his wife, and . . . he imputed Harrison owed him . . . a grudge and . . . he (prisoner) would seek an opportunity to kill him." Manuel settled the grudge but also assured his own death by hanging.[10]

There were several other reasons why some slaves would kill whites. Bondsmen were prevented from seeing their own wives. Others were threatened with or were actually being sold. Such transactions undoubtedly involved separation from either a nuclear or extended family. Moreover, some of the slaves involved in such killings were en route from Maryland to the unknown dangers of the Deep South. For them the risk of hanging was less terrifying than was the thought of being "sold to Georgia." Similar considerations figured in the behavior of several runaways who were caught only after they had killed, or nearly killed, someone who was trying to apprehend them. One maroon was convicted of just such an attempted murder but later pardoned. As he was being driven to his owner's home from jail, "some person unknown" shot and killed him.[11]

Self-defense could only rarely serve as effective legal protection for slaves whose attempts to save themselves caused the death of a white person. There was no such thing as lawful defense against a white person's use of coercion in the process of "correcting" slaves. In fights between slaves and whites, the slave would normally receive the doubt while the white person would get the benefit of the doubt. There were exceptions. In 1818 a Henrico County slave was found not guilty of stabbing to death James F. Miller, a white man: it was a rare case of

10. Trial of Manuel, June 12, 1818, King George County, C.S., box 3, and VEPLR. For a similar case, see trial, September 10, 1830, New Kent County, C.S., box 5, and discussion in Johnston, *Race Relations in Virginia*, 307–308.
11. Family separation: trial, October 7, 1826, Brunswick County, C.S., box 5, and VEPLR; trial, January 7, 1802, Prince Edward C.C.O.B. (1797–1802), 488–89, and C.S., box 2. Threatened sale: trial of Major Jackson, March 29, 1810, Goochland, C.S., box 3, and VEPLR. En route from Maryland: trials of January 4, 1799, Southampton County, C.S., box 1, and VEPLR. For related details, see Southampton County Court Minutes (1793–99), 423, (1799–1803), 6, 46–48, 67–68. Runaways: trials of February 7, 1824, Monroe County, September 26, 1803, Mecklenburg County, August 18, 1818, Pittsylvania County, March 17, 1808, Charles City County, and January 4, 1819, Princess Anne County, C.S., boxes 1–5, and VEPLR. For more on the last case, after which the vigilante execution occurred, see materials in folder for December 1–11, 1818, and affidavit of February 19, 1819, VEPLR. Another dramatic case involving a maroon is in a trial of June 24, 1823, Norfolk County, C.S., box 4, and Herbert Aptheker, "Maroons Within the Present Limits of the United States," in Richard Price (ed.), *Maroon Societies: Rebel Slave Communities in the Americas* (Garden City, N.Y., 1973), 158–59.

exoneration on the basis of self-defense. Yet even in this instance a group of people close to Jacob strongly disagreed. After someone complained about his conduct to Boar's Head Swamp (Antioch) Baptist Church in eastern Henrico County, Jacob confessed to his fellow church members that he had indeed stabbed Miller, "but he did it in vindication of his own life and . . . he did not feel Guilty of any sin in so doing." The voting members rejected this defense, declaring that Jacob could have escaped danger without killing Miller. Jacob was promptly excommunicated, never to be restored. This action caused a sharp split among the church members, however. "As several of the Black Brethren withdrew" when Jacob was excommunicated, "the Church thought it disorder in them" and mounted an investigation. The black members and the completely white voting membership of the church had a fundamental disagreement about a slave's defensive violence.[12]

The exact nature of the incident is unknown, but circumstantial evidence does suggest its character. Perhaps Jacob had been in a "tipling house" brawl precipitated by rowdy white men. Miller and those who testified against Jacob were free white people who owned neither slaves nor land and little personal property. They seem to have been accustomed to violence. Within two years, one of them was the object of an attempted murder by several other white men. Ephraim Gathright, Jacob's master, may have been part of this violent group. There is also a hint of a long-standing relationship between the Miller and the Gathright families. Like the whites involved in the incident and in Jacob's trial, Gathright had low social status. He had only recently inherited the one other adult slave he owned. (Jacob had belonged to other members of the Gathright family since the Revolution.) Gathright had also just inherited a modest 114 acres in Henrico and 224 acres of timberland in adjacent Charles City County. Unlike many other members of the Gathright family, Ephraim was not a member of Boar's Head Baptist Church.[13]

12. Shepherd, *Statutes at Large*, I, 125, stated that a "negro or mulatto" could plead self-defense when "wantonly assaulted." See also *American Digest*, XLIV, cols. 1060–63, para. 65. Trial of Jacob, July 6, 1818, Henrico C.C.M.B. (1816–19), 393, 410; Boar's Head Swamp (Antioch) Baptist Church Minute Book (1787, 1791–1828), July–August, 1818, in VBHS.

13. Boar's Head Swamp Church Minute Book, April, 1822, and Membership List; Henrico C.C.M.B. (1816–19), 393; Henrico County Land and Personal Property Taxes (1816–20), in VSL; expenses of William Mayo, jailer, November 18, 1820–August 1821, Virginia Auditor's Office, Auditor's Item 147, Criminal Charges, box 7, VSL; U.S. Manuscript Census, 1810, Henrico, 113, and 1820, Henrico, 101A; Joyce H. Lindsay, *Marriages*

There was one kind of case in which a slave accused of murdering a white person could hope for mercy, even though convicted of the fact of the killing. That would be killing for hire by, or on the instigation of, a white person. Benjamin Cluverius' Hanover apparently sneaked up to William Temple's window one night in 1809 and shot him. Temple survived and testified. Another guilty party existed, however. Baylor Gwathmey had asked a slave to do the job in retaliation for Temple's having accused that slave of stealing brandy. Cambridge not only refused Gwathmey's request but testified about the transaction. Gwathmey had instead persuaded Hanover to try to kill Temple in return for payment. According to Cambridge, Gwathmey told Hanover that he and his wife "would be furnished." When both Gwathmey and Hanover were accused of the offense, Gwathmey increased his troubles by trying to persuade Cambridge to alter his testimony. Cambridge did not; Gwathmey was jailed; Hanover was transported rather than hanged.[14]

Gabriel's 1799 attack on Absalom Johnson fell into still another category of violence, that used in commission or protection of another illegal action. Trying to save himself, Jupiter, and Solomon from punishment for hog stealing, Gabriel "maimed" Johnson by biting off part of his ear. Johnson's life was not endangered, so Gabriel, who would in 1800 lead a large-scale plot to rebel against slavery itself, had the chance to survive for another year. Sometimes that happened to slaves who used violence in highway robbery. Isaac gave directions to a white couple who were on their way from the Goochland courthouse to a friend's plantation at sunset on a summer night in 1814. Afterwards he ran ahead of them, hid behind a tree, then clubbed the man and knocked down his wife, who consequently nearly died. Struggling to find money in Peter Mason's pocket, Isaac yelled at him, "God damn you where is your money?" He then ran away with the Masons' belongings and their horse and saddle.[15]

---

of Henrico County, Virginia 1680–1808 (N.p., 1960), 35; Henrico County Deeds (1789–92), 105, (1819), 21, (1819–20), 120–21, (1823–24), 95, VSL; Henrico County Wills (1787–1802), 117–18, 253–54, (1802–1809), 319, 429–30, (1816–22), 137–39, 148–49, 281–82, 322–23, VSL. No will for James F. Miller appears in these records.

14. Trial of Hanover, July 27, 1809, King and Queen County, C.S., box 2, and VEPLR. What happened to Gwathmey is unknown. For a similar case, see trial of Shadrack, August 18, 1818, Pittsylvania County, C.S., box 4, and VEPLR.

15. Schwarz, "Gabriel's Challenge"; trial of Isaac, July 1, 1814, Goochland C.C.O.B. (1813–17), 121–24, and C.S., box 3.

The Goochland authorities charged Isaac only with highway robbery and the theft of the Masons' clothes and wallet, valued at $50.
Isaac was transported rather than hanged. Perhaps the testimony of
Tom, another slave, helped him. Tom had told Isaac that if he was
guilty of the robbery, "for God's sake to let it be the last time." Isaac
replied that "if he got clear of that offence it should be the last time."
Also, Isaac's master may have protected him by testifying that Isaac
had been a "humble obedient negro" who was "by no means . . . of
violent turbulent habits, though he has been suspected of dishonesty."
Transportation would remove any threat; execution was apparently
regarded as unnecessary. That conclusion would hold for several other
slaves convicted of violent robberies. One of the few exceptions is
significant. Convicted of assaulting and robbing Isaac Brown on a
Charles City County highway in the fall of 1819, Stephen was hanged
the day before Christmas. Yet the victim was by no means of high
status. Instead, he was a free black man. Moreover, Stephen's defense
counsel was none other than young John Tyler, gentleman, the future
president of the United States. Stephen was almost the only slave to be
executed for violent robberies between 1801, when transportation became possible, and 1831, the end of the period under consideration.
Yet his execution is somewhat surprising since all the other slaves
executed for robbery allegedly had committed their offenses against
whites.[16]

It was more than the race or the status of the victim that influenced
the fate of a slave convicted of robbery. It was the degree of physical
danger associated with the robbery. The slave of a recently deceased
mayor of Norfolk did not have a chance when Norfolk County justices
accepted testimony that he had robbed Ralph and Mary Keeling on a
county road. The problem was not that he had stolen goods valued at
$13.50—many a transported slave had stolen more. What doomed
Tom to execution was that he had apparently clubbed Ralph Keeling,

16. Trial of Isaac, July 1, 1814, Goochland C.C.O.B. (1813–17), 121–24, and C.S., box
3; trial of Stephen, November 18, 1819, Charles City County, C.S., box 3. Executions:
trials of Joe, October 10, 1795, Elizabeth City County, Daniel, September 30, 1798,
Petersburg, Lewis Amigo, October 8, 1798 (Chesterfield C.C.O.B. [1796–99], 597), Nat,
October 25, 1798, Northampton County, Peter, November 27, 1799, Petersburg, Jack and
Jerry, July 5, 1805, Berkeley County, Moses, September 28, 1807, Hanover County, Ned,
October 8, 1810, Chesterfield County, George and Jack, August 23, 1826, Princess Anne
County, and Levin, August 23, 1826, Accomack County, C.S., boxes 1–5, and VEPLR. For
the August 4, 1829, trial of Claiborne for robbing a free black man, see C.S., box 5. The
judges recommended mercy because of Claiborne's "previous good character." He was
transported.

was regarded as abusive and insulting to the couple, and then had acted rather directly on the assumption that Mary Keeling kept her money "in her bosom." Not finding any cash, he undressed her more, still to no avail.[17]

It was slave violence of any sort that whites feared most. Besides the physical suffering and even death that could result, a complete reversal of power could also be a consequence of such attacks by slaves. When John Cornish questioned whether a white man had properly identified a slave assailant, his reasoning revealed whites' basic assumption in dealing with black slaves. "Who would stand and let a negro approach him with a stake in his hand, under such circumstances?" The slave was reportedly "sultry obstinate and hardened to the last." It is no wonder. The man to whom he was hired out seemed to be boasting or at least complaining when he stated that a dozen lashes with a whip would not hurt Jack "as he had them so often before." But it is also not surprising that whites would respond with official violence to a slave who would hit someone on the head with a fence rail. A white man convicted of the same offense would probably be jailed, not corporally punished, but there would be an official response in either case.[18]

There are, however, some cases that defy categorization or explanation. In 1828 the only event that aroused the white people of Louisa County as much as the election of Andrew Jackson was the five-day trial and conviction of the slave Sydnor for the murder of Nancy Green, a thirteen- or fourteen-year-old white person. After having been missing for three and one-quarter years, she was found in a shallow grave. The coroner's inquest established strangulation as the cause of death. The corpse was naked and both legs were almost completely broken off at the knees, only small portions of flesh retaining the lower legs. After sifting through the confusing evidence, the court found Sydnor guilty and sentenced him to death. The efforts of Richard Sandidge, Sydnor's master and his father, were partly responsible for the reduction of the mulatto slave's sentence to transportation. But the

17. Trial of Tom, July 20, 1818, Norfolk County, C.S., box 4, and VEPLR. Tom, the property of the estate of Thomas Newton, was not hanged—he escaped from jail.
18. John Cornish to William H. Roane, September 25, 1826, with file for Jack's case, August 23, 1826, Princess Anne County, VEPLR. The disposition of the case is recorded in C.S., box 5, at September 25, 1826. Billy Fitzhugh of Essex pointed a gun at two robbery victims in 1787, yet received benefit of clergy. He did not fire the gun, that is. Trial, November 21, 1787, Essex C.C.O.B. (1784–87), 391.

mystery centered on why Sydnor had killed Nancy Green. The oyer and terminer judges accepted the story that Sydnor and a white man had detained Nancy in order to have sex with her and to place her at the sexual disposal of other men. So the citizens of Louisa County were treated to the spectacle of a white man who had covered up his own sexual exploitation of a slave woman he owned, trying to save the life of a slave, his son, charged with murdering a young white woman in the sexual exploitation of whom the slave had allegedly participated.[19]

Even though it is not certain that Sydnor killed Nancy Green, much of the testimony made clear that Nancy was the victim of the same kind of brutality and ill-will that permeated several other relationships on Sandidge's plantation. Frank Tannenbaum once observed about slavery that "nothing escaped, nothing and no one." Sandidge could employ legal maneuvers to try to erase his past; Sydnor could claim he was trapped; others could and did place all the blame on Sydnor. Yet slavery was the nearly irresistible force from which all the participants in this tragic episode were trying to escape. Everyone's behavior was a response to conditions in a slave society, but few human reactions to slavery were sufficiently strong to withstand its corrosive influence.[20]

In 1825, the year Nancy Green disappeared, the slave Rachel told John Hamlin, her Lunenburg County master, about a plot against his life. Hamlin's response helped to seal his fate. He promised that if any of his slaves told him of such conspiracies again, he "would give them one thousand lashes for he was afraid of none of them, and if they chose to do it, let them do it." Thus when a plot matured in 1827 and Rachel knew about it, she took Hamlin at his word. He died quickly in one of his fields and at the hands of several of the men he thought were his to own. The defense counsel for Hamlin's slaves knew the laws and the courts well enough not to argue provocation in order to have the murder charge reduced to manslaughter. The slave code could hardly conceive of a slave committing manslaughter against her or his owner. But Richard J. Cralle did at least state that "the severity, and privations which they [the convicted slaves] endured under the discipline of

19. Trial of Sydnor, December 12, 1828, Louisa C.C.O.B. (1826–31), 285–97, and C.S., box 5, and VEPLR. The trial record is quite full, but letters filed with the state executive complete the picture of this case.

20. Frank Tannenbaum, *Slave and Citizen: The Negro in the Americas* (New York, 1946), 115.

a most rigid master, must in conscience at least, weigh something in the extenuation of its malignancy." Not fearing his slaves, Hamlin brutalized them and thereby encouraged some of them to kill him.[21]

But Cralle's conscience failed to impress the citizens of his county or the governor and the council as they reviewed the cases. There was a strong belief that mercy would virtually encourage a repetition of the killing on other plantations. So seven slaves hanged and two went into exile for this group homicide. Fear was at the core of such killings. Nearly seventy-five years later, a Lunenburg resident who was two years of age at the time of Hamlin's violent death described him as "the victim of an awful tragedy having been burnt to death by his negroes." This distortion of the event—Hamlin's corpse was burned; he had not been burned alive—reflects the terror that a slave or slaves killing a white person could produce. The story of Dr. Robert Berkeley's death in 1818 was told long after the event. A similar tale of an 1820 slaying of a prominent master is still known in Sussex County, and many accounts of such killings probably circulate in relatively accurate versions in other counties.[22]

Fear of violence can be groundless. In specific cases, whites' fear of slave violence was, and slaves' fear of white brutality was. But such fears did generally have a solid basis in reality, slavery being nearly a state of war. It was usually unpredictable when certain slaves would violently kill their masters, overseers, or other whites. Moreover, it was ordinarily beyond anticipation when such killings would increase in a certain time or place. One never knew when ordinarily moderate owners would turn brutal and sadistic. But two trends were certain. When slaves' violence against whites increased, the official response would grow more harsh. Slaves had every opportunity to know that that happened. A decline in murder convictions always followed a rise, reflecting increased controls and slaves' own restraint in the face of nearly certain execution or transportation of those who were caught (see Tables 23, 24).

Particularly between 1785 and 1831, violent slave behavior toward

21. Trials, March 20, 1827, Lunenburg County, C.S., box 5, and VEPLR, which contains extensive materials.

22. Captain Richard Irby, "Extracts from Old Places and Old People" (Typescript, 1899, in looseleaf notebook, Nottoway County Public Library); R. E. Griffith, Sr., "Notes on Rock Hill," *Proceedings of the Clarke County Historical Association*, III (1943), 47–52. The Sussex County story concerns the killing of Colonel David Mason (see trial of Bob, July 12, 1820, Sussex County, C.S., box 4).

whites generally coincided with insurrection episodes. The two periods of greatest white fear of slave insurrection were 1790 to 1802 and
1829 to 1831. (See Table 27.) The obvious upward trends in convictions
of slaves for murdering white people directly coincide with or immediately precede those two periods. Apparently groundless insurrection
scares occurred, especially in 1802 and 1829, but large-scale plots and
actual outbreaks also unquestionably occurred, such as Gabriel's Plot
in 1800 and Nat Turner's Revolt in 1831. These two episodes constituted the peak of insurrectionary planning or activity by slaves in
Virginia between 1785 and 1831. The years 1800 and 1831 also end the
times of sharpest increase in convictions of slaves for murdering
whites.[23]

Such analysis is not comprehensive, however, since it leaves out
slaves' killing of other slaves. Tables 23 and 24 highlight the three most
distinctive characteristics of homicides committed by slaves against
slaves. First, of the 216 slaves who were executed or transported for
murder between 1785 and 1834 and whose victims are known, only 57,
or 26.4 percent, had killed slaves.[24] Second, very few had worked with
accomplices. Third, the killing of slaves from other plantations was
not predominant as it was in the early and mid-eighteenth century.

There is some evidence from the 1785 to 1831 period that slave
informers then feared for their lives. Lewis, a slave who implicated
several men in the 1802 conspiracy scare, declared that he knew his
confession "would cause his death, for he spoke against his color, and
the blacks would kill him." When two whites in Spotsylvania County
reported the Boxley conspiracy of 1816 to the state government, they
asked that the information be kept secret to protect a slave informer
against "the rage of the people of her own colour, as we have been
informed that the life of a negro man in Louisa who informed of the
conduct of Boxley in assembling his associates there, has been
endangered."[25]

23. A similar relationship existed between poisoning and insurrection trials from the
1750s through the 1770s. There was a subsequent rise in poisoning and administration
of medicine convictions in the 1790s and late 1820s.

24. The figures do not include slaves convicted of manslaughter of other slaves and
granted benefit of clergy. No slaves were transported or executed for assault or for
attempted murder of a slave. Only twenty-three slaves were executed or transported for
murder of unidentified victims between 1785 and 1834.

25. James M. Bell and Waller Holladay to Governor W. C. Nicholas, March 1, 1816,
VEPLR (also in draft in Holladay Family Papers, 1728–1931, sec. 72, VHS, and printed in
CVSP, X, 433–36). Such disloyalty of one black person against slaves could work in other

Table 27. Selected Slaves Tried for Conspiracy and Insurrection, 1785–1834

	Tried	Convicted	Punishment Unknown	Pardoned	Corporal Punishment	Transported	Executed	Escaped; Died in Prison
1785–89	1	1	0	0	1	0	0	0
1790–94	4	4	0	0	0	0	4	0
1795–99	7	7	0	0	1	0	6	0
1800–1804	97	64	2	12	1	12	36	0
1805–1809	11	4	0	0	0	2	2	0
1810–14	6	5	0	0	0	5	0	0
1815–19	26	12	0	0	1	6	5	0
1820–24	1	0	0	0	0	0	0	0
1825–29	1	0	0	0	0	0	0	0
1830–34	89	45	0	1	0	21	23	1
Total	243	142	2	13	4	46	76	1

SOURCES: See Appendix One.
NOTE: These statistics are selective in that even though they include data on all slaves executed or transported for insurrection, they cover only some of the slaves found not guilty, pardoned, or given lesser sentences for insurrection.

Such death threats and killings were obviously related to the enslavement of all involved. It is less readily apparent how a killing motivated by a seemingly personal emotion such as jealousy could possibly have a connection with the unique aspects of slavery. On a January night in 1801, the Henrico slave Stephen arrived at the plantation of Miles Turpin early in the evening partly to ask a female slave a straightforward question. Would she have him? Her rejection of him provoked him to exclaim, "Then I am determined to murder this night." All Stephen had to do to find his victim was to return to the woman's cabin in the middle of the same night and rouse him out of her bed. Stephen challenged Aaron with a "chunck of fire." In spite of another slave's efforts to calm him, Stephen mortally wounded Aaron. Within a few months, the Commonwealth of Virginia caused Stephen's death in return.[26]

It would be superficial to conclude that Stephen acted only out of jealousy. The killing was more complex than that. Stephen belonged to Lucy Redford, Aaron to Miles Selden, and the woman to Miles Turpin. Neither of the rivals lived on the same plantation as the woman, but each probably had a different opportunity to compete for her attention. Stephen had visited the plantation early in the evening while running an errand for Lucy Redford. Aaron, however, was obviously somehow able to bed down for the night. The woman may have preferred Aaron to Stephen anyway, but slavery still made the situation much more difficult, perhaps impossible, for all concerned. Jealousy would figure in other killings. As petitioners for the life of John put it, he had been motivated by "the strongest passion that can possibly aggitate the human mind namely jealousy." In 1818, this Caroline County slave caught his wife in bed with Sam. What had complicated this case was that Dr. John Thornton, John's owner and the only authority to whom he could appeal for legal protection against Sam, had been unable to enforce his order that Sam never come to his plantation. Thus made legally helpless, John "took the law into his own hands."[27]

---

ways than informing, however (see *CVSP*, IX, 298, X, 436; trial, January 9, 1826, King and Queen County, VEPLR). Lewis may have been "playing his part" in a social ritual, telling authorities what they wished to hear, but his fears may also have been well founded. See Wyatt-Brown's skeptical analysis in *Southern Honor*, 426–27.

26. Trial of Stephen, February 2, 1801, Henrico County, C.S., box 2, and VEPLR.

27. *Ibid.*; trial of John, August 12, 1818, and accompanying materials, Caroline County, VEPLR. For a similar case, see trial of Clara, September 2, 1816, Spotsylvania C.C.M.B. (1815–19), 129–30, and C.S., box 3, and VEPLR. John escaped from jail.

Jealousy and insults could combine in the same incident with tragic results, as in Peter's mortal attack against John in Essex County. Some seemingly harmless insults led to killings. This raises questions about our understanding of slaves' perceptions of their status relative to one another. A case in point is that of Julius, a fifty-five-year-old Rockbridge County slave. While he was cutting wood with another slave in early 1817, a dispute arose over the truth of a tale concerning a panther. Julius called Ned "an ungodly man," Ned retorted that "he was no more ungodly" than Julius, and the two started fighting. Julius ended the fight and Ned's life as well with a blow of his ax. Why did the two men take such offense at the epithet *ungodly*? The word did mean a great deal because of who they were and their previous relationship. Julius and Ned responded openly to verbal challenges. But Julius' owner testified to his previous "good character and behavior." Killing had not been among the ways Julius reacted in an argument. So the key to this case was the past interaction between the two men. According to a white witness, Julius told him after the incident that he and Ned had carried on a grudge for two years. The most recent flare-up had been at a corn husking in the fall of 1816, several months before the killing. Then the two had argued; in the course of scuffling with each other, Ned had butted Julius. Julius refused to forgive him. The relationship could have improved thereafter, but did not.[28]

Several months after Julius killed Ned, a forty-three-year-old slave named David threw a wood-handled, iron and steel mattock at Isaac, a co-worker. This Harrison County incident did not represent an old grudge. The bondsman Squire testified that only the day before, the two men had been friendly and had been singing hymns together. But when the two began to dig up some iron ore under Squire's direction, David lifted up a piece of sandy ore and Isaac immediately broke off a chunk with his shovel. When David told Isaac not to do that again since the ore would "moulder fast enough" by itself, Isaac declared that he had a right to check the quality of the ore. In spite of Squire's efforts to stop the altercation, the two kept at it until Isaac called David "a mean negro" several times. David finally retaliated by throwing his heavy tool at Isaac.[29]

28. Trial of Peter, October 16, 1826, Essex C.C.O.B. (1823–26), 511–14, and C.S., box 5, and VEPLR. See also Tragle (ed.), *The Southampton Slave Revolt*, 450. Trial of Julius, February 15, 1817, Rockbridge County, C.S., box 3, and VEPLR.
29. Trial of David, July 15, 1817, Harrison County (now West Virginia), C.S., box 3, and VEPLR.

Close friends Matthew and Mike fell into a mortal quarrel in Northampton County during the late spring of 1816. At issue was the possession of some Chesapeake Bay crabs. The two struggled with each other from the dubious vantage points of separate canoes. The shoving match subsided temporarily when Mike retreated, but when he returned later on, demanding his hat, the real brawl began. Saying he would make Mike "sip sorrow by ladles full," Matthew refused to give him his hat. Mike yelled that he would have the hat or die, and Matthew hit him with an oak oar. The blow knocked Mike into the water, where he drowned. There had been no previous dispute. In fact, the two had been brought up together since infancy and had a high regard for each other. The clerk of the court that condemned Matthew reported that he had now "almost lost the little portion of reason he has received from nature, by the alarm and agitation which his situation has occasioned." The death was really accidental, then, even though some would hastily blame Matthew for lack of self-restraint.[30] There is no reason to try to justify what Matthew did. That would be a presumptuous denial of the sincerity of his grief as well as a violation of nearly universal ethical precepts. David also probably regretted the loss of his friend Isaac; even Julius may have wished he could turn back the clock for Ned's sake as well as for his own. But the fifty-seven executions or banishments of slaves for killing other slaves between 1785 and 1831 indicate that this sort of event occurred fairly regularly, though perhaps not so often as slaves' killings of white people did. In both cases, one of the most important elements of causation was the circumscribed status of assailant and victim. When a slave killed a slave, it was significant that one person of low status was in conflict with another person of the same status.

The status of all slaves within a slave society was by definition low. The status of each slave relative to other slaves depended in turn on her or his ability to defend the few vestiges of status the slave society allowed. When a former Virginian slave came up against a black driver in Georgia whom he hated, he "let him have it in old Virginia stile, (which generally consists in gouging, biting, and butting)." One vestige of status was the position any slave was able to uphold in the eyes of other slaves. Even that was jeopardized by slaveowners. All slaves were forced by their situation to depend completely on what they did have, be it family, skills, reputation, or honor, for their status in their own

30. Trial of Matthew, June 3, 1816, Northampton County, VEPLR.

community. Should any person threaten these signs of standing in the slave community, that person endangered everything. Some slaves could stand this sort of jeopardy; others could not. Some slaves found themselves having to defend their last vestiges of status against fellow slaves.[31]

One other kind of killing by slaves presents a special analytical problem. Given the rule of *partus sequitur ventrem*—the condition of the child follows the condition of the mother—the only way a mother could prevent an infant from remaining a slave was to run away with the baby—a dangerous and improbable course of action—or to commit infanticide. But which babies were consciously saved from slavery, which were in fact murdered, which were stillborn, which were aborted late in pregnancy, and which were the victims of various diseases or hazards to which the newborn were particularly vulnerable? White officials appear to have had an even harder time detecting the private action of infanticide by slaves than the hidden behavior of poisoners.[32] Between 1785 and 1831, only eight women reached the notice of Virginia's auditor because of their execution or transportation for infanticide. Three were hanged and the other five were transported.[33] Among the most important of the circumstances that differed in these cases were the perceptions of different white judges. On

31. Grimes was born in King George County in 1794 and later lived in Rappahannock County before being sold to Georgia (Grimes, *Life of William Grimes*, 37); trials of Bill Williams, September 12, 1807, Norfolk city, Randall, June 8, 1809, New Kent County, Davey, January 29, 1810, Fauquier County, Moses, April 5, 1823, Nansemond County, and Patrick, February 21, 1831, Culpeper County, C.S., boxes 2–6, and VEPLR. For a discussion of the possible role of honor in slaves' relationships with one another, see Edward L. Ayers, *Vengeance and Justice: Crime and Punishment in the Nineteenth-Century American South* (New York, 1984), 133.

32. Not only are the opinions of judges to be suspected in such cases, but skepticism must reign concerning the ability of authorities to detect all cases in which slave mothers killed their newborn infants in order to save them from slavery.

33. In Essex, Henry, Southampton, and Spotsylvania counties between 1786 and 1865, there were only two trials of slaves for infanticide, both of which ended with exonerations. There were no such cases at all in Brunswick and Henrico counties and in the city of Richmond between 1786 and 1799. In recorded cases, sentencing was inconsistent. Transportation was the penalty for a thirty-year-old woman convicted of killing her four-year-old, as it was for a weaver who was convicted of killing her three children. In 1818 an eighteen-year-old was found guilty of killing her newborn infant; a woman of the same age received the same verdict for the same offense in 1827. The first was hanged, but the second was transported. Trials, July 28, 1824 (Louisa C.C.O.B. [1822–26], 259–61), September 7, 1815, Powhatan County, November 9, 1818, Buckingham County, and May 21, 1827, Prince Edward County, C.S., boxes 3–5, and VEPLR. The ages of transported slaves are in "A List of Slaves and Free Persons of Color received into the Penitentiary . . . 1816 to . . . 1842," C.S., box 10.

September 7, 1815, the oyer and terminer justices of Powhatan County heard the charge against Jenny of murdering her three young children. They believed they had the evidence to find her guilty and sentence her to hang for drowning them. But because she was pregnant again, she did not hang. That allowed time for some county residents to compile a petition for mercy on the grounds that Jenny was insane. The county judges responded to this public pressure with an inquiry into the truth of the claim of insanity. As might be expected, the standards of the white community rather than scientific observation established whether she was in fact insane. Conflicting reports came into the governor and the council, who concluded there was reasonable doubt as to her responsibility for her actions.[34]

In 1819 the state executives responded similarly to the case of Lucy, the twenty-two-year-old slave of Thomas Balton of Lewis County. Insanity was not the problem this time. Instead, a person or persons unknown tried to assure that the only clue to the father's identity would be that the child was a mulatto. Petitions and a private letter established, however, that Lucy had given birth to a mulatto child once before and feared for her life should she have another. Neither the identity of the white father nor the fact of threats against Lucy's life could be entered as trial evidence, however. Presumably the source of this evidence was a slave who could not testify against a white person. Moreover, the child may either have been abandoned or born dead rather than killed.[35]

All the women convicted of infanticide had uniformly been treated and identified as slaves. As a result, one had a mulatto child but could not name the father, another could not adequately defend herself against the charge of infanticide, and a third had been so desperate about running away from her owner that she had killed her four-year-old child. Slavery played a crucial role in the paternity, birth, or death

34. Trial of Jenny, September 7, 1815, Powhatan County, C.S., box 3, and VEPLR, especially inquiry and pardon papers of February, 1816; Virginia Council Journals, 1815–16, pp. 56, 61, VSL. For a similar case, see trial of Letty, July 24, 1822, Brooke County (now West Virginia), C.S., box 4, and VEPLR. Johnston, *Race Relations in Virginia*, 308, discusses this case.

35. Trial of Lucy, November 4, 1819, Lewis County (now West Virginia), C.S., box 4, and VEPLR. There was a similar circumstance in the trial of Letty, July 24, 1822, Brooke County (now West Virginia), C.S., box 4, and VEPLR. A hanging for infanticide appears to have resulted from testimony that the accused stated her intentions, even though she subsequently expressed sorrow for the act (trial of Milley, June 15, 1826, Patrick County, C.S., box 5, and VEPLR).

of these unfortunate children. Slavery was like an unindicted co-conspirator or a perpetrator in many infanticides committed by slave women.

Thus did slavery continue to make an essential difference between any homicide committed by slaves and killings for which whites were directly responsible. A few killings over the years from 1785 to 1831 would not have required a strong public response. But convictions of slaves for first-degree murder of whites became more frequent in several key periods, giving rise to the notion that "the slaves" were out of control if "some" slaves went so far as to plan and openly bring about the destruction of the very people who were supposed to be their complete masters.

10. *Authorities and Banditti*

The powerful image of Nat Turner looms large in the history of slavery in North America, so large that it threatens analysis of the context in which the rebellion he led in 1831 took place. Nat Turner was important, of course, but he was neither alone nor isolated. If he and his allies killed fifty-seven white people in 1831, other bondspeople, whether individually or in groups, killed more than one hundred whites between 1785 and 1831, seventy-four of them during Nat Turner's lifetime. Judges found forty-four slaves guilty of conspiring or acting with Turner, sending twenty-three of them to the gallows, but other judges convicted ninety-six enslaved Afro-Virginians of rebellion or conspiracy to rebel between 1785 and 1831, eighty-four of them after Turner's birth and before the Southampton revolt exploded. Forty-one such convicts were hanged between 1800 and 1816 alone. Moreover, the oyer and terminer courts of Turner's home county, Southampton, had amassed a great deal of experience in dealing with the illegal behavior of their county's black residents. Again, in Turner's lifetime, twenty-six Southampton slaves had been formally accused and nine convicted of various kinds of attacks on whites; numerous others were found guilty of endangering or destroying whites' property.[1]

A single case can illustrate the importance of context to analysis of slave plots or rebellions. In October, 1799, a small but revealing fracas

---

1. The statements by Stephen B. Oates, in *The Fires of Jubilee: Nat Turner's Fierce Rebellion* (New York, 1975), 59, that in Southampton "only seven slaves had ever been convicted of crimes" before 1831 and that "most of the neighboring counties had similar records" are mistaken.

Map 4. Virginia Counties, 1825

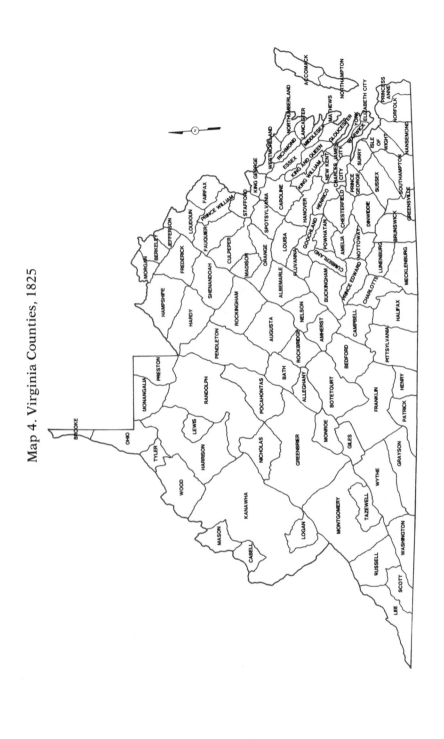

took place in Henrico County. Gabriel, a slave who belonged to Thomas Henry Prosser, fought with Absalom Johnson, a white former overseer who had recently begun to rent part of Colonel Nathaniel Wilkinson's plantation. The trouble began when Johnson caught Wilkinson's slave Jupiter stealing a hog. Solomon, Gabriel's brother and another slave of Prosser's, apparently threatened Johnson. Gabriel did far more. He struggled with Johnson and bit off "a considerable part" of his left ear. Johnson retaliated by bringing all three slaves before the Henrico County Court. On October 7, 1799, five justices of oyer and terminer tried Gabriel for the capital crime of maiming John- son, unanimously concluding that "the said Gabriel is Guilty of the Crime with which he stands accused." Acting as regular county jus- tices, the same men convicted Jupiter of the misdemeanor of hog steal- ing. They also reviewed Johnson's complaint concerning Solomon's threats but then dismissed it.[2]

Three of the five justices would try the same three slaves again about a year later for a capital crime. In that instance, these slaves had clearly engaged in something more than "criminal conduct"— Gabriel, Jupiter, and Solomon plotted to defy slavery itself. Partici- pants in an insurrectionary plot of major proportions in 1800, Gabriel and Jupiter would die on the gallows, the former for leading the con- spiracy and the latter for actively supporting it. Solomon would be condemned to die for his collaboration with Gabriel but would escape execution by incriminating other slaves.[3]

Although the 1799 incident did not cause the 1800 plot, it definitely reflected the ever-present possibility that small-scale criminalized re- sistance by slaves would lay the foundation for large-scale, collective rebellion. The members of the Henrico County bench misinterpreted the conflict, because they treated Gabriel, Jupiter, and Solomon as just three more criminals. The slaves could have made their last ap- pearance before the bar in 1799, but they built on their experience in 1799 in order to shape the plot in 1800. Gabriel was the "Main Spring and Chief Mover" in the private and public confrontation of 1799, as he would be in the insurrectionary conspiracy of 1800.[4] But his behavior

2. Schwarz, "Gabriel's Challenge," 283–309. Gabriel and Solomon had been owned by Prosser at least since Gabriel was seven or eight years of age (Henrico County Per- sonal Property Tax, 1783, 1784, VSL).
3. See Mullin, *Flight and Rebellion*, 136–61.
4. Certificate of the examining magistrates to Governor Monroe, September 8, 1800, VEPLR; Mullin, *Flight and Rebellion*, 147.

in both cases corresponded to a general pattern of interaction between slaves and white authorities that had become widespread by the end of the eighteenth century and that would reach its flash point in the 1820s and particularly in 1831.

The conflict that flared up so often between 1785 and 1831 was collective and based on competing ideologies. It was not just personal. Some people knew that at the time. Noting in 1802 that the recent insurgency by an unknown number of slaves in the South resulted in part from the events in Saint Domingue, President Jefferson declared that slave rebels "are not felons, or common malefactors, but persons guilty of what the safety of society, under actual circumstances, obliges us to treat as a crime, but which their feelings may represent in a far different shape."[5] Slave rebels were nevertheless bound to be treated as criminals in Virginia before and long after 1776. A successful revolutionary such as Jefferson had to look back at 1776 as he tried to understand some other accused revolutionaries in 1802. But the bloodiness as much as the triumph of the black revolution in Saint Domingue made it rather unlikely that oyer and terminer justices in Virginia would ever see things from the perspective of these rebels. Jefferson would support execution in exceptional cases and transportation in most in order to hold "the wolf by the ears." In other words, he believed in a process that would, in spite of his opinion, reinforce most white citizens' view of slave insurrectionaries as nothing but common felons. That in turn would encourage some other slaves to reject totally the legitimacy of the authorities who called them criminals.

The "divergent concepts of revolution" discussed earlier account partially for the existence of so fundamental division of opinion as that which prevailed between slave rebels and white authorities in Virginia. Such division was especially strong between 1785 and 1831, partly because of what had happened before. Rumors of insurrection

5. Thomas Jefferson to Rufus King, July 13, 1802, in Thomas Jefferson Papers, microfilm reel 226, Library of Congress. John M. Sink, *Political Criminal Trials: How to Defend Them* (New York, 1974), 1–2, showed how collective actions that are also illegal still create the situation recognized by Jefferson. Sink counseled that when a defendant had been involved in an "admitted crime intended as a political protest," the defense must make the jury "see things the way the defendant saw them." In 1981 a supporter of the insurgent provisional wing of the Irish Republican Army in Northern Ireland said it in another way: "I'll wear no convict's uniform nor meekly serve my time, / That Britain might make Ireland's fight 800 years of crime" (Cable News Network broadcast, May 17, 1981).

spread in 1785; they continued to appear during the next forty-five years.[6] The catastrophe feared by whites nearly occurred in 1800 and actually took place in 1831.

Insurrection episodes were often bigger and more dramatic manifestations of the same rejection of white authorities' claim to legitimacy that led other slaves to attack white people. In fact, a surge in convictions of slaves for certain major crimes is a leading indicator of the coming of a regional scare, plot, or outbreak as opposed to isolated insurgencies or mutinies (see Table 27).[7] There was a steady rise in such convictions through the 1785 to 1789, 1790 to 1794, and 1795 to 1799 quinquennia, after which the massive plot in 1800 and the scare in 1802 surfaced. Moreover, at about the same time these episodes occurred, the number of convictions for major crimes dropped. The same pattern recurred, prefiguring the relatively small regional plot of 1816 and dramatically rising just before the 1831 revolt, once again declining during the same quinquennium. Certain kinds of major convictions made the difference in this pattern. It was not convictions of slaves in general, as the uneven trends in the most numerous convictions for stealing indicate, but the convictions of slaves for murdering white people that truly prefigured insurrectionary scares and events.

However, slaves who aided, abetted, participated in, or planned insurrections did not necessarily otherwise act in ways that white

6. Insurrection scares, major and minor, that did not result in the trials listed in the Appendix occurred in 1786 (Cumberland), 1806 (James and York, and city of Richmond), 1808 (city of Norfolk), 1812 (Henry and surrounding region), 1823 (city of Richmond and environs), and 1829 (Eastern Shore). W. T. Moulson to Governor Henry, May 6, 1786, Robert Anderson to Governor Cabell, April 4, 1806, Robert Taylor to Governor Cabell, April 8, 1806, Note from the Council, April 9, 1806, William Sharp to General Mathews, and enclosed depositions, November 14, 1808, "Confessions made before us John Floyd and Henry Edmundson, Justices . . . 2nd April 1812," John G. Joynes to Governor Giles, August 13, 1829, John Eyre to Governor Giles, August 27, 1829, all in VEPLR; Virginia Executive Letter Books, 1823–30, p. 51; Virginia Council Journals, 1823–24, p. 13; *Genius of Universal Emancipation*, Vol. III, No. 37 (January, 1824), quoting Baltimore *American*, December 24, 1823. See also Austin Steward, *Twenty-Two Years a Slave and Forty Years a Freeman* (Reading, Mass., 1969), 27–39. An undated scare in Prince William County stemmed from a violent clash between patrollers and a prominent slaveowner's slaves. After several blacks were killed and many whites demanded insurrection trials, "Col. Alexander" still insisted that the slaves could defend themselves against patrollers' attacks.

7. In *American Negro Slave Revolts*, Aptheker did not look for geographical or temporal patterns other than those that related to his argument concerning the widespread existence of rebelliousness. Although his treating the United States made it impossible for him to give extensive attention to Virginia, his book contains much good material on the jurisdiction.

authorities regarded as criminal. From the perspective of 1800, the behavior of Gabriel, Jupiter, and Solomon in 1799 was a sort of stepping-stone to the insurrectionary planning in 1800. It did not have to be, though. Indeed, most of the slaves tried for conspiracy and insurrection had not previously confronted or defied the legal power of government and the criminal code and courts for slaves. Besides those three, Daniel, the property of John Brooke, was the only other person accused in 1800 who had been tried before. Charged in 1797 with stealing a blanket worth 15 shillings from a white man, Daniel was acquitted then just as he was in his 1800 conspiracy and insurrection trial. Otherwise, not one of the Spotsylvania slaves tried for the Boxley plot of 1816 or the Southampton slaves prosecuted for Turner's Revolt had previously been tried for a felony in a county slave court. In other words, the process by which many slave insurrectionaries moved toward the choice for revolution certainly did not have to include an eye-opening confrontation with the criminal courts for slaves.[8]

On the other hand, many, but not necessarily all, slave insurrectionaries emerged from slave communities that had exhibited major illegal behavior. Prior association was an important factor. Open violence was more prevalent in Southampton County during the thirty years before Nat Turner's Revolt than in most other counties. Spotsylvania County, scene of a plot in 1816 and a small insurgency in 1831 as well, also experienced a great deal of illegal slave behavior of major proportions in the early nineteenth century. Gabriel's fellow slaves in Henrico County and Richmond had troubled white leaders with open resistance that went beyond slaves' actions in most of Virginia. Yet the few cases of suspected insurrection in Brunswick and other counties such as Nottoway may have related to the distinct threat of poisoning attacks.[9] Even though few slaves in these areas had stood trial for a felony before—execution or transportation helped to ensure that—there are several instances of different slaves belonging to the same

8. Schwarz, "Gabriel's Challenge," 283–309; trials of Daniel, October 28, 1797, September 13, 1800, Henrico C.C.O.B. (1796–98), 446–47, (1799–1801), 379–80. Since I have not surveyed the post-1785 trial records of several counties in which insurrection charges were made, I did not apply this test to any slaves other than those tried in Brunswick, Essex, Henrico, city of Richmond, Southampton, and Spotsylvania.

9. Henrico and Richmond figure in Schwarz, "Gabriel's Challenge," 283–309. In Spotsylvania, eleven slaves were convicted of murder or poisoning between 1785 and 1831 alone. One other was convicted of rape, another of attempted rape. Three received guilty verdicts in arson trials.

owner appearing in felony and also in conspiracy and insurrection trials.[10]

The direct connections among slaves suspected of insurrection are also suggestive. In Henrico County, different slaves who belonged to Paul Thilman of Hanover County were convicted of insurrection in both 1800 and 1802, and three of Thomas Henry Prosser's slaves were found not guilty of rebellion in 1806, six years after a half dozen Prosser bondsmen had been convicted of that offense. Similarly, three Robert S. Coleman slaves were found not guilty in the Boxley plot, and another of his slaves was transported after being convicted of participation in the 1831 Spotsylvania incident. One incident raises the question whether tradition—or "long memory"—could have encouraged plotting. Three Caroline slaves transported for taking part in Gabriel's Plot belonged to Charles Carter of Shirley, his plantation in Charles City County. His relative Charles Carter had experienced collective slave unrest in 1755. Although that took place in Lancaster County, did Carter's relocated slaves spread traditions concerning this incident? In 1769 the same Charles Carter's slaves had participated in an uprising in Hanover County.[11]

While slave insurrectionaries were clearly not common felons, what they did had some similarity to what many slaves convicted of other major crimes had done. A Southampton conspiracy illustrates the reason why the difference between conspiracy and insurrection on the one hand and first-degree murder on the other was political as well as

10. Three slaves who belonged to James Price, owner of two found not guilty in the Gabriel episode, were found guilty of an unspecified felony in 1789 in Henrico and of stealing in 1797 and in 1798 in the city of Richmond (Henrico C.C.O.B. [1789–91], 16; Richmond city Hustings C.O.B. [1797–1801], 14, 231). Balak, found guilty of insurrection in Spotsylvania County in 1801, belonged to Stephen Johnston, who also owned two slaves convicted and sentenced to death for preparation and administration of medicine in 1795 and another slave found guilty of grand larceny in 1796 (Spotsylvania C.C.O.B. [1795–98], 90–91, 248–49; Spotsylvania C.C.M.B. [1798–1802], 177). Robert Ricks of Southampton County owned a slave who was tried for insurrection in 1801, another tried for burglary and theft in 1820, and still another tried for the same offense—in fact, the massive burglary of David Vallance's store in Jerusalem—in 1821 (Southampton C.C.M.B. [1799–1803], 152; Southampton C.C.O.B. [1819–21], 135, 332–33).

11. Mary Frances Berry and John W. Blassingame, *Long Memory: The Black Experience in America* (New York, 1982); Lieutenant Governor Dinwiddie to Charles Carter, July 18, 1755, in *The Official Records of Robert Dinwiddie, Lieutenant-Governor of Virginia, 1751–1758* (2 vols.; Richmond, 1884), II, 102; Mullin (ed.), *American Negro Slavery*, 94–95 (from the *Virginia Gazette* [R], January 25, 1770); *JHB*, May 28, 1770, p. 28. Prosser's Ben escaped prosecution in 1800 by testifying against several slaves. The chances are good that the Ben prosecuted in 1806 was the same "Prosser's Ben," but there is no evidence that he actually was.

legal. In 1799, several slaves being shipped through Southampton County on their way from Maryland to Georgia killed their new owners. These slaves had not planned with other slaves from the Southampton and southeastern Tidewater region. They had attended no local barbecues or Baptist meetings. Nor had they, since no one could have, subscribed to Garrison's *Liberator* or read David Walker's *Appeal*. But they chose to kill their owners rather than face bondage in Georgia. They had responded together to their common situation.[12] They were convicted of conspiracy and insurrection, and they hanged. Twenty-eight years later, nine slaves conspired to kill their owner, John Hamlin of Lunenburg County, in order to stop his intolerable behavior toward them. Although this killing sent shock waves through the area, and seven of the convicted slaves were hanged and two transported, the charge filed against each one was murder, not conspiracy and insurrection.[13]

This apparent contradiction only reflected that Virginia's lawmakers and judges, from 1723 to 1865, consistently believed that a conspiracy of slaves to rebel had something in common with a conspiracy of slaves to murder white people. Thus, oyer and terminer justices—in their discretion and their fear, anger, or concern—had to determine whether a particular incident constituted which sort of conspiracy. As many writers on slavery have noted, reports of slave insurrection plots may frequently have resulted from widespread fear rather than from real planning.[14] But the fear of insurrection derived

12. Approximately one-quarter of the killings of whites by slaves resulted from conspiracies between 1785 and 1834 (153 slaves were convicted for killing 101 white people).
13. Trials of Isaac, Hatter Isaac, Old Sam, and Tom, October 25, 1799, Southampton C.C.M.B. (1799–1803), 46–47, and C.S., box 2; trials of David, Archer, Billy, Nathan, Big Stephen, Tom, Sam, Little Stephen, and Robin, March 19, 1827, Lunenburg County, C.S., box 5, and VEPLR. One of the victims of Isaac and his cohorts had apparently committed a white-collar crime—he was accused of embezzlement from the Georgia treasury (Ulrich B. Phillips, *American Negro Slavery: A Survey of the Supply, Employment and Control of Negro Labor As Determined by the Plantation Regime* [New York, 1918], 188–89).
14. Hening, *The Statutes at Large*, IV, 126, VI, 105; Shepherd, *Statutes at Large*, I, 122–25, II, 77–78. Slaves knew about feared plots; many slaves may have known whether the feared plots really existed. Slaves also knew that whites were more vulnerable at some times than at others. One knew about the forthcoming War of 1812 because "it was heard from the poor people in the neighbourhood and by hearing the news papers read." Slaves in Gabriel's Plot were aware of the French threat and also knew that patrols in their area had recently been decreased (Colonel Tompkins to Governor Giles, July 18, 1829, VEPLR; Virginia Executive Council Journal, 1828–29, August 4, 1829, p. 138; "Confessions made . . . 2nd April 1812," VEPLR; Mullin, *Flight and Rebellion*, 148–49, 151–52). Other contemporary comments on insurrection scares are in George McIntosh to Gover-

as much from the possibility and the occasional reality as it did from white guilt or panic. If anyone in government blithely assumed in the early summer of 1831 that the absence of capital convictions of slaves for insurrection since 1818 meant that a major insurrection was unlikely to happen in the near future, or ever, he was ignoring the steadily rising number of slaves convicted of murdering white people between 1818 and 1831. He was also making too little of the insurrection scare that so unsettled Tidewater Virginia in 1829. Some white leaders discounted reports. They may have been in error. In fact, fear of a plot could even have led to discovery of a real plot in its infancy, thus choking it off at the most opportune time.[15]

More and more slaves became involved in insurrectionary talk or behavior, and the legal context had some influence on their thinking and action because laws and courts were used frequently to suppress rebellious slaves. Blacks knew that white leaders regarded, prosecuted, and punished as insurrectionary certain kinds of talk and behavior—regular trials, whippings, sentences of transportation, and hangings were a constant reminder. Slaves also became increasingly aware of the changing political context in which they and slaveholders lived. They knew that Virginia's legislators had fine tuned the harsh prerevolutionary slave code so that it would serve, paradoxically, as a republican slave code.[16] Born in 1776, Gabriel had to come to terms with this and other aspects of American republicanism in 1799 and 1800. In 1799, Gabriel confronted the government of a white man,

---

nor Wise, December 22, 1856, in VEPLR; and Edmund Ruffin, *The Diary of Edmund Ruffin*, ed. William Kauffman Scarborough (2 vols.; Baton Rouge, 1972, 1977), II, 207–209. See also Wyatt-Brown, *Southern Honor*, 402–34.

15. Trials of George, Plato, and Grandison, January 27, 1818, Goochland C.C.M.B. (1811–18), 438–43, and C.S., box 3—actually a charge of conspiracy to murder. Before that, the Boxley plot was the incident nearest in time. On the 1829 incident, see trial of Sam, July 25, 1829, Essex C.C.O.B. (1826–30), 574, and VEPLR. See also Clement Eaton, *The Freedom-of-Thought Struggle in the Old South* (New York, 1964), 91–92. News of a December uprising of slaves on a steamer bound from Norfolk to New Orleans and a January account of four Kentucky slaves who stood on the gallows and "attempted to justify the deed they had committed" undoubtedly contributed to the fears experienced in the winter of 1829–30 (Aptheker, *American Negro Slave Revolts*, 98; Richmond *Enquirer*, January 28, 1830).

16. Virginia even passed a special law in 1798 concerning whites who aided slave insurrectionaries (Shepherd, *Statutes at Large*, II, 77–78; Ira Berlin, *Slaves Without Masters: The Free Negro in the Antebellum South* [New York, 1974], 3–107). As Pauline Maier has pointed out, American revolutionaries rejected the notion that citizens in the new republic would find it necessary to resort to revolution ("Popular Uprisings and Civil Authority in Eighteenth-Century America," *WMQ*, 3rd ser., XXVII [1970], 33–35).

Absalom Johnson, as well as republican slaveholders' power in the courtroom, where the positive legislation in Virginia's aging slave code as well as common law dictated procedure and results. But former overseer Johnson could not overawe Gabriel in the fields, and the republican judges in Henrico failed to employ their full power against Gabriel. Unknowingly, they left him free, once Thomas Henry Prosser paid his bond for good behavior, to plan rebellion with other slaves and perhaps with a white Frenchman.[17]

Changes in the peculiar institution outside the Old Dominion also affected rebellious Afro-Virginians. They knew about the Saint Domingan slaves who had gone through one form or other of revolution.[18] Perhaps they also knew that British abolitionists were cooperating with and encouraging the growing American movement. And they definitely were aware that British soldiers in the War of 1812, as they had during the Revolution, welcomed runaway slaves to freedom in exchange for their support of the British war aims. It was once again rather difficult for republican owners to recover their "stolen property" when the hostilities ended. What is more, the British in the West Indies had long since adamantly refused to share in the increased international supply of slaves that resulted from the Old Dominion's instituting transportation in 1801. Part of the reason was that British imperial authorities were moving closer to complete abolition of slavery in their Caribbean possessions. Moreover, Virginian slaves could not help but know that when Denmark Vesey, a free black influenced by West Indian contacts, led an unsuccessful insurrection plot in Charleston in 1822, he provoked more than reprisals against himself. He also caused a great deal of uneasiness in Virginia, accounting in part for a sudden shift in legislation concerning free blacks convicted of crimes and a significant tightening of the criminal code for slaves.[19]

Virginia's leaders were by no means defenseless, however. They

17. Schwarz, "Gabriel's Challenge," 283–309.
18. Berlin, *Slaves Without Masters*, 40–42; Jordan, *White Over Black*, 381–82; Willis Wilson to Governor Lee, August 21, 1793, Mayor Thomas Newton to Governor Brooke, June 9, 11, 23, 19, 1795, Andrew Dunscomb to Lieutenant Governor Wood, September 18, 1795, Petition of French refugees, July 30, 1795, all in VEPLR, and *CVSP*, VI, 490, VIII, 254–55, 260, 264, 277–78, 298.
19. Aptheker, *American Negro Slave Revolts*, 25–27; Cassell, "Slaves of the Chesapeake Bay Area," 144–55; George Goosley to Governor Monroe, June 5, 24, 1802, Mayor Thomas Newton to Governor Monroe, September, 1802, all in VEPLR, and *CVSP*, IX, 305–306, 309, 320; Berlin, *Slaves Without Masters*, 183; *Supplement to the Revised Code of the Laws*, 147, 234. From 1835 to 1864, one-sixth of the slaves convicted of assault against a white person with intent to kill went to the gallows, most between 1845 and 1854.

knew, and slaves knew as well, that slaveholders had reason to expect the federal government to help defend their government and society against domestic insurrections.[20] There was solid evidence that the federal government supported the slave system as well as the public safety. The government had always upheld the return of fugitive slaves.[21] Moreover, the District of Columbia's federal criminal court for Arlington County, Virginia, regularly heard charges against slaves, convicting 100 percent of those actually brought to trial in one eight-year period.[22] More important, when there first arose the real need for U.S. troops to suppress a slave insurrection, the call to a federal commander came from a mayor, and not the governor. And troops were sent. According to one former slave, Richmond's white authorities constantly made sure slaves knew that federal troops would be able to crush a slave revolt.[23]

This international, national, regional, and local context was important, but slaves themselves were at the center of collective resistance. It was black Virginians who initiated the plots and the one revolt. Government officials knew that well enough not to put all the blame for Nat Turner's Rebellion on non-Virginians. Governor Floyd saw certain key figures within Virginia as planners and leaders of revolt—the slave preachers. Floyd charged that white Virginians had been guilty of "resting in apathetic security," allowing "magistrates and laws" to become "more inactive." The watchmen had not been at the gate or at any of their other posts.[24]

Floyd had learned as long before as 1812 that slaves might act very

20. Article I, Section 8, empowered Congress "to provide for calling forth the Militia to execute the Laws of the Union, suppress Insurrections and repel Invasions," and Article IV, Section 4, declared that "the United States shall guarantee to every State in this Union a Republican form of Government, and shall protect each of them against Invasion; and on Application of the Legislature, or of the Executive (when the Legislature cannot be convened) against domestic Violence." The second part of the latter reinforced the promise of protection. It provided for interstate extradition of fugitive criminals and slaves.

21. Even during the Civil War, when Congress decreed that no fugitive slaves would be returned to disloyal owners, the one exception was a slave wanted for a crime (*Statutes at Large of the United States of America, 1789–1873* [17 vols.; Boston, 1850–73], XII, 354, 589).

22. These were jury trials. U.S. District Court, Arlington County Criminal C.M.B., in VSL. See also Catterall, *Judicial Cases*, IV, 154–210.

23. Tragle (ed.), *The Southampton Slave Revolt*, 16–20, 269–72; Henry Box Brown, *Narrative of the Life of Henry Box Brown* (Boston, 1849), 38–40.

24. Governor Floyd to South Carolina Governor Hamilton, November 19, 1831, Floyd to Virginia Senate and House of Delegates, December 6, 1831, both in Tragle (ed.), *The Southampton Slave Revolt*, 275–76, 432–33. See also Oates, *The Fires of Jubilee*, 147–54.

much on their own. At the age of twenty-nine, he had for six years been practicing medicine in Montgomery County, Virginia; he was also a justice of the peace and a major in the militia there. He joined another justice in the interrogation of a slave suspected not only of murdering his master in Henry County but of complicity in a regional insurrectionary plot. In his report, Floyd cited the imminent war with Great Britain, but most of the slave's statement referred to the organizing efforts by two slave conjurers, Goomer, a North Carolinian, and Jack, the property of a Henry County widow. Tom, the slave being questioned, was executed upon being convicted of murdering his owner. In his statement to the Montgomery justices, he named prominent citizens whom the conspirators planned to poison or shoot. These were anything but outside agitators. They could well become internal enemies.[25]

Even in the conspiracy that Tom described, there were two essential elements that testified to slaves' determination and ability to plan insurrection on their own. First, the plot was focusing on locations as far as eighty miles apart—Lynchburg, Blacksburg, and Henry County, as well as Rockingham County in North Carolina. Second, the rebels had targeted the white leaders of Henry County, knowing that success would breed terror. Even their trust in the two conjurers was based on one kind of reality. However much Floyd the medical practitioner might dismiss Goomer and Jack as manipulators of superstitious slaves, Jack had had the power to convince Tom that he "could not be hurt" for killing his owner and that Goomer "would conjure me clear." Moreover, Goomer clearly had access to poison, which he was willing to distribute to the other slaves, and some confederates had the money to buy guns or the plan to take them from a store. If that were not enough, the slaves hated whites enough to carry the plot forward. Speaking about the famous fire in 1811, Tom reported that "the negroes in the neighbourhood said they were glad that the people were burnt in Richmond and wished that all the white people had been burnt with them—That God Almity [sic] had sent them a little Hell for the white people and that in a little time they would get a greater."[26]

---

25. "Confessions made . . . 2nd April 1812," VEPLR. A sketch of Floyd's career is in Tragle (ed.), *The Southampton Slave Revolt*, 249; the trial of Tom, April 14, 1812, is in Henry C.C.O.B. (1811–20), 77–79, and C.S., box 3. See also Aptheker, *American Negro Slave Revolts*, 252–53.

26. Many people died in the Richmond Theatre Fire (see Virginius Dabney, *Rich-*

Even whites' images of inhuman or monstrous slave insurrectionaries testify to the hostility of slave rebels toward whites. One newspaper writer called Gabriel a "hardened miscreant," which was relatively mild. But another prefigured Jefferson's 1820 statement about
wolves. "In a word," he wrote in early September, 1800, "if we will
keep a ferocious monster in our country, we must keep him in chains."
He regarded the danger as so great that liberty could not coexist with
it. "The slave-holder can never be a Democrat." Other observers por-
trayed slave rebels as "misled" or "deluded," but whites shocked by
the Turner revolt relied on the most violent labels they could summon
up, referring to Turner and his confederates as "murderous insurgents," "savages," "lawless wretches," "banditti," and a "fiend-like
band of desperadoes."[27]

The ideological importance of slaves' hostility was apparent to some
whites. In 1801, John Randolph of Roanoke, like St. George Tucker,
recognized in Gabriel's Plot evidence of the rebels' "sense of their
rights, and contempt of danger, and a thirst for revenge." In 1802,
Governor Monroe cited as a cause of unrest the "growing sentiment of
liberty existing in the minds of the slaves." Jefferson expressed his
understanding of slaves in rebellion in response to the 1802 executions. By 1820, however, this architect of a republic founded on natural right had so succumbed to fear of southern slaves that he said: "We
have the wolf by the ears; and we can neither hold him, nor safely let
him go. Justice is in one scale, and self-preservation in the other."[28]

Some phrases that whites used to describe slave insurrectionaries
further illuminate the ideology of those blacks. The notions of law-
lessness, insurgency, and banditry best reflect slave rebels' total rejection of slaveowners' authority over the slave society of Virginia. Some
writers also referred to slaves in general as "our internal enemy." This

---

mond: *The Story of a City* [Garden City, N.Y., 1976], 90–92). Among the victims was a
daughter of the lawyer who defended Gabriel at his 1799 trial. At the same time, a
Richmond slave saved many of the theatergoers ("Diary of Charles Copland, 1788–
1822," VSL, reprinted in *WMQ*, 1st ser., XIV [1905–1906], 224–27).

27. *Virginia Herald* (Fredericksburg), September 23, October 4, 1800; Tragle (ed.), *The
Southampton Slave Revolt*, 43, 48, 73, 74, 96, 123, 431; Oates, *The Fires of Jubilee*, 120.

28. John Randolph of Roanoke to Joseph H. Nicholson, in William C. Bruce, *John
Randolph of Roanoke, 1773–1833* (2 vols.; New York, 1922), II, 250–51; [Tucker], *Letter to
a Member of the General Assembly*, quoted in Mullin (ed.), *American Negro Slavery*, 117;
Jefferson to John Holmes, April 22, 1820, in *The Writings of Thomas Jefferson*, ed. Paul L.
Ford (10 vols.; New York, 1892–99), X, 157–58; Monroe to Assembly, January 16, 1802,
VEPLR.

:ared during insurrection scares rather than after the dis-
.ots or the suffering involved in the Turner killings. It con-
ɔbservers' sense of their own vulnerability. It sometimes
ed fervent requests to the state government for guns and
ammunition for the militia.[29]

This perception of an internal enemy, lawless, insurgent, and bent
on banditry, derived from more than the presence of a large number of
slaves in Virginia. It was a response to something more than behavior
that resembled that of bandits, the lawless, or insurgents in many
societies of the world at that time. Slave rebels were not Barbary
pirates descending on travelers' ships or native Americans attacking
settlers' homes. They were insurgents, working from within the slave
society. The reference in the U.S. Constitution to "domestic Violence"
covered attacks on government as well as slave insurrections. But the
internal enemy had more than time-bound, specific grievances, such
as those of Shays, the Whiskey Rebels, and the followers of Fries and
Dorr. It was the situation, the condition of slaves that not only gave
them reason to become enemies of slaveholders but also made it necessary for them to consider insurrection. It was the only way, if successful, that they could force whites to carry out the general emancipation they otherwise refused even to plan.

The crisis in which Tidewater Virginia found itself in 1829, William
Presson explained to Governor Giles, grew "out of the heterogeneous
population of our Country, especially in this section of our state." The
officer later referred to "our Continual exposure to the hatred of those
unfortunate and enfatuated beings, a hatred existing from and Conse-
quent upon their relative situations in society." There was the heart of
the matter, understood in part by Presson in 1829, sensed by other
white Virginians at other times, and openly discussed in the slavery
debates in 1831 and 1832. In a diverse population, those people fixed
by law, custom, and force in a "relative situation" at the bottom of
society would not only feel hatred for those at the top, they would
naturally be predisposed, should the opportunity arise, to defy law
and custom with force in order to improve their position.[30]

29. Thomas M. Bayley to Governor Monroe, January 30, 1802, William Presson to
Governor Giles, July 31, 1829, both in VEPLR; Petition of thirty-one Chesterfield County
citizens to Governor Floyd, September, 1831, VEPLR; Aptheker, *American Negro Slave
Revolts*, 25.
30. William Presson to Governor Giles, July 31, 1829, in VEPLR. Presson was asking
for arms. On the debates, see Freehling, *Drift Toward Dissolution;* and Theodore M.
Whitfield, *Slavery Agitation in Virginia 1829–1832* (Baltimore, 1930).

There was limited opportunity. Numbers were in the slaves' favor. On August 7, 1829, state officials considered which counties actually needed more arms in order to be prepared for the rumored insurgency. No counties in the Western Federal District were in want, they concluded, but the number of slaves made it imperative to send military supplies to certain other counties and cities. The list of needy and endangered places was rather large; it included sixty-one counties and four cities, or every jurisdiction east of the Shenandoah Valley. The test was the number of slaves. Using inexact figures, the authorities determined that the white population of these areas at 459,324 was but 34,000 higher than the black population of 421,019. Their subtraction was incorrect but their point was valid, especially in light of the mistaken notion that Virginia's racial balance had really changed in whites' favor by 1829. Confined largely to the Western Federal District, that change affected state politics, but certainly had not yet profoundly transformed the potential for slave insurrection in the Tidewater, Piedmont, and Southside regions.[31]

Some would-be insurrectionaries in the period beginning in 1785 and ending in 1831 tried to organize in ways that revealed their thorough understanding of what was necessary for them to be able to do battle with their enemy. Many were willing to form alliances with white men who also resented their own disadvantaged position in Virginian society. Gabriel and his fellows perhaps relied on at least one Frenchman for military advice; the fugitive Gabriel relied on a white Methodist captain of a boat in order to escape as far as Norfolk. In 1802 a convicted conspirator supposedly told his followers he had organized not only blacks and mulattoes but also "the common or poor white people." Planners in Louisa, Orange, and Spotsylvania counties formed a coalition with white radical George Boxley in their aborted 1816 uprising. Boxley appeared to outsiders to be the leader of the conspiracy, but that may only have been a matter of temporary convenience. One convicted slave hinted at this. Boxley called for help to release some other suspected insurrectionaries, and the slave reportedly said that "when I was ready, you were not."[32]

Whatever movement Afro-Americans made from rebellion to revo-

31. Virginia Executive Council Journal, 1828–29, August 7, 1829, pp. 141–43; Miller, *The Wolf by the Ears*, 241; Tragle (ed.), *The Southampton Slave Revolt*, 119–23.

32. Mullin, *Flight and Rebellion*, 143, 151–54; Arthur quoted in Johnston, *Race Relations in Virginia*, 36; trials of Ned, Matt, and Kitt, March 5, 1816, Louisa C.C.M.B. (1815–18), 41. For a comment on the reliability of Arthur's trial, see Wyatt-Brown, *Southern Honor*, 426–27.

lution between the early 1700s and the early 1800s, individual slaves had to change from victims into rebels and finally into revolutionaries in order to participate in a planned, large-scale insurgency. The will to rise up was present. A significant number of the slaves convicted of attempted murder or murder of whites had acted on the basis of rebellious intentions. The statements of several insurrectionaries also testify to the existence of a revolutionary consciousness. Gabriel and the other plotters in 1800 wished to take control of the Richmond area away from white leaders. In 1802 a convicted conspirator reportedly wanted black people to "take the country of Virginia." According to him, "white people have had the country long enough." The planners in the Henry County area in 1812 insisted that "they were not made to work for the white people but they (the white people) were made to work for themselves and that they (the negroes) would have it so." They believed that it was possible to control the whites because "there were ten negroes for one white man," a notion as revealing of the plotters' perception of their opportunity as it was statistically mistaken. Some of the Boxley conspirators told interrogators that they had hoped to be "over the white people." Other slave insurrectionaries had revenge or their own freedom in mind, but all the revolutionaries knew what had to be overturned. When Nat Turner heard "the Spirit" say in 1828 that "the time was fast approaching when the first should be last and the last should be first," he not only accepted a scriptural saying but also embraced a slave insurrectionary's understanding of the structure of a slave society.[33]

But slave insurrectionaries in Virginia had something more in mind than destroying the old order. What raised their thinking, planning, and action above mere anarchy and revenge was their standard of political legitimacy. The matter was not simply one of strategy and tactics; nor was it a problem of developing widespread hatred for those who maintained slavery, though that was one prerequisite for success. Instead, the more fundamental consideration was the alternative authority to which slave rebels looked in their quest to reject established authority. In order to identify slave insurrectionaries'

33. Genovese, *From Rebellion to Revolution;* Mullin, *Flight and Rebellion,* 157–58; Arthur quoted in Johnston, *Race Relations in Virginia,* 36; "Confessions made . . . 2nd April 1812," VEPLR; Edward Herndon to James Frazer, April 5, 1816, in Felix G. Hansford Papers, West Virginia Collection, West Virginia University Library, Morgantown; Spotsylvania C.C.M.B. (1815–19), 70; Turner, *Confessions,* in Tragle (ed.), *The Southampton Slave Revolt,* 310.

standards for what was lawful and legitimate, we must bypass one of the dominant revolutionary rationales of the time, the republicanism of the American Revolution. We must, rather, identify the competing symbols of authority, the leaders whom the slave rebels chose.

Those leaders often proved to have been already established leaders within the slave communities. Some leaders assumed authority in rebellions because they had been tested before and during planning. The "Main Spring and Chief Mover" in the 1799 confrontation between Absalom Johnson and three slaves, Gabriel maintained that role throughout the competition for leadership in 1800. White authorities gave backhanded acknowledgment to his status when they tried to capture him and get a confession from him. As another slave testified, he followed Gabriel because he believed that decisive, imposing man "would carry the business into execution." Gerald Mullin's definitive analysis of Gabriel's leadership emphasizes his ability to "make decisions, delegate responsibilities, and pursue routine tasks to their completion in order to avert the strong possibility of disaster." But since Gabriel was "a man imbued not so much with messianic fervor as with a grim sense of what had to be done," also required were the preaching of his brother, Martin, and the scriptural references of Ben Woolfolk to command the allegiance of numerous slaves to the plot as well as to Gabriel's leadership.[34]

Martin's power to command respect reflects not only the authority of slave preachers within their own communities but their legitimacy as leaders of rebellion. When Governor Floyd blamed slave preachers for the killings in 1831, he was more correct than he could have known. In Virginia, the preacher Martin was a key figure in Gabriel's Plot. A preacher named Will was accused of involvement in the Boxley plot, and William Grady's Anthony, transported with Anthony's son-in-law Tom for joining with Boxley, was a member of Piney Branch Baptist Church.[35] County and state officials insisted that Boxley "pretends to be religious" and that he based his cooperation with slave rebels on

34. Schwarz, "Gabriel's Challenge," 283–309; Mullin, *Flight and Rebellion*, 147–49. Mullin (ed.), *American Negro Slavery*, 224–26, compares Gabriel, Denmark Vesey, and Nat Turner.
35. Tragle (ed.), *The Southampton Slave Revolt*, 275–76, 432–33; Richmond *Enquirer*, March 13, 1816; trials of Will, March 5, 1816, and Anthony, April 1, 1816, Spotsylvania C.C.M.B. (1815–19), 54–55, 70–72, and C.S., box 3; Piney Branch Church Minute Book (1813–51), 2–8 (membership list), and entry for March 23, 1816, VBHS and VSL photostat, excluding Anthony from the church for "Inserection."

theological notions. Indeed, while a fugitive from justice in Ohio, Box-ley adopted "Methodist dress" and preached to free blacks in support of runaway slaves. Nat Turner's accomplishments as a preacher and prophet are well established. It is significant that early in his career, other slaves so trusted his "superior judgment" and status that they allowed him to plan their "roguery" (or stealing) even though he re-fused to participate in it.[36]

The ability of slave preachers to act as authorities within their com-munities is apparent. What needs more attention is the timing of ma-jor conflicts between them and white-dominated churches. There was severe discord within the Baptist churches of the area of which Spot-sylvania County is the center before the Boxley plot and also in the southeastern Tidewater region in the years before the Turner Re-bellion. The issue was the legitimacy of slave preaching. The Boxley plot may have begun in the summer or fall of 1815. Soon after that, Piney Branch Church took up the question whether slaves could law-fully preach. On the fourth Saturday in November, a committee made its report that they could not. By February 24, 1816, the very day on which a slave woman informed her master of the Boxley conspiracy, the Piney Branch congregation set up a committee of three white men to "consult with our Black Brethren the reason of their absenting themselves from the places of worship." A month later, the church excommunicated Anthony. It was not until May that black members of the church explained their absence, though they reportedly did so to the satisfaction of the white members.[37]

There was a long history of discord in the Baptist churches of the southeastern Tidewater, much of it revolving around some slave

36. Jailor's Notice, May 15, 1816, and Governor's Proclamation, May 18, 1816, both in VEPLR; *Virginia Herald* (Fredericksburg), May 29, June 2, 1816; James M. Bell and Waller Holladay to Governor W. C. Nicholas, March 1, 1816, in VEPLR (also in draft in Holladay Family Papers, sec. 72, VHS, and printed in *CVSP*, X, 433–36). Bell and Holla-day accused a white itinerant Methodist preacher of marginal participation in the plot. Boxley's preaching career after he fled from Virginia is described in a hostile letter from Jacob W. Reader to Governor Preston, August 2, 1819, in VEPLR. Oates, *The Fires of Jubilee;* Tragle (ed.), *The Southampton Slave Revolt,* 307; Sobel, *Trabelin' On.*

37. Sobel, *Trabelin' On;* Albert J. Raboteau, *Slave Religion: The "Invisible Institution" in the Antebellum South* (New York, 1978), 238–39; Aptheker, *American Negro Slave Re-volts,* 59n14; Piney Branch Church Minute Book (1813–51). Boxley's marriage of 1805 appears on page 4 of the Marriage Register (1793–1833) kept by the Reverend Jeremiah Chandler, who became minister of Piney Branch Church in 1813. See also Richmond *Enquirer,* March 13, 1816; and Bell and Holladay to Governor Nicholas, March 1, 1816, in VEPLR.

preachers. It did not necessarily cause insurrection, but it was crucial to the context of slave rebellion. In South Quay Baptist Church in Nansemond County, from which David Barrow removed himself in 1798 because of his antislavery opinions, a preaching dispute began in March, 1810. Shortly thereafter an insurrection scare, for which slave preachers were blamed, unnerved the area's whites and caught the state government's attention. First cited for excessive drinking and "exercising public functions contrary to the rules of this church," Tom expressed repentance before the congregation in July, 1810. By December he was again in trouble, this time for stealing as well as intoxication, but in September, 1811, he won another restoration with a new statement of repentance.[38]

The general question of preaching by black brethren resurfaced in December, 1812, leading eventually to the December, 1813, decision that "whereas Bror. Tom (of Battle) professes to be called of God to preach, it was agreed that he be permitted to exercise his gift" the next February. At that time, two more slaves were to be considered as candidates to preach. This hopeful action came to nothing. In July, 1814, the congregation directed the minister to "strictly forbid Bror. Tom (of Battle) to exercise at all in a public way" and to warn other uncalled brethren to await the church's decision. Once again, also in July, 1814, Tom stood accused of "drinking to excess," repented, and was restored, but he did not figure in the church's proceedings again.[39]

Within seven years, two slaves showed the members of South Quay Baptist Church how far slaves' hostility to white authorities could go. In 1821, member James Powell and his wife fell victim to an ax held by a slave hired out to him. The slave and his convicted accomplice had also been accused of burning the Powells' corpses inside their house. One year later, slave member York presented a lesser but nonetheless real threat to white church members. At the same time that members allowed Davy, a slave soon to be emancipated, to preach, they "cited" York for preaching without permission. Admonished in March, 1823, "not to exercise in publick" until the church could consider his qualifi-

38. Carlos R. Allen, Jr., "David Barrow's *Circular Letter* of 1798," *WMQ*, 3d ser., XX (1963), 440–51; South Quay Church Minute Book (1775–1827), 71, VSL (photostat); trial of Sam, June 6, 1810, Isle of Wight C.C.O.B. (1810–13), 51, and VEPLR, and C.S., box 3; several letters and documents, May–June, 1810, in VEPLR; Andrew Reid, Jr., to Samuel McD. Reid, June 8, 1810, in Phillips Papers, Sterling Memorial Library, Yale University; South Quay Church Minute Book (1775–1827), 103, 107, 110, 114.

39. South Quay Church Minute Book (1775–1827), 119, 126–28, 130.

cations, York was finally restored to good standing in September, 1824, but still not given permission to preach. York was called to account in December, 1827, not only for preaching but for doing so "while so much intoxicated, that the audience were greatly disgusted with his Conduct and Conversation." After what must have been an agonizing personal conflict for York, he repented in March, 1828. The congregation unanimously voted not to allow him to preach and also not to allow any members to hear the preaching of excommunicants. York's resentment simmered until 1829, when he was finally expelled for having "reproach'd the Church, and slandered its members."[40]

Problems of order with which congregations regularly contended went beyond individual cases of stealing, adultery, and intemperance. At Southampton's Black Creek Baptist Church, authorities noted in December, 1822, that black attendance was falling off. At a conference some months later, several black members stated their grievances, but the conference members concluded that they were not sufficiently "serious" to warrant further consideration. By 1825, the minister's antislavery statements so harmed church unity that most of the members agreed to "put him out of fellowship." Further conferences concerning the black communicants were held in 1829. The members of South Quay Baptist Church thought it necessary in late 1830 to silence a slave for "having spoken disrespectfully of the Church and some of its members" when they refused to baptize another slave.[41]

The white Baptists' worries about the rebelliousness of the black Baptists were sometimes realistic, but their preventive measures were inadequate as a means of suppressing rebellious thinking. Four Sussex slaves went to the gallows merely for stating that they would join in the killing of whites during the Turner Revolt; three more were transported for the same offense; still another died during an attempt to escape from jail. At least three of these verbal insurrectionaries, as well as two more transported from Southampton and one more found

40. Trials of Abel and Celia, June 28, 1821, Southampton C.C.O.B. (1819–21), 321–27, and C.S., box 4; South Quay Church Minute Book (1775–1827), 9, 177, 185–86, 189, (1827–61), 15–17, 28.

41. South Quay Church Minute Book (1827–61), 33; Black Creek (Southampton County) Baptist Church Minute Book (1818–62), 22–23, 39, 43, 48–52, 63–64, VSL; Sobel, *Trabelin' On;* Gary W. Williams, "Colonel George Blow: Planter and Political Prophet of Antebellum Sussex," *VMHB,* XC (1982), 445n52. Keeping "order among the enslaved communicants" was a perennial problem (see, for example, Antioch [Racoon Swamp, Sussex County] Baptist Church Records, I [1772–1837], 54, VSL).

not guilty there, were members of Antioch (Racoon Swamp) Baptist Church. According to the subsequently challenged testimony of the slave Beck, some of the convicted advocates of insurrection had made their rhetorical stands outside that church. The church expelled all such members and, like many other Baptist churches in the area, dramatically regimented its slave membership and instituted strict rules for their admission to the church and conduct during service.[42] Elsewhere, slave members of Mill Swamp Baptist Church in Isle of Wight County stood trial in the Surry court for insurrectionary utterances. One was found guilty and transported despite Edmund Ruffin's angry objections; three others and four nonmembers were found not guilty. But the church still excommunicated them as well as several other slaves who belonged to Richard H. Cocke, the owner of the church members.[43]

Other slave authorities shared in the leadership of and support for rebellion. Nat himself had the reputation of being a Baptist preacher, though at least one white hotly denied that he was. The reputation of one of Nat Turner's most trusted confederates reflected the authority held by a few conjurers in some insurrectionary situations. Soon after the Turner Revolt, Nelson, the slave of Jacob Williams, was reported to be a slave preacher. In fact, Nelson was probably a sorcerer or conjurer. According to trial testimony of Caswell Worrell, Nelson's overseer, Nelson had foretold catastrophic events a few days before the revolt exploded. Indeed, Nelson claimed that "anybody of his practice could tell these things." Even though Nat Turner reportedly looked down on the trickery of conjurers, he strongly trusted Nelson. Indeed, he had himself relied upon omens and signs to chart his rebellion. Nat still did not want to be confused with a conjurer.[44]

42. Trials of Boson, Frank, and Nicholas (Antioch members) and Ned, Squire, Booker, Solomon, and Shadrack (not members), September 1, 2, 12, 1831, Sussex C.C.O.B. (1827–35), 248–56, and C.S., box 5; Williams, "Colonel George Blow," 444–45. Beck's testimony in the trials of Frank and Solomon, Nicholas, and Booker included references to the Racoon Meeting House. Trials of Jim and Isaac, September 22, 1831, Southampton C.C.M.B. (1830–35), 110–11. On the trials and other materials, see Tragle (ed.), *The Southampton Slave Revolt*, 99, 213–15, 240–41; "A List of Slaves and Free Persons of Color received into the Penitentiary . . . 1816 to . . . 1842," C.S., box 10; Antioch Church Records, I, 63; *Minutes of the Virginia Portsmouth Baptist Association . . . Surry County, Virginia . . . May . . . 1832* (Norfolk, 1832), 25–26.
43. Black Creek Church Minute Book (1818–62), 86–89; Mill Swamp (Isle of Wight County) Baptist Church Minute Book, 96–97, 102–105, VSL; South Quay Church Minute Book (1827–61), 48.
44. Tragle (ed.), *The Southampton Slave Revolt*, 80. Robert E. Lee called Nelson a

Nat Turner's apparent contempt for conjurers did not derive from his experience as an insurrectionary but from his aspiration to prophecy. A few conjurers appear to have been accepted by other slaves as sufficiently authoritative to lead insurrectionary plots. The conjurers Goomer and Jack figured in the reported 1812 planning of slaves for rebellion in Henry County. Goomer's status so impressed Jack that he said "he would make haste and learn all he could (being at the time nearly equal to Goomer in conjuration) and get as high as he could." Tom's execution undoubtedly undercut Goomer's and Jack's claims. But within a few years, the slave conjurer Old Matt had spread fear in Cumberland County. After 1822, many white Virginians knew what a crucial role the shaman Gullah Jack had played in the Vesey Plot. They could not afford to ignore conjurers who might become insurrection leaders, competing with established white authorities for the "obedience" of slaves.[45]

White people mostly referred to European models when trying to understand an insurrectionary such as Nat Turner or collective maroonage of the type practiced by Robert Ricks, Bob Ferebee, General Sampson, and Mingo along the North Carolina–Virginia border and near the Dismal Swamp. To some whites, all these men were brigands or banditti. Those labels caught the flavor of such slaves' tactics, their living off the land and hiding in secure strongholds or staying on the run. Those labels also acknowledged the ability of some slave men to lead bands of followers and constituted unwilling recognition of the communitarian bases for maroons or insurrectionaries. Unlike officials of established counties or states, they were organized to jeopardize property and, if need be, to endanger people. These bands pre-

---

preacher, but also mistakenly identified him as the possession of Mrs. Caty Whitehead. He had received his information from troops that had been in Southampton (Lee to Mary Lee [Fitzhugh] Custis, in Mary Anna Randolph [Custis] Lee to Mary Lee [Fitzhugh] Custis, n.d. [probably September, 1831], in Lee Family Papers, VHS). Lee also repeated local reports that a slave preacher in Norfolk was another leader of the plot. See also trial of Nelson, September 3, 1831, Southampton C.C.M.B. (1830–35), 87–88, and in Tragle (ed.), *The Southampton Slave Revolt*, 192–94; Turner, *Confessions*, in Tragle (ed.), *The Southampton Slave Revolt*, 308; Oates, *The Fires of Jubilee*, 62.

45. "Confessions made . . . 2nd April 1812," VEPLR; trial of Tom, April 14, 1812, Henry C.C.O.B. (1811–20), 77–79, and C.S., box 3; trials of Matthew, Old Matt, and Daniel, December 23, 1816, Cumberland County, C.S., box 3, and VEPLR; "A List of Slaves and Free Persons of Color received into the Penitentiary . . . 1816 to . . . 1842," C.S., box 10; Aptheker, *American Negro Slave Revolts*, 225; Eugene D. Genovese, *Roll, Jordan, Roll: The World the Slaves Made* (New York, 1974), 593–94; Genovese, *From Rebellion to Revolution*, 8–10, 44–50.

sented the same kind of counterimage of society to frightened and outraged whites as pirates had to merchants and governmental authorities. Whites branded the Mingos, Ferebees, Ricks, Sampsons, and Nat Turners as the worst kind of outlaws since they threatened to undermine the legal foundations of society. But whites had to marshal some of the strongest powers of society against them in order to defeat them.[46]

The capacity of organized maroons and insurrectionaries in Virginia to evoke in whites the images of warfare, even of past Indian wars, testifies to their status as competing sources of legitimacy and authority for many slaves.[47] That very capacity helps to explain why white officials' quick reaction to insurrection and to insurrection scares was to execute those slaves convicted of being ringleaders and willing participants. The problem of competing authorities also influenced the frequent punishments, ranging from lashings to execution, of slaves who merely stated insurrectionary intentions, support for slave rebels, or agreement with the proposition that slaves had a right to freedom. Many of the slaves listed in Appendix One were in this category. Talk was not cheap, since a slave's verbal support of insurrection in any form would, if unanswered by white authorities, gain practical strength and authority of its own. That authority would proceed from sharing the belief in the right of revolution against slaveholders. When free blacks such as David Walker in Massachusetts or fellow insurrectionaries in Henrico, Southampton, and other counties argued in favor of slave revolt, they too had great potential for becoming competing authorities for slaves to follow. It was not just a question of their being able to publish their opinions, as in David Walker's case, or their enjoying greater mobility and access to the outside world than did most slaves, as in the case of free blacks. It was again a matter of

46. At least one observer of the Turner Revolt compared the attacks to a "former incursion of the Indians upon white settlements" (Richmond *Enquirer*, August 30, 1831, quoted in Tragle [ed.], *The Southampton Slave Revolt*, 43).

47. Marcus Rediker, " 'Under the Banner of King Death': The Social World of Anglo-American Pirates, 1716 to 1726," *WMQ*, 3rd ser., XXXVIII (1981), 203–27. For use of the term *brigands*, see Tragle (ed.), *The Southampton Slave Revolt*, 48. On General Sampson, see Williams, "Colonel George Blow," 435; and Hugo Prosper Leaming, "Hidden Americans: Maroons of Virginia and the Carolinas" (Ph.D. dissertation, University of Illinois at Chicago Circle, 1979), 324–574. The well-known hysteria that followed Nat Turner's Revolt included the killing and "half-hanging" and pelting with eggs of Richmond slaves. This constituted a community response to a danger faced by the white community just as did vigilante efforts to suppress "bandits." See Brown, *Narrative*, 37–38.

communal sharing of revolutionary sentiments. Should free black insurrectionaries grow in number, they would extend the community that shared a commitment to insurrection, thereby conferring further legitimacy on the idea.[48]

Alliances with such white radicals as George Boxley, the higher-law doctrine of the new abolitionists, and the theological tenets of the Quaker and evangelical abolitionists undoubtedly gave some slave rebels a stronger sense of their own legitimacy, but leaders such as Gabriel, Nat Turner, the preachers, and the conjurers reflect the indigenous roots of slave rebels' authority.[49] That they did have authority within their own communities makes clear why they were not lawless, anarchistic, or antinomian. They sorely tried established institutions not only because they rejected the legitimacy of slavery and of the governments that backed it but because they had their own system of law and authority. Although that system was partly derived from and influenced by white institutions, it contained an implicit and original claim to sovereignty. Slave rebels knew by experience that an *imperium in imperio* was impossible. That was why they chose insurrection as opposed to smaller-scale resistance. That is also why white authorities took them so seriously as to suppress them and to do so with the full force of their government. White leaders were upholding their claim to legitimacy and authority as well as protecting their safety.

There was one essential element of authority that slave rebels in Virginia never held between 1785 and 1831.[50] That was the kind of

48. David Walker, *Appeal to the Colored Citizens of the World* (Boston, 1829; rpr. New York, 1969). For the official Virginia reaction to this work, see Governor Giles to House of Delegates Speaker, January 6, 1830, and Giles to Boston Mayor Harrison Gray Otis, February 19, 1830, both in Virginia Executive Letter Books, 1823–30, pp. 333–34, 343–44, VSL, and Virginia Council Journals, 1829–31, p. 8. Of people incarcerated in the Virginia Penitentiary before 1825, only two spent more than the forty months in solitary confinement experienced by a free black man convicted of insurrection in 1802 (*Report of the Joint Committee to Examine the State of the Penitentiary Institution* [Richmond, 1826], in *Virginia House Journal*, 1825–26, Appendix). The slaves known to have been tried for insurrectionary statements include, besides those discussed in relation to the Turner Revolt, Arch, Lewey, and Daniel (in 1808), Sam and Dennis (in 1810), Harry (in 1821), and Sam (in 1829).

49. The case of white insurrectionary George Boxley is *sui generis* and bears further examination than is possible here.

50. Some slaves may have rejected slave leaders just as a few apparently resented Nat Turner himself because of the reprisals or tightened controls imposed by enraged, revengeful, or frightened whites in the aftermath of the Southampton revolt. One Virginia slave exclaimed some years later that Nat Turner "had better never been born than to have left such a curse upon his nation" (Mary J. Bratton [ed.], "Field's Observations: The Slave Narrative of a Nineteenth-Century Virginian," *VMHB*, LXXXVIII [1980], 93).

success measured by attainment of control. The number of trials of slaves for insurrection dropped sharply after 1831. Fifteen would be convicted, and a smaller percentage—26.7—of the convicted than before would go to the gallows. It would not be until the 1860s that former slaves and free blacks would fight collectively against slaveowners and their allies in Virginia, that time in the uniform of a government that claimed sovereignty over people who honored competing authorities defined by the Union as insurrectionaries or rebels. Thus came full circle what had been happening ever since the first slave insurrection in Virginia, but particularly between 1785 and 1831.

Slave Aaron Harris' opposition to Turner during the revolt arose from his knowledge of the superior numbers of whites available to fight the Prophet, not from a rejection of the slaves' right to revolt. The famous defense of Dr. Blunt by his slaves may have resulted from their appreciation that more guns and nooses supported his authority than that of Nat Turner (Oates, *The Fires of Jubilee*, 92, 107).

11. *The End of Slave Crime*

The slave communities of Virginia suffered much wrenching change during the same years that free Virginians went into economic and political decline and then began to recover. So the most important single question to ask about convictions of slaves for major crimes in the antebellum Old Dominion is how they changed from earlier periods as well as between 1830 and 1865. If one asked Governor Floyd in 1849, all the changes had been for the better: "The 'curse' of slavery has not filled our land with felony and crime. We have no riots, mobs, arson and wholesale murder to mourn over, to punish or to countenance. We have no work-houses crowded with famishing and unprovided wretchedness; no swarms of beggars infesting our cities; no onerous poor rates levied to support everlasting pauperism. All is peace, quiet and order. From one extremity of the land to the other, there is felt in every ramification of society, perfect and absolute personal security." One might be tempted to dismiss this rosy picture of a slave society as southern nationalist defensiveness and anti-abolitionist hyperbole, especially in view of the changes made but a year before in the criminal code for slaves and the subsequent upward trend in convictions of slaves for major crimes. But Floyd's statement concentrates on collective violence and social decay more than on individual incidents. Here is the crux of any analysis of convictions of slaves for major crimes: large, collective challenges to white domination were rare. It was primarily individual offenses that truly challenged the perfect and absolute security of which Floyd boasted.[1]

---

1. Message of Governor Floyd to the House of Delegates, December 3, 1849, in *Virginia House Journal*, 1849–50, p. 26. Floyd may also have relied only on his own experience, as

Map 5. Virginia Counties, 1850

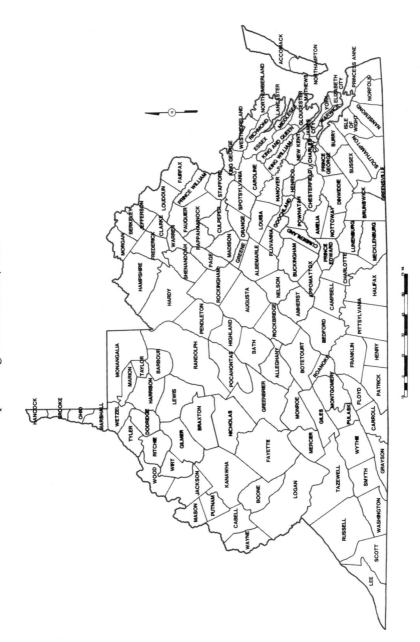

Many aggressive slaves acted during the last years of slavery in Virginia. One hundred eighty-five, excluding insurrectionaries, were convicted of killing someone; another one hundred eighteen were found guilty of attempted murder; fifteen assaulted whites with sufficient violence to provoke justices to order their transportation out of the state. Forty-seven poisoned someone, said the oyer and terminer justices. The same authorities were convinced that no fewer than one hundred nine slaves had resorted to arson in order to attack white enemies and that at least two hundred fifteen had stolen large amounts of property from whites. Seventy-six were accused and found guilty of attempting to rape or actually raping white women, and eighty more went to the gallows or out of the state for offenses whose nature officials did not bother to record. Twelve slaves were detected making insurrectionary statements or plotting in the thirty years before the Civil War began. Among the twelve, only two were executed, both in 1840. Prosecutions would increase during the Civil War, but three slaves were executed between May, 1861, and February, 1865.

The essential change in the pattern of serious crimes that slaves were found guilty of committing after 1830 is that individual offenses became, more than in most other periods in Virginia's history, the only collective threat Afro-Americans in bondage presented to slaveholding. Demonstrably collective offenses, such as insurrection, decreased steadily after 1831. In addition, running away became sufficiently widespread that it was the most threatening of all acts of resistance in which Virginian slaves ever engaged on an individual or group basis. It elicited a personal, social, judicial, political, and constitutional response for the simple reason that it was not only economically devastating to its "victims," it was more likely to happen, and to increase, than was killing, arson, or other actions that presented an obvious danger to whites.

Insurrection endangered slavery, but insurrection faded out. Running away, especially with the aid of abolitionists, grew steadily in importance. At least one other individual offense, arson, increased, and later seemed to become epidemic, in a way that first provoked officials to enact new provisions in the criminal code for slaves. Only

---

did North Carolina judge Thomas Ruffin, when he commented in an 1849 decision that he had *heard* of no more than six killings of whites by slaves since 1810 (*State v. Caesar*, 31 N.C. 421 [1849]). For the criminal code for slaves in 1849, see Stroud, *A Sketch of the Laws*, 77–80; and *The Code of Virginia*, Title 54, Chapter 200.

the Civil War and emancipation ended the increasingly tense situation that developed in the 1850s between slave and slaveowner. Yet the history of that tension and the contradictory underlying assumptions lived on in a new form, making Reconstruction and later years violent, bloody, and tense.

The background of these changes was the dramatic decline of Virginia and the crushing transformation of the slave communities between 1830 and 1865. The once proud and prosperous leader of the nation lapsed into economic seediness, social stagnation, and political alienation.[2] The state's largest export seemed to be its people, both free and unfree. Industrialization in some areas helped the economy to rebound in the 1850s, yet fear of abolitionism and resentment toward the federal government led a majority of white Virginians to choose secession in 1861. Yet the people over whom so many whites were arguing suffered near decimation between 1830 and 1860. The United States censuses for 1820 through 1860 indicate one reason why. Not only did the slave population of the Old Dominion decrease sharply between 1830 and 1840, but certain segments of that population had particularly large losses. And that influenced the future of slave crime.

It was precisely those slaves who were statistically overrepresented among convicted felons transported from Virginia who also suffered the biggest loss through involuntary migration to the Deep South. Those slaves statistically more likely to be convicted of major crimes in the 1830s and 1840s became less numerous, thus eliminating any chance for convictions to rise until there could once again be large growth in that sector of the population. Such growth would start to occur by the 1850s, but would have no impact, of course, after 1865.

Young slave men made all the difference. Male slaves aged twenty-four to thirty-five were 39.12 percent of all male slaves transported from Virginia between 1816 and 1842. Census data place this figure in context. Young male slaves were 28.4 percent of the slave population of eastern Virginia in 1830. Those between the ages of ten and twenty-three throughout the United States were 30.5 percent. The comparable figures for 1840 were 29.7 percent for enslaved Afro-Virginian men aged ten to twenty-three, and 31 percent for all male slaves of those

2. Virginius Dabney, *Virginia, the New Dominion* (Garden City, N.Y., 1971), 275–83, is a useful summary. See also David R. Goldfield, *Urban Growth in the Age of Sectionalism: Virginia, 1847–1861* (Baton Rouge, 1977), 1–6; Jack P. Maddex, Jr., *The Virginia Conservatives, 1865–1879* (Chapel Hill, 1970), 5–17; and Freehling, *Drift Toward Dissolution.*

ages in the United States. Male slaves who were between fourteen and twenty-five in 1830 then suffered the greatest loss of population of any group of Virginian slaves between 1830 and 1840. Moreover, male slaves between twenty-four and thirty-five were almost 28 percent in 1830 and 26.4 percent in 1840 of the population of male slaves ten years of age and older in eastern Virginia.[3]

Such involuntary out-migration forced suffering and change not only on the slaves "sold to Georgia" but also on slaves who stayed in Virginia. In newspapers, pamphlets, and letters, white Virginians lamented and proposed solutions for the devastating economic decline the Commonwealth experienced in the antebellum period. As slaves in Virginia watched the departure of some of their best young men and women, all of them sons or daughters and a significant portion of them husbands or wives, fathers or mothers, of slaves left behind, they undoubtedly had a great deal of sorrow, pain, and resentment to express as well. Some expression might appear in the abolitionists' publications; none of it, however, would appear in print in Virginia. But the various slave narratives make clear that being sold was one of the worst catastrophes inflicted by slaveholders on their alleged property. The U.S. census makes clear that slave communities in the Old Domin-

---

3. "A List of Slaves and Free Persons of Color received into the Penitentiary . . . 1816 to . . . 1842," C.S., box 10; U.S. Census Office, *Fifth Census; or, Enumeration of the Inhabitants of the United States. 1830; as corrected at the Department of State* (Washington, D.C., 1832), 85; U.S. Census Office, *Sixth Census or Enumeration of the Inhabitants of the United States as Corrected at the Department of State, in 1840* (Washington, D.C., 1841), 210; U.S. Census Office, *The Statistics of the Population of the United States*, Vol. 1, *Population and Social Statistics*, 68–70; U.S. Bureau of the Census, *Negro Population, 1790–1915* (Washington, D.C., 1918), 166. In "Changes in the Slave Population of the Virginia Tidewater and Piedmont, 1830–1860: A Stable Population Analysis," William J. Ernst computes a relatively higher decline in the group aged five to fourteen in 1830, but it is only the decline attributable to forced migration. The figures herein include the decline that resulted from a lower number of births as well. The lack of statistics by age groups of slaves prior to the 1820 census makes it impossible to determine whether the overall decline in the fourteen to twenty-five age group between 1830 and 1840 resulted more from forced migration or from decreased births between 1805 and 1816. Ernst's paper is in University of Virginia, Corcoran Department of History (History Club), *Essays in History*, XIX (1975), 75–83. Computations concerning slaves sold by Franklin & Armfield from Alexandria, Virginia, to New Orleans between 1828 and 1836 show that more than half of the males were between seventeen and twenty-eight (Donald Sweig, "Reassessing the Human Dimension of the Interstate Slave Trade," *Prologue*, XII [Spring, 1980], 5–21). See also John Thomas Schlotterbeck, "Plantation and Farm: Social and Economic Change in Orange and Greene Counties, 1716–1860" (Ph.D. dissertation, Johns Hopkins University, 1980), 136–47; and Michael Tadman, "Slave Trading in the Ante-Bellum South: An Estimate of the Extent of the Inter-regional Trade," *Journal of American Studies*, XIII (1979), 195–200.

ion had to endure involuntary out-migration in extraordinary numbers between 1830 and 1860. One computation places the total at 281,142, or nearly the 1790 slave population of the state. The same estimate offers annual averages of 11,800 (in the 1830s), 8,200 (in the 1840s), and 8,000 (in the 1850s). Only during the eighteenth century had there been shifts in Virginia's slave population that can reasonably be compared to the massive change between 1830 and 1860. But neither the growth due to heavy importation from 1700 to the 1770s nor the sharp loss because of the many escapes during the Revolution had the socially destructive force of the antebellum change.[4]

In that context, hundreds of slaves participated in the last days of the peculiar institution in the Old Dominion. Those days were occasionally dramatic, but often predictable. For example, the frequency of slaves' mortal attacks on whites did not change dramatically between Turner's Revolt and the Civil War.[5] Table 28 pinpoints those jurisdictions in which the number of convictions ranked highest when weighed against slave population. Twentieth-century residents of the United States would probably look first at the cities of Petersburg and Richmond in the expectation that homicides occur more frequently in urban areas. But in the context of racial slavery, slaves' mortal and violent attacks on whites were most frequent on plantations. The rank-

4. James B. Gouger, "The Northern Neck of Virginia: A Tidewater Grain-Farming Region in the Antebellum South," in David C. Weaver (ed.), *Essays on the Human Geography of the Southeastern United States* (Carrollton, Ga., 1977), 82–85; Charles H. Ambler, *Sectionalism in Virginia from 1776 to 1861* (Chicago, 1910), 108–13; Frederic Bancroft, *Slave-Trading in the Old South* (Baltimore, 1931), 384–86; John W. Blassingame, *The Slave Community: Plantation Life in the Antebellum South* (Rev. ed.; New York, 1979), 173–74; Kenneth M. Stampp, *The Peculiar Institution: Slavery in the Ante-Bellum South* (New York, 1956), 237–44, 265–71; Eugene D. Genovese, *Roll, Jordan, Roll: The World the Slaves Made* (New York, 1974), 452–58; Sweig, "Reassessing the Human Dimension," 5–21. Governor Henry Lee had observed as early as 1792 that the forced separation of slave families had contributed to slave unrest (Governor Henry Lee to Robert Goode, May 17, 1792, in Virginia Executive Letter Books, 1792–94, pp. 5–7, VSL).

5. There is reason to be confident that murder convictions are closer to the "dark figure" of unrecorded offenses than are other convictions. Death records kept by counties from 1853 are one indication that courts did not miss a large number of homicides. See, for example, Hurley Rowland Gray, Jr., and Marion Joyner Watson, *Death Records of Southampton County, Virginia, 1853–1870* (Suffolk, Va., 1971); New Kent County Death Register, 1853–96, VSL; and Norfolk County Death Register, 1853–80, VSL. I have compared these with C.S., boxes 1–10, and have found no deaths of whites at the hands of slaves not covered by court trials. Since not everyone cooperated with registration procedures, this is indicative, and not conclusive, evidence. That slaves' assaults on whites would become matters of common knowledge is apparent in sources such as W. R. Bland to John Will, February 16, 1849, in "Letters from Home, Nottoway County, Virginia, Written to: the John W. Irby Family in Panola County, Mississippi, 1848 to 1875" (Typescript in Nottoway County, Va., Library).

Table 28. Minimal Rate of Killings by Slaves, 1830–1864

	Prince William	Amherst	City of Richmond	Powhatan	Petersburg	Nottoway	Goochland	Fluvanna	Prince Edward
Slaves convicted of murder[a]	7	9	12	7	4	6	4	3	5
Slaves convicted of murdering whites	6	6	6	6	0	2	4	2	3
Slaves convicted of murdering slaves (excluding infanticide)	0	2	6	1	3	2	0	1	2
% slave, 1830	41.2	49.1	39.5	64.2	34.3	68.5	55.1	46.1	68.3
% slave, 1860	31.4	45.7	30.9	64.4	31.1	73.2	57.6	48.2	62.0
Mean slave poulation, 1830–60	2,866	5,983	8,871	5,322	4,224	6,520	5,800	4,418	7,926
Minimal rate of killing	2.44	1.50	1.40	1.30	0.95	0.92	0.69	0.68	0.63
Minimal rate of killing whites	2.09	1.00	0.68	1.10	0.00	0.31	0.69	0.45	0.38
Minimal rate of killing slaves	0.00	0.33	0.68	0.20	0.71	0.31	0.00	0.23	0.25
Growth rate of slave population, 1830–60	Decline	Decline	+2.6	Decline	+2.3	Decline	+0.24	+0.92	Decline

SOURCES: C.S., boxes 1–10; miscellaneous county court order and minute books; U.S. Census Office, *The Statistics of the Population of the United States*, Vol. I, *Population and Social Statistics*, 68–72.

[a] Includes slaves convicted of killing free black and unidentified victims, so the sum of the next two lines does not necessarily equal this figure. Moreover, these figures are not to be taken as the maximum number of such killings.

ing of Fluvanna, Prince William, and Prince Edward counties suggests that demographic predominance of slaves in that environment was by no means an absolute determinant of such attacks. The history of each county—that is, the personal histories, or decisions, of hundreds of slaves and whites—was the only absolute determinant.

The old patterns continued. Slaves killed by themselves or cooperated with fellow Afro-Virginians, especially when the victim was the assailant's owner. Overseers were beaten in the fields; two members of First African Baptist Church were convicted of killing their owner's wife and son in 1852. Whites were no more subject to prosecution for killing or beating slaves than before, so some slaves fought back.[6] There were diverse reasons for these homicides. Some men or women refused to be whipped again; others were trying to prevent the whipping of loved ones.[7] One violently attacked whites in order to avoid capture as a runaway. Some assaulted or killed whites during robberies.[8] The changing nature of Virginia's economy and of slavery affected such attacks, as in the case of a Chesterfield County slave who

6. Trials of Ben, Moore, Edward, Thom, George, and Robert, August 13, 1857, Henrico C.C.M.B. (1856–57), 473–75, 479–83, and C.S., box 9, accounts; trials of Jane Williams and John Williams, August 9, 1852, Richmond city, C.S., box 8; Virginius Dabney, *Richmond: The Story of a City* (Garden City, N.Y., 1976), 139; Sobel, *Trabelin' On*, 210; Richmond *Enquirer*, July 30, August 3, 10, 1852. Some evidence of the few whites convicted of violence against slaves is in Essex C.C.O.B. (1830–33), 423 (not guilty), 591 (not guilty), (1847–58), 228 (not guilty); Spotsylvania C.C.M.B. (1832–38), 128 (not guilty); Spotsylvania C.C.O.B. (1843–49), 112, 124 (defaulted through nonappearance), 324 (bound to the peace for assault and battery against the slave of another owner), (1849–58), 3 (to Superior Court for trial); Southampton C.C.M.B. (1861–70), 192, 201, 204 (to Circuit Court for trial); *Commonwealth* v. *Richard Turner*, 26 Va. Rep. (1827), 560–64; *Souther* v. *Commonwealth*, 48 Va. Rep. (1851), 338–42; William H. Richardson, Secretary of the Commonwealth, to J. M. Wynee, June 30, 1848, and Richardson to Pittsylvania County Clerk, June 30, 1848, both in Virginia Executive Letter Books, 1849–56, pp. 10–11, VSL; Blassingame (ed.), *Slave Testimony*, 429–30; *Weevils in the Wheat*, 255, 319–20.

7. Trial of Humphrey, March 14, 1836, Caroline County, C.S., box 6, and VEPLR; trial of Phoebe, April 6, 1836, Essex C.C.O.B. (1833–36), 334–38 and C.S., box 6; trial of Daniel, June 28, 1847, Halifax C.C.O.B. (1847–50), 8–13, and C.S., box 8; trial of Henry Gunn, May 8, 1850, Henrico County, C.S., box 8, and *Religious Herald* (Baptist), May 16, 1850; trials of Thomas and Alfred, November 17, 1856, Amherst C.C.O.B. (1855–59), unpaginated, C.S., box 9, and VEPLR, and *Governor's Biennial Messages to the General Assembly . . . December 7, 1857* (Richmond, 1857), 173–74. In Loudoun County six enslaved men protected their mother from a whipping (Blassingame [ed.], *Slave Testimony*, 221–22).

8. Trial of Thom (a runaway from Alabama back to Amherst County, from which his owner had moved), August 20, 1860, Amherst C.C.O.B. (1854–64), unpaginated, and C.S., box 9; trials of John, January 1, April 2, 1839, Spotsylvania C.C.O.B. (1838–43), 82, 134–35, and C.S., box 6; trial of Henry, June 16, 1851, Dinwiddie County, C.S., box 8; trial of Ben, July 7, 1851, Henrico County, C.S., box 8; trial of Sydney, December 2, 1852, Nottoway County, C.S., box 8; trial of Patrick, August 18, 1855, Bedford C.C.O.B. (1855–57), 108, and C.S., box 8; trial of Spot, May 7, 1860, Lynchburg city, C.S., box 9.

struck out at a factory supervisor who had hit him. But most of the attacks took place in the traditional agricultural context. Changes in the law and some judges' increased understanding of the impossible situations in which slaves might find themselves allowed four slaves to be convicted only of second-degree murder of whites and twenty-two others to be transported rather than executed for killing white people between 1830 and 1865.[9]

Some slaves' hostility and hatred stand out in several of the cases. In 1838, Randolph came out of the woods to where his master was showing a slave woman how to use a crosscut saw. To her surprise, Randolph brought his ax down on George Thornley's skull. William M. Hamilton, Thornley's overseer, ran to the scene and ordered Randolph to account for himself. "Master Hamilton," he said, "I'm afraid I shall be hung. I've knocked master in the head and chopped out his brains." After looking at Thornley's corpse, Randolph showed none of the remorse that some other slaves did after committing murder. Instead, he declared that "he felt as if he should like to chop him to pieces even down to his shoes: that he had killed him and would do it again." As might be expected, neither the Louisa County Court nor state authorities showed any mercy, and Randolph was hanged in July. The fear that such attacks raised in white people reflected their perception of real hatred. They might now and then forget that it existed, but news of killings, attempted homicides, and particularly violent attacks on whites by slaves was always available.[10]

The most dramatic changes in the slave communities of Virginia strongly affected some of the attacks and killings. Besides the runaways who killed to protect their flight, there were slaves who responded most violently to being sold. Some white people understood how owners' using that threat as a means of control led slaves to resort to homicidal or otherwise violent methods to avoid such a fate. The threat had worked well, some Preston County petitioners argued in 1836, but it had also meant that slaves' "hatred to the south and southern purchasers of their Race has been increased to a degree of *desperation* so much so that the *best* of them has no *morral* hesitancy in

9. Trial of Reuben, March 24, 1832, Chesterfield County, C.S., box 6, and VEPLR; *The Code of Virginia* (1860).
10. Trial of Randolph, June 11, 1838, Louisa C.C.M.B. (1835–39), 337–38, and C.S., box 6; Petition against reprieve of Caesar, VEPLR. (See his trial for attempted murder, October 26, 1836, Fluvanna County, C.S., box 6.)

killing what they call a sale [*sic*] driver." Execution was an unjust punishment, the petitioners concluded, for a crime "which we have *indirectly* taught him to Commit." Unwilling to accept this appeal for the security of slaves, the governor and the council rejected the petition and allowed the execution of Ned for killing his new owner, James Martin of Mississippi.[11]

The availability of guns in a slave society was likely crucial to most whites' relative security. In the more than eighty cases in which court clerks recorded the weapon used by slaves who had killed or assaulted either free or enslaved people between 1830 and 1865, only five involved guns. In two cases, the assailants had taken their white victims' guns. Most slave assailants used knives or agricultural implements; a great many simply beat their victims. No matter what some slaves wanted to do to certain white people, the weapons at their disposal allowed them to do only so much.[12]

Jealously, insults, and fighting continued to lead to homicide or serious injuries among slaves during the last thirty years of bondage in Virginia. Owners took those actions seriously.[13] Not only would slaves appear before the county and city courts regularly on the charges of murder and manslaughter when slaves had been attacked by slaves, but after the state abolished benefit of clergy for slaves in 1848, more and more men and women were executed—nineteen of them—for killing another slave. Fifty were forced into exile for that from 1830 to 1865. Twice as many slaves were hanged or deported for murdering slaves of a different owner.[14] The old rules continued to apply. One defense lawyer went so far as to claim that an 1857 prosecution of a slave for murder of a slave violated the Fifth and Sixth Amendments to the Constitution since there had been no indictment by a grand jury

11. Trial of Ned, May 21, 1836, Preston County (now West Virginia), in June, 1836, folder and 1836 rejected claims folder, VEPLR.

12. Trial of Ned, May 21, 1836, Preston County (now West Virginia), June, 1836, folder, VEPLR; trial of Dick, May 12, 1853, Louisa County, C.S., box 8; trials of Buck (principal), John, and Harris (accessories), August 4, 1853, Sussex County, C.S., box 8; trials of Alfred and Thomas, November 7, 1856, Amherst C.C.O.B. (1855–59), unpaginated, and C.S., box 9; trial of Frank, March 16, 1864, Scott C.C.M.B. (1860–66), 426–27, and C.S., box 9.

13. For one planter's efforts to reduce violence among slaves, see "Code of laws and regulations," *ca.* 1857 (MS in Eppes Family Muniments, 1722–1948, VHS); Nicholls, " 'In the Light of Human Beings,' " 67–78; and Richard Eppes Diary, March 25, 1861, in Eppes Family Muniments, 1722–1948, VHS.

14. As had always been the case in Virginia, owners could not sue other owners for the value of a murdered slave or collect insurance if both the killer and the killed belonged to them (*American Digest,* XLIV, cols. 1054–58, para. 1325).

and the defendant was denied trial by jury. However philosophically valid that desperate measure was, the Appomattox County oyer and terminer justices overruled the attorney and had Reuben hanged.[15]

The slaves who might become involved in desperate struggles with other slaves could also endanger white people. Lee was one of the slaves whom his master, Paschal Bracey of Mecklenburg County, so feared that he always wore a gun. Lee died in 1846 as the result of a violent quarrel with another slave. When the bondsman of a Charlotte County woman faced execution for murdering a slave, the prosecuting attorney informed Governor Wise that Julius was "under a terribly bad character. His brother Albert was transported some years ago." Albert had provoked that sentence by attempting to kill another slave. He had succeeded in killing a slave in 1852, but he had gotten off then with a conviction for voluntary manslaughter. Albert had manifested a willingness to defy white authority as well as to attack other slaves, however. Over a year before his attempted murder conviction, he had been found guilty of giving forged identity papers for a free black to a slave. Like those slaves who truly tried to protect overseers from slaves' attacks, the slaves who attempted to subdue Albert when he challenged his victim recognized that a slave who could kill a white person might, for whatever reason, also be capable of killing a black person. This notion helps to explain why a cook whose testimony had helped to

15. Trial of Reuben, September 10, 1857, Appomattox County, C.S., box 9. The defense counsel was Thomas I. Fitzpatrick. Controversy over the judicial statement against black citizenship in the recent Dred Scott decision might have influenced this legal clash. For court action concerning the assault of a slave by a slave, see Melvin Herndon, "From Scottish Orphan to Virginia Planter; William Galt, Jr., 1801–1851," VMHB, LXXXVII (1979), 337; trial of Namon, July 5, 1839, Henry C.C.M.B. (1839–49), 30 (the punishment was fifty lashes); trial of Ballard, April 11, 1864, Henry C.C.M.B. (1859–64), 494 (punishment of thirty-nine lashes). Between 1830 and 1865, there were fourteen slaves convicted of killing slaves who belonged to the same owner; courts convicted thirty-six slaves of killing slaves who were the property of other masters or mistresses. Some of the same factors as before were present—jealousy, for example. To his female victim, Robin was said to have promised that "by God if I don't enjoy you, no body else shall; if you don't have me, the worst will become of you" (trial of Robin, February 20, 1844, Pittsylvania C.C.O.B. [1844–45], 12, 15–21, and C.S., box 7. See also trial of Julius, February 4, 1856, Charlotte County, April, 1856, folder, VEPLR). Fighting sometimes led to a homicide. In one instance, the assailant and his victim worked for the same owner, James H. Grant, at his factory. They had fought over two marbles with which they had been gambling. According to a white witness, "it is very common for the negro boys engaged in Mr. Grant's Factory to amuse themselves by boxing and scuffling" (trial of Julius, January 13, 1856, Richmond city, VEPLR). In another case, the victim had called the attacker a "liar" because of the way he had been "talking about the gals" (trial of Bob, October 1, 1846, Mecklenburg County, C.S., box 8, and VEPLR).

get a slave hanged for murder of an overseer stated that she simply did not like that slave.[16]

The number of convictions of slave women for infanticide rose sharply after 1851, however. One woman was convicted in 1833 and one in 1834, but nine were sentenced to transportation between 1851 and 1858. Abolition of benefit of clergy in 1848 and general revision of the criminal code for slaves in 1848–1850 were the causes of this increase. But the changes reflect public authorities' concern over the incidence of infanticide. They partly wished to protect a capital investment, but their concern also had something to do with the relationship between slavery and the killing of slaves by slaves. Keziah, the property of Henry L. Carter, covered the mouth of her newborn child in order to keep the baby from crying and giving away what had been her secret pregnancy. Carter testified at her trial that she had a very good reputation but was "very much ashamed at . . . having had a child." That was Carter's perception; he had gained it from observing Keziah. Therein lies a clue to the political relationship between slave and owner that influenced so many aspects of slavery. Whatever Keziah's values were, the legal system for slaves could force her to bend to white leaders' values.[17]

Rape prosecutions were bound to be even more fraught with questions of legitimacy and authority than were infanticide trials. But there was an ominous change that occurred in antebellum Virginia. For the first time, threats or instances of lynching slaves suspected of

16. Trial of Bob, October 19, 1846, Mecklenburg County, C.S., box 8, and VEPLR; informant concerning Paschal Bracey was Susan Bracey Sheppard, a descendant; trial of Julius, February 4, 1856, Charlotte County, April, 1856, folder, VEPLR; trial of Albert, September 7, 1852, Charlotte County, C.S., box 8; trial of Robin, August 1, 1842, Northampton County, C.S., box 7 (a slave tried to protect an overseer); trial of Smith, June 18, 1856, Goochland County, C.S., box 9, and VEPLR (the cook's testimony).

17. Trial of Keziah, May 5, 1834, Henrico C.C.M.B. (1833–35), 106–107, and C.S., box 6. See also trial of Ally, February 18, 1833, Fairfax County, C.S., box 6; trial of Caroline, April 23, 1851, Hanover County, C.S., box 8; trial of Fanny, August 3, 1852, Albemarle County, C.S., box 8; trial of Lucy, September 16, 1852, Richmond city, C.S., box 8; trial of Charlotte, September 13, 1854, Richmond city Hustings C.M.B. (1853–55), 262, and C.S., box 8; trial of Lucy, May 1, 1855, Richmond city, C.S., box 8; trial of Opha Jane, April 7, 1856, Powhatan C.C.O.B. (1851–56), 501, and C.S., box 9, and VEPLR; trial of Mary Jane Willis, October 6, 1856, Hardy County (now West Virginia), C.S., box 9, and VEPLR; trial of Suckey, June 16, 1857, Culpeper C.C.M.B. (1853–58), 420–21, and C.S., box 9, accounts; trial of Marietta, November 9, 1858, Loudoun C.C.M.B. (1856–58), 448, and C.S., box 9. The Culpeper judges recommended transportation of Suckey because of the absence of malice in her action, which they attributed instead to "a sense of shame and pride of character."

raping or otherwise sexually assaulting white women began to occur regularly. White leaders do not appear to have made strenuous efforts to suppress such lynchings since so many whites shared hostility toward slaves accused of sexual attacks against white females. When counsel for Jim, the property of Robert V. Davis, won the third continuance in the trial of Jim for attempting to rape Mrs. Sarah E. Gregory, her husband Samuel F. Gregory moved quickly behind the seventeen-year-old suspect and cut him from ear to mouth. Jim tried to run, but fell bleeding on the floor. He survived the attack, was guarded thereafter, then found guilty and transported out of the Old Dominion. On the day Jim was sentenced, Samuel Gregory was examined for having assaulted Jim with a knife with intent to kill. After but one continuance, the court dropped the charge—the reason was lack of probable cause.[18]

It is rather difficult to know whether the incidence of what whites called rape by slaves of white women became more frequent after the 1830s. A change in the law indicates that whites perceived an increasing problem. In 1837 the legislature denied benefit of clergy to bondsmen convicted of either attempted rape or rape of a white woman. The legislature had in 1823 eliminated castration as the punishment for attempted rape, which soon drove up the statistics of slaves being sentenced to death for attempts. But that new law had not raised the number of executions or the confidence of influential whites that sexual aggression by slaves would decrease. Nor did the 1837 law increase the number of slaves executed or transported for attempted rape. Moreover, the number of slaves sentenced to death for rape of white women declined steadily while the percentage of slaves transported rather than executed rose steadily. In the midst of this downward

18. Trial of Jim, August 16, 1858, and proceedings concerning Gregory, Prince Edward C.C.O.B. (1853–62), 281, 283, 288, 292, and C.S., box 9; Richmond *Enquirer,* September 24, 28, 1858; Herbert Clarence Bradshaw, *History of Prince Edward County, Virginia* (Richmond, 1955), 285. For vigilante action and lynching threats, see trial of John, November 20, 1838, Jefferson County, C.S., box 6; and Virginia Council Minutes, 1838–39, pp. 214–15, 218–19, 221. Trial of Anthony, December 3, 1846, King George C.C.O.B. (1839–47), 508, and C.S., box 8, and VEPLR. A letter concerning the trial of Anthony asserted that if the victim had been from a "rich family," the governor knew "he Never would have gotten to jail" (VEPLR). In another case, the twelve-year-old victim's mother said that if the court did not have the defendant hanged, she would have him shot (trial of Anderson, October 6, 1856, Spotsylvania County, VEPLR). In the trial records concerning George, August 11, 1856, Mathews County, September, 1856, folder, VEPLR, the rumor of an acquittal on the second day had led to a general determination to hang George anyway. See also P. F. Howard to Governor Wise, undated but received August 29, 1859, in VEPLR.

statistical trend, however, one governor would declare to the legislature in 1857 that rape, like arson, was "on the increase, and ought to be
severely guarded against."[19]

Unless white mobs were in fact lynching more slaves, the frequency
of slaves raping white women did not rise in antebellum Virginia.
Instead, white fear of black sexual assault did. That led to the extremely volatile situation in postbellum Virginia with which historians are so familiar. The pressure of opinion was intense and judicial
jeopardy was high before the Civil War. In 1842, former slave Lewis
Clarke wrote angrily in the *National Anti-Slavery Standard* that rape of
white women was a "crime for which more black men are hung than
for any other."[20] Whether this was true elsewhere, it was not quite true
in the Old Dominion. Between 1830 and 1865, Virginia sheriffs hanged
more than twice as many slaves for murdering whites—at least seven-
ty-eight—as for raping or trying to rape white women—at least thirty-
six. More significant is the percentage of slaves sentenced to death and
denied benefit of clergy who were actually executed rather than transported when charged with either crime. From 1785 to 1829 the percentage for rape was 92.7; for murder it was 86.2. From 1830 to 1865
the comparable figures were 57.1 percent and 51.0 percent. In the
representative counties of Essex, Henry, Southampton, and Spotsylvania, the simple conviction rates for murder and rape of whites
between 1830 and 1865 were, respectively, 63.6 percent and 66.7 percent. Only assault and attempted murder prosecutions yielded higher
percentages, and then the number of those convicted who were executed was somewhat lower than in the case of rape.

However, rationality was not totally absent. Petitions still came to
the executive to pardon or grant mercy to convicted rapists. There
were a few prosecutions of slaves for raping free black women, and
even one sentence of deportation for raping an enslaved woman.[21]

19. *Supplement to the Revised Code*, 280–81; *Acts of the General Assembly*, 1836–37;
Governor's Biennial Messages . . . 1857, p. 151.

20. Blassingame (ed.), *Slave Testimony*, 155.

21. Trial of Coleman, November 17, 1856, Mecklenburg C.C.O.B. (1853–58), 353, and
C.S., box 9, and VEPLR, which includes (in December, 1856, folder) a citizens' petition
and letters from Mrs. Nelson to Governor Wise, December 9, 28, 1856. For slaves' assaults
against free black and enslaved victims, see trial of Charles, July 29, 1857, Halifax
C.C.O.B. (1856–57), 341, and C.S., box 9, accounts; trial of Ned, June 9, 1859, Fredericksburg city Hustings C.O.B. (1855–60), 346; Fredericksburg *News*, June 14, 1859; trial of
John, December 2, 1850, Spotsylvania C.C.O.B. (1849–58), 78 (sentenced to transportation for rape of a slave); trial of William, April 12, 1858, Loudoun C.C.M.B. (1856–58),
314, 332 (charge made against slave for rape of an enslaved woman, but later dropped).

When courts began to take action, albeit infrequently, against slaves suspected of raping slave women, and the same courts gave less harsh sentences than before to slaves convicted of raping or attempting to rape white women, threats and instances of lynching predictably increased. In another era, the early 1890s, all lynchings in Virginia of black men accused of sexually assaulting white women took place after courts had acted in a manner that the various mobs thought too lenient. The lynchings did not occur before the judicial process began. The apparent judicial reform during the 1850s resulted from many causes, not the least of which was the general campaign to improve the conditions of slavery so as to prevent slaves and abolitionists from attacking it.[22] The declining level of prosecutions for rape and attempted rape in the representative counties of Essex, Henry, Southampton, and Spotsylvania, and the decrease in executions of Virginian slaves for the same offense suggest that the reformers had been shrewd. Slaves were not going to take chances unless pushed extremely hard. When the pushing decreased, so did slaves' violence.

The essential question for this study is whether postemancipation interaction merely continued old trends or created new ones. One must avoid reading meanings appropriate to the period after 1865 back into the pre-1865 pattern, yet the search for evidence that lynching or a rape complex originated in the slave era cannot but yield continuities.[23] The simple rule seems to have been that when enough whites trusted the courts, lynching would not occur. Slaveowners had their reasons to trust the courts of oyer and terminer. Many white Virginians apparently believed in the early twentieth-century crimi-

22. Kerry Johnson, "The Fever Breaks: Virginia Lynchings, 1885–1895" (Honors paper, Department of History and Geography, Virginia Commonwealth University, 1980); Genovese, Roll, Jordan, Roll, 49–70; Aptheker, American Negro Slave Revolts, 60; Wayne Edward Barry, "Against Their Master's Will: A Judicial History of Virginia's Manumission Law, 1800–1860" (M.A. thesis, University of Minnesota, 1979), 61–100. Blassingame gives some support to this notion of proslavery reform in his statistics on slaves' participation in churches in Virginia and elsewhere (The Slave Community, 344–56, 360), but see his note of caution about the data (337–40).

23. An excellent study of the relationship between lynching and interracial sexual tensions is Jacquelyn Dowd Hall, Revolt Against Chivalry: Jessie Daniel Ames and the Women's Campaign Against Lynching (New York, 1979), 129–57. See also Wyatt-Brown, Southern Honor, 51, 453–58. Lawrence J. Friedman's entry "Rape Complex, Southern" in The Encyclopedia of Southern History is a useful reference, but see also Johnston, Race Relations in Virginia, 257–63; Susan Brownmiller, Against Our Will: Men, Women, and Rape (New York, 1975), 210–55; and Catherine Clinton, The Plantation Mistress: Woman's World in the Old South (New York, 1982), 199–231, 293–94n42, a valuable commentary on published studies of interracial sexual relations.

nal courts of Virginia. Lynching was relatively less frequent in the Old Dominion than in other states. Between 1885 and 1930, only 1 in 5 lynchings of black Virginians resulted from accusations of rape of a white woman. Fewer than 20 black men so accused were lynched. In the years from 1908 to 1930, there were 29 black men electrocuted after convictions for sexual offenses against white women. Moreover, at least 52 of the 205 black citizens executed in the state between 1908 and 1962 had been convicted of attempted rape or rape. Disproportionate as that number was in relation to white convicts, those men were executed rather than lynched.[24]

Tensions concerning sexual aggression by slaves resembled many other tensions that were inherent in the slave society of Virginia. Usually below the surface of daily interaction, they sometimes flared into dramatic incidents of violence or accusation. But the courts also had to deal with slaves' secret behavior that had the same potential as did assault, killing, or sexual offenses to turn the world of white supremacy and slavery upside down, yet it was harder to detect and therefore harder to combat. Those slaves presented a special challenge in Virginia during slavery's last years. It may be that fewer slaves took risks in late antebellum Virginia, but as many slaves as ever appear to have been working underground with such weapons as poisoning, stealing, arson, and even insurrectionary plotting. If a slave did not actually do any of those things, the mere threat would continue to keep slaveowners and other whites somewhat on the defensive, even as the threat of being whipped kept slaves somewhat on the defensive.

Poisoning and administering medicine convictions are the best examples of how some slaves continued to try to undermine their enemies.[25] Legislators reflected the uneasy state of public opinion when in 1843, some ninety-five years after the passage of the original law, they made it a capital offense without benefit of clergy for any slave to administer or cause to be administered "any medicine, deadly poison,

24. Bernard Peyton Chamberlain, *The Negro and Crime in Virginia* (Charlottesville, 1936), 66–68; William J. Bowers, *Executions in America* (Lexington, Mass., 1974), 386–94. For the years before 1908, aggregate statistics of executions of free Virginians are unfortunately available only from newspaper accounts.

25. On the limited role of conjurers in late antebellum Virginia, see *Weevils in the Wheat*, 223; "Voudouism in Virginia," undated article from unidentified newspaper, *ca.* 1875, George William Bagby Scrapbook, 1866–76, pp. 110–11, Bagby Family Papers, 1824–1960, sec. 36, VHS. One Virginian former slave had great contempt for conjurers, whom he accused of being frauds (Henry Clay Bruce, *The New Man: Twenty-Nine Years a Slave. Twenty-Nine Years a Free Man* [York, Pa., 1895; Miami, Fla., 1969], 52–59).

or other noxious and destructive substance or thing, with intent thereby to murder." In recognition that Afro-Americans favored this kind of attack, the legislation covered slaves, free blacks, and mulattoes. Slaves could go on providing health care with their owners' permission, since such permission precluded intent to murder. The assumption in this provision was that owners would not direct slaves to do their killing for them. Nevertheless, county oyer and terminer justices could execute or transport slaves for poisoning if mere intent, as opposed to illness or death, could be proved beyond slaveholders' reasonable doubts. After the 1843 legislation went into effect, thirty-one slaves received the sentence of death for this offense when whites were the victims, twenty-five of them being transported and six executed. Pardons and reversals of convictions by a higher court indicated that judges and other authorities did not regard it as essential to use all the powers they had. What seemed essential was to remove from the Commonwealth any slave suspected of being willing to use poison.[26]

There was an important change in the nature of the substances used. Prosecutors still presented evidence of the use of Jamestown weed, roots, arsenic, and glass, but after 1830, they also displayed laudanum, morphine, and opium. Afro-Americans were now using more Euro-American weapons and still mostly against whites. Many more slaves were convicted of poisoning other slaves after 1830 than had been convicted in the years between 1785 and 1829—eleven as opposed to two. Thirty-nine slaves were found guilty of poisoning twenty-three white victims; the eleven had been convicted of poisoning six fellow slaves. Most significant was the composition of the group of slaves convicted of poisoning. Women had been involved in fifteen, or 65.2 percent, of the twenty-three killings of whites; nineteen, or 48.7 percent, of the slaves convicted of these killings were women. Most frightening to slaveowners was the connection of attacker and victim in the four cases in which infants or children had been poisoned. All slaves convicted of these attacks were women.[27]

Attacks within white families were lethal and unnerving. If a father

26. *Acts of the General Assembly*, 1842–43, pp. 59–60. Pardons occurred in the trial of Eady, August 8, 1836, Buckingham County, and trial of Jane, April 27, 1846, Brunswick County, VEPLR. A rare reversal took place in the case of Elvira, April 22, 1864, Petersburg city Hustings C.O.B. (1861–67), 377–78, and C.S., box 9, and excerpted in Catterall, *Judicial Cases*, I, 254.

27. A slave mother once used the threat of poisoning to try to keep a slave man from marrying her daughter (trial of Robin, February 20, 1844, Pittsylvania C.C.O.B. [1844–45], 12, 15–21, and C.S., box 7). Trial of Nelly, June 21, 1834, Bedford County, C.S., box 6;

found ground glass in his food, he feared for his own life and the lives of his wife and children.[28] One house servant claimed she had given a fatal overdose of opium to a baby in order to "get out of the trouble of nursing it."[29] While white families were vulnerable, black families could be particularly threatening, as Edward Haynie, a Northumberland County planter, learned in 1854. As many as ten bondspeople in his "family" may have been involved in a plot to kill him with poison. They were all related to one another.[30]

But slaves' primary weapon between 1830 and 1865 was arson. The conviction rate was extraordinarily low between 1830 and 1865, so it was more effective and less dangerous than poisoning. Unlike poison, however, arson could normally be used only against whites. And it was used frequently from 1830 to 1865 since the number of convictions grew and since the low simple conviction rates give rise to the suspicion that guilty verdicts were but the visible manifestations of a veritable epidemic. Some of the increase in the number of transportees after 1848 resulted from elimination of benefit of clergy. Yet arson prosecutions in the representative counties of Essex, Henry, Southampton, and Spotsylvania tell the story. From 1785 to 1829, there were nine prosecutions of slaves for arson in those jurisdictions. Between 1830 and 1865, the number rose to sixteen, a gain of more than 40 percent during years when the slave population of three of those counties declined. In the case of Henry County, the slave population had risen, but there was only one prosecution of a slave for arson in that county.[31]

---

trials of Roberta and Eliza, August 1, 1849, Brunswick County, C.S., box 8; trial of Fanny, February 15, 1860, Richmond city Hustings C.M.B. (1859–60), 250–51, and C.S., box 9; trial of Permelia, July 16, 1860, Amherst County, C.S., box 9. The first three women hanged; the last two were transported.

28. Trial of Martha, April 1, 1857, King William County, C.S., box 9, and Aylett Family Papers, 1776–1945, sec. 52, VHS. The latter contains evidence used in defense of Martha by William Roane Aylett, then a young lawyer just out of the University of Virginia.

29. Trial of Eady, August 8, 1836, Buckingham County, VEPLR. In "The Westover Journal of John A. Selden," *Smith College Studies in History*, VI (July, 1921), 298, Selden briefly described the day-long trial of a slave for poisoning his master's son with corrosive sublimate in a brandy toddy. "He was condemned," Selden noted, "but by the dissent of one magistrate (Hubbard), to be transported." Trial, July 21, 1859, Charles City C.M.B. (1848–60), 569–70, and C.S., box 9.

30. Trials of Joe, Tracy, Jasper, Robert Lewis, William, Daniel, Isaac, Sam Taylor, Polly, and Austin, April 13, 1854, Northumberland C.C.O.B. (1852–61), 122–32, and C.S., box 8. All ten were transported.

31. Trial of Jenny, May 9, 1836, Henry C.C.M.B. (1827–38), 292, and C.S., box 6, and VEPLR. Jenny was found guilty and transported. There was an increase in white concern about slave arson in Virginia in the 1850s and 1860s (Aptheker, *American Negro Slave Revolts*, 146–49).

There is some significant correlation between the ratio of slaves to whites and the number of convictions for arson between 1830 and 1865 (see Table 29). The correlation is strongest where that ratio was lowest, however. Four of the top five jurisdictions had a slave minority, but only one of the last five did so; four of the lower five had more slaves than whites, but in only one of the upper five did slaves outnumber whites. Like the thirty-one women who were 31.6 percent of the convicted arsonists, the many slaves in counties and cities with a slave minority had a weapon that was quite powerful—no matter how overpowered or outnumbered they might be. Women and outnumbered slaves were by no means the only ones to rely on arson.

As in the years 1785 to 1829, the overwhelming majority of incidents and convictions between 1830 and 1865 were in Piedmont, northern, and western Virginia. Of the seventy-nine burned structures that court clerks identified, more than half were agricultural, including barns with unspecified contents, stables, tobacco barns, and hay, grain, or corn barns. Concentration of arson convictions continued to be in the grain regions, as in the earlier years, but the learning process that had

Table 29.   Minimal Rate of Arson Incidents, 1830–1865, per 1,000 Slaves

County or City	Incidents	Mean Slave Population, 1830–60	Rate	Rank	% Slave	
					1830	1860
Richmond city	10	8,871	1.13	1	39.5%	30.9%
Wythe County	2	1,988	1.01	2	17.2	17.6
King George County	3	3,486	0.86	3	56.8	55.9
Madison County	3	4,476	0.67	4	46.2	50.7
Henrico County	4	6,751	0.59	5	46.6	35.2
Powhatan County	3	5,271	0.57	6	64.2	64.4
Loudoun County	3	5,472	0.55	7	24.4	25.3
Goochland County	3	5,828	0.51	8	55.1	57.6
Caroline County	4	10,549	0.38	9	60.5	57.8
Charlotte County	3	9,162	0.33	10	61.8	63.8

SOURCES: C.S., boxes 1–10; miscellaneous county court order and minute books; U.S. Census Office, *The Statistics of the Population of the United States,* Vol. I, *Population and Social Statistics,* 68–72.

NOTE: Minimal rate computed as ratio of arson incidents for which one or more slaves were executed or transported to the mean slave population, 1830–1860. Rate is minimal because it cannot take unreported incidents into account.

been at work then also continued. There were more attacks on tobacco barns and more of the most frightening kind of fire, that in dwellings, which constituted nearly one-third of the structures burned. Density of population and structures, fear of fire, and the higher probability of dwellings becoming targets all drove up the rate of convictions in the city of Richmond. The old fear of urban fires being set by slaves intensified as Richmond grew larger and larger.[32]

The motives for arson were similar to the motives for the various kinds of physical attacks on white people. There were cases of white instigation, but most testimony focused on bondspeople alone. Some of Edmund Ruffin's slaves kept burning structures on his property in reaction to an overseer they hated. Puzzled for several years, Ruffin eventually got the point. Other slaves used arson to retaliate against patrollers who had harassed them. Slave arsonists included one man whose wife had just been sold—and he was himself about to be. A pregnant woman was obviously overworked by her master, a physician, despite his professional knowledge of the risks and pain; a relative of hers set fire to his barn. A slave who had been engaged in a long-standing feud with a white man opened a new stage of combat by burning his enemy's barn. And a woman in Charles City County who asserted that "the white folks are getting too high" burned a home in order to set things right. As convicted arsonists, these slaves had not always succeeded in gaining their objectives, but that did not necessarily matter because other slaves often used arson without getting caught.[33] Arson could become an unusually dangerous weapon if used by enslaved rebels, a situation that became quite possible in the 1850s.

32. Henry Box Brown asserted that Richmond whites lived in constant fear of slaves, especially of arson by slaves (Narrative, 38–39). See also Rodney Dale Green, "Urban Industry, Black Resistance, and Racial Restriction in the Antebellum South: A General Model and a Case Study in Urban Virginia" (Ph.D. dissertation, American University, 1980), 551–54.

33. Edmund Ruffin, The Diary of Edmund Ruffin, ed. William Kauffman Scarborough (2 vols.; Baton Rouge, 1972, 77), II, 553–54; trial of Lee, November 22, 1860, Amelia County, C.S., box 9; trial of Jesse, February 18, 1856, Warren C.C.M.B. (1853–61), 108–10, and C.S., box 9, and March, 1856, folder, VEPLR; trial of Venable, who acted on behalf of the abused pregnant woman, August 25, 1856, Cumberland C.C.O.B. (1851–57), 502, 504, 509–13, and C.S., box 9, and VEPLR, which contains the sixty-three-page record of this trial; trial of London, June 30, 1838, Washington C.C.M.B. (1837–39), 178, and C.S., box 6; trial of Ann, February 22, 1856, Charles City County, April, 1856, folder, VEPLR; Aptheker, American Negro Slave Revolts, 148. It remained possible for whites to persuade or coerce enslaved blacks to do their burning for them (see trial, June 2, 1856, Spotsylvania C.C.O.B. [1849–58], 428, 439; trials of John Woods and Roy Green, May 19, 1856, Jefferson County [now West Virginia], C.S., box 9, and VEPLR). A character in

Stealing was, however, still the most frequently prosecuted major crime. Whites persisted in blaming or privately punishing slaves for theft, but they also tried to prosecute when they could, which was probably not as often as they would have liked. Richard Eppes of Eppes Island on the lower James River learned in November, 1851, how difficult it could be to bring enslaved suspects to court. After becoming concerned about some property missing from his plantation, Eppes joined a patrol late on a Saturday night. The group waited near the river until 3:00 or 4:00 A.M., when they heard a boat with muffled oars approaching. When several men left the boat to take some articles to a woman's house, the patrollers were convinced they had found a slaves' fencing operation in progress, and they leaped into action. One slave eluded Eppes and got to the boat even as Eppes fell into the water. A patroller mistook Eppes for a slave and knocked him flat, after which he was weak and "flighty." Two of the slaves managed to get to a boat as well and pushed off. Yet those blacks gave up, because the patrollers might have had guns. The captured slaves proved to be the cook and the carpenter of Mr. Carter of the nearby plantation, Shirley. Eppes did not say whether he expected to find field hands, but he had been reminded that any slave might take from white people.[34]

Stealing by slaves continued to be part of the social landscape in Virginia from 1830 through the Civil War.[35] But convictions for theft resulting in transportation or execution decreased slightly, even though convictions for other major crimes rose dramatically from 1850 on. There were some changes in the criminal code for slaves. In 1828 a new law made $20 the threshold for capital stealing. Burglary remained a capital crime, though justices could grant benefit of clergy.

William Faulkner's "Barn Burning" reflected the once widespread white southern understanding of this kind of interracial "cooperation" when he asked Abner Snopes, who was about to burn an enemy's barn by himself, " 'Ain't you going to even send a nigger? . . . At least you sent a nigger before!' " (*Collected Stories of William Faulkner* [New York, n.d.], 21). See also Wyatt-Brown, *Southern Honor*, 384.

34. Eppes would later be unsuccessful in his efforts to determine which of his slaves had broken into his storehouse and stolen some shad: "Gave each a severe whipping but could not get them to confess." Richard Eppes Diary, November 13, 1851–January 8, 1852, Eppes Family Muniments, 1722–1948, VHS.

35. William Wells Brown referred to his first owner as "the man who stole me as soon as I was born" (*Narrative*, in Gilbert Osofsky [ed.], *Puttin' On Ole Massa: The Slave Narratives of Henry Bibb, William Wells Brown, and Solomon Northrup* [New York, 1969], 179). Bibb, *Narrative, ibid.*, 59–60, 79, 125, 131, 146–47, 165–67; *Weevils in the Wheat*, 78, 116, 124 (Nottoway County), 139, 181, 201–202, 244–45, 252, 266–67; Genovese, *Roll, Jordan, Roll*, 599–609. It was obviously still possible for whites to make or persuade slaves to steal for them.

Statistics from Essex, Henry, Southampton, and Spotsylvania counties indicate that theft prosecutions of slaves occurred with the same frequency after 1848 as before. The records of the compensations paid for executed or transported slaves show, however, that slightly fewer of the slaves convicted of theft across Virginia received the harshest available punishments.[36] Convictions reveal that bondsmen stole money and banknotes more often than before. Otherwise, they concentrated on much the same items (see Tables 30 and 31).

A most important shift took place in another one of the patterns of convictions for major stealing after 1830. More than 16 percent of theft convictions had occurred in larger towns and cities between 1785 and 1829; that percentage jumped to 35.8 between 1830 and 1864. (The percentage of incidents was 35.5.) In spite of some strengthening of police forces and local constabularies, urban slaves who wished to steal large amounts of goods or money increasingly took advantage of the ample opportunities provided by cities (see Tables 32 and 33). White citizens complained and white authorities struggled, but such stealing could not be ended.[37] Moreover, in spite of many whites' strenuous efforts to remove or suppress free blacks, they concentrated heavily in towns and cities, making stealing that much easier for slaves and free blacks who wished to collaborate.[38] The disruptions of the Civil War only intensified stealing by slaves in urban Virginia.[39]

36. *Supplement to the Revised Code*, 242; *Acts of the General Assembly*, 1847–48, pp. 124–26. From 1830 to 1848, there were thirty-five prosecutions, or 1.9 per year; from 1849 through 1865, there were thirty prosecutions, or 1.9 per year.

37. Ira Berlin, *Slaves Without Masters: The Free Negro in the Antebellum South* (New York, 1974), 242–43, 330; Richard Wade, *Slavery in the Cities: The South, 1820–1860* (New York, 1964), 183–93. In *American Slavery As It Is* (New York, 1839), 150, Theodore P. Weld (or his source) confused two Virginia cities, reporting a burglary conviction to have taken place in Alexandria. Not only did the trial actually take place in Norfolk, but the slaves who, according to Weld, were "to be hung," ended up being transported, as was true for almost all slaves convicted of burglary in Virginia courts during the antebellum years. See trials of Arthur and John, January 28, 1839, Norfolk city, C.S., boxes 6, 7; "A List of Slaves and Free Persons of Color received into the Penitentiary . . . 1816 to . . . 1842," C.S., box 10; and *Norfolk Directory for 1851–1852* (Norfolk, 1851), 52, 78. Collaboration between slaves and whites certainly continued. See *Smith v. Commonwealth*, 10 Leigh 695 (1840), excerpted in Catterall, *Judicial Cases*, I, 198.

38. The Richmond City Sergeant's Register, March 13, 1841–May 8, 1846, in VHS, shows one urban authority's constant involvement in apprehending runaway slaves, slaves at large, and free blacks without registers, or identity papers. See the trial of Bob, May 12, 1860, Culpeper County, June, 1846, folder, VEPLR, for a good illustration of how an "urban temptation" led not only to a theft but to a pardon, since the temptation was so great and Bob's owner was willing to remove him from Virginia. See also Green, "Urban Industry, Black Resistance, and Racial Restriction," 468–558.

39. Ruffin, *Diary*, II, 480–81. There was a rash of convictions in Richmond during the

Table 30.   Items Stolen by Slaves Transported or Executed, 1830–1864

	Clothes/ Fabric	Food/ Livestock	Banknotes/ Money	Horses	Total
1830–34	5	1	5	3	14
1835–39	5	1	3	1	10
1840–44	9	6	8	1	24
1845–49	4	5	4	1	14
1850–54	5	4	5	0	14
1855–59	2	1	3	0	6
1860–64	2	1	0	0	3
Total	32	19	28	6	85
Percentage	37.6%	22.4%	32.9%	7.1%	100%

SOURCES: C.S., boxes 1–10; miscellaneous county court order and minute books.
NOTE: These 85 cases represent only part of the slaves transported or executed for theft. Court clerks did not always record the items stolen. Some slaves stole items in more than one category.

Slaves increasingly saw another kind of opportunity for stealing in cities. The familiar story of how Henry Box Brown was shipped out of Richmond to Philadelphia reflects the efforts of slaves to "steal themselves" from cities.[40] There was an intensive judicial and governmental response to such escapes, whether they began in cities or on plantations. Between 1800 and 1838, five people served terms in the Virginia Penitentiary for persuading slaves to run away, and one person received the same punishment for furnishing a slave with free papers. Late in 1859, however, three white and two black people were in the

Civil War. Trials of John, October 12, 1863, Henry and John, January 11, 1864, Joe, July 13, 1864, Henry, August 10, 1864, Ben, September 13, 1864, Curtis, November 17, 1864, John, December 12, 1864, and Abner, February 15, 1865, C.S., box 9. Including three of these slaves, all fifty-four of the slaves found guilty of felonies by the Richmond city Hustings Court from September, 1863, through August, 1864, had been tried for property crimes (John Breeden, "Crime and Justice in Wartime Richmond" [Undergraduate paper, History 486, Virginia Commonwealth University, 1977]).

40. Brown, *Narrative; The Code of Virginia* (1860), 513–18, 792–96; "Report of the Committee Appointed at a Meeting of the Citizens of the City of Richmond and Henrico County," 1835, VSL; T. B. Robertson to Governor Wise, July 30, 1856, in VEPLR (a recent loss of seven slaves who escaped via schooner in spite of inspection laws); Sherrard Clemens to Governor Smith, November 12, 1847, VEPLR; Catterall, *Judicial Cases*, I, 208–11, 216–19, 221, 247; Federal Writers' Project, Virginia, *The Negro In Virginia* (New York, 1940), 138; Genovese, *Roll, Jordan, Roll*, 653–54; Patricia P. Hickin, "Antislavery in Virginia, 1831–1861" (2 vols.; Ph.D. dissertation, University of Virginia, 1968), I, 71–106; Green, "Urban Industry, Black Resistance, and Racial Restriction," 471–84, 494–500, 511–37, 681, 710–13, 803–804.

Table 31. Items Stolen by Slaves, 1830–1864

	Clothes/Fabric			Food/Livestock[a]			Liquor			Money/Banknotes			Hogs[b]		
	T	G	C[c]	T	G	C	T	G	C	T	G	C	T	G	C
Essex	3	3	0.0%	2	1	0.0%	0	0	0.0%	2	1	0.0%	1	0	0.0%
Henry	3	3	0.0	0	0	0.0	2	2	100.0	1	0	0.0	0	0	0.0
Southampton	2	1	0.0	2	2	0.0	0	0	0.0	0	0	0.0	0	0	0.0
Spotsylvania	10	9	88.9	22	15	60.0	7	5	80.0	3	0	0.0	5	5	60.0

SOURCES: C.S., boxes 5–10; miscellaneous county court order and minute books.
NOTE: There was only one trial and conviction for horse stealing in these four counties between 1830 and 1864.
[a]Livestock excludes hogs
[b]All misdemeanor cases
[c]T = Tried, G = Guilty, C = Percentage of convicted slaves who collaborated with other slaves

Table 32.   Major Stealing Incidents per 1,000 Slaves, 1830–1864

Jurisdiction	Incidents, 1830–64	Mean Slave Population, 1830–64	Incidents per 1,000 Slaves
1. Richmond city	40	8,871	4.50
2. Fredericksburg	2	1,204	1.66
3. Petersburg	6	4,224	1.42
4. Lancaster County	3	2,655	1.13
5. Gloucester County	6	5,669	1.06
6. Prince William County	3	2,866	1.05
7. Powhatan County	5	5,322	0.94
8. Henrico County (outside Richmond)	6	6,546	0.92
9. Northumberland County	3	3,449	0.87
10. Stafford County	3	3,596	0.83
11. Accomack County	3	4,695	0.64
12. Cumberland County	3	6,781	0.44
13. Louisa County	4	9,612	0.42
14. Fauquier County	4	11,009	0.36
15. Albemarle County	4	12,686	0.32

SOURCES: C.S., boxes 5–10; miscellaneous county court order and minute books; U.S. Census Office, *The Statistics of the Population of the United States*, Vol. I, *Population and Social Statistics*, 68–72.
NOTE: More than one slave could have been convicted of participation in any one of these incidents.

penitentiary for helping slaves to escape and four whites and one black were incarcerated for "carrying off slaves," an offense related to running away yet not connected with slave stealing. Of these convicts, one white person was in the penitentiary for the fourth time, this time for life, for aiding slaves' escapes. Others faced terms of anywhere from two to forty years. For all nine of the white convicts, excluding the one serving the life term, the mean sentence was 13.67 years; the figure for the four black inmates was 8.75 years. Lawmakers and the judiciary seem to have feared more what free whites would do on behalf of fugitive slaves, though it is equally possible that free blacks had to be much more cautious than whites if they even bothered to stay in the hostile environment of the Old Dominion. A Southampton County free black paid a high price for helping runaway slaves in early 1862. He was sold into slavery.[41]

41. *Report of the Joint Committee on the Penitentiary (Virginia House Journal*, 1839, doc. 41), 9; *Annual Report of the Board of Directors of the Penitentiary Institution, 1858–1859*

Table 33.   Major Stealing Incidents, 1830–1864

	Northern Neck/ Middle Peninsula	Central Piedmont	Southeastern Tidewater
1830–34	9	8	1
1835–39	0	6	1
1840–44	2	13	0
1845–49	2	9	1
1850–54	4	6	0
1855–59	2	10	1
1860–64	0	10	1
Total	19	62	5
Mean Slave Population, 1830–60	41,980	59,356	44,891
Incidents per One Thousand Slaves	0.45	1.04	0.11

SOURCES: C.S., boxes 5–10; miscellaneous county court order and minute books; U.S. Census Office, *The Statistics of the Population of the United States*, Vol. I, *Population and Social Statistics*, 68–72.

NOTE: Northern Neck/Middle Peninsula: Essex, Gloucester, King and Queen, King George, King William, Lancaster, Mathews, Middlesex, Richmond, and Westmoreland counties. Central Piedmont/Upper Tidewater: Charles City, Chesterfield, Goochland, Hanover, Henrico (outside Richmond), New Kent, Powhatan, and Prince George counties and Petersburg and Richmond cities. Southeastern Tidewater: Elizabeth City, Isle of Wight, James City, Nansemond, Norfolk, Princess Anne, Southampton, Surry, Sussex, and Warwick counties, and Norfolk city.

Prosecution of slaves for running away was bound to be less frequent than for other offenses. Those who succeeded were beyond prosecution. But some were prosecuted, and some of the slaves who helped runaways were convicted. During 1832, residents of Northampton County labored as strenuously to keep slaves in the county as they did to throw free blacks out. They were unsuccessful in retrieving all the slaves who had used a whaleboat to flee to New York, but they did seize

(*Virginia House Journal*, 1859, doc. 13), 26; Southampton C.C.M.B. (1861–70), 60. Another free black won acquittal on the same charge in December, 1863 (Southampton C.C.M.B. [1861–70], 134). For other cases, see the materials on Nelson Talbert Gant, September–October, 1846, folder, VEPLR; Judge J. W. Edmunds to Governor Smith, June 12, 1846, in VEPLR; trial records from Hampshire County (now West Virginia), May 27, 1856, and Richmond city, August 12, 1856, VEPLR (latter in September 9–23 folder); Virginia Council Journals, 1840–41, p. 100. When the Union army neared Richmond, more and more slaves were caught helping others to escape "from the state." They were all sold out of the state (trials of William, Catharine, John, and Peter, March 17, May 9, 1864, January 12, February 14, 1865, city of Richmond, Pardons, April–December, 1864, and January–April, 1865, VEPLR).

one of them. The county oyer and terminer judges concluded that since Isaac had been granted benefit of clergy for another conviction two years earlier, he would now have to be hanged for stealing a whaleboat worth $132. Isaac was not hanged, however; the forty-two-year-old slave was transported out of Virginia in chains that belonged to the state government. The last two trials of slaves in Essex County before bondage ended were for aiding runaways, and had the same result. Two men who had aided three other slaves in their April, 1863, escape were also sentenced to transportation. The same fate awaited a slave tried in Richmond but a month before the war ended. No other trials resulted in the sentence of transportation or execution.[42]

Many whites greatly feared that the same black and white abolitionists who encouraged slaves to flee also wanted them to rebel. This accusation contained more and more truth through the 1840s and the 1850s. Black and white abolitionists either changed their minds or made public their views about the necessity of using violence to effect the fundamental change that persuasion and politics had not done.[43] But during the same years white Virginian judges heard few cases of slaves charged with insurrection. That did not necessarily mean that slaves stopped trying to rebel collectively. It is more likely that collective rebelliousness became increasingly secretive. The thinking and acting were now primarily underground, and white authorities were nervously aware of that—whether or not they accurately identified the slaves involved in plots.

Seditious speech and writing appeared to present the greatest

42. Virginia Council Journals, 1832–33, pp. 156, 169–70. There was a similar case in Accomack County in 1836 and 1837 (see Virginia Council Journals, 1836–37, pp. 143, 184, 195–96). See also Abel P. Upshur to Governor Floyd, October 4, 1832, in *CVSP*, X, 578–79; Norma Lois Peterson, *Littleton Waller Tazewell* (Charlottesville, 1983), 254; and trial of John, March 13, 1865, Essex C.C.O.B. (1853–63), 888–89.

43. Robert B. Abzug, "The Influence of Garrisonian Abolitionist Fears of Slave Violence on the Antislavery Argument," *JNH*, LV (1970), 15–28; John Demos, "The Antislavery Movement and the Problem of Violent Means," *NEQ*, XXXVII (1964), 501–26; Robert C. Dick, *Black Protest: Issues and Tactics* (Westport, Conn., 1974), 127–60; Lawrence J. Friedman, *Gregarious Saints: Self and Community in American Abolitionism, 1830–1870* (Cambridge, England, 1982), 196–222; Leslie Friedman Goldstein, "Violence as an Instrument for Social Change: The Views of Frederick Douglass (1817–1895)," *JNH*, LXI (1976), 61–72; Carleton Mabee, *Black Freedom: The Nonviolent Abolitionists From 1830 Through the Civil War* (London, 1970); Lewis Perry, *Anarchy and the Government of God in Antislavery Thought* (Ithaca, 1973), 231–67; Jeffery Rossbach, *Ambivalent Conspirators: John Brown, the Secret Six, and a Theory of Slave Violence* (Philadelphia, 1982). For the argument that abolitionists had little impact on slave resistance in Virginia, see Green, "Urban Industry, Black Resistance, and Racial Restriction," 468–558.

threat to white leaders. A Loudoun County slave stood trial in June, 1839, for having writings printed that questioned the right of masters to own slaves. Gerard was found guilty, sentenced to hang, reprieved to be sold and transported out of the United States, but finally died while waiting in the penitentiary for exile. During the same month of March, 1840, in which the state had paid Gerard's owner her compensation money, five slaves in nearby Fairfax County faced the more serious charge of insurrection. But three were found not guilty, and even though Alfred was transported and Spencer was executed, they had been convicted of assault of three white men with intent to kill, not of insurrection. The execution indicates that white authorities took the attack quite seriously, but the elimination of the insurrection charge suggests that they wished to publicly reject the possibility that an organized attack on whites was political.[44]

The context in which seditious speech took place was all-important. Just as running away became an ideologically charged action after northern abolitionism grew in strength, so even the suggestion of rebellion by slaves became more threatening to the white community. As several Southampton County slaves learned in 1840, white people who had nine years earlier experienced one of the most effective slave rebellions in United States history would be especially nervous about what slaves might say. As Davy testified at the September trial of Nicholas, about fifteen or sixteen slaves were standing around the well at Barnett's Meeting House on Sunday, August 23. Davy claimed that he heard Nicholas say, "By God boys you must all get ready: the people are coming out from Town [Petersburg] to destroy all the white people and boys you must be ready by next Thursday (Sussex Court day) and destroy the white people as they are going to court—we will then go to the Courthouse and kill all they could, after which they would go towards So'hampton Courthouse killing all that came in the way." According to the slave Booker, Nicholas added that their objective was a rendezvous with the British at Petersburg or Norfolk, "where the British had been and taken or removed all the large guns." The key to

---

44. Trial of Gerard, June 1, 1839, Loudoun County, C.S., box 7, and VEPLR, and Virginia Council Journals, 1839–40, p. 61; trials of Alfred and Spencer, March 11, 1840, Fairfax C.C.M.B. (1835–42), 250, and C.S., box 7; "A List of Slaves and Free Persons of Color received into the Penitentiary . . . 1816 to . . . 1842," and "Slaves transported and Executed *pd for* 1 October 1839 to 30 Sept 40," C.S., box 10. For white defendants in insurrection or abolition cases, see Hickin, "Antislavery," I, 399–403, II, 505–508, 742–43.

the plan was to meet "General Harrison," their leader, in nearby Sussex County.[45]

There were many insurrection scares between 1832 and 1865. The most serious ones resulted in court cases; less serious ones elicited public comment and precautionary action.[46] Free blacks received particularly close attention, and slaves' church activities created a great deal of concern for whites in spite of the 1832 prohibition of slave preaching. White people who began to act in a suspicious manner also ran into distrust and fear.[47] But a non-Virginian who conspired and attacked without the aid of any slaves brought all the white fears of abolitionist-provoked slave insurrection to a head. This was, of course, John Brown, who led the Harpers Ferry Raid of October, 1859. Assuming that slaves were eager to rebel despite the heavy odds against them, Brown did not make adequate advance preparations among the slaves and free blacks in northern Virginia and Maryland near Harpers Ferry. Brown did study the 1850 census, but he could not know

45. Trials of Nicholas, Nelson, Solomon, Daniel, Abram, James, and Davy, September 2, 1840, Southampton C.C.O.B. (1839–43), 210, 217, 220–23, and C.S., box 7. The pardon, transportation, or execution of the various slaves can be traced in C.S., boxes 7, 10 ("A List of Slaves and Free Persons of Color received into the Penitentiary . . . 1816 to . . . 1842" and "Slaves transported and Executed pd for 1 Oct. 40 to 30 Sept. 41"), and Virginia Council Journals, 1840–41, p. 85. One was executed. None of these sources supports an explanation of why he was, however. On the "British" rumor, see S. B. Emmons to Mr. Greene, September 24, 1831, in Tragle (ed.), The Southampton Slave Revolt, 115. On the William Henry, or "General," Harrison story, see Genovese, From Rebellion to Revolution, 128–29; Aptheker, American Negro Slave Revolts, 83, 332; and Hickin, "Antislavery," I, 303. Two 1843 cases involved circumstantial evidence of meetings for obscure purposes (trial of Charles, April 17, 1843, trial of Frederick, April 24, 1843, King William County, C.S., box 7, and VEPLR).

46. Trial of Beverley, February 1, 1857, New Kent County, C.S., box 9, and Governor's Biennial Messages . . . 1857, p. 174. On the 1856 scare, see assorted material in VEPLR; Religious Herald (Baptist), December 18, 1856; Charles B. Dew, "Black Ironworkers and the Slave Insurrection Panic of 1856," JSH, XLI (1975), 321–28; Stampp, The Peculiar Institution, 138; and Aptheker, American Negro Slave Revolts, 84–85.

47. Berlin, Slaves Without Masters, 188–89, 343; Minutes of the Virginia Portsmouth Baptist Association, . . . Surry County, Virginia . . . May . . . 1832 (Norfolk, 1832), 25–26; G. Millan to Governor Floyd, September 9, 1833 (on a white carpenter's suspicious actions), in CVSP, X, 587; a white man was examined in 1843 for threatening to arouse slave insurrection and was discharged (Southampton C.C.O.B. [1839–43], 655); "Order respecting apprehended disturbances," June 1, 1846, VEPLR; Stampp, The Peculiar Institution, 137; Luther R. Boxley to Waller Holladay, January 3, 1850, in Holladay Family Papers, 1728–1931, sec. 30, folder 3, VHS; Religious Herald (Baptist), May 16, 1850; Jennings C. Wise, The Military History of the Virginia Military Institute from 1839 to 1865 (Lynchburg, 1915), 102–103 (on an 1858 scare related to slave ironworkers at Pewe Iron Works, Lexington); Clement Eaton, The Freedom-of-Thought Struggle in the Old South (New York, 1964), 104; Aptheker, American Negro Slave Revolts, 95 (on an 1864 scare in Richmond city). The sporadically enforced prohibition of slave preaching, passed March 15, 1832, is in Acts of the General Assembly, 1831, p. 20.

that the slave population of the area had declined by nearly 10 percent since then. The wife and seven children of Dangerfield Newby, one of Brown's five free black confederates, were still in slavery near Warrenton, Virginia, but Newby apparently could or would not take full advantage of that connection to help Brown. Equally important, Brown greatly underestimated the capability and willingness of Virginia whites to respond to his attack.[48]

Brown's failure to mobilize enough slaves near Harpers Ferry had the predictable result that he did not receive support from enough of them during the early stages of the raid. But some slaves did take action. Local whites reacted furiously and hysterically because they feared abolitionists and did not know how many allies Brown had recruited. But they were also making sure that local slaves did not answer Brown's call. Nearby Fairfax County had been the scene of five insurrection trials nineteen years earlier, within living memory of much of the population. None of those suspects had been convicted of insurrection, but the accusations reflected white authorities' fears of slave rebellion. The 1839 conviction of Gerard for having antislavery literature printed had occurred in Loudoun, the next county to Jefferson, in which Harpers Ferry was located. Most ominous of all, there had been a recent surge in arson incidents for which slaves were convicted in Jefferson and several nearby counties.[49]

Even though not enough slaves helped Brown, a significant number responded to the raid in what had become a traditional, destructive, antiwhite fashion. Brown's raid coincided with a wave of slave arson. In proceedings that began on November 28, 1859, in Berryville, Clarke County (about twenty miles south of Harpers Ferry), Jerry was found guilty and Joe, another slave, jailed but released after both were

48. Oates, *To Purge This Land with Blood: A Biography of John Brown* (New York, 1974), 211–12, 224, 274–76, 282–83, 287.

49. Madison and Loudoun counties were fourth and seventh in arson convictions per slave population between 1830 and 1865 (Table 29). For nearby cases, see trial of Charlotte, March 23, 1840, Clarke County, C.S., box 7; trial of George, April 22, 1830, Culpeper County, C.S., box 5; trial of Jim, March 22, 1859, Culpeper C.C.M.B. (1858–64), 105–107, and C.S., box 9; trial of Tulip, February 28, 1833, Fauquier County, C.S., box 6; trials of John Woods and Roy Green, May 19, 1856, Jefferson County (now West Virginia), C.S., box 9, and VEPLR; trial of Harrison, May 9, 1854, Loudoun C.C.O.B. (1852–54), 337, 340, and C.S., box 8; trial of Mary, April 12, 1858, Loudoun C.C.M.B. (1856–58), 313–14, 319; trials of Lucinda, Jacob, and Alberta, May 22, 1834, September 26, 1839, September 22, 1859, Madison County, C.S., boxes 6, 9; trial of Jake, February 24, 1856, Page C.C.O.B. (1855–61), 74–75, and C.S., box 9; trial of Landon, March 4, 1839, Prince William County, C.S., box 6; trial of Lucy, April 1, 1834, Rappahannock County, C.S., box 6; trial of Jesse, February 18, 1856, Warren C.C.M.B. (1853–61), 108–10, and C.S., box 9.

charged with using arson to make insurrection with other "unknown" slaves. According to the oyer and terminer judges, who would otherwise have included Francis McCormick, Jerry's and Joe's owner, Jerry had burned houses and wheat stacks worth more than $11,000 on November 12, when John Brown and many other observers of the upheaval that followed the raid were well aware that numerous fires erupted during the night. At the same time that Jerry and Joe stood trial, Francis McCormick's Hopewell and George Jones, a free black, fell under suspicion of complicity in the insurrectionary arson. Neither was found guilty, but Hopewell's master and Jones both had to post bonds. Many white people in the area thought that slaves started the many fires, but as usual had trouble getting evidence against specific men and women. As the black abolitionist Henry Highland Garnet remarked at a meeting in honor of Brown, "all that was needed was a box of matches in the pocket of every slave, and then slavery would be set right."[50]

Edmund Ruffin confided to his diary in May, 1861, that a "conspiracy discovered and repressed is better assurance of safety than if no conspiracy had been heard of or suspected." Ruffin and several other James River planters did uncover a conspiracy that month. They regarded it as insurrectionary, but all that was happening apparently was widespread running away to the Union lines.[51] And there were more hangings of slaves convicted of such offenses as assault of a white

50. Oates, *To Purge This Land*, 322, 342; Benjamin Quarles, *Allies for Freedom: Blacks and John Brown* (New York, 1974), 100–101, 107–108, 117, 159; Jean Libby, *Black Voices from Harpers Ferry: Osborne Anderson and the John Brown Raid* (Palo Alto, Calif., 1979), 175–77; proceedings concerning Jerry, Joe, Hopewell, and George Jones, November 28, 1859, and later, Clarke C.C.M.B. (1858–62), 98–100, 104–105, 107, 114–16; N. O. Sowers to Samuel McCormick (son of Francis McCormick), October 29, 1924, in McDonald Family Papers, VHS. Sowers remembered the slaves' trials taking place while he was one of the guards at the gallows for John Brown.

51. Ruffin, *Diary*, II, 35; Eppes Diary, May 8–9, 13, 15, 1860; John R. Pindie to Governor Letcher, May 17, 1861, Petition from Inhabitants of Trevilian Depot, Louisa County, May 20, 1861, "Hairston" to Governor Letcher, May 25, 1861, and W. Eppes to Hill Carter, May 25, 1861, all in VEPLR; "The Westover Journal of John A. Selden," 314–15 (brief account of June 4–5, 1861, trial of slaves for plotting insurrection; insufficient evidence led to their receiving thirty-nine lashes and being discharged); Aptheker, *American Negro Slave Revolts*, 95; James H. Bailey, *Henrico Home Front, 1861–1865* (Richmond, 1963), 6–9, 20. On general southern fears of insurrection and slave resistance during the war, see Armstead L. Robinson, "In the Shadow of Old John Brown: Insurrection Anxiety and Confederate Mobilization, 1861–1863," *JNH*, LXV (1980), 279–97; Leon F. Litwack, *"Been in the Storm So Long": The Aftermath of Slavery* (New York, 1979), 13–18, 29–30, 49, 59–63, 140, 147–48, 425–30; and Genovese, *Roll, Jordan, Roll*, 99–100, 128–33.

person with intent to kill. Some nervousness existed in counties such as Amherst, Princess Anne, and Mecklenburg in 1861, but no plot to attack whites ever seemed to emerge from the familiar background of rumors, fears, plotting, and even preparation. After Virginia's Governor Letcher reacted to the Emancipation Proclamation with a declaration that all Union soldiers should be treated as agents of slave insurrection, a few oyer and terminer judges found a new way to use insurrection statutes against slaves. Convicted of helping Union soldiers to raid plantations for mules, horses, and food, two bondsmen from Nottoway and one from Mecklenburg went to the gallows.[52] There were some dramatic killings of owners by their slaves in 1863, and one group in Amherst County stole the gun they used from a nearby military guard.[53]

When Union forces defeated the Rebels, slavery ended without the benefit of an uprising by bondspeople, except in the figurative sense with so many former slaves in uniform. However, what whites called slave crime lived on as a specter. By April, 1865, Virginia was but one of the defeated states of the Confederacy. By December of the same year, ratification of the Thirteenth Amendment ensured that slavery, which had ended in fact the previous spring, was now impossible before the law as well. Yet, just as the Union's 1862 abolition of the Fugitive Slave Act of 1850 excepted runaway slaves wanted for crimes, so the Thir-

52. Trial of Denson, November 8, 1860, Princess Anne County, C.S., box 9, and VEPLR; trial of Sam, May 21, 1861, Mecklenburg County, C.S., box 9; Governor Letcher's declaration in *CVSP*, XI, 238–43; trials of Fed, July 18, 1864, Mecklenburg County, Bob, Nottoway County, August 4, 1864, and another Bob, Nottoway County, January 5, 1865, Pardons, January–April, 1865, VEPLR. (These boxes contain unsuccessful and successful efforts to gain pardons. The results are noted in the governor's hand, so these documents have served as evidence of actual executions even though the Auditor's Office did not record them and the Treasury cash journals for this period are missing.) An Augusta slave was convicted and sentenced to die for insurrection on November 28, 1864, but evidence that he had been coerced led to his pardon (trial of Andy, Pardons, January–April, 1865, VEPLR).

53. Trials of Sarah, Jane, Bet, Seaton, Armstead, and George, May 18, 1864, Amherst C.C.O.B. (1859–64), unpaginated, at date. For a similar case, see trials of Landon, Joe, Jaque, and Charles, July 6, August 4, 1863, Powhatan County, Treasury cash journal, 1862–64, and Pardons, August, 1863, VEPLR. Other attacks are in trial of Clara Ann, October 21, 1861, Culpeper C.C.M.B. (1858–64), 365, and C.S., box 9; trials of William and William, December 19, 1861, Prince Edward C.C.O.B. (1861), 419, 421, 426, 432; trial of Ellen, December 3, 1862, Albemarle County, C.S., box 9; *Weevils in the Wheat*, 44; trial of John, December 5, 1862, Henrico C.C.M.B. (1861–63), 192, and Treasury cash journal, 1862–64, and Bailey, *Henrico Home Front*, 84–85, 116–17. Four slaves were convicted of poisoning two white people, but none of the victims had died (trials of Thea and Liddy, September 15, 1862, Mecklenburg County, and of Abram and Harriett, March 9, 1864, Charlotte County, C.S., box 9).

teenth Amendment excluded from its prohibition of slavery any punishment "for crime whereof the party shall have been duly convicted."[54] And for varying lengths of time, everyone remembered the old laws and trials. Long-standing as was the relationship between people the white authorities of Virginia had called slaves and the criminal code those same authorities had developed and enforced partly in order to support their identification of almost all black people within the borders of the Old Dominion as slaves, the ghost of slave crime would continue to haunt many Virginians for years after 1865.

54. *Statutes at Large of the United States of America, 1789–1873* (17 vols.; Boston, 1850–73), XII, 354, 589.

Conclusion

In August, 1706, five slaves in Westmoreland County, Virginia, the birthplace of George Washington about a quarter of a century later, were hanged. They had been convicted of burglarizing a storehouse and stealing assorted goods worth 20 shillings or more. One hundred sixty years later, two Spotsylvania freedmen stood trial on the charge of burglarizing a house and stealing goods worth $100. The differences between their situation and that of the five Westmoreland slaves were substantial. The Spotsylvanians were free and the others were slaves; the former were found not guilty and the latter were executed. But John Fletcher, the man who claimed that the two freedmen had burglarized and stolen his property, would have seen that the two groups of defendants had something in common. He had cut off one ear of each freedman. Having expected that the Spotsylvania authorities would regard criminal behavior by blacks as necessitating strong reprisal, Fletcher was undoubtedly dumbfounded to be sent to the Circuit Court on the charge of attempted murder. Had Fletcher lived for another one hundred years, however, he would have learned that a majority of white Virginians—indeed, a majority of white Americans—believed as he did that there was something especially dangerous about crimes committed by black former slaves or their descendants, particularly when the victim was white.[1]

That belief has a great deal to do with my central theme, which is the struggle between slaves and slaveowners as manifested in the changing and diverse connections of bondage and slave crime. That belief

1. Westmoreland C.C.O.B. (1705–21), 32a–32b, 37a, 150; *EJC*, III, 128; Spotsylvania C.C.O.B. (1858–71), 330–31.

derived not only from a long history of racism in Virginia and from the central fact of white Virginia's historical role as the Mother of Slavery in English North America but also, as this study has repeatedly emphasized, from many slaves' efforts against the domination inherent in the peculiar institution and white supremacy. Many enslaved people were particularly dangerous to slavery; Afro-Americans have always challenged white supremacy. In other words, since a significant number of black Virginians implicitly or explicitly demonstrated their refusal to accept racism and slavery by violating the Old Dominion's criminal code for slaves, whites who believed in white supremacy and the peculiar institution were bound to perceive such slaves as rebellious and dangerous. Even those slaves who killed other slaves faced laws and courts that treated them as more dangerous than whites who killed free blacks, slaves, or other whites. Whites' ideology and fear did encourage insurrection scares and extensive precautions, but they also gave many slaves no choice but to fight back. Thus that kind of slave and bondspeople who endangered fellow slaves was consigned to the same category of special criminal.

Slavery thus made a great difference to those men and women who chose to violate the slave code; such slaves significantly influenced the nature of slavery. But the experiences of several thousand convicts in Virginia make clear how diverse were slavery's effects on those of its victims who were also convicted of crimes and what variable and profound effects slaves found guilty of crimes had on human bondage. The history of crime, however defined, is also the history of the societies in which such crime occurred. The slavery on which the slave society of the Old Dominion was based was not an undifferentiated, immutable institution. Rhys Isaac has commented that "the study of slavery has too much been conducted as though the slaves could be understood in isolation from the whole society of which they were a part, and as though there were no evolution in slave culture or transformation in the ways blacks interacted with whites."[2] Given the nature of the conflict between slaves and the criminal code and courts, it is nearly impossible to make the mistake to which Isaac refers when one studies enslaved Virginians convicted of crime. Much prosecuted crime is a form of interaction between people and, as the English legal forms "Rex v." and "Commonwealth v." assert, also between a society's

2. Isaac, *The Transformation of Virginia*, 308n.

institutions and its people. Moreover, the forms and content of oyer and terminer trials encompassed a deep-seated conflict between many Afro-Virginians' and Euro-Virginians' perceptions of the same acts. Both kinds of interaction changed dramatically over time as both white and enslaved, as well as free black and Native American, sectors of Virginia's society evolved.

Because of its longevity and size, the slave society of Virginia was bound to have multiple and changing characteristics. For many years after 1700, hereditary thralldom in Virginia was primarily rural and agricultural. By 1800, however, more and more slaves worked in mines, factories, and other nonagricultural places. An increasing number lived in towns and cities. In both the rural and urban contexts, many were hired out or even hired themselves out. Moreover, the bondspeople themselves changed. They enlarged and strengthened their own communities. Many were forcibly transplanted Africans; thousands more became or were born Afro-Americans. Like their owners, blacks sometimes lived in the Tidewater, other times in the Piedmont or Southside, and to a lesser extent in western Virginia. So it was not simply that slavery as such influenced prosecuted slave behavior. In addition, the varieties and changes in the institution affected that behavior.

The location and the nature of conspiracies or rebellions in favor of slave authorities and against slaveholders' authority illustrate the workings of the process. The only constant factor in all the conspiracies and the one real rebellion, Nat Turner's, was the slavery against which slaves wished to rebel. The plots in the early eighteenth century occurred in the context of new communities. There was a strong African presence in at least one case, but the insurrectionaries all suffered from isolation and numerical weakness in relation to whites. By the 1760s, evangelism provided a new basis for some rebel leaders' claim to legitimacy, and the enlarged slave population gave increased numerical force to the slaves in relation to whites. Gabriel's Plot of 1800 took place in an area that was becoming urbanized and whose diversified agricultural and commercial economy encouraged mobility among slaves. The Boxley plot represented not only the old influences of evangelism and mobility among slaves but the new impulse of white abolitionism. By the time Nat Turner led the bloody revolt of 1831, economic decline and the rise of a relatively independent free black community in Southampton County created new factors that figured in a real rebellion. The very failure of Turner's Revolt to over-turn slavery in Virginia may have decreased the authority of rebels who advocated collective insurrection. For that or some other reason, including the possibility that flight to the North or to Canada grew in popularity among slaves as the most efficacious form of resistance to enslavement, there was no major plot or rebellion among Virginian slaves after 1831 until the close proximity of Union forces during the Civil War so jeopardized slaveholders as to make mass escapes possible.

The changes and varieties in slavery did not result solely from "out-side" forces or the decisions of powerful whites. The discussion of factors in slave plots or rebellions indicates the role many slaves played in modifying the society of Virginia. But those who were con-victed of crimes played a special role in changing and diversifying slavery.[3] The rhythm of challenge and response was fairly constant. Did outlying and other dangerous slaves threaten slaveholders in late seventeenth-century Virginia? Then slaveholders judged it necessary to create the segregated courts of oyer and terminer. Once the plots in the early eighteenth century constituted a clear and present danger, laws concerning insurrection were stiffened as well as enforced. When slaves in some parts of Virginia resorted to poisoning to threaten or destroy some slaveholders or even fellow Africans or Afro-Americans, the House of Burgesses created and certain oyer and terminer judges enforced new and special laws concerning administration of medicine.

Even the locus of public authority over slaves shifted in response to some attacks. As various kinds of convictions became more prevalent in the Old Dominion, slaveholders initially gained more local control over trials of slaves accused of those crimes. Even after local judges lost much of their power over free suspects to a new, more centralized court system, they retained their extensive powers over slave defen-dants. But after more and more blacks persisted in individually and collectively challenging owners' hegemony, the state government in-creasingly involved itself in slave control. The "anxious oppressors" in the 1830s, 1840s, and 1850s insisted repeatedly that they not only faced extreme danger from slaves inspired to revolt by northern aboli-

3. I argue this with respect to slaves' impact on Virginia's criminal code for slaves in "Forging the Shackles," 125–46. While I read *There Is a River* after writing much of this book, I strongly agree with Harding's theme of changing, diverse means of struggle against domination.

tionists but also stood to suffer even more should they end slavery, thus removing the only shackles many southern white leaders thought strong enough to control blacks.

It was manifestly not just the dramatic plots in 1800 and 1816, the scares in 1802, 1829, and 1856, or even the devastating revolt in 1831 that led white Virginia's leaders and the mass of white Virginians to conclude that there was a real threat from within their society. As convincing were the many individual killings, poisonings, assaults, and threats as well as other attacks by slaves that revealed to so many whites the hostility with which numerous black Virginians perceived them. White Virginians were often mistaken about the source of rebellious slaves' inspiration. They saw ghosts at times, ringing the alarm for plots that did not exist; but those whites who declared that it was possible for slaves to rebel were correct. That no white officials saw either Gabriel's Plot or the Turner Revolt coming was one kind of proof that those who thought they had discovered a plot had better act. But they had only to remember the dramatic individual incidents in their own county or town to believe that at least some slaves were willing to risk everything to strike out at slaveholders at any time.

Another change in the social history of the Old Dominion illustrates the more permanent influence of those Afro-Virginians who struggled against white authorities and the slave code. That change was the abolition of slavery in 1865 and the development of a new relationship between blacks accused of crimes and white Virginians in authority. Comparison of free blacks in criminal courts before 1865 and freedmen in courts after emancipation provides some perspective on the manner in which slaves tried to control their lives in spite of the slave code. Well before 1865, many white Virginians were fond of repeating that blacks were better off in bondgage. Concurrent with this notion was the impression held by many, but not all, whites that free blacks were more inclined to criminal behavior, especially stealing, than were slaves, and that the presence of free blacks in any concentration contributed to the danger of insurrection. Since plantation authorities dealt with slaves' minor offenses, there was no way for people at the time, any more than historians today, to measure whether slaves or free blacks broke the laws and rules of white supremacy more often. Not even the comparison of convictions of free blacks and of slaves for major crimes would be particularly illuminating. Free blacks would logically stand a greater chance of being convicted for the same kind of behavior since they—"slaves without masters"—suffered from racial subordination in the courts yet did not have the benefit of owners' self-interested intervention. More important, whites' relatively greater supervision of slaves made it easier to prevent slaves' violations of the criminal code.[4]

Given the observable judicial situation with which free blacks had to deal should they be tried for offenses defined by Virginia's criminal code, they were in a particularly precarious position. The criminal code and the judicial system for slaves certainly changed in significant ways over the years, making the risk of being punished for a crime higher or lower for them, depending on the circumstances. But there were some rather dramatic changes in the status of free blacks within the judicial system and in their treatment by the criminal code, especially after their number began to increase steadily and some were suspected of insurrectionary plotting or activity. Subject, like the rest of the state's free population, to terms in the Virginia Penitentiary after the late 1790s, free blacks suddenly in the 1820s could be sold into slavery as the punishment for major crimes. Almost as quickly as this penalty affected thirty convicts, the Virginia legislature abolished it in favor of the old system. But within a few years, the anxious reaction to Nat Turner and the "abolitionist peril" led to still another drastic change. Thereafter most felony trials of free blacks would no longer be by white judge and jury, but only by white judges of oyer and terminer, as in the trials of slaves. The result would still be execution for all convictions of first-degree murder and for some rape convictions and penitentiary terms for other offenses. Before the criminal law, free blacks were "neither slave nor free" and both enslaved and free.[5]

Comparison of the position of freedmen after 1865 with that of slaves and free blacks before then further illuminates the status of slaves in the criminal courts. Before legal abolition, free blacks were threatening anomalies to whites. Legislators' attempts to deal with free black offenders reflected white perceptions of the problem posed by free Afro-Virginians in a slave society. After 1865, however, all black people were legally free, but whites easily perceived most blacks as

---

4. Berlin, *Slaves Without Masters*, 183, 186–87, 360–62; Russell, *The Free Negro*, 164–67.
5. Schwarz, "Forging the Shackles"; Guild, *Black Laws*, 161–70; Stroud, *A Sketch of the Laws*, 77–80.

former slaves, relegating them to inferior status for that as well as for their race. Depending on the will of various former owners, some freedmen might appeal to powerful white patrons for protection in court. But for those freedmen who refused or lacked such patrons, the white-dominated criminal courts of Virginia became especially perilous. Freedmen's Bureau courts lasted but a short time; bureau agents had some influence in a few county courts, almost none in others. Black people were eventually able to testify in cases involving whites, but in criminal trials of blacks for various offenses, white supremacy demanded that the word of most whites would prevail over that of most blacks. The number of blacks on juries was gradually whittled down to nothing. When conviction of blacks for various crimes kept them off juries and also served the political purpose of keeping them from voting—voting Republican, Readjuster, or Populist, that is— conviction became all the more attractive to whites.[6]

Black Virginians may have been no better off in the state's criminal courts after abolition than before, yet they were better off than blacks in some other states. White Virginians' fear of aggressive slaves was constant and sometimes particularly strong. In the late nineteenth and early twentieth century, white fear of black crime was also persistent and periodically hysterical. Before 1865, white leaders' insistence that major slave crimes be tried in courts of law ensured at least some protection for slave defendants and convicts. After 1865, the rule of law still provided relative protection to black Virginians. Statistics on lynchings from 1885 to 1930 indicate that in older slave societies such as Virginia and South Carolina fewer black people were lynched

6. Convention of the Colored People of Virginia, Alexandria, 1865, *Proceedings . . .* (Alexandria, 1865), 24; Henderson H. Donald, *The Negro Freedman* (New York, 1952), 179–90, a source to be used cautiously; Donald G. Nieman, *To Set the Law in Motion: The Freedmen's Bureau and the Legal Rights of Blacks, 1865–1868* (Millwood, N.Y., 1979), 9–10, 12, 22, 96–98, 119, 122–24; Flanigan, "The Criminal Law of Slavery," 189–219, 264–400; U.S. Bureau of Freedmen, Records of the Assistant Commissioners for the State of Virginia, 1865–69, NARS Microfilm, M1048, rolls 59–61; Spotsylvania C.C.O.B. (1858–71), 330–31, 346, 352–54, 478, 484–86, 490, 493, 546, 551, 554, 595–96 (freedmen's position was most insecure). Other valuable material is in Virginia Department of Corrections, Register of Convicts, Penitentiary, 1865–84, VSL; Virginia Penitentiary, Board of Directors, *Annual Report* (1878), 26–27, (1879), 24–25, (1880), 31, (1881), 33; Virginius Dabney, *Richmond: The Story of a City* (Garden City, N.Y., 1976), 229; Michael B. Chesson, *Richmond After the War, 1865–1890* (Richmond, 1981), 183; Guild, *Black Laws,* 170ff.; Franklin Johnson, *The Development of State Legislation Concerning the Free Negro* (Westport, Conn., 1979); Leon F. Litwack, *"Been in the Storm So Long": The Aftermath of Slavery* (New York, 1979), 274–91; Charles E. Wyne, *Race Relations in Virginia, 1870–1902* (Charlottesville, 1961), 135–36.

after abolition than in the younger ones such as Georgia and Missis-sippi. That was partly because of the kind of control state authorities were able to exercise over potential trouble spots. Preservation of the rule of law required the suppression of lynching. While riots and lynchings certainly occurred in the Old Dominion, white authorities still maintained white supremacy through the semblance of the rule of law and the use of the criminal courts, just as slaveowners had ulti-mately done before 1865. The racist and deadly "efficiency" of the courts is apparent. Almost 87 percent of the men and women executed by the Commonwealth of Virginia between 1908 and 1962 were black. Every man executed for rape was black. Disfranchisement of almost all blacks after 1902 meant that virtually no black people had con-sented to these conditions.[7]

The history of Afro-Virginians' challenges to the colony and the state's criminal code and courts demands recognition not only of the constants involved—the proslavery, white supremacist, and racist rel-egation of free and enslaved blacks to a debased status—but also of the diverse ways in which black Virginians mounted those challenges and white authorities tried to prevent or suppress them. Virginian slaves give historians good reason not to limit their study of slave societies to any one perspective, factor, or period. The several thousand slaves' conflicts and confrontations with slaveholders or other slaves over at least one hundred sixty years illustrate changes over time and varia-tions from slave to slave and place to place. The job of writing a general history of the changes and variations in Old Dominion slavery from 1619 to 1865 still needs to be done. But a significant cross-section of that history is in the story of those people to whom slaveholders had to pay official attention.

The challenges by Virginian slaves to their owners and other whites shed light on the developing picture of slave communities. It is nearly a truism that given the powerful presence of slaveowners and other authorities, slave communities could not be truly autonomous in the Old Dominion. Slaves could not ordinarily ignore absentee owners or isolate themselves in maroon communities as could many enslaved

7. Kerry Johnson, "The Fever Breaks: Virginia Lynchings, 1885–1895" (Honors pa-per, Department of History and Geography, Virginia Commonwealth University, 1980); John Hammond Moore, "The Norfolk Riot, 16 April 1866," *VMHB*, XC (1982), 155–64; Chesson, *Richmond*, 103–104; William J. Bowers, *Executions in America* (Lexington, Mass., 1974), 386–94; Charles S. Mangum, *The Legal Status of the Negro* (Chapel Hill, 1940), 369.

Jamaicans, for example.[8] But one of the primary means of achieving individual or group identity is conflict with other individuals or groups. The illegal behavior of slaves acting by themselves, with a few fellow slaves, or with such groups as Nat Turner's followers, all set determined bondspeople against equally determined whites, first in private, informal environments, then in official, public contexts. Competing rituals, meanings, symbols, and perceptions impelled such conflicts. But once slaves' actions became matters for the criminal courts, they constituted both the strongest direct challenge slaves could offer to white authority as well as the most extreme intervention of whites' powerful institutions in the lives of individual slaves or slave communities. Short of full-scale insurrections, which were rare, these conflicts were the most dramatic individual events, as opposed to long-term trends, that occurred in slave societies in North America. By pitting the most daring slaves against the most powerful whites, they may even have prepared slave communities for some aspects of the struggle for self-determination after 1865.

That conclusion suggests part of the power the history of slavery in Virginia has had over the history of the Old Dominion since 1865. It is no accident that black people faced the kinds of laws, courts, or mobs they did for many decades after 1865. Whites' perception of Afro-Virginians not only as black but also as former slaves or descendants of slaves has had everything to do with the way the majority of whites have perceived and tried to control black people. Every society defines and punishes crimes. Slave societies such as Virginia defined and punished slave crimes, however, in a distinctive way. Thus slaves in such societies had to deal with the criminal law and courts in a different way than other people did. When former slave societies such as Virginia have used various means to place blacks in a debased position before the law, many people have continued to reject and sometimes to challenge such a system. No one had to learn the basics of this old conflict.

8. For Peter Kolchin's overargued yet provocative discussion of this problem in the historiography of the slave community, see his "Reevaluating the Antebellum Slave Community: A Comparative Perspective," *JAH*, LXX (1983), 579–601.

Appendix Slaves Hanged or Transported for Conspiracy and Insurrection, 1785–1831

Trial Date	Slave/Owner	County	Verdict, Sentence, Outcome
1. Aug. 19, 1785	Will/Edward Dodson	Mecklenburg	30 lashes
2. July 2, 1792	Jack/Thomas Parramore	Northampton	Hanged
3.	Daniel/Rosey Rose		Hanged
4.	Matthew/Major Andrews, orphan		Hanged
5. Aug. 16, 1793	Roger/John Wills, Jr.	Warwick	Hanged
6. Jan. 2, 1799	Burgess/Richard H. Corbin	Middlesex	Hanged
7.	Billy, alias Billy Weeks/John Hopkins (Richmond city)		Hanged
8. Oct. 25, 1799	Sam/Joshua Britt (Georgia)	Southampton	Hanged
9.	Isaac/Harris Spears (Georgia)		Hanged
10.	Hatter Isaac/Harris Spears		Hanged
11.	Jerry/Harris Spears		Hanged
12.	Sam/Harris Spears		Benefit/39 lashes

Trial Date	Slave/Owner	County	Verdict, Sentence, Outcome
13. Sept.-Oct., 1800	Solomon/Thomas Henry Prosser	Henrico	Hanged
14.	Peter/Thomas Henry Prosser		Hanged
15.	Tom/Thomas Henry Prosser		Hanged
16.	Gabriel/Thomas Henry Prosser		Hanged
17.	Watt/Thomas Henry Prosser		Transported
18.	Martin/Thomas Henry Prosser		Hanged
19.	Frank/Thomas Henry Prosser		Hanged
20.	Will/John Mosby, Sr.		Hanged
21.	John/Mary Jones (Hanover)		Hanged
22.	Isaac/William Burton		Hanged
23.	George/William Burton		Not Guilty
24.	Isham/William Burton		Hanged
25.	Abraham/Thomas Burton		Pardoned
26.	Michael, alias Mike/Judith Owen		Hanged
27.	Ned/Ann Parsons		Hanged
28.	Billy/Roger Gregory		Hanged
29.	Charles/Roger Gregory		Hanged
30.	Martin/Roger Gregory		Not Guilty
31.	Frank/Nathaniel Wilkinson		Not Guilty
32.	Jupiter/Nathaniel Wilkinson		Hanged
33.	Sam/Nathaniel Wilkinson		Hanged
34.	Daniel/Nathaniel Wilkinson		Not Guilty

35.	Sawney/William Young	Hanged
36.	Gilbert/William Young	Hanged
37.	Ned/William Young	Pardoned
38.	William/William Young	Hanged
39.	Daniel/John Brooke	Not Guilty
40.	Isaac/James Allen	Hanged
41.	Harry/Thomas Austin (Hanover)	Not Guilty
42.	Ned/Thomas Austin	Not Guilty
43.	Joe/Thomas Austin	Not Guilty
44.	Laddis/John Williamson	Hanged
45.	Billy, alias Billy Chicken/Dabney Williamson	Not Guilty
46.	Lewis/Dabney Williamson	Transported
47.	Peter/Allen Williamson	Pardoned
48.	Ben, alias Ben Woolfolk/Paul Graham (Caroline)	Pardoned
49.	Sam, alias Sam Graham/Paul Graham	Hanged
50.	Stephen/Thomas Wingfield (Hanover)	Not Guilty
51.	George/Estate of Jacob Smith, in poss. of Ann Smith	Hanged
52.	Dick/Jesse Smith	Guilty/Hang/Outcome unknown
53.	Joe/Temperance Baker (Hanover)	Not Guilty
54.	George/Izard Bacon	Not Guilty
55.	Michael/Thomas Goode	Hanged
56.	Sam, alias Sam Bird/Jane Clarke	Hanged
57.	James, alias Jim Allen/James Price	Not Guilty

Trial Date	Slave/Owner	County	Verdict, Sentence, Outcome
58.	Moses/James Price		Not Guilty
59.	James/Elisha Price		Pardoned
60.	Absalom/William Price		Not Guilty
61.	Solomon/Estate Joseph Lewis		Pardoned
62.	Jacob/Thomas Woodson		Pardoned
63.	Billy/Estate Ambrose Lipscombe		Pardoned
64.	Billy/Nathaniel C. Lipscombe (Hanover)		Pardoned
65.	Dick/Paul Thilman (Hanover)		Pardoned
66.	Randolph/Nancy Leftwich (King William), in poss. of Paul Thilman		Pardoned
67.	Bristol/Paul Thilman		Not Guilty
68.	Jack, alias Jack Bowler/Estate William Bowler (Caroline)		Transported
69.	Emanuel/Drewry Wood		Not Guilty
70.	Jordan, alias Thomas Jordan Martin, free black		Breach of Peace
71.	King/Philip Norborne Nicholas	Richmond city	Transported
72.	Brutus, alias Julius/William Anderson (Caroline)		Not Guilty
73.	Ralph/Mrs. Elizabeth Page		Not Guilty
74.	Scipio/Paul Thilman	Caroline	Pardoned
75.	Thornton/Paul Thilman		Transported
76.	Ben/Charles Carter		Transported

77.		Jack, alias Jack Gabriel/Charles Carter	Transported
78.		John Fills/Charles Carter	Transported
79.	Oct. 20, 1800	Peter/Estate William Presler Claiborne	Dinwiddie	Hanged
80.	Feb. 18, 1801	Jack/Ethelred Edmunds	Southampton	Not Guilty
81.		Tom/Robert Ricks		Not Guilty
82.		Dick/Drewry Cotton		Not Guilty
83.		Phil/William Crichlow(?)		Not Guilty
84.		Phill/Alan McNeil		Not Guilty
85.	Feb. 19, 1801	Austin/William Cram		Not Guilty
86.		Ned/James Bell		Not Guilty
87.		Sam/Jeremiah Drake		Not Guilty
88.		Tom/Elizabeth Moore		Not Guilty
89.		Peter Whitehead/ Samuel Kello, but freedom suit in progress		Not Guilty
90.		Abraham Browne, free black		Not Guilty
91.		Peter Joe, free black		Not Guilty
92.		Sam Bink(?), free black		Not Guilty
93.		Crumwell Scott, free black		Not Guilty
94.		Amos Ricks, free black		Not Guilty
95.	Feb. 20, 1801	Balak, commonly Young Balak/ Stephen Johnston	Spotsylvania	39 lashes
96.	Jan. 7, 1802	Joe/Estate Batt. Jones	Nottoway	Hanged
97.		Bob/John Royall		Hanged
98.	Feb. 3, 1802	Isaac/Estate Joseph Wilkes, in poss. of widow, Henrietta	Brunswick	Hanged

Trial Date	Slave/Owner	County	Verdict, Sentence, Outcome
99.	Phill/Randolph Hagood		Hanged
100. Apr. 23, 1802	Sancho/John Booker	Halifax	Hanged
101.	Frank/Archer Robertson		Hanged
102.	Martin/Henry Bass		Hanged
103.	Abram/William Smith		Hanged
104.	Absalom/John Hilliard		Hanged
105. Apr. 26, 1802	Jeremiah/Estate John Cornick (Princess Anne Co.)	Norfolk city	Hanged
106.	Ned/Estate William Walke		Transported
107. May 5, 1802	Glasgow/Paul Thilman, later Benjamin Pollard	Hanover	Transported
108.	Tom/Paul Thilman		Transported
109. May 17, 1802	Arthur/William Farrar (Goochland)	Henrico	Transported
110.	Stephen/David Price (Goochland)		Not Guilty
111. Jan. 14, 1805	Abraham/William Fitzhugh	Stafford	Hanged
112.	Robin/William Fitzhugh		Transported
113.	Cupid/William Fitzhugh		Transported
114. May 10, 1806	Ben/Thomas Henry Prosser	Henrico	Not Guilty
115.	Ned/Thomas Henry Prosser		Not Guilty
116.	Isaac/Thomas Henry Prosser		Not Guilty
117.	Harrison/William Clopton		Not Guilty

118.	Nov. 7, 1808	Arch/Gray Samuel	Caroline	Not Guilty
119.		Lewey/Robert Chap-man		Not Guilty
120.		Daniel/Elizabeth Broaddus		Not Guilty
121.	Dec. 27, 1808	Jacob/John Ligon	Nelson	Hanged
122.	June 6, 1810	Sam/John G. Periner (Nansemond)	Isle of Wight	Transported
123.		Dennis/William Blunt		Not Guilty
124.	Mar. 31, 1813	Kit/Lucy L. Paradise (Williamsburg)	James City	Transported
125.		Tassy/Lucy L. Para-dise		Transported
126.		Anthony/Lucy L. Paradise		Transported
127.	Apr. 23, 1813	Sam/Enoch Jeffries	Fauquier	Transported
128.	Mar. 5, 1816	Will/Robert S. Cole-man	Spotsylvania	Not Guilty
129.		Phill/Robert S. Cole-man		Not Guilty
130.		Jack/Robert S. Cole-man		Not Guilty
131.		Tom/Thomas Cole-man		Not Guilty
132.		Charles/George Twy-man		Hanged
133.		Peter/George Twy-man		Transported
134.		Emanuel/George Twyman		Hanged
135.		James/John Hailey		Not Guilty
136.		Peter/Hezekiah Ellis		Not Guilty
137.		Winston/Thomas Lipscomb		Not Guilty
138.		Armistead/Thomas Lipscomb		Not Guilty
139.		Edmund/Thomas Lipscomb		Not Guilty
140.		Lewis/James M. Bell		*Nolle Pros.*

Trial Date	Slave/Owner	County	Verdict, Sentence, Outcome
141.	Dick/John Day		Not Guilty
142.	Gloster/John White		Transported
143.	Abram/Thomas Bowby(?)		Not Guilty
144.	Peter/Benjamin Robinson		Not Guilty
145.	Anthony/William Grady		Transported
146.	Tom/Richard Estes		Transported
147.	John/M. Queser(?)		Not Guilty
148.	George Boxley, white man		Escaped
149.	Lewis/John M. Sale		Not Guilty
150.	Tomkin/Samuel Cole	Louisa	Transported
151.	Matt/Francis Jordan		Transported
152.	Tom/Sarah Gardner		Hanged
153.	Ned/Joseph Boxley		Hanged
154.	Mack/Joseph Boxley		Hanged
155. July 8, 1818	Ned/Elizabeth Collins	Essex	Misdemeanor trespass/30 lashes
156. Aug. 10, 1821	Harry/Robert Gordon	Richmond city	Not Guilty
157.	Oakley Philpotts, white man		Not Guilty
158. July 25, 1829	Sam/William L. Waring	Essex	Not Guilty
159. Aug.-Nov., 1831	Daniel/Richard Porter	Southampton	Hanged
160.	Tom/Caty Whitehead		Discharged
161.	Jack/Caty Whitehead		Transported
162.	Andrew/Caty Whitehead		Transported
163.	Stephen/Thomas Ridley		Hanged
164.	Curtis/Thomas Ridley		Hanged

165.	Isaac/George H. Charlton (Greensville)	Transported
166.	Hark/Estate Joseph Travis	Hanged
167.	Nelson/Jacob Williams	Hanged
168.	Davy/Levi Waller	Hanged
169.	Dred/Nathaniel Francis	Hanged
170.	Nathan/Nathaniel Francis	Transported
171.	Sam/Nathaniel Francis	Hanged
172.	Tom/Nathaniel Francis	Transported
173.	Davy/Nathaniel Francis	Transported
174.	Hardy/Benjamin Edwards	Transported
175.	Isham/Benjamin Edwards	Transported
176.	Sam/James W. Parker	Not Guilty
177.	Jim/William Vaughan	Not Guilty
178.	Bob/Temperance Parker	Not Guilty
179.	Davy/Joseph Parker	Not Guilty
180.	Daniel/Solomon Parker	Not Guilty
181.	Frank/Solomon Parker	Transported
182.	Davy/Elizabeth Turner	Hanged
183.	Joe/John C. Turner	Hanged
184.	Nat/Estate Edwin Turner	Hanged
185.	Matt/Thomas Ridley	Not Guilty
186.	Lucy/Estate John T. Barrow	Hanged
187.	Moses/Estate Thomas Barrow	Hanged
188.	Jim/Richard Porter	Not Guilty
189.	Jack/Everett Bryant	Not Guilty

Trial Date	Slave/Owner	County	Verdict, Sentence, Outcome
190.	Stephen/James Bell		Not Guilty
191.	Jim/Samuel Champion		Transported
192.	Isaac/Samuel Champion		Transported
193.	Preston/Hannah Williamson		Not Guilty
194.	Jack/Nathaniel Simmons		Treason/discharged
195.	Shadrack/Nathaniel Simmons		Treason/discharged
196.	Sam/Peter Edwards		Hanged
197.	Archer/Arthur W. Reese		Not Guilty
198.	Jack/Estate William Reese		Hanged
199.	Moses/Estate Joseph Travis		Transported
200.	Nat, alias Nat Turner/Putnam Moore, infant		Hanged
201.	Ben/Estate Benjamin Blunt		Hanged
202.	Nelson/Estate Benjamin Blunt		Not Guilty
203.	Nathan/Estate Benjamin Blunt		Hanged
204.	Arnold Artes, free black		Discharged
205.	Thomas Hatchcock, free black		To Superior Court
206.	Berry Newsom, free black		To Superior Court
207.	Exum Artis, free black		To Superior Court
208.	Isham Turner, free black		To Superior Court
209. Sept. 1, 12, 1831	Boson/William Peters	Sussex	Escaped/Caught/ Transported

210.		Frank/William Peters	Killed in escape attempt
211.		Ned/Estate Charles Stuart	Hanged
212.		Squire/George Goodwyn	Transported
213.		Solomon/Nancy Sorsby	Hanged
214.		Nicholas/Hannah Williamson	Hanged
215.		Booker/Samuel Parsons	Hanged
216.		Shadrack/Ann Key	Transported
217.	Sept. 5, 16, 1831	John, alias John Claiborne/Richard H. Cocke	Surry	Transported
218.		Moses/Richard H. Cocke	Not Guilty
219.		George/Richard H. Cocke	Not Guilty
220.		Cyrus/Richard H. Cocke	Not Guilty
221.		Mason/Joseph Parham	Not Guilty
222.		Harry/Thomas Simpson	Not Guilty
223.		Joe/Thomas Simpson	Not Guilty
224.		Allen/Ann Hart	Not Guilty
225.	Sept. 8, 1831	Jacob/Robert Crutchfield	Spotsylvania	Transported
226.		George/Peachy Faulconer	Transported
227.		Solomon/Robert S. Coleman	Transported
228.	Sept. 10, 1831	Meschak/Littlebury Orgain	Greensville	Transported
229.	Sept. 12, 1831	Jack of Niles/Estate William Woods	Nansemond	Hanged
230.		21–23 other unidentified slaves and free blacks	Not Guilty

Trial Date	Slave/Owner	County	Verdict, Sentence, Outcome
231. Sept. 13, 1831	Kitt/John A. J. Heath and Benjamin Heath	Prince George	Transported
232. Sept. 26, 1831	Charles/Robert W. Ross	Brunswick	Pardoned
233.	Lewis/Estate William Gholson		Not Guilty
234. Sept. 27, 1831	Tom/G. Drummond		Not Guilty
235.	John/John M. Lundie		Not Guilty
236. Sept. 30, 1831	Davy Thomas, free black	Isle of Wight	To Superior Court

The primary source for all trials is ideally the county court order books or minute books. When available, they are cited. VEPLR often contains trial records. The compensation records in C.S., boxes 1–10, are invaluable. The primary sources for other trials are listed after the number of the trial. Where relevant, some useful secondary sources on the trial or incident are listed. Aptheker, *American Negro Slave Revolts*, discusses so many of these incidents that he will not be cited repeatedly. I am grateful to Professor Douglas Egerton of Le Moyne College for pointing out some errors in an earlier version of this table.

1. Mecklenburg C.C.O.B. (1784–87), 392.

2–4. Jordan, *White Over Black*, 391–92.

8–12. Parramore, *Southampton County*, 65; Southampton C.C.M.B. (1799–1803), 46–48, 67–68.

13–69. Henrico C.C.O.B. (1799–1801), 372–403, 408–10, 416, 445. Jack Bowler was sentenced to be hanged, but for unexplained reasons was transported ("A List of Slaves Reprieved for Transportation & Sold by the Commonwealth," March 8, 1806, VEPLR; Professor Egerton correctly notes that one accused slave died in jail; notes on bottom of "Negroes Condemned by the County Court of Caroline, for conspiracy in the year 1800, and their valuation," inexplicably filed with a receipt of July 15, 1809, for a transported slave, VEPLR).

70–72. Richmond City Hustings C.O.B. (1797–1801), 473–74.

73–77. Virginia Council Journal, 1799–1801, pp. 340, 342.

74–77. "Negroes Condemned by the County Court of Caroline."

78. Professor Egerton and I disagree as to whether this prosecution was connected to Gabriel's Plot. Adequate documentation is not available.

79–93. Southampton C.C.M.B. (1799–1803), 151–54; Parramore, *Southampton County*, 65–67.

94. Spotsylvania C.C.M.B. (1798–1802), 177.

95–105. Jeffrey J. Crow, "Slave Rebelliousness and Social Conflict in North Carolina, 1775 to 1802," *WMQ*, 3rd ser., XXXVII (1980), 96, 98–100; Ruth Henshaw, "A New England Woman's Perspective on Norfolk, Virginia, 1801–1802; Excerpt from the Diary of Ruth Henshaw Bascom," ed. A. G. Roeber, *Proceedings of the American Antiquarian Society*, LXXXVIII, part 2 (October, 1978), 306–307, 312, 316, 321–22; Wyatt-Brown, *Southern Honor*, 402–34.

108–109. Henrico C.C.O.B. (1801–1803), 328.

110–12. *Virginia Herald* (Fredericksburg), January 4, 8, 1805; Ruth Coder Fitzgerald, *A Different Story: A Black History of Fredericksburg, Stafford, and Spotsylvania, Virginia* (Greensboro, N.C., 1979), 65.

113–16. Henrico C.C.O.B. (1805–1807), 454–55.

117–19. Caroline C.C.O.B. (1807–1809), 346–48; warrants and indictments, October 31, 1808, Caroline County Historical Papers, box 3, Slave Insurrection, 1808, VSL.

121–22. Isle of Wight C.C.O.B. (1810–13), 50–51.

127–53. Spotsylvania C.C.M.B. (1815–19), 52–72, 85–87; Louisa C.C.M.B. (1815–18), 38–41; Johnston, *Race Relations in Virginia*, 100–101; William H. B. Thomas, " 'Poor Deluded Wretches!' The Slave Insurrection of 1816," *Louisa County Historical Magazine*, VI (1974–75), 57–63.

154. Essex C.C.O.B. (1817–21), 145–46.

155–56. Richmond City Hustings C.M.B. (1821–24), 13; Henrico and Richmond city docket, September 22, 1821, and April 23–October 29, 1821, Criminal Charges, Box 7, Virginia Auditor's Item 147, VSL.

157. Essex C.C.O.B. (1826–30), 574.

158–236. Southampton C.C.M.B. (1830–35), 72–123, 131, also printed and calendared in Tragle (ed.), *The Southampton Slave Revolt*, 173–245; Brunswick C.C.O.B. (1829–32), 333–35; Greensville C.C.O.B. (1827–32), 432–33; Isle of Wight C.C.O.B. (1830–34), 124–25; Nansemond: Virginia Council Journal, 1831–32, p. 114, and John Thompson Kilby to Governor Floyd, September 16, 1831, VEPLR; Prince George: Virginia Council Journal, 1831–32, p. 131, and Ruffin, *Diary*, II, 207–209; Spotsylvania C.C.M.B. (1829–32), 328–29, 334, 336–37; Surry C.C.O.B. (1829–33), 307, 310–13, 315; Sussex C.C.O.B. (1827–35), 248–56.

Bibliography

Published Primary Sources

Acts of the General Assembly. Richmond, 1807–65.

Blackstone, William. *Blackstone's Commentaries: . . . with . . . Reference to the . . . Commonwealth of Virginia.* Edited by St. George Tucker. 5 vols. Richmond, 1803.

———. *Commentaries on the Laws of England.* 4 vols. Philadelphia, 1771–72.

Blassingame, John W., ed. *Slave Testimony: Two Centuries of Letters, Speeches, Interviews, and Autobiographies.* Baton Rouge, 1977.

Brown, Henry Box. *Narrative of the Life of Henry Box Brown.* Boston, 1849.

Calendar of Virginia State Papers and Other Manuscripts, 1652–1869, Preserved at the Capitol in Richmond. Edited by William P. Palmer *et al.* 11 vols. Richmond, 1875–93.

Carter, Landon. *The Diary of Colonel Landon Carter of Sabine Hall, 1752–1778.* Edited by Jack P. Greene. 2 vols. Charlottesville, 1965.

Catterall, Helen T. *Judicial Cases Concerning American Slavery and the Negro.* 5 vols. Washington, D.C., 1924–26.

Century ed. of The American Digest: A Complete Digest of All Reported American Cases from the Earliest Times to 1896. 50 vols. St. Paul, 1897–1904.

Charles City County Court Orders, 1664–1665, Fragments, 1650–1696. Edited by Beverley Fleet. Virginia Colonial Abstracts, XIII. Baltimore, 1961.

The Code of Virginia. Richmond, 1849.

The Code of Virginia. 2nd ed. Richmond, 1860.

Corpus Juris Secundum. A Complete Restatement of the Entire American Law as Developed in All Reported Cases. 155 vols. to date. Brooklyn, 1936–.

Creecy, John Harvie. *Princess Anne County Loose Papers, 1700–1789.* Richmond, 1954.

Criminal Proceedings in Colonial Virginia. Edited by Peter Charles Hoffer and William B. Scott. American Historical Association, American Legal Records, X. Athens, Ga., 1984.

Executive Journals of the Council of Colonial Virginia. Edited by H. R. McIl-waine *et al.* 6 vols. Richmond, 1925–66.

Flaherty, David H. "A Select Guide to the Manuscript Court Records of Virginia." *American Journal of Legal History,* XIX (1975), 112–37.

Greene, Evarts B., and Virginia D. Harrington. *American Population Before the Federal Census of 1790.* 1932; rpr. Gloucester, Mass., 1966.

Grimes, William. *Life of William Grimes the Runaway Slave.* New York, 1825.

Guild, June Purcell. *Black Laws of Virginia.* Richmond, 1936.

Hening, William Waller. *The Statutes at Large, Being a Collection of All the Laws of Virginia.* 13 vols. Richmond, 1809–23.

Historical Statistics of the United States: Colonial Times to 1970. 2 vols. Washington, D.C., 1975.

Jones, Alice Hanson. *American Colonial Wealth: Documents and Methods.* 3 vols. New York, 1977.

Journals of the Council of the State of Virginia. Edited by H. R. McIlwaine *et al.* 5 vols. to date. Richmond, 1931–.

Journals of the House of Burgesses, 1619–1776. Edited by J. P. Kennedy and H. R. McIlwaine. 13 vols. Richmond, 1905–15.

Legislative Journals of the Council of Colonial Virginia. Edited by H. R. McIl-waine. 3 vols. Richmond, 1918–19.

Minutes of the Council and General Court of Colonial Virginia. Edited by H. R. McIlwaine. 2nd ed. Richmond, 1979.

Mullin, Michael, ed. *American Negro Slavery: A Documentary History.* New York, 1976.

Rawick, George P., ed. *The American Slave: A Composite Autobiography.* 41 vols. Westport, Conn., 1972–79.

Revised Code of the Laws of Virginia. 2 vols. Richmond, 1819.

Revisors of the Code of Virginia [John M. Patton and Conway Robinson]. *Report of the Revisors of the Code of Virginia Made to the General Assembly in July, 1849, Being Their Final Report, and Relating to the Criminal Code.* Richmond, 1849.

Roberts, Ralph. "A Slave's Story." *Putnam's Monthly,* IX (June, 1857), 614–20.

Rose, Willie Lee, ed. *A Documentary History of Slavery in North America.* New York, 1976.

Shepherd, Samuel. *Statutes at Large of Virginia, from October Session 1792, to December Session 1806, Inclusive.* 3 vols. Richmond, 1835.

Starke, Richard. *The Office and Authority of a Justice of the Peace.* Williamsburg, 1774.

Stroud, George M. *A Sketch of the Laws Relating to Slavery in the Several States of the United States of America.* 1856; rpr. New York, 1968.

Supplement to the Revised Code of the Laws. Richmond, 1833.

Tragle, Henry Irving, ed. *The Southampton Slave Revolt of 1831: A Compilation of Source Material.* New York, 1971.

[Tucker, St. George]. *Letter to a Member of the General Assembly of Virginia on the Subject of the Late Conspiracy of the Slaves, with a Proposal for their Colonization.* Richmond, 1801.

U.S. Census Office. *The Statistics of the Population of the United States.* Vol. I.
　Population and Social Statistics (Washington, D.C., 1872).
Van Schreeven, William James, *et al.,* eds. *Revolutionary Virginia: The Road to
　Independence.* 7 vols. Charlottesville, 1973–83.
Virginia and West Virginia Digest. Vol. 1–. St. Paul, 1944–.
Webb, George. *The Office and Authority of a Justice of the Peace.* Williamsburg,
　1736.
Weevils in the Wheat: Interviews with Virginia Ex-Slaves. Edited by Charles L.
　Perdue. Charlottesville, 1976.
Whitelaw, Ralph T. *Virginia's Eastern Shore: A History of Northampton and
　Accomack Counties.* 2 vols. Richmond, 1951.
Winfree, Waverly K., ed. *The Laws of Virginia: Being a Supplement to Hening's
　The Statutes at Large, 1700–1750.* Richmond, 1971.

Published Secondary Sources

These works treat subjects directly related to this study—slaves and crime,
slavery in Virginia, and Virginia.

Aptheker, Herbert. *American Negro Slave Revolts.* New ed. New York, 1974.
Ayers, Edward L. *Vengeance and Justice: Crime and Punishment in the Nine-
　teenth-Century American South.* New York, 1984.
Ballagh, James Curtis. *A History of Slavery in Virginia.* Baltimore, 1902.
Berlin, Ira, and Ronald Hoffman, eds. *Slavery and Freedom in the Age of the
　American Revolution.* Charlottesville, 1983.
Billings, Warren M. "Pleading, Procedure, and Practice: The Meaning of Due
　Process of Law in Seventeenth-Century Virginia." *Journal of Southern His-
　tory,* XLVII (1981), 569–84.
Bogger, Tommy L. "Slave Resistance in Virginia During the Haitian Revolu-
　tion 1791–1804." *Hampton Institute Journal of Ethnic Studies,* V (1978), 86–
　100.
Breen, T. H., and Stephen Innes. *"Myne Owne Ground": Race and Freedom on
　Virginia's Eastern Shore, 1640–1676.* New York, 1980.
Breen, T. H., James H. Lewis, and Keith Schlesinger. "Motive for Murder: A
　Servant's Life in Virginia, 1678." *William and Mary Quarterly,* 3rd ser., XL
　(1983), 106–20.
Cassell, Frank A. "Slaves of the Chesapeake Bay Area and the War of 1812."
　Journal of Negro History, LVII (1972), 144–55.
Comparative Perspectives on Slavery in New World Plantation Societies. Edited
　by Vera Rubin and Arthur Tuden. *Annals of the New York Academy of
　Sciences,* CCXCII (1977).
Dargan, Marion. "Crime and the Virginia Gazette, 1736–1775." *University of
　New Mexico Bulletin, Sociological Series,* vol. II, no. 1 (1934), 1–61.
Ernst, William J. "Changes in the Slave Population of the Virginia Tidewater
　and Piedmont, 1830–1860: A Stable Population Analysis." University of
　Virginia, Corcoran Department of History (History Club), *Essays in His-
　tory,* XIX (1975), 75–83.

Ethridge, Harrison M. "The Jordan Hatcher Affair of 1852: Cold Justice and Warm Compassion." *Virginia Magazine of History and Biography*, LXXXIV (1976), 446–63.

Flanigan, Daniel J. "Criminal Procedure in Slave Trials in the Antebellum South." *Journal of Southern History*, XL (1974), 537–64.

Freehling, Alison Goodyear. *Drift Toward Dissolution: The Virginia Slavery Debate of 1831–1832*. Baton Rouge, 1982.

Frey, Sylvia R. "Between Slavery and Freedom: Virginia Blacks in the American Revolution." *Journal of Southern History*, XLIX (1983), 375–98.

Genovese, Eugene D. *From Rebellion to Revolution: Afro-American Slave Revolts in the Making of the Modern World*. Baton Rouge, 1979.

———. "Jurisprudence and Property Relations in Bourgeois and Slave Society." In Elizabeth Fox-Genovese and Eugene D. Genovese, *Fruits of Merchant Capital: Slavery and Bourgeois Property in the Rise and Expansion of Capitalism*. New York, 1983.

Gray, Lewis Cecil. *History of Agriculture in the Southern United States to 1860*. 2 vols. New York, 1941.

Greenberg, Douglas. *Crime and Law Enforcement in the Colony of New York, 1691–1776*. Ithaca, 1976.

———. "Crime, Law Enforcement, and Social Control in Colonial America." *American Journal of Legal History*, XXVI (1982), 293–325.

Hay, Douglas, et al., eds. *Albion's Fatal Tree: Crime and Society in Eighteenth-Century England*. New York, 1975.

Higginbotham, A. Leon, Jr. *In the Matter of Color: Race and the American Legal Process: The Colonial Period*. New York, 1978.

Hindus, Michael S. *Prison and Plantation: Crime, Justice, and Authority in Massachusetts and South Carolina, 1767–1878*. Chapel Hill, 1980.

Hindus, Michael S., and Douglas Lamar Jones. "Quantitative and Theoretical Approaches to the History of Crime and Law." *Newberry Papers in Family and Community History*, No. 77–46. Chicago, 1977.

Hoffer, Peter C. "Disorder and Deference: The Paradoxes of Criminal Justice in the Colonial Tidewater." In *Ambivalent Legacy: A Legal History of the South*. Edited by David J. Bodenhamer and James W. Ely, Jr. Jackson, Miss., 1984.

Hughes, Sarah S. "Slaves for Hire: The Allocation of Black Labor in Elizabeth City County, Virginia, 1782 to 1810." *William and Mary Quarterly*, 3rd ser., XXXV (1978), 260–86.

Isaac, Rhys. *The Transformation of Virginia, 1740–1790*. Chapel Hill, 1982.

Johnston, James Hugo. *Race Relations in Virginia and Miscegenation in the South, 1776–1860*. Amherst, Mass., 1970.

Jordan, Winthrop D. *White Over Black: American Attitudes Toward the Negro, 1550–1812*. Chapel Hill, 1968.

Kay, Marvin L. Michael, and Lorin Lee Carey. " 'The Planters Suffer Little or Nothing': North Carolina Compensations for Executed Slaves, 1748–1772." *Science & Society*, XL (1976), 288–306.

Kulikoff, Allan. "The Origins of Afro-American Society in Tidewater Maryland and Virginia, 1700 to 1790," *William and Mary Quarterly*, 3rd ser., XXXV (1978), 226–59.

———. "A 'Prolifick' People: Black Population Growth in the Chesapeake Colonies, 1700–1790." *Southern Studies*, XVI (1977), 391–428.

———. *Tobacco and Slaves: The Development of Southern Cultures in the Chesapeake, 1680–1800*. Chapel Hill, 1986.

Langbein, John. "Albion's Fatal Flaws." *Past and Present*, No. 98 (February, 1983), 96–120.

McColley, Robert. *Slavery and Jeffersonian Virginia*. 2nd ed. Urbana, 1973.

Miller, John Chester. *The Wolf by the Ears: Thomas Jefferson and Slavery*. New York, 1977.

Mintz, Sidney W., and Richard Price. *An Anthropological Approach to the Afro-American Past: A Caribbean Perspective*. Philadelphia, 1976.

Morgan, Edmund S. *American Slavery—American Freedom: The Ordeal of Colonial Virginia*. New York, 1975.

Morris, Thomas D. " 'As If Injury was Effected by the Natural Elements of Air, or Fire': Slave Wrong and the Liability of Masters." *Law & Society Review*, XVI (1982), 569–99.

Mullin, Gerald W. *Flight and Rebellion: Slave Resistance in Eighteenth-Century Virginia*. New York, 1972.

Nash, A. E. Keir. "Fairness and Formalism in the Trials of Blacks in the State Supreme Courts of the Old South." *Virginia Law Review*, LVI (1970), 64–100.

———. "A More Equitable Past? Southern Supreme Courts and the Protection of the Antebellum Negro." *North Carolina Law Review*, XLVIII (February, 1970), 197–242.

———. "Negro Rights, Unionism, and Greatness on the South Carolina Court of Appeals: The Extraordinary Chief Justice John Belton O'Neall." *South Carolina Law Review*, XXI (Spring, 1969), 141–90.

———. "Reason of Slavery: Understanding the Judicial Role in the Peculiar Institution." *Vanderbilt Law Review*, XXXII (1979), 7–218.

Nicholls, Michael L. " 'In the Light of Human Beings': Richard Eppes and His Island Plantation Code of Laws." *Virginia Magazine of History and Biography*, LXXXIX (1981), 67–78.

Nieman, Donald G. *To Set the Law in Motion: The Freedmen's Bureau and the Legal Rights of Blacks, 1865–1868*. Millwood, N.Y., 1979.

Noonan, John T., Jr. *Persons and Masks of the Law*. New York, 1976.

Oates, Stephen B. *The Fires of Jubilee: Nat Turner's Fierce Rebellion*. New York, 1975.

Parramore, Thomas C. *Southampton County, Virginia*. Charlottesville, 1978.

Phillips, Ulrich B. "Slave Crime in Virginia." *American Historical Review*, XX (1915), 336–40.

Preyer, Kathryn. "Crime, the Criminal Law and Reform in Post-Revolutionary Virginia." *Law and History Review*, I (1983), 53–85.

———. "Penal Measures in the American Colonies: An Overview." *American Journal of Legal History*, XXVI (1982), 326–53.

Quarles, Benjamin. *The Negro in the American Revolution*. Chapel Hill, 1961.

Radzinowicz, Sir Leon. *A History of the English Criminal Law and Its Administration from 1750*. 3 vols. London, 1948–56.

Robert, Joseph C. *The Road From Monticello*. Durham, 1941.

Roeber, A. G. *Faithful Magistrates and Republican Lawyers: Creators of Virginia Legal Culture, 1680–1810*. Chapel Hill, 1981.

Russell, John H. *The Free Negro in Virginia, 1619–1865*. 1913; rpr. New York, 1969.

Saunders, Robert M. "Crime and Punishment in Early National America: Richmond, Virginia, 1784–1820." *Virginia Magazine of History and Biography*, LXXXVI (1978), 33–44.

Schwarz, Philip J. "Clark T. Moorman, Quaker Emancipator." *Quaker History*, LXIX (1980), 27–35.

———. "Forging the Shackles: The Development of Virginia's Criminal Code for Slaves." In *Ambivalent Legacy: A Legal History of the South*. Edited by David J. Bodenhamer and James W. Ely, Jr. Jackson, Miss., 1984.

———. "Gabriel's Challenge: Slaves and Crime in Late Eighteenth-Century Virginia." *Virginia Magazine of History and Biography*, XC (1982), 283–309.

———. "The Transportation of Slaves from Virginia, 1801–1865," *Slavery and Abolition: A Journal of Comparative Studies*, VII (1986), 215–40.

Scott, Arthur P. *Criminal Law in Colonial Virginia*. Chicago, 1930.

Sobel, Mechal. *Trabelin' On: The Slave Journey to an Afro-Baptist Faith*. Westport, Conn., 1979.

Tate, Thad W., Jr. *The Negro in Eighteenth-Century Williamsburg*. Charlottesville, 1972.

Tushnet, Mark. *The American Law of Slavery, 1810–1860: Considerations of Humanity and Interest*. Princeton, 1981.

Watson, Alan D. "Impulse Toward Independence: Resistance and Rebellion Among North Carolina Slaves, 1750–1775." *Journal of Negro History*, LXIII (1978), 317–28.

———. "North Carolina Slave Courts, 1715–1785." *North Carolina Historical Review*, LX (1983), 24–36.

Whitfield, Theodore M. *Slavery Agitation in Virginia 1829–1832*. Baltimore, 1930.

Wyatt-Brown, Bertram. *Southern Honor: Ethics and Behavior in the Old South*. New York, 1982.

Newspapers

Daily Richmond Examiner, 1847–65.
Richmond *Enquirer*, 1804–65.
Virginia Gazette, 1736–80.
Virginia Herald (Fredericksburg), 1816–59.

Dissertations and Theses

Albert, Peter Joseph. "The Protean Institution: The Geography, Economy, and Ideology of Slavery in Post-Revolutionary Virginia." Ph.D. dissertation, University of Maryland, 1976.

Barry, Wayne Edward. "Against Their Master's Will: A Judicial History of Virginia's Manumission Law, 1800–1860." M.A. thesis, University of Minnesota, 1979.

Bogger, Tommy Lee. "The Slave and Free Black Community in Norfolk, 1775–1865." Ph.D. dissertation, University of Virginia, 1976.

Deal, Joseph Douglas. "Race and Class in Colonial Virginia: Indians, Englishmen, and Africans on the Eastern Shore During the Seventeenth Century." Ph.D. dissertation, University of Rochester, 1981.

Flanigan, Daniel. "The Criminal Law of Slavery and Freedom, 1800–1868." Ph.D. dissertation, Rice University, 1973.

Green, Rodney Dale. "Urban Industry, Black Resistance, and Racial Restriction in the Antebellum South: A General Model and a Case Study in Urban Virginia." Ph.D. dissertation, American University, 1980.

Henderson, William Cinque. "Spartan Slaves: A Documentary Account of Blacks on Trial in Spartanburg, South Carolina, 1830 to 1865." Ph.D. dissertation, Northwestern University, 1978.

Hickin, Patricia P. "Antislavery in Virginia, 1831–1861." 2 vols. Ph.D. dissertation, University of Virginia, 1968.

Howington, Arthur F., III. "The Treatment of Slaves and Free Blacks in the State and Local Courts of Tennessee." Ph.D. dissertation, Vanderbilt University, 1982.

Kulikoff, Allan Lee. "Tobacco and Slaves: Population, Economy, and Society in Eighteenth-Century Prince George's County, Maryland." Ph.D. dissertation, Brandeis University, 1976.

Leaming, Hugo Prosper. "Hidden Americans: Maroons of Virginia and the Carolinas." Ph.D. dissertation, University of Illinois at Chicago Circle, 1979.

Morgan, Timothy. "Turmoil in an Orderly Society: Colonial Virginia, 1607–1754: A History and Analysis." Ph.D. dissertation, College of William and Mary, 1976.

Nicholls, Michael L. "Origins of the Virginia Southside, 1703–1753: A Social and Economic Study." Ph.D. dissertation, College of William and Mary, 1972.

Parent, Anthony S., Jr. " 'Either a Fool or a Fury': The Emergence of Paternalism in Colonial Virginia Slave Society." Ph.D. dissertation, University of California, Los Angeles, 1982.

Schlotterbeck, John Thomas. "Plantation and Farm: Social and Economic Change in Orange and Greene Counties, 1716–1860." Ph.D. dissertation, Johns Hopkins University, 1980.

Thomas, Arthur D. "The Second Great Awakening in Virginia and Slavery

Reform, 1785–1837." Ph.D. dissertation, Union Theological Seminary in Virginia, 1981.

Manuscripts

Colonial Williamsburg Research Department
  Miscellaneous manuscripts on microfilm
Garrett Evangelical Theological Seminary Library, Evanston, Ill.
  William Colbert Journal
  Ezekiel Cooper Collection
  Thomas Rankin Journal
  Richard Whatcoat Journal
National Archives and Records Service, Washington, D.C.
  Bureau of Freedmen, Records of the Assistant Commissioners for the State of
    Virginia, 1865–1869 (microfilm)
  Miscellaneous Papers of the Continental Congress, 1770–1789 (microfilm)
  Papers of the Continental Congress (microfilm)
Surry County Court, Office of the Clerk, Surry, Va.
  Criminal proceedings vs. Free persons, Slaves, etc. From 1742 to 1822
University of New Orleans, Earl K. Long Library
  Supreme Court of Louisiana Collection
University of Virginia, Alderman Library
  Landon Carter Papers
  Lee Family Papers, 1742–95
  Miscellaneous Petitions, Virginia Legislative
  Col. Richard Morris Papers
Virginia Baptist Historical Society, Richmond
  Baptist Church Records
    Boar's Head Swamp Church (Antioch), Sandston
    Chesterfield
    High Hills Baptist Church, Sussex County
Virginia Historical Society, Richmond
  Aylett Family Papers, 1776–1945
  Bagby Family Papers, 1824–1960
  George Carter of Oatlands Letterbook, 1807–19
  Charles City County Records, 1642–1842
  Eppes Family Muniments, 1722–1948
  Grigsby Family Papers
  Holladay Family Papers, 1728–1931
  Lee Family Papers
  George Bolling Lee Papers
  McDonald Family Papers
  Louise (Anderson) Patten Papers
  Richmond City Sergeant's Register
  Virginia Colonial Records Project microfilms (also available at Alderman
    Library, University of Virginia, and at Virginia State Library)

Virginia State Library, Richmond
  Baptist Church Records
    Antioch (Racoon Swamp) Baptist Church, Sussex County
    Black Creek Baptist Church, Southampton County
    Goose Creek Baptist Church, Bedford County
    Lower Banister Baptist Church, Pittsylvania County
    Meherrin Baptist Church, Lunenburg County
    Mill Swamp Baptist Church, Isle of Wight County
    Morattico Baptist Church, Lancaster County
    Northwest Baptist Church, Norfolk County
    Piney Branch Baptist Church, Spotsylvania County
    Saylor Creek Baptist Church, Prince Edward County
    South Quay Baptist Church, Nansemond County
    Tomahawk Baptist Church, Chesterfield County
  Caroline County Historical Papers
  Condemned Slaves
  Colonial Papers
  County and city records
    Court minute and order books
    Death registers
    Deeds
    Inventories
    Tithables
    Wills
  Council Journals
  Criminal Charges
  Department of Corrections, Register of Convicts
  Executive Letter Books
  Land Taxes
  Legislative Petitions
  Personal Property Taxes
  Richmond County Criminal Trials, 1710–1754
  Sussex County Court [Loose] Papers
  Treasury Cash Journal
  U.S. District Court, Arlington County, Criminal Court
      Minute Books
  Virginia Executive Papers, Letters Received
      Pardon Papers
West Virginia University Library, West Virginia Collection
  Felix G. Hansford Papers
Yale University, Sterling Memorial Library
  U. B. Phillips Papers

Index